Restoring the Kingdom

Princeton Theological Monograph Series

K. C. Hanson, Charles M. Collier, D. Christopher Spinks,
and Robin Parry, Series Editors

Restoring the Kingdom

The Role of God as the "Ordainer of Times and Seasons"
in the Acts of the Apostles

Michael A. Salmeier

PICKWICK *Publications* · Eugene, Oregon

RESTORING THE KINGDOM
The Role of God as the "Ordainer of Times and Seasons" in the Acts of the Apostles

Princeton Theological Monograph Series 165

Pickwick Publications
An Imprint of Wipf and Stock Publishers
199 W. 8th Ave., Suite 3
Eugene, OR 97401

www.wipfandstock.com

ISBN 13: 978-1-61097-098-3

Cataloguing-in-Publication data:

Michael A. Salmeier

Restoring the kingdom : the role of God as the "ordainer of times and seasons" in the Acts of the Apostles / Michael A. Salmeier.

Princeton Theological Monograph Series 165

xii + 212 pp. ; 23 cm. Includes bibliographical references and index(es).

ISBN 13: 978-1-61097-098-3

1. Bible. N.T. Acts—Criticism, interpretation, etc. 2. Bible. N.T. Acts—Criticism, Narrative. I. Title. II. Series.

BS2625.52 S21 2011

Manufactured in the U.S.A.

Contents

Preface

THE GENESIS FOR THIS WORK CAME WHEN I WAS AN ASSISTING PASTOR AT A FOURSQUARE church in Anaheim, California (I mention the origin because, while this is a work intended primarily for scholarly engagement, it is my hope that it will have a positive impact on the church). My co-worker and I began teaching through Acts in a small Sunday School class. I say "began," because we did not get very far. However, it was while preparing for those class sessions that I noticed the ubiquity of divine involvement in the narrative and began wondering about the significance in Jesus' reply to the disciples (Acts 1:7–8). Was the Father setting times and seasons related to the kingdom's establishment? Did this phrase explain God's involvement throughout the plot? These questions drove the doctoral research proposal for which I was accepted at University of Oxford. During the three years there the effort to answer these inquiries produced a successful doctoral thesis and, after a few more years of revising and reshaping, this book.

The questions are important since, I believe, answering them goes a long way towards understanding Luke's purpose in writing Acts. Initial impressions and expectations affect how the reader thinks about the work and what the reader will look for as he or she reads. Many have argued that the geographic pattern (Jerusalem, Judea, Samaria, and the ends of the earth) Jesus presents to the disciples sets the agenda for missional expansion. This, however, only deals with half of Jesus' statement and there has been little attention given to the other half. It is the contention of this work, then, that giving attention to first half of Jesus' reply helps to unfold Luke's aims in assuring the reader concerning what has taken place, while explaining Luke's theology concerning God and His Kingdom.

Various portions of this book were presented at sessions of the Evangelical Theological Society or to the New Testament Seminar at the University of Oxford. I am thankful to all those who listened to and provided feedback during those sessions. Gratitude is also extended to John Muddiman of University of Oxford and Bruce Longenecker, now of Baylor University, who were the readers for my doctoral thesis. Their suggestions impacted the reshaping this project underwent. Special thanks go to my doctoral supervisor, Robert Morgan. I learned much from his guidance and prodding.

Completion of a book project does not come without the help of friends and family. I so appreciate the support I received from my colleagues and students at Life Pacific College. The encouragement and friendship they have offered has been invaluable. Michael Wilkins and Clint Arnold, both of Talbot School of Theology, encouraged me to continue pursuing publication. My parents, Milo and Patt Salmeier, along with my two sisters and their families have always been a support to me. I hope seeing this work in print makes them proud. I especially thank my wonderful wife, Jonelle. Without her love, support, and sacrifice this book would not see the light of day.

I must express my appreciation to the editorial staff at Pickwick and the Princeton Theological Monograph Series. It is an honor to work with you. Finally, I would be remiss not to thank Luke's God. Without Him, in so many ways, this book could not exist.

General Abbreviations

κτλ	καί τά λοιπά, and the remainder
ET	English translation
LXX	Septuagint
OT	Old Testament
WT	Western Text

Biblical Texts

Old Testament

Gen	Genesis
Exod	Exodus
Lev	Leviticus
Num	Numbers
Deut	Deuteronomy
Josh	Joshua
Judg	Judges
1 Sam	First Samuel
2 Sam	Second Samuel
1 Kgs	First Kings
2 Kgs	Second Kings
1 Chr	First Chronicles
2 Chr	Second Chronicles
Esth	Esther
Ps (Pss pl.)	Psalms
Isa	Isaiah

Jer	Jeremiah
Ezek	Ezekiel
Dan	Daniel
Hos	Hosea
Joel	Joel
Amos	Amos
Obad	Obadiah
Mic	Micah
Hab	Habakkuk
Zeph	Zephaniah
Hag	Haggai
Zech	Zechariah
Mal	Malachi

New Testament

Matt	Matthew
Mark	Mark
Luke	Luke
Acts	Acts

Apocrypha

Tob	Tobit
Jdt	Judith
Wis	Wisdom of Solomon
Sir	Sirach
Bar	Baruch
1 Macc	First Maccabees
2 Macc	Second Maccabees
3 Macc	Third Maccabees
Pr Azar	Prayer of Azariah

Pseudepigrapha

Apoc. Bar.	Apocalypse of Baruch
As. Mos.	Assumption of Moses
1 En.	1 Enoch (Ethiopic Apocalypse)
2 En.	2 Enoch (Slavonic Apocalypse)
4 Ezra	4 Ezra
Jos. Asen.	Joseph and Aseneth
Jub.	Jubilees
L.A.B.	Liber antiquitatum biblicarum
Pss. Sol.	Psalms of Solomon
Sib. Or	Sibylline Oracles
T. 12 Patr.	Testament of the Twelve Patriarchs
T. Benj.	Testament of Benjamin
T. Dan	Testament of Dan
T. Iss.	Testament of Issachar
T. Jos.	Testament of Joseph
T. Jud.	Testament of Judah
T. Levi	Testament of Levi
T. Naph.	Testament of Naphtali
T. Job	Testament of Job
T. Mos.	Testament of Moses
T. Sol.	Testament of Solomon

Qumran Documents

1QM	War Scroll from Qumran Cave 1
1QS	Rule of the Community, Manual of Discipline from Qumran Cave 1
1QSb	Appendix B, Rule of Benediction to 1QS from Qumran Cave 1
4Q215	T. Naph. from Qumran Cave 4.
4Q252	Commentary on Genesis A, from Qumran Cave 4.
4Q403-5	Songs of the Sabbath Sacrifice or Angelic Liturgy, Scrolls 403-5, from Qumran Cave 4.

4QFlor   *Eschatological Midrashim* from Qumran Cave 4.

11QT   *Temple Scroll* from Qumran Cave 11.

Hellenistic, Rabbinical, and Early Church Writings

Ant.   Josephus *Antiquities of the Jews*

War   Josephus *Jewish War*

Legat.   Philo *Legatio ad Gaium*

Praem.   Philo *De Praemiis et Poenis*

QE   Philo *Quaestiones et Solutiones in Exodum, I*

Vit. Ap   Philostratus *Vita Apollinii*

m. Qidd.   *Mishnat Qiddushin*

Apol.   Tertullian *Apologeticus*

Reference Works

BAGD   Walter Bauer, William F. Arndt, F. W. Gingrich, and F. W. Danker. *Greek-English Lexicon of the New Testament and Other Early Christian Literature.* 2nd ed. Chicago, 1979.

BDF   Frederich Blass and Albert Debrunner. *A Greek Grammar of the New Testament and Other Early Christian Literature.* 3rd ed. Chicago: University of Chicago Press, 2000.

PGM   *Papyri graecae magicae: Die grieshischen Zauberpapyri.* Edited by K. Preisdanz. Berlin, 1928.

1

Portrait Characteristics and Method

As the Book of Acts opens, Luke[1] relates Jesus speaking about the things concerning the "kingdom of *God*" (1:3), the promise of the *Father* (1:4), and explains that it is this *Father* who has established "times or periods [seasons] . . . by his own authority" (1:7). Further, three passive constructions implicate God in Jesus' ascension (1:2—ἀνελήμφθη; 1:9—ἐπήρθη; 1:11—ὁ ἀναλημφθεὶς). This divine involvement continues throughout Acts as "the narrator constantly has God intervening, saving or consoling his people."[2] From the first chapter on, the narrative unfolds in a way that demonstrates the principal agent is "the powerful arm of God,"[3] and Acts, therefore, is "a discourse about God."[4] Luke emphasizes that events unfold at God's "behest" and "in accordance with His plan."[5]

While most commentators have noted this ubiquitous divine involvement, scholarly attempts at analyzing Luke's portrayal of God have been surprisingly few. Haenchen's comments, typical in their brevity, begin with, "[I]t is God (the Father) who occupies the dominant place" and end some ninety (English) words later after short statements about God being "placed over" Christ, the Creator, the one who designed the plan of salvation, the worker of miracles, and the one who raised Jesus.[6] For a character who "occupies the dominant place" such limited discussion does not seem sufficient. Bovon, in surveying thirty years of Luke-Acts research, notes that the divine role in the Acts narrative was "strangely overlooked in numerous works."[7] This lacuna confirms (at least for Lukan studies) Dahl's lament that God is the neglected topic in New Testament theology.[8] Since this

---

1. "Luke" is a convenient designation for the author and is not intended to make any statement about who this Luke is or about whether a Luke actually wrote either Acts or the Gospel assigned by tradition to that name.

2. Marguerat, *First*, 9.

3. Ibid., 9.

4. Ibid., 85.

5. Marshall, *Luke*, 104.

6. Haenchen, *Acts*, 91.

7. Bovon, *Luke*, 53. Bovon ("God," 67–80) subsequently addressed this issue, but demonstrated just three ways that Luke presents God: 1) the image of access through a doorway; 2) the choice between money and life; and 3) the key of knowledge (73–78). His data are primarily from the Gospel and tend to be colored by his existentialist approach, which is most clear when he interprets Acts 17:26 as calling the reader, whether gentile or Jew, to an internal meeting with God (80). This conception of the inner-self is a modern perspective and one not likely shared by ancient peoples.

8. Dahl, "Neglected," 153–63.

theme is neglected in NT theology and because it is recognized as being central to the Acts narrative, analyzing Luke's presentation of God seems an important endeavor.

Portrait Characteristics

Given the limited discussions of how Luke portrays God in Acts, no standard method for analyzing such portrayals has developed in the literature. This chapter begins, therefore, by outlining what such an analysis should look like. Ten criteria, which will need to be met by the current study, will be examined, demonstrating how the failure to meet these criteria weakens the other studies.[9] It will then be argued that by employing what literary theorists call *characterization* these desiderata can be achieved. In keeping with this, it will be demonstrated that the initial statements about God in Acts 1:1–8 suggest that God will be portrayed as controlling the narrative events, including the kingdom's possible restoration to Israel. Thus, examining the characterization of God in Acts should prove fruitful for understanding Luke's narrative.

Ten Characteristics for a Proper Portrait of God in Acts

It is important to define what an effective presentation of Luke's portrayal of God might look like. The ten features discussed below emerge from analyzing scholarly discussion on God in Acts and from principles seen as important in literary characterization study. These characteristics provide criteria for the model developed here.

An appropriate study should attend to the narrative figure "God." To see this factor's importance it is helpful to explore the focus found in a few analyses. For Cadbury,[10] Luke's emphasis on divine intervention was probably the author's "conscious intention." Everyone and everything is under God's guiding hand. Accordingly, Acts emphasizes how the author understands history including its completion, for it is apparent that: "God has set a day, he has elected the witnesses, he has fixed upon the judge, he has appointed the way."[11] This divine guidance is detailed and immediate as evidenced in how God initiated the mission to Macedonia (Acts 16:6–10).

Marshall[12] sees Luke portraying God as the source for salvation. He traces how Luke uses several titles for God, beginning with Luke characterizing God as *Savior* (Luke 1:47). For Marshall, God, in line with OT[13] rather than Greek influences, is the Creator

9. The works discussed here are not exhaustive, but were chosen because they include Acts in their analysis and because they give significant space to Luke's portrayal of God. For simplicity, works using a historical-critical approach (including source/redaction criticism) are combined with those that incorporate some form of literary analysis even though the latter are more recent and proceed from different assumptions about the way information is gleaned from the text.

10. Cadbury, *Making*, 303–6.

11. Ibid., 305.

12. Marshall, *Luke*, 103–14.

13. OT will be used as a conventional designation for the Hebrew Scriptures and does not indicate a theological evaluation of them.

who causes all the narrative events to unfold according to plan. This plan is expressed in salvation-history, presenting Luke's God as the God over salvation-history.

For Squires, Luke understands the divine plan as showing that: 1) God is the primary actor throughout Luke-Acts. 2) God directs the life of Jesus and the church by performing signs, wonders, healings, and exorcisms. 3) Epiphanies function to declare the divine will and divine guidance of history. 4) Divine purpose is emphasized through prophetic fulfillment (especially important in the passion narrative and the mission to the gentiles). Finally, 5) divine necessity is inherent to Jesus' life, death, and the apostolic mission.[14] Squires then demonstrates these conclusions, showing how such themes agree with the way divine providence was conceived by contemporary historians such as Josephus, Diodorus Siculus, and Dionysius of Halicarnassus.

Together these studies concentrate on divine guidance, God's plan, God's effect, or salvation. They do not focus specifically on God. It seems true that Luke's work emphasizes divine guidance, but this theme does not represent a comprehensive picture of God. Regarding Marshall, while the Lukan God does control salvation-history, it does not follow that *savior* is Luke's primary designation for God, since this may leave out too much characterizing data. Squires details how the divine *plan* is described and developed but not how *God* is portrayed. His focus is *impersonal* rather than *personal*. Despite many helpful insights, these writers do not appear to present Luke's portrayal of God completely, failing to consider God directly.

A clear account of the literary and theological predecessors (the possible sources for the author's literary, theological or philosophical model—i.e., Greek or Jewish) for the portrayal should be stated. Cadbury's work gives the outline for a Lukan theme (divine control), but does not illuminate how the author nuances this divine control. Does it come from a Greek or Jewish background? Squires concentrates on Hellenistic influences over Jewish ones for understanding how Luke presents the divine plan. He notes that the Septuagint is influential,[15] and that the themes he discusses in relation to Hellenistic sources already appear there (particularly in the Deuteronomist's perspective). However, *providence* and *divine intervention* (themes Squires traces in Josephus and Josephus' influences—Diodorus Siculus, and Dionysius) are particularly evident in Second-Temple Jewish works like 2 Maccabees.[16] Unlike Josephus but like Luke, that work's author does not de-emphasize divine intervention.[17] Again, dissimilar to Josephus, Luke seems to reject notions about *Justice* and *Fate* (compare how the Maltans misunderstand Paul's deliverance in Acts 28:1–10). Thus, Squires' concentration on non-Jewish influences seems suspect, particularly since it downplays the Jewish precedents.

The portrait must be consistent (coherent) enough to show that the text's major themes support it. In some studies it is unclear how various themes relate to the portrayal of God.

14. Squires, *Plan*, 2–3.

15. Ibid., 121.

16. See Doran, *Temple*, 98–99; van Henten, *Maccabean*, 44.

17. See Feldman, "Portrayal," 159; *Studies*, 568; Sterling, "Presence," 116, 129.

For instance, Marshall's study does not demonstrate how some issues he discusses (fate, necessity, election) present God as the God of Salvation. Gaventa sketches Luke's characterization of God, pointing out that Luke does not introduce God (God is already known to the reader). Luke portrays God as the "God of Israel," yet the one who has acted in Jesus, for gentile inclusion, and who continues to act through those who believe in Jesus' name.[18] Thus, Gaventa indicates that the "God of Israel" is not a sufficient title for God because God does more than just relate to Jews. While this is true, the reader will seek to develop a consistent portrait that understands how to relate the God of Israel to the One acting in Jesus, for the gentiles, and through believers. Gaventa does not attempt to explain this relationship, coming short in forming a consistent portrait.

Brawley[19] uses narrative theory to demonstrate the "theocentric" nature of Luke-Acts. He seeks to show how characterization reveals the presentation of God, suggesting that 1) God "acts toward an intended future," providing "salvation for the enemies of God and inclusion in God's kingdom (Luke 1:71; 13:29; Acts 2:34)." 2) That future is "peace (Luke 1:79; 2:14; Acts 10:36)." 3) "The intended future also includes judgment (Luke 3:17; 13:28; Acts 10:42; 17:31)" because enemies have to be overthrown and wickedness vanquished.[20] Ultimately however, Brawley believes that an attempt "to inquire into the character of God is an effort to fix that character. But, it remains elusive."[21] Complexity and narrative gaps render "God's character indeterminate," frustrating attempts to epitomize it.[22] Brawley, therefore, thinks that it is impossible to come to a consistent understanding about how Luke portrays God.

Brawley's presentation leaves questions unanswered—how consistently is God acting towards this end portrayed? What, if any, fulfillment of that end has taken place? Brawley seems to assume that a consistent characterization of God is impossible. However, there is a substantial difference between the character of God in Luke-Acts becoming "fixed" and Luke's reader forming a consistent picture of God. Brawley acknowledges that readers construct characters from various traits which they combine "into coherent wholes."[23] Further, since the reader fills narrative gaps through textual and extra-textual (commonly held beliefs and knowledge) information, gaps do not inhibit this process. This suggests that, even with God, the reader will attempt such a construction. Thus, the characterization process Brawley employs indicates that readers come to a consistent picture of God even though Brawley does not look for it. Despite Brawley's valuable discussion of characterization, his attempt to analyze the Lukan portrait seems incomplete since it does not look for the coherent portrait that characterization anticipates.

---

18. Gaventa, *Acts*, 28–31.

19. Brawley, *Centering*, 110–24. Separately, Brawley ("Abrahamic," 109–32) analyzes how Luke connects God to Abrahamic covenant traditions, making a case for God as the one who fulfills Abrahamic promises. As Brawley admits, this is simply part of the "entire scope of the characterization of God" (130). Similarly, Brawley, "Promises," 279–96.

20. Brawley, *Centering*, 122.

21. Ibid., 123.

22. Ibid.

23. Ibid., 107.

Bibb classifies God as a character using Hochman's grid,[24] finding Luke's God to be a rather robust character that changes, enters into conflict, and receives specific stylizations that distinguish God from other characters.[25] Hochman's grid, however, depends on similarities between characters and human persons. Conflict, change, and stylization, which make sense for finite creatures, do not apply to an infinite God in the same way. Thus, this aspect of Bibb's analysis needs to be more carefully nuanced. However, what most seems to leave Bibb's work incomplete is that he is more interested in determining what type (flat, round, person-like) of character God is, rather than understanding the comprehensive, constructed character God and how that character functions in the narrative. While Bibb notes that God directs and initiates plot action in both volumes,[26] he does not identify how this fits into a coherent picture of Luke's God or what impact that portrayal might have on the reader.

Who the reader is and what his or her role in the process is must be identified since this affects how the text is perceived. Bibb does not define who Luke's implied reader is, pointing to a Greek and Jewish audience without suggesting how this is possible.[27] When Squires mentions a "reader familiar with the Hebrew scriptures" and a pagan reader "unfamiliar with the differences between Judaism and the emerging faith of Christianity,"[28] he appears to assume two entirely different implied readers. Squires may be thinking about actual readers. However, he claims interest in cues that reveal the text's apologetic intention.[29] Implied readers follow these cues whereas actual readers may or may not. Thus, possible responses by (accidental) actual readers cannot be relied on to determine the text's apologetic aims. Neither Squires nor Bibb, therefore, clearly identify the reader and the reader's role in understanding how God is presented.

The study should not focus on direct statements, titles, speeches, etc., without looking at other narrative elements as well. Marshall's study is limited to (relatively few) specific titles associated with God. In several articles Mowery investigated direct statements about God (those made by other characters in the narrative or by the narrator concerning direct divine action or involvement). Mowery shows that God can be considered the God of the past (Israel's history), of the passion account, of the future, of the Spirit, and finally of the Acts events.[30] In the passion account, Mowery investigates words ($\delta\epsilon\tilde{\iota}$, $\mu\epsilon\lambda\lambda\omega$) that indicate the event occurs by divine necessity, concluding that, while direct divine involvement in the passion is not stated in the Gospel, it is expressed clearly in Acts.[31] Elsewhere, Mowery suggests that Luke virtually limits the epithet *Father* to Jesus' lips and Luke el-

---

24. See Hochman, *Character*, 88–89.

25. Bibb, "Characterization," 276–83.

26. Ibid., 295.

27. Ibid., 197.

28. Squires, *Plan*, 58.

29. Ibid., 52–53.

30. Mowery, "Direct," 197–202.

31. Ibid., 567–72.

evates the term θεός over other terms for God.[32] Finally, Mowery investigates the titles *Lord*, *God*, and *Father* for their theological value.[33]

Mowery's analysis, however, does not provide a coherent picture of God. He does not consider indirect statements about God. Further, references to other supernatural agents and their relationship to God receive only brief discussion.[34] These omissions seem critical, as evidenced when Mowery concludes that in Acts 2:1–13 the reader learns "that 'a sound came from heaven' (2:2), that 'tongues of fire' appeared to the disciples (2:3), that they were filled with the Spirit (2:4a) and that they spoke in other tongues 'as the Spirit was giving them utterance' (2:4b), no verse in this story explicitly declares that God gave the Spirit."[35] However, Acts 1:4–5 has already informed the reader that the "promise of the Father" is associated with being "baptized with the Holy Spirit" that would take place "not many days from now." Thus, when the Spirit comes, the reader knows that this is a divine sending—it is the Father's promise. This conclusion is confirmed by the Spirit coming from *heaven*—a term often used as a divine circumlocution (the location for the divine voice in Luke 3:22; 9:35). Thus, looking solely at explicit statements is misleading. Both Mowery and Marshall's studies focused on particular narrative elements (direct statements, titles), which, therefore, prevented their analysis from being comprehensive.

Reconstructions reflecting the "actual" history or "what must have happened" should not drive the exegesis. This can be seen from Jacob Jervell's work.[36] According to Jervell, Luke's God is exclusively Israel's God.[37] The gentiles who are added to the church are "God-fearers" and there is no mission to the heathen. God is never labeled the God of the nations, but God has forced the Way to include these God-fearers. Because the divine will has been imposed, Luke is compelled to express that the church is the *people of God*, and its history is Israel's history.

Given the surveys of Israel's history in Acts 7 and 13, the Acts narrative does seem to present God as Israel's God. However, Jervell too greatly emphasizes "pagan" exclusion. Paul's two speeches to generally "heathen" audiences (Acts 14:15–18; 17:22–34)[38] report little success. Still, since "heathens" receive a message and at least some believed (disciples in Lystra—14:20–22; some men, Dionysius, and Damaris in Athens—17:34) it is implied that the mission was not closed to them. Further, in both speeches, although God has allowed the nations to go their way (14:16; cf. 17:30), God retains a witness among them (14:17; 17:23–27—the unknown God, testified to by Greek poets). Consequently, God has always been the providential God for all nations not just for Israel. Finally, Acts 17:31 finds

---

32. Mowery, "Disappearance," 355–58.

33. Mowery, "Lord," 82–101.

34. Mowery, "Direct," 197.

35. Ibid., 202.

36. Jervell, *Theology*, 18–25. This is Jervell's most concise statement about the Lukan God (see also Jervell, *Apostelgeschichte*, 92–99).

37. Jervell, *Theology*, 18.

38. Schneider ("Gottesverkündigung," 280–96) explored these passages in relation to proclamation concerning God in Hellenistic settings. He shows that several NT sources, including Luke, point to a particular method for proclaiming God to "heathens."

Paul stating that God has set a day for judging all the world (οἰχουμένην). The implication is that God, as ruler over the entire world, has the right to judge all humanity. God may have made himself known in a unique way to Israel, but Luke does not ignore divine rule over the nations. Jervell's historical reconstruction has caused his conception of the Lukan God to miss the larger portrait. Jervell's historical reconstruction, then, drives his exegesis by too narrowly defining the recipients of the message and overlooking other data that suggests God was not to be understood simply as Israel's God.

It is vital that the narrative focus is understood and followed. Daniel Marguerat notes the remarkable diversity in divine interventions in Acts,[39] but suggests inconsistencies in how these are presented. Acts 1–7 show a "concentration" in manifestations and "collective wonders," while during the final narrative stages "the divine materializes essentially in favour of individuals, especially Paul."[40] Marguerat identifies the difference between Acts 1–7 and the Pauline period (Acts 13–28) in the latter being "chronologically closer to the post-apostolic period, the time of Luke."[41] Thus, the Spirit's activity has changed—as time elapses, the Spirit, and therefore God, focuses only on individuals rather than the community.

This analysis, however, misses the narrative focus. Acts 1–7 focuses on the general community, where, nevertheless, individuals are recipients of or manifest divine activity. After Acts 7, Luke focuses more on individuals (Philip, Peter, Paul). Thus, it is only appropriate that, in this latter, individually-focused portion, the divine should materialize in their favor. Further, having assumed what seems unproven (that the Spirit's activity has changed because the focus has changed), Marguerat then takes a truism (the Pauline period is chronologically closer to the writer's time than is Acts 1–7) and makes it a theological point about why divine activity had changed—the Apostolic age was ending. However, since narrative evidence for a change in divine action is absent, the truism reveals little. Marguerat, therefore, missed a change in narrative focus, which challenges his theological conclusions.

The study should account for how characters relate to other characters, and how direct statements, indirect statements, and actions affect the picture. For Marguerat, the diversity in divine interventions in Acts has no "equal" in Luke's Gospel apart from the infancy narratives (Luke 1–2) and Jesus' death (Luke 24).[42] The Gospel is focused on Christology, which then is balanced in Acts "between the poles" of Christology, Pneumatology, and "theology." Consequently, Marguerat appears to think these divine interventions are missing from Luke's Gospel because Jesus' activity is separate from the Spirit's and God's.

However, because of interrelationships in Luke's Gospel, Marguerat distinguishes Jesus' Christological activity from God and the Spirit's role too quickly and too easily. Filled with the Spirit, Jesus is led by the Spirit into the wilderness to do battle with Satan (God's

39. Marguerat, *First*, 88.

40. Ibid., 88.

41. Ibid., 113.

42. Ibid., 88.

activity—Luke 4:1).[43] Jesus returns to Galilee in the "power of the Spirit" and announces that the "Spirit of the Lord" (i.e., God) is upon him (4:18), indicating a close relationship between Jesus and the Spirit in the Gospel. Consequently, since the Spirit is God's Spirit, what Jesus does would seem to be what God does. Demons recognize Jesus' relationship to God ("Holy One of God"—4:34; "Son of God"—4:41). Jesus forgives sins, the work of God alone (5:21), and heals to demonstrate that this is accomplished. Jesus commands "even the winds and the water, and they obey him" (8:25), indicating control over nature. Further, divine activity is not confined to Jesus, since Jesus gives the twelve (9:1) and then the seventy (-two) power to heal disease and to have victory over the demonic (10:9, 19). Indeed, even those not specifically included in the twelve (or the seventy (-two)?) have power over demons (9:49–50). That power over demons manifests divine power seems apparent from Jesus' declaration that he casts out demons by the "finger of God" (11:20). Thus, divine interventions are not absent from Luke's Gospel narrative. Indeed, Jesus appears to be God's intervention in history. Jesus' interrelationship with other characters in Luke's Gospel shows the interlinking of Christology, Pneumatology, and "theo–logy." So, when Marguerat splits these, he misses the role that the relationship between characters plays in characterization.

Any investigation should allow for the strategies used by ancient authors to lead readers to 'proper' conclusions about plot development. Marguerat observes: "Except for a few rare occasions, the narrator never directly ascribes the action of the narrative to God."[44] Instead, Luke allows these works to be clarified by the "word of the witness." For Marguerat, then, divine action is not obvious in the story and can only be seen retrospectively. Nevertheless, what Marguerat sees as distinctive in Luke-Acts (retrospective clarification by speech from witnesses) is typical for Hellenistic writing. When action is portrayed in such literature it "often includes speeches by one or more characters, which provide implicit commentary or explanation on preceding narrative events and potentially guide the evolving judgments and understanding of the readers."[45] Further, chapter 3 will argue that Marguerat incorrectly assesses the narrator's capabilities with regard to ascribing actions to God. Hellenistic-period writers (like their modern counterparts), then, often chose to use reliable characters to be their mouthpiece, guiding the reader's attention to certain details. This practice need have no specific theological significance and a proper analysis should be aware of such strategies.

Jerome Neyrey analyzes the Acts presentation of God using native (Greek and Israelite) understandings about the deity—benefaction, providence, and theodicy.[46] Using the patron/client model, Neyrey shows God to be the Great Patron who acts for the benefit of clients (Jesus, the disciples, all believers). Jesus, then, brokers this divine

---

43. See Ladd (*Theology*, 48–53, 65–68) concerning the battle between God and Satan in the Synoptics. Brawley (*Centering*, 85) suggests this conflict remains important throughout the Lukan narrative (see also chapter 4).

44. Marguerat, *First*, 90.

45. R. Thompson, "Believers," 331.

46. Neyrey, *Render*, 82–105.

benefaction.[47] Divine providence is demonstrated in creation, by exerting foreknowledge and executing the divine plan, providing insight into the future, benevolently controlling history, and judging sinners justly.[48] Such providential action allows the reader to see divine benefaction within history.[49] Finally, Luke offers a theodicy to support the divine beneficence and providence—the unjust do not go without judgment since God has fixed a day and a judge.[50]

Neyrey's presentation is consistent since the providence and theodicy themes point to divine benefaction. However, while Neyrey shows that these elements would be familiar to a reader, he does not explain the narrative role this portrayal would have. Luke is writing theology through a history that appears to offer an explanation for something. How does God fit in this explanation? Is Luke's reader supposed to learn anything or receive any benefit from God providentially advancing the mission? To understand Luke's characterization of God, the analysis should seek to explain how that characterization functions in the plot and for the reader.

Finally, *the portrait should consider how initial characterizations provide the foundation, which the narrative develops, allowing the opportunity either to reassess or confirm the original picture.* For Marguerat, "Luke's God *redirects* history in order to inscribe it in his plan." God retains the "initiative to *change* the direction of history."[51] Therefore, God is represented as manipulating a history that usually operates without direct divine control. However, the initial impression given the reader is that God has fixed (ἔθετο), not redirected or changed, "times and periods" (Acts 1:7). The verb τίθημι, with the accusative, refers to establishing, fixing, or arranging.[52] It does not connote change or alter. Later, Acts 17:26 mentions God setting (ὁρίζω—to determine, fix or appoint)[53] appointed "times" and "boundaries." The implication here, apparently, is that not only the time, but the duration and locations for human existence are under divine control. Thus, for Luke, God *directs and determines* history rather than redirecting or changing it. Marguerat fails to account for this initial impression.

The process literary theorists call *characterization* provides for the satisfying of these criteria. The process, to be further outlined below, focuses on the character being depicted, allowing concentration on God as a character (first criterion). Characterization studies are generally interested in the co-textual element (how the same or similar characters are portrayed in other works).[54] Thus, such studies look at how other works (particularly antecedents—second criterion) portray the same character.

47. Ibid., 83–92.

48. Ibid., 93–94.

49. Ibid., 96.

50. Ibid., 96–103.

51. Marguerat, *First*, 108, emphasis added.

52. BAGD, 816.

53. Ibid., 580.

54. See Shepherd, *Narrative*, 78–79.

Characterization expects the reader to construct a generally consistent character portrait as the narrative develops. Due to this interest, the model delineates the role played by the reader, the author, and the text.[55] Further, characterization incorporates how readers construct characters using various narrative features (direct and indirect statements, actions, interactions with other characters, etc.).[56] Thus, since readers are vital to the model, characterization fits the third, fourth, fifth, and eighth criteria.

Because characterization aims to analyze *textual* cues that signal how the reader is to construct the character, it is not interested in reconstructing an 'actual' historical situation (sixth criterion). However, the historical task is not jettisoned; rather, in this "text-specific" approach there is a recognition that the text arises within a cultural framework.[57] Therefore, in order to present the character constructed by the reader, elements from the literature and society contemporary to the implied reader must be understood. Thus, historical *investigation and understanding* are important, but historical *reconstruction* is not. At the same time this text-specific approach focuses on how the narrative develops (seventh criterion). Further, in allowing for cultural idiosyncrasies, characterization must be interested in how authors use characters and plot (ninth criterion).

Finally, characterization theorists argue that the reader develops a portrait by anticipating plot and character based on information in the text. From the original characterization, the narrative stimulates and guides responses from the reader causing the initial perspective to be re-examined, modified, or confirmed.[58] The initial picture sets a tone that can then be altered, but, nevertheless, is important to the reader's impressions (tenth criterion). Characterization, then, dovetails with the criteria.

Initial Impressions: A God who Ordains Times and Seasons—Acts 1:1–8.[59]

Because the reader's character construction begins with the initial characterization, the opening verses of Acts should suggest how God will be portrayed throughout. There, Jesus has instructed his followers concerning the "kingdom of God," and he tells them to await the "promise of the Father," the baptism "with the Spirit." The reader, then, would wonder what exactly this promise is and when it will be fulfilled,[60] anticipating that the story will reveal answers to these questions. Therefore, when in 1:8 the Spirit is associated with power for witness that will reach to the "ends of the earth," the reader is led to expect that the Spirit will play a central role in this witness. These initial references to God and the Spirit lead the reader to anticipate that the narrative features divine activity.

Jesus' disciples ask if he is now going to restore the "kingdom to Israel" (1:6). His answer is that it is not theirs "to know the times or periods that the *Father* has set by his own authority" (1:7). This response leaves "the question of the restoration of the kingdom to

55. Darr, *Character*, 16.

56. Ibid., 44–47.

57. Ibid., 14.

58. Ibid., 30–32.

59. See chapter 4 for more on Acts 1:1–11.

60. Brawley, *Centering*, 17–18.

Israel open."[61] Thus, more narrative questions arise for the reader—when will the kingdom be restored? What is that kingdom (is it the same thing as the kingdom of God)? Will the narrative describe the restoration?

The narrative also raises questions about this *Father*. One clue for understanding a character's role in the story is to look at the identity (name) and attributes ascribed to that character.[62] Picking up on that, fatherhood in OT thought often pictures a father as the "ancestor of a clan or family, and thus the one who gives an inheritance to his children." In application to God it suggests "God's purposes and blessings for Israel (Isa 63:16; 64:8; Jer 3:19; 31:9),"[63] providing "the basis for hope for the future" since at Jer 31:9 and at Isa 63:16 "the exiles call upon God as Father in distress and hope for deliverance and return to the land."[64] As Father, God is concerned with His children's inheritance, blessings, and deliverance. The restored kingdom, therefore, would relate to the Father's role in granting inheritance and delivering his children from enemy oppression. The Spirit, as well, is associated with the divine role as Father, for as the Father's promise, the Spirit would be a blessing given by the Father.[65]

The Father is described as the one who establishes things "by his own authority" (1:7). God, like a human father, is an authoritative figure to whom honor and obedience is due.[66] Further, the Father sets "times or periods"—determining when the kingdom will be restored. When Jesus' ascension is mentioned (1:2), the reader cannot be certain that it is God who took Jesus up (that has not been revealed), but the passive ($\dot{\alpha}\nu\epsilon\lambda\acute{\eta}\mu\phi\theta\eta$) implies that Jesus did not take himself up. This suggests that Jesus did not choose the day for his ascension. Further, Jesus does not immediately grant the Father's promise; rather it waits a someday soon (1:5)—here, by implication, a day that the Father chooses.

It seems, therefore, that the reader will initially understand God as the one who controls narrative events. The promise concerning the Spirit relates to a witness that is expected to continue throughout the narrative. This promise is also connected to a Father who blesses his children, and who has the authority and responsibility to establish the "times or periods" for such blessings. Further, the narrative raises questions concerning the kingdom's restoration, which is also tied to the divine will. The divine Father grants the inheritance and brings deliverance, while also controlling the time for these events. Thus, Acts begins with a portrayal of God as the *ordainer of times and seasons* (periods). As the narrative unfolds, the reader anticipates God controlling the events, even down to their timing. Divine involvement would be expected in relation to the kingdom being restored and related issues such as the coming of the Spirit, fulfilled promises to Israel, and the mission to the "ends of the earth." This initial conception will be re-examined, altered, or confirmed as the story unfolds, but represents the reader's initial construction.

61. Ibid., 43.

62. Shepherd, *Narrative*, 78–79.

63. M. M. Thompson, *God*, 59. See also chapter 2.

64. Ibid., 62.

65 Tannehill, *Narrative*, 13.

66. M. M. Thompson, *God*, 58.

Further Observations

Some further observations are necessary concerning the concentration on Acts and God in Luke's account. This study concentrates on the book of Acts. The limitation does not deny the unity of Luke-Acts but simply narrows the focus. Given that Acts starts with a reference back to the former work (Acts 1:1) Luke's Gospel must be treated as part of the reader's extra-text. This allows the Acts portrayal of God to be explored while maintaining the relationship between the two Lukan works.

In Acts God is a character with whom other characters interact and relate. This kind of depiction would have been familiar to Luke and his reader since from Genesis on the biblical reader is led to think about humanity in relationship to God (Gen. 1:26).[67] A God presented in narrative form, interacting with and intervening in human affairs, is an assumption held by such readers.[68] This study, therefore, will attempt to analyze the God presented in the narrative—what does Luke say about God? What does God do? How does Luke relate human and divine actions in his narrative world? How does Luke use this portrayal? Nevertheless, Luke's narrative world and the real world are not identical. In a narrative world logical connections are made that cannot be so easily defined in the external world. Thus, the relationship between God in Acts and a real, external God is difficult to determine and will be evaluated in various ways based on the presuppositions each evaluator brings to the issue. George Stroup comments, "one of the most significant limitations to every interpretive act is the tradition and community within which the interpretation takes place. The same event may have a wholly different interpretation in one tradition from what it has in another."[69] Inherent in each tradition are beliefs about what could and could not be true about God. Such analysis, however, is beyond this study's scope.

Method

In order to clarify how Luke's portrayal of God will be analyzed, the following discussion sketches the major factors in characterization and outlines the *reader-response* method that will be used. The chapter closes with an overview of how this study will proceed.

Elements in Characterization Theory

Two main questions need to be answered—what is a *character* and what is *characterization*? The answers provide a foundation for investigating any narrative figure. They also raise special concerns to be addressed in studying God as a character.

What is a character? Any figure in a narrative is a character. While this response picks out an instance of a character, it does not explain what one is. Therefore, narratologists have suggested that a character is a collection of the traits or qualities associated with a

---

67. See Miles, *God*, 14. Also chapter 2.

68. So Patrick, *Rendering*, 26–27.

69. Stroup, *Promise*, 118.

narrative figure.[70] Every literary figure has at least one trait—that quality associated with the action the figure performs[71] (a person who rescues another figure is, if nothing else, a rescuer). Most literary figures in modern literature have more than one trait; therefore, Chatman indicates that a character should be understood as a "paradigm" (a structure constructed from these qualities).[72]

Some suggest that a character is merely the words on the page (nothing more or less than a literary construct). This belief creates a problem for both fictional and non-fictional literature. For non-fiction literature, such as Acts,[73] whose characters apparently refer to real persons outside the text,[74] the idea that the figure is simply the words on the page is difficult to maintain. Even for purely fictional narratives this position has been challenged since characters, as imitations of people, take on a greater reality in the readers' minds (readers treat them as people).[75] Hochman argued that a character can be abstracted (treated as real) if the critic so chooses. When controlled by the text such abstraction is legitimate. Importantly, Hochman concludes that, "a considerable number—if not the great majority—of literary texts demand that we abstract the characters from them in the course of analyzing them in order to grasp the implicit or explicit logic of their actions, their worlds, and their thematic concerns."[76] Therefore, it seems that characters can be treated as both people and words.

As a construct in a literary work, a character is connected to the story told in the narrative. However, in modern fiction, characters are generally conceived to be more than mere plot agents. According to Chatman, characters and events are interdependent narrative aspects (the plot influences the character, the character influences the plot).[77] Rimmon-Kenan adds that how much a character is subordinated to plot depends on the narrative type (character- versus plot-driven) and on what focus the reader chooses (whether the reader is interested in attending to the character over the plot).[78] In a related issue, literary theorists have presented many different models for character typology (from Forster's

70. Chatman, *Story*, 126.

71. Ibid., 109.

72. Ibid., 126.

73. Even if there are unreliable elements in Acts, the narrative itself purports (and has been treated as such) to recount real events. Narrative approaches remain applicable since Acts is a narrative and the difference between fiction and non-fiction, "does not result from the presence or absence of particular formal features: forms and conventions typical of fictional narratives may be present in non-fictional narratives as well" (Merenlahti and Hakola, "Reconceiving," 37–38).

74. Merenlahti and Hakola ("Reconceiving," 40–43) assume that, since characters refer to real, external people or groups, these characters allegorically represent some group in the author's contemporary setting. They, thus, seem to commit the intentional fallacy—assuming that biographical information about the author is going to reveal his or her intentions in a specific text (see Darr, "Narrator," 48 n. 11). There is no reason to assume that characters refer to any person or group other than that given in the text.

75. Chatman, *Story*, 118.

76. Hochman, *Character*, 166.

77. Chatman, *Story*, 113; Hochman, *Character*, 21–29.

78. Rimmon-Kenan, 35–36.

flat and round characters[79] to Hochman's robust grid containing eight continuums of polarity).[80] In keeping with the realist emphasis, the tendency has been to opt for more person-like models such as Hochman's as opposed to flat types.[81]

Some, nevertheless, doubt that characters in ancient narratives can be treated as independent from the plot or as anything more than ideal representations (types). The issue arises because, following Aristotle's *Poetics*, it is believed that in ancient narratives persons were necessary only to perform action. Character (*ethos*) was added later.[82] Thus, ancient characters were just plot agents, showing no development or change—merely ideal representations. This issue has received attention in recent applications of characterization to the New Testament.[83] The majority conclusion has been that, although the characters in Acts should not be understood in the modern sense, characterization is not hampered by subordination to action and/or flat character types. Therefore, it seems valid to proceed (at least cautiously) with this method.

Can God be considered a character in Acts? Certainly God is involved in the Acts events even if divine actions are not directly narrated. At least one trait associated with God (*ordainer of times and seasons*) has been suggested and it is implied that God was involved in Jesus' ascension. This indicates a character, but, as Craig notes, "the portrayal of God is unique because most aspects typically associated with character—appearance, social status, place of residence, etc.—have no bearing on God at all."[84] This may be overstated—it was already shown that God is identified in the Acts narrative as Father (a social-status position),[85] and the narrative informs the reader where the divine residence is not (in dwellings "made with human hands"—7:48).[86] Still, if characters are modeled after humans, God seems a difficult figure to analyze. While human characters in the Bible tend to variability, God is presented in a relatively constant manner (different narratives across time generally portray God similarly). Although particular emphases in one narrative or another can be identified, "there is likely to be as much continuity between these documents as there is contrast or difference."[87] However, this is actually a positive for the presentation of God. God's characterization is relatively constant, so the "biblical narrative seldom employs the correction of first impressions in order to illuminate the character of

---

79. Forster, *Aspects* (1963).

80. Hochman, *Character*, 88–89.

81. Hochman's norm for classification is "resemblance to real people, which means some form of realism or naturalism of representation" (*Character*, 90).

82. See Chatman, *Story*, 108–13.

83. See the discussion in, among others, Burnett, "Characterization," 3–28; Fowler, "Characterizing," 97–104; Gowler, *Host*, 78–174. On characterization in ancient Greek literature see Pelling, *Characterization* (1990). Many authors (Alter, *Art* (1981); Fokkelman, *Reading* (1999); Humphreys, *Character* (2001); Sternberg, *Poetics* (1985)) indicate how significant characterization is in OT narrative.

84. Craig, "Character(ization)," 160. Likewise, M. M. Thompson, "God's," 185.

85. So Malina, *World*, 94–121.

86. Noted by Bibb, "Characterization," 268.

87. M. M. Thompson, "God's," 185–86.

God,"[88] which suggests that Luke's initial characterization of God will have an enduring role in the narrative.

Further, there is an expectation in narratives that even the flattest character is revealed through the narrative's dynamic interaction; even if that characterization remains relatively constant.[89] Also, even though the numerous narratives about God multiply the avenues to knowing about God, "the reader's conception of God is also the most textually bound," because these other avenues cause the specific portrayal in the narrative to "assume greater significance in building the character of God."[90] The narrative focuses the reader's attention on specific details about God that are important for the story. Thus, there seems to be sufficient reason to treat God as a character (although a somewhat different one) in Acts.[91]

What is Characterization? Characterization is the "assembling of various character-indicators distributed along the text-continuum and, when necessary, inferring the traits from them."[92] Readers construct the character from the data (actions, speeches, etc.) in the text used to portray that character.[93] This picture is clarified by outlining the various textual indicators.

According to Rimmon-Kenan,[94] two, basic, textual-character-indicator types exist—direct definition and indirect presentation. Direct definition is authoritative and *names* traits by adjectives, abstract nouns or other speech types. However, in order to succeed as characterization such qualities must be named by a reliable textual source (a dependable narrator or character).

Indirect characterization *illustrates* the trait in various ways, leaving it to the reader to infer the implied quality. The actions, speech, external appearance, and environment of the character all contribute. Whether the action is habitual or singular, a committed or omitted act, something can be inferred about the character. The actor's speech style, dress or physical features, and surroundings (whether physical or social-cultural) add to the trait paradigm. Further, these traits can be reinforced by the analogy (comparison or contrast) between characters (Stephen, Peter, and Paul in Acts) or by using analogous names (Eutychus ['Lucky']—20:8). From these textual cues the reader forms a mental image of the character.

In summary, a character, as understood in this study, is a trait paradigm assembled from textual cues. Characterization is the process of constructing that paradigm from the

88. Ibid., 186.

89. Ibid.

90. Ibid.

91. One further reason for thinking that God can be treated as a character is the helpful results from such studies in the OT. See, for instance, Patrick, *Rendering* (1981); Humphreys, *Character* (2001); and Miles, *God* (1999).

92. Rimmon-Kenan, *Narrative*, 59.

93. Hochman, *Character*, 38–39. Easterling ("Constructing," 87) argues that this kind of activity was expected in ancient literature and drama.

94. See Rimmon-Kenan, *Narrative*, 59–71.

textual indicators. Although modern psychological notions should not be attached, the character is neither simply the words on the page, nor just a plot functionary—both are important. While God is a special case needing individual consideration, God can be treated as a character in the Acts narrative. Using information from direct definition and drawing conclusions from actions, speech, environment, and appearance, the reader assembles a portrait of God.

A Pragmatic Reader-Response Approach

Because the reader's involvement in characterization is crucial, it is necessary to specify the reader's role. While the characters in Acts are more than words on the page, because they are portrayed in a written work, those characters are also bound by the text. Rashkow argued that a biblical character's realism makes it more difficult to assign motives to that character since in real life people do not always know why others do what they do. Similarly, the way information about the character is presented or withheld in a text does not parallel the real world. There is no real-world narrator to provide authoritative signals about a person's truthfulness, reliability, etc. In response to this problem Rashkow poses a reader-response approach, where the reader supplies the character's missing psychology so as not to be trapped by plot necessities in developing the portrait of the character.[95]

This study adopts a reader-response model proposed by John Darr—a "pragmatic" approach intended to balance theory and text.[96] This model attends to author, text, and reader, with the reader playing a powerful role since "readers 'build' characters, and critics 'build' readers."[97] Texts are designed to evoke responses from the reader and meaning is formed through the reader's interaction with the perspectives in the text.[98] Based on textual cues, the reader produces a conception of the story (a narrative world). This conception becomes the interpretive object and, therefore, becomes the focus for any attempts to understand the text.[99] Writing, reading, and interpretation, nevertheless, are conditioned and enabled by cultural context. Thus the critic has to be aware of the reader's "extra-

---

95. Rashkow, "Image," 106–08.

96. Darr, *Character*, 14. Darr is dependent on Iser, *Act* (1978). Reader-response proposals take varying forms. Some, often characterized as radical reader-response or reader-reaction methods, seek to attack the supposed authoritarian structures inherent in the text. Rather than follow textual cues and rhetorical strategies used by the author, these approaches (often deliberately) undermine such markers. While these methods are valid ways to read and can be helpful in exposing textual biases often ignored by commentators, they are less useful for presenting Luke's portrayal of God. See Vanhoozer, "Reader," 306–12.

97. Darr, *Character*, 16.

98. Tompkins ("Reader," 203–4) argued that in classical antiquity effect (emotive response) was more important than meaning. Once the author had engaged the reader/hearer's emotions *meaning* was superfluous. Moessner ("'Managing,'" 61–80) effectively refutes this notion, arguing that in a *diegesis* (like Luke-Acts) the author intended not just to prompt an effect (the author's proper ordering of the text interrelates plot and impact with authorial intention), but to convey "certain" knowledge (i.e. a specific meaning) that engages the correct response.

99. Darr, *Character*, 20.

text"—the common-knowledge, historical and cultural background information that is shared between the implied author and the implied reader.[100]

While there are several possible readers (implied, intended, and actual), the focus is on the implied reader (in Acts, a first-century reader). Darr considers the implied reader as the one "for whom the account was written,"[101] but it must be understood that this reader is constructed not only from the role set out for the reader by the implied author but also through the critic's disposition (the critic makes decisions about what the reader is like and what choices the reader would make). Such a reader combines both the critic's cultural horizon and the historical and cultural horizon in the textual world.[102] Thus, the critic's particular interests, commitments and knowledge affect the proposed reader, meaning that the analyst's knowledge can be a problem. However, the analyst can try to overcome the difference between the two horizons through investigation into the history and culture described in the text.

The reader is expected to have extra-textual information including basic religious, historical, political, geographical, and ethnic data.[103] In Luke's narrative, it appears that this reader possesses a somewhat "stereotyped knowledge" about contemporary cities and peoples and has some familiarity with popular Greco-Roman literature (cf. Acts 17). Consequently, it is assumed that the reader will recognize allusions to ideas found in Greco-Roman writings well-known at the time. More securely, since Luke repeatedly quotes the Jewish scriptures in Greek, this reader seems familiar with OT ideas found in the LXX. That the Greek OT is quoted so extensively in arguments from Scripture suggests that author and reader held these texts to be authoritative. While some have suggested that Luke's LXX usage indicates that the readership is gentile,[104] it need only imply that the reader spoke and read Greek—something that both Diaspora and some Palestinian Jews did.[105] When the authority attached to the OT is combined with the

---

100. Ibid., 22. Iser (*Act*, 79) calls this the "repertoire."

101. Darr, *Character*, 26. Darr's designation seems confused here. Iser (*Act*, 35–37) distinguishes between the implied reader, a position from which the perspectives of the text (narrator, characters, plot, and fictitious reader) are viewed and the intended reader (Iser's "fictitious reader"), a perspective within the text. Iser's implied reader combines the "role offered by the text and the real reader's own disposition" (*Act*, 37), which differs from Rimmon-Kenan (*Narrative*, 89), who considers it to be constructed from the text alone.

Although some might question whether the critic's involvement makes this approach too subjective, it is no more subjective than any other interpretive method. All investigative techniques involve presuppositions, imagination, and interpretive judgments. Thus, Gadamer (*Truth* (1982)) seems correct that historical-critical techniques cannot really re-create the intended meaning (neither can literary methods), since recovering the author's and reader's psyche is impossible. Nevertheless, being guided by the text and by investigation into the culture and beliefs seemingly shared by the author and reader, a good approximation can be attained.

102. Darr, *Character*, 26.

103. Gowler (*Host*) includes in the extra-text socio-cultural scripts like honor/shame, dyadic personality, limited good, kinship/household, and purity rules. While this is a helpful addition, it will not have as much emphasis here.

104. Fitzmyer, *Luke*, 57–59

105. Second Maccabees, written in Greek, is most likely written from Palestine for Jews in Egypt (see Stemberger, *Leib*, 6–7). Thus, at least some non-Diaspora Jews spoke and wrote Greek. Moreover, Fernández Marcos (*Septuagint*, 263) points out that 2 Macc 7:6 quotes Deut 32:36 from the LXX, which suggests the LXX was used by Palestinian Jews.

emphasis on Jewish institutions (temple, Law, Scripture) and Jewish piety and practice, it seems likely that the implied reader is significantly sympathetic to Jewish tradition (at least as a God-fearer).[106] Jervell and Esler have made strong cases for seeing a large Jewish contingent as well as God-fearers among Luke's original readership.[107] Rather than choose one side to this dual readership, it seems best to imagine the reader as being significantly aware of and sympathetic to Jewish traditions, while also being familiar with *popular* Hellenistic-period ideas.

This implied reader is interested in following the role set for it in the text, developing a portrait by following plot and characterization in a sequential manner. Initial pictures are re-examined and modified as more data is provided. Since no narrative contains all the information the reader is expected to have, the reader has to supply the missing data from the extra-text in order to understand the presentation.[108] A consistent character is constructed by correlating the portrait in the text with elements from the extra-text. This correlation is not done randomly, being informed as much as possible by textual cues (the more obscure the information might be, the more textual evidence should be offered before including it). Thus, in analyzing the portrayal of God in Acts, much of the discussion will involve stating what the reader encounters, what the reader will assume from the extra-text, and what conclusions the reader draws from this process.

During the reading process, the reader identifies with some characters and/or is distanced from others by their portrayal in the text. The narrative stimulates (raising questions, expectations) and guides responses, pushing the reader to re-evaluate beliefs and values.[109] Plot, setting, and stereotypical information affect how readers perceive the character's speech and behavior. However, how a reader perceives a character is most profoundly influenced by that person or group's interaction with other characters, specifically

---

106. Darr, *Character*, 27–28. See chapter 5 for how important Jewish institutions, piety, and practice are in Acts. Support for Luke's interest in those sympathetic to Judaism is strengthened if Luke is a Jew, but this is debated. In responding to J. T. Sanders (*Jews* (1987); "Jewish," 51–75), Salmon ("Insider," 76–77) suggested that Sanders *assumes* Luke was not a Jew. Salmon proposed that Luke's language and descriptions marked him as an "insider" so that in criticizing the Jews he is really offering self-criticism (Tiede [*Prophecy*, 7] also described Luke as depicting an intra-family dispute). Sanders ("Who," 452–54) correctly critiques Salmon's insider/outsider language because it is not necessarily true that an outsider would be unable to use the descriptions and distinctions an insider uses. However, Sanders misses Salmon's real point—the specific things that Luke points out in his narrative focus attention on Jewish details. In particular, Luke's emphasis on Torah-observance by Jewish Christians suggests that it is unlikely that Luke was a gentile. Sanders ("Who," 453) responded that Luke was simply showing that Christian Torah-observance was better than Jewish Torah-observance. However, Luke makes no attempt to denigrate how the Jews observe the Law. It is their rejection of Jesus and the divinely offered salvation that is the problem. Sterling ("'Opening,'" 201) declared that there is now an *opinio communis* that Luke is either a Jew or a God-fearer attached to the synagogue. If Luke is one or the other it is likely that his reader is also.

107. Jervell, *Luke*, 175–77; Esler, *Community*, 24–26, 30–45; see also Ravens, *Luke*, 11–16. Tyson ("Jews," 24–25) argued that Luke's implied reader was a God-fearer. It would follow that Luke was interested in writing to an audience that had associated itself with Judaism. However, Tyson's further conclusion that Luke is attempting to push the reader away from Judaism is not supported by the way Jewish piety, heroes, and hopes are portrayed throughout Acts (see chapter 5).

108. See Rimmon-Kenan, *Narrative*, 128–30.

109. Darr, *Character*, 30–32.

the protagonists.[110] In Acts, the reader will develop the characterization primarily through indirect means (actions, plot, setting, speech, etc.), since Luke offers little direct definition.[111] Luke's reader, nevertheless, remains dependent on the narrator because the narrator controls the story, determining how the reader is to perceive the indirect characterization.[112]

Summarizing, this reader-response method seeks to construct the character from the textual cues, while being aware of the narrative world's historical and social location. It provides the 'psychological' position (the analyst's, informed by other factors) necessary for the comprehending motives and making decisions. It is text-centered, but considers the author's and reader's roles (since the author embeds the narrator and reader's textual roles). It does not reconstruct the real history described by the text. Neither does it seek to provide the historical situation for the writing. Both constructs are speculative and are often in danger of forcing interpretations onto the text, rather than seeking to explore the ideology in the text. While this method is limited by the gap between the analyst's and the text's historical, social, and possibly religious location, it provides a useful investigative model.

Summary and Prospect

This chapter has defended analyzing the characterization of God and offered an outline of how to do so. Ten criteria that an analysis of Luke's portrayal of God should satisfy were identified. Characterization was presented as allowing the achievement of these desiderata. Now, using Darr's reader-response model and the characterization process described above, it is possible to explore Luke's portrayal of God as the *Ordainer of Times and Seasons*, the one who restores the kingdom.

Some special problems facing this study (separating Acts from the Gospel, speaking about God, considerations about ancient characters and about God as a character) were identified, but other issues remain. Previous portrayals of God influence the reader's expectations concerning God in a particular narrative.[113] OT and Second-Temple literature offer other characterizations of God that, given the reader's significant awareness of and sympathy with Jewish traditions, are likely to affect expectations. Therefore, chapter 2 begins by identifying seven conceptions about God found in Acts 1:1–8 which will then be analyzed for how they contribute to these expectations.

Chapter 2 also addresses the way that portrayals of God are developed in works that can be considered roughly similar to Acts. A look at 2 Maccabees and Josephus' *Antiquities* (Books 15–17), will suggest a role for these books' portrayal of God—a role the reader might also expect to be found Acts.

Chapter 3 discusses the parameters of this study. While divine actions and descriptions are not often directly given in the narrative, such direct characterization is not required.

110. Ibid., 41.

111. Ibid., 44. Also Bibb, "Characterization," 284–85.

112. See chapter 3.

113. M. M. Thompson, "God's," 185–86.

Nevertheless, it is necessary to know where to look for the presentation of God. A case is presented for attending to the narrator's role in leading the reader to conclusions about divine action. Luke also portrays Jesus in so close an analogy to God that, particularly as Lord, Jesus' actions should be seen as divine actions. Likewise, the Spirit is presented as marking the divine presence, promise, and will.

Building on these elements, chapters 4–6 explore the characterization of God in Acts. The initial characterization that God is the *ordainer of times and seasons* is confirmed through Luke's presentation, which implies that God restores the kingdom in the resurrected Davidic king (chapter 4), offers that kingdom to Jews, Samaritans, and gentiles (chapter 5), and controls the kingdom (and narrative) events right through to Paul's imprisonment in Rome (chapter 6). An epilogue sketches the reader's accumulated portrait that God, as the *ordainer of times and seasons*, is the restorer of the kingdom.

2

The Reader's Background Conceptions

CHAPTER 1 INDICATED THAT THE IMPLIED, FIRST-CENTURY READER IS FAMILIAR WITH the LXX and is significantly sympathetic to Jewish traditions. As such, the ways God is presented in the OT and Second-Temple Judaism seem to provide extra-textual material from which the reader would draw to fill in narrative gaps. The reader need not be familiar with each text, but it is reasonable that even a God-fearer would know major themes about the Jewish God. Examining these presentations should provide some idea about the narrative expectations their appearance in Acts would prompt for the reader. Also, taking a closer look at how God is portrayed in literature written in the same general vein as Acts is likely to suggest what narrative function the reader might expect the characterization of God to have.

Because there are various OT and Second-Temple Jewish conceptions about God, the focus must be narrowed to material that is likely to have affected the reader. The reader is 'cued' to supply extra-textual information when confronted with unexplained narrative data. Images that appear early-on in narratives require the reader to be more dependent on extra-textual information to understand them. Gunn and Fewell note that when "the divinity is only lightly sketched in the narrative" readers "will often bring to the story a conception of God from other stories." Although the authors are referring to stories where God is "minimally" portrayed, this principle would function at narrative beginnings.[1] In this light, the focus will be placed on seven ways (conceptions) God is presented in the opening verses, which, chapter 1 argued, suggest a characterization of God that is likely to impact the portrayal throughout Acts. Thus, the images here warrant investigation.

Following this are outlines of the portrayal of God in two Hellenistic-Jewish writings—2 Maccabees and Josephus' *Antiquities* books 15–17.[2] These sketches suggest areas for comparison with Acts, but, more importantly, provide a framework for understanding how the reader might expect Luke to use the characterization of God. This discussion will argue that the Acts reader will see the initial characterization of God pointing to a God who controls everything and fulfills promises, in particular the restoration of the kingdom, and will expect the portrayal of God to support claims made in the narrative.

1. Gunn and Fewell, *Narrative*, 85.

2. This study treats Josephus' work (while possibly written contemporary to or even after Luke-Acts) as another way that God is portrayed in Hellenistic-Jewish historiography. It represents a possible way to present God available in the general cultural environment.

Background Conceptions about God

In Acts 1:1–8 God appears to be a being with a *kingdom* (1:3), who makes *promises* (1:4), and establishes "times or periods" (1:7). These ideas suggest beliefs about 1) God as King, 2) God of Promises, and 3) God controlling History/Time. The reference to *establishing* implies that God acts with purpose, suggesting conceptions about 4) the divine Will/Plan. Behind everything is a picture reflecting 5) God as Personal—a character that appears in narratives, speaking and acting in personal (relational) ways. Further, God can be identified as 6) "Father" (1:4). Finally, the reference "to the ends of the earth" (1:8) suggests that 7) God stands in some relation to the nations.[3] These conceptions of God will be discussed as they appear in OT and Second-Temple literature.[4]

God in the OT [5]

God as a Character/Personal. In Genesis God is introduced as a character that is "directly and immediately present."[6] God has a linguistic style, being individuated through first person and self-referential speech (Gen 3:26; Exod 3:6).[7] There are adaptations to this picture since God receives significantly less dramatic depiction from 1 Samuel through to the post-exilic narratives. In these texts, the narrator does not have access to the divine inner-life (emotions, thoughts), with such access becoming more and more the domain of the prophets.[8] However, even this more-or-less unseen God is constructed as a character involved in the story because God is connected to the events "enough for a reader to ascribe the whole grand scheme of things to the divinity's desire and deed"[9] (cf. 2 Sam 15–20). Throughout the OT, the God portrayed had to "strike the reader again and again" as the one already known, requiring the narrator to "draw his character according to the image in the common mind."[10]

3. The category headings allow for ideas to be grouped whether or not the first-century reader would have titled them the same way. It is not suggested, for instance, that either in OT or in Second-Temple Judaism God was thought to be personal in the modern sense. Rather, God was portrayed within narratives as entering into relationships with humans and in human-like ways.

4. Since in these verses Jesus mediates the divine word to the disciples, an eighth category could be suggested—God and Human Agency. However, Jesus' role is addressed elsewhere in this work—chapter 3 argues that in Acts Jesus is to be included in the characterization of God and is not simply a mediating figure (Neyrey [*Render*, 85–89] discusses Jesus as a mediator figure, but admits that Jesus is uniquely given divine roles). Further, a primary way the characterization of Jesus affects the portrayal of God (as the Davidic king) is addressed in chapter 4.

5. The reason for only limited reference to modern critical notions about when and how the OT corpus developed is because the Acts implied reader would not know them. Thus, the texts are considered in their final form.

6. Humphreys, *Character*, 3.

7. Patrick, *Rendering*, 39.

8. Ibid., 22–23; cf. Dennis, *Looking*, 92–93.

9. Gunn and Fewell, *Narrative*, 81.

10. Patrick, *Rendering*, 46, 58. He argues that "out of character" portraits were absorbed into the overall biblical characterization of God, creating an "incomparable" God who is both consistent and mysterious (*Rendering*, 52–56).

The determination to make man in the divine image could be seen as "an unmistakable invitation to make some sense of God in human terms."[11] Although this text focuses on man being made in God's image not God in man's,[12] it appears correct that this passage implies a "point of contact" between humans and God, one expressed in personality.[13] Such notions are enhanced by the way anthropomorphic (God's arm, Isa 53:1; hand, Deut 26:8; voice, Ps 29:3; ear, Ps 116:2; eyes, 2 Chr 16.9) and anthropopathic (God's wrath, Exod 4:14) images are used throughout the OT.[14] These personal notions are placed in tension with images reflecting divine transcendent control over creation. God creates without effort and divine knowledge surpasses that of every creature. However, the "transcendent God wears a human face," knows human emotions, and thus is able to relate to humanity.[15]

The relationship between God and the people is described using terms like love, expressing careful supervision and concern by one person for another.[16] Even the giving of the divine name, YHWH (Exod 3:14), is a highly personal feature since, "To know this real name was to have power over the person and to be able to make an intimate relationship with them."[17] When this name is revealed Moses and Israel are invited into a personal relationship with God.

In light of this background image, the reader should be comfortable with conceiving of God as a personal being, able to enter into relationships with human beings. Anthropomorphic and anthropopathic metaphors used for God would be acceptable. Further, while the reader may not be surprised if God speaks during the narrative, he would just as likely expect to follow divine involvement in the narrative flow rather than in direct actions alone. Finally, the reader is likely to anticipate some continuity between the current and earlier portrayals of God. Thus certain questions will arise: Is the God portrayed in Acts consistent with the portrait in the OT? Is there a determined attempt by the author to show that the same God active in the OT is active in Acts?

God as King. The image reflecting God as King is so common in the OT that it could be considered a "common possession" for all eras in Israel's history.[18] This kingship is ultimately based in the divine creation of the world—Ps 33:6–9 implies that God is a sovereign who creates by uttering decrees from the throne. Such a conception is in keeping with ancient Semitic depictions about creator gods as kings who use their power to defeat chaos.[19] Acknowledging God as King could have been known even in the Mosaic period given that the Ark is identified as the divine throne, and that there is some sugges-

---

11. Miles, *God*, 14.

12. See Baly, *God*, 28; Fretheim, *Suffering*, 10–11; Zimmerli, *Theology*, 37.

13. R. Mason, *Pictures*, 4.

14. See Baly, *God*, 50; Eichrodt, *Theology*, 258; Patrick, *Rendering*, 19–22, 38.

15. R. Mason, *Pictures*, 89–90; Patrick, *Rendering*, 16–18.

16. Mills, *Images*, 46; cf. R. Mason, *Pictures*, 4.

17. Mills, *Images*, 31; cf. Eichrodt, *Theology*, 206, 273–76; Patrick, *Rendering*, 30–32.

18. Patrick, "Kingdom," 72.

19. Cf. Eichrodt, *Theology*, 194; R. Mason, *Pictures*, 107; Zimmerli, *Theology*, 41. R. Mason (*Pictures*, 93–96) discusses the Egyptian and Babylonian King/Creator concepts.

tion that a heavenly court attends YHWH.[20] This conception, nevertheless, appears most frequently in the Psalms.[21]

The king was supposed to defend and judge the people.[22] As King, God orders the social world[23] using divine power against rebellious factors within the kingdom (those who oppress the poor and the weak) and against external forces which disrupt the peace and prosperity of God's people (cf. Ps 72).[24] Indeed, divine kingship is ultimately seen in peace (prosperity, health and justice) being produced for Israel (Pss 47, 93, 95, 97, 98).[25] In Isa 52:7–10 God's absolute sovereignty is extended to all nations and this universal rule becomes the ideal way to express the divine majesty (Ps 95:3; Obad 21). Divine control over the nations offers hope to the exiled people because God can return the nation from its dispersion (Ezek 12:1–16; 33:23–29; Isa 41:25–27; 43:15). At the same time, this absolute sovereignty functions to invalidate all other lordships for Israel.[26]

The image that God is King is a "base metaphor" relating to other factors:[27] 1) Israel's earthly king was a vassal to the real divine sovereign.[28] As such, the king could act as a model for understanding the divine kingship, suggesting that "the king of Israel makes the domain of Yahweh visible on earth."[29] This belief leads the Chronicler to refer to the Davidic kingdom as the 'kingdom of YHWH' (1 Chr 28:5; 2 Chr 13:8).[30] The Davidic king was to be an agent of God in bringing peace, security and rest to the people (Ps 89:22–26; 2 Sam 7:10–11).[31] At the same time, 2) the idea that God is King implies that the temple is the royal palace,[32] 3) makes commandments royal decrees,[33] and 4) presents the Day of the Lord as the King's final establishment of order.[34] Therefore, this image is central to the OT portrayal of God, providing hope and order for the people.

Luke's reader should expect God, as King, to be the ultimate power behind everything. Specifically, the image is likely to focus attention on the "kingdom of God" being established (God's reign over all nations, producing peace (including social justice) for the people). The tie to the Davidic kingdom could lead the reader to expect a Davidic king

---

20. Eichrodt, *Theology*, 195.

21. Ibid., 196.

22. Baly, *God*, 140.

23. Brueggemann, *Theology*, 238; Patrick, "Kingdom," 74.

24. R. Mason, *Pictures*, 103–4; cf. Mills, *Images*, 5–6.

25. R. Mason, *Pictures*, 108.

26. Brueggemann, *Theology*, 239–40; Eichrodt, *Theology*, 199.

27. Mettinger, *Search*, 92.

28. Baly, *God*, 140; Mills, *Images*, 47. This is typical among ancient Near-East peoples, see Patrick, "Kingdom," 74–75.

29. Zimmerli, *Theology*, 92 (discussing Ps 2); cf. R. Mason, *Pictures*, 102–3.

30. Albertz, *History*, 547: the Chronicler evaluated the "time of David and Solomon as the goal and climax of the Israelite foundation history."

31. See Strauss, *Messiah*, 35–36.

32. Mettinger, *Search*, 101.

33. Brueggemann, *Theology*, 181; Patrick, "Kingdom," 75.

34. Mettinger, *Search*, 109.

would be restored, just as seems to be suggested by the question the disciples ask (Acts 1:6). The reader may also place great importance on the temple and the Law due to their relationship to God's kingdom, suggesting a possible concern with how these factors are treated in the Acts portrayal of God.

God over History/Time. The idea that God rules over history/time also begins with the divine role in creation. Everything, including humankind is dependent upon the Creator. Israel experienced this in the way God controlled its past[35]—God rescued Israel from Egypt and established it in the land. These actions lived on, not just in memory, but in the people's thought and prayer life (cf. among others, Josh 2:10; 24:5–7; Judg 6:13). The God who controls history establishes kings and judges rulers who are unfaithful to God (1 Kgs 19).[36] Israel, therefore, experienced divine control over history through cycles of blessing, judgment, and restoration.[37] Thus, history is seen as the means by which God is disclosed to the people. It seems, "reality without the working of God does not yet exist" for them.[38]

Such control over history depicts divine power constantly at work, whether indirectly or directly bringing things (events) into existence. Joseph could say that God sent him ahead into Egypt to preserve Jacob's family (Gen 45:7), even though his brothers did not act with this intention.[39] Such divine action brought about interaction with other nations, demonstrating that God controls their histories as well;[40] an idea that comes to full expression in Daniel. Here, God controls the entire world, intervening in every nation's temporal affairs (Dan 2:36–44). Dates may be given according to the reigns of Babylonian kings, but in 2:21 it is Daniel's God who removes and sets up kings, changing "times and seasons." In Daniel 5 God has numbered the days of Belshazzar's reign and in Daniel 7 God is pictured as the "Ancient One," furthering the relationship between God and time.[41] This control over time and history is also portrayed in Psalm 90, which contrasts man's brief life with God's eternity and ability to use time for divine purposes.[42]

With this idea the reader is likely to expect God to control all the narrative events, even when this does not appear to be so. Indeed, the reference to "times or periods [seasons]" in Acts 1:8 may lead the reader to recall the same phrase from Daniel 2, emphasizing divine control over kings and kingdoms within world history. It would, therefore, create expectations about the kingdom's restoration to Israel and the divine role in that. The reader, consequently, seems likely to be interested in how and when this restoration is to take place.

---

35. Eichrodt, *Theology*, 231; Westerman, *Elements*, 39.

36. Briend, *Dieu*, 19.

37. Westerman (*Elements*, 55) identifies this cycle in Israel's history.

38. Westerman, *Elements*, 12.

39. Baly, *God*, 72; Fretheim, *Suffering*, 75.

40. Westerman, *Elements*, 13, 102.

41. Mills, *Images*, 123–24. She is following Davies, *Daniel*, 81–120.

42. See Mills, *Images*, 111–12.

God's Will/Plan. The divine will or plan is often associated with works done by the unseen God. The narrator or a character in the narrative sees the divine purpose in retrospect (cf. Gen 45:7). Through an event being predicted and then fulfilled, characters (and readers) are led to relate events to the divine plan.[43] Specifically, this will/plan seems to be associated with promises to Israel, and, therefore, in and beyond the exile, to Israel's future hope (Isa 55; Jer 29:11).[44]

The opening chapters of Genesis appear to express divine personal decision through the narrated actions. These rational, creative acts imply a God who plans.[45] Similarly, Isa 46:11 uses the word for creation when describing God using nations for the divine purpose (cf. 2 Kgs 19:25; Isa 37:26).[46] Human plans can oppose God, but ultimately such plans will be brought to destruction (Isa 7:5–7; 8:9–10). Sometimes, however, the divine will is enigmatic (David punished for numbering the people). Yet, the OT retains the view that God was always set on providing for God's people,[47] even if the divine will was seen in wrath being poured out on Israel (Amos 5:18; Zeph 1:15; Ezek 20).

In the OT, the divine plan is singular (Isa 5:19; 14:26; 19:17) and not simply separate acts in history.[48] In some cases this suggests that events are shaped in advance (cf. Isa 37:26), but ideas about foreordination are not to be pressed too far since room is left for human freedom.[49] The emphasis is on divine freedom since, while God has securely promised certain items (the Davidic kingdom), the prophets include conditional formulas in their restatements (Isa 7:9).[50] Finally, the divine plan moves toward a goal—that divine majesty would be manifest.[51] This manifestation affects not only the future, but also the present, providing order to the social and political environment.[52] Through the Law, God provides a social and religious structure that models the divine plan for the people.[53] The belief that God punishes the guilty even when they seem to go unpunished (2 Sam 3:39), suggests notions about how important the divine purpose was for ordering human social life. Thus, the divine plan is not simply seen in hopes for Israel as a nation, but also in the hope for a properly ordered society before God.

Again, this image seems likely to lead Luke's reader to expect divine control over the narrative events. Everything should work toward the divine purpose being fulfilled. The reader may associate this with the promise about the Davidic kingdom and hope for Israel, but also with concerns for peace and social order. The reader would, however, realize that

43. Kort, *Story*, 26.

44. Brueggemann, *Theology*, 355–56; Zimmerli, *Theology*, 68.

45. Mills, *Images*, 10–11.

46. R. Mason, *Pictures*, 38–39.

47. Eichrodt, *Theology*, 262–63.

48. Mettinger, *Search*, 143; Patrick, *Rendering*, 113.

49. Patrick, *Rendering*, 113.

50. Mettinger, *Search*, 145–47.

51. Mills, *Images*, 87.

52. Brueggemann, *Theology*, 190–91; Eichrodt, *Theology*, 209–10; Mills, *Images*, 39; Patrick, *Rendering*, 73–74.

53. Eichrodt, *Theology*, 242–43.

God's purpose is often worked out enigmatically. It is likely, then, for the reader to look for assurance that the divine plan is being fulfilled as the narrative unfolds.

God of Promises/Covenant.[54] Central to the belief about God as promise-maker is that God is both powerful and reliable enough to change life for the covenant people—God is able to fulfill promises.[55] Although God promises (to Noah) not to destroy the earth, for Israel the divine promises begin with the Abrahamic covenant (Gen 17:4–7).[56] This promise expresses a desire by God to bless the entire world and not just Israel; however, Israel latches on to the promise of *land*. For Israel, God "moves through history, obligated and propelled by this utterance."[57] Israel's life is tied to this promise,[58] even though the promise becomes conditioned upon fidelity. The land is a divine gift to Israel as God fulfills promises to Abraham and Moses (Deut 9:5; Josh 24:13), but God can take it away when Israel acts unfaithfully. The consequences of infidelity eventually lead to hopes for a restored land (Amos 9:11–15). Thus, the land-promise remains a central factor in Israel's thought.

The Davidic kingdom (2 Sam 7:5–16; Ps 89) represents the second key promise. Even during the monarchy, the prophets take up this subject (Isa 11:1–5), announcing a new king who will restore justice and well-being. Indeed, this promise is never forgotten, being constantly reinterpreted and made relevant to new situations, leading to messianic expectations.[59]

For Israel, the God of Promises is also reflected in deliverance from Egypt. In Exod 3:8 God's promise to deliver lays the groundwork for rehearsing divine deeds. That God had fulfilled promises to deliver in the past (the Exodus) sets the stage for continued promise-fulfillment thinking beyond the exile.[60] At the same time, the Exodus provides the background to the covenant proper in Exod 34. Here, God is committed to those bound by the covenant (to being Israel's God), yet this commitment does not mean God would overlook sin (34:7).[61] The pledge to be the people's God is taken up repeatedly in the exilic period (Jer 11:4; Ezek 11:20; 14:11) and puts God on display before the nations: divine power to deliver the people is being judged by these nations.[62] Israel, therefore, attributes the restoration from exile to God's commitment to the covenant (Isa 54:7–10).[63] Consequently, this commitment to the people is seen as a secure promise.

---

54. While references to covenant in Acts may seem limited, chapter 5 will suggest that (through the importance placed on Law, temple, and Abraham) Acts implies an ongoing covenantal interest.

55. Brueggemann, *Theology*, 164.

56. Mills, *Images*, 19–20.

57. Brueggemann, *Theology*, 169.

58. Fretheim, *History*, 53–54; McKenzie, *Theology*, 142.

59. Von Rad, *Theology*, 311; Strauss, *Messiah*, 37–38.

60. Zimmerli, *Theology*, 30–31.

61. Brueggemann, *Theology*, 217–18; Fretheim, *Suffering*, 27.

62. Brueggemann, *Theology*, 299.

63. Ibid., 154.

Given references to divine promises, the Acts reader seems likely to expect that promises to Israel were about to be fulfilled. The reader might think chiefly about the promises of land and the Davidic kingdom, but may also recall the promise to bless all the nations. The Apostles' question (Acts 1:6), which follows the reference to the divine promise, concerns the elements *kingdom* and *Israel*. Since Jesus does not deny that these promises would be realized, the reader would continue to expect evidence that God is now (or soon will) fulfill them.

God and the Nations. The Table of Nations (Gen 10) unites all nations under the Creator without distinguishing Israel from others.[64] All nations were created to be in a harmony that was disrupted by Babel. The promise to Abraham, which becomes addressed to Israel, seeks to remedy this situation by causing Israel to be a blessing to the nations (Isa 19:24–25; 42:6–7; Mic 4:1–4).[65] However, throughout most of the narrative works there are few references to foreigners worshipping God and Israel blessing other nations. An exception (1 Kgs 8:41–43) expects that foreigners would pray to Israel's God. This image is transformed into a future ideal where all nations will follow suit (8:60).[66]

The eighth-century prophets are the first to tie God to international politics as Assyria (Isa 10), Egypt (Isa 19), and Tyre (Isa 23) are pictured under God's control.[67] Subjection to divine judgment was extended to all nations (Pss 75, 94). Yet, Israel remains the only nation that God has "known" (Amos 3:2), suggesting its exclusivity. As such, Israel expected God to put things right by suppressing foreign nations (Pss 9:5; 43:1; 44:7–11).[68] The oppression by foreign nations also leads the prophets to deny that other gods even exist since the God of Israel has complete claim over all nations (Isa 45:5), even if that means God uses the nations to judge Israel.[69] Eventually, this oppression leads to Israel equating its national enemies with God's enemies (Joel 3:1–17).[70] Thus, beliefs about God and the Nations envision a tension—although the prophets expected that all evil powers would finally be destroyed and divine rule established (Zech 14:3–9; Isa 13:4–9; 66:15), they also saw the nations living in harmony under divine rule (Isa 2; Mic 4).

The Acts reader should pick up on this tension. Since the images discussed so far emphasize God fulfilling promises to *Israel*, the reader could see the witness as involving divine judgment upon the nations. However, Jesus' words seem to suggest a positive message that begins with Israel and moves out to the nations (the nations being blessed through Israel). Thus, the reader will have to determine whether this witness "to the ends of the earth" is to be understood positively or negatively.

---

64. Von Rad, *Theology*, 162.

65. Baly, *God*, 123–24.

66. Noth, *History*, 91.

67. Payne, *Theology*, 131.

68. Baly, *God*, 165–66.

69. Mills, *Images*, 63.

70. R. Mason, *Pictures*, 137–38.

God as Father. References to God as Father occur only about twenty times in the OT. Divine fatherhood is applied corporately to Israel, but individually only the king is called "son of God."[71] Semitic views about the father evoke ideas about rule, ownership, and general authority mixed with ideas associated with love.[72] The father is considered the one who provides the inheritance.[73] Parents have obligations toward the children (paternal love—Ps 103:13), but children also have the responsibility to act in keeping with the family.

Father expresses the divine commitment to and care for Israel. It suggests a "peculiar intimacy" between Israel and God.[74] Like a father, God blesses God's child, Israel (Isa 42:6; 43:1). Yet, the father also chastises his treacherous child (Jer 3:19; Hos 11:1–9). With rebuke, there, nevertheless, is always the balancing compassion that willingly takes back the penitent child (Jer 31:20).

While this image stems from the divine claim on all people as Creator,[75] the main emphasis is on the claim to be Israel's creator—Israel was established as God's child through the Exodus (Deut 32:6; Hos 11:1). In this redeeming act God shows a kinsman relationship to Israel, protecting the "family."[76] It is this belief in the redeeming Father that gives hope amidst despair in the exilic prophecies (Isa 64:8–12). While Israel has failed to live up to its family obligations (cf. Mal 2:10), God remains the compassionate Father.[77]

The special relationship between king and God is most clearly seen in Ps 2:7, which states that God has begotten the king (cf. Ps 89:27). This idea appears to develop from the belief that God had promised David He would establish God's kingdom through him (2 Sam 7). The image, then, sees the divine relationship as father to all Israel mediated to the people through the king.[78]

This conception, once again, seems to lead the Acts reader to expect that God is interested in Israel's welfare. God is the Father of Israel, and in this time when foreigners rule over them, God should be acting to redeem the people. Further, if the term Father is strongly linked to the relation in which Jesus stands to God, the idea that Jesus is the promised Davidic king would resonate powerfully with other images that focus on the kingdom of Israel.

Thus, based on these OT images appearing in Acts 1:1–8, Luke's reader will likely read Acts with expectations that God is set to restore the kingdom to Israel. Most images also focus attention on divine control over events and people. However, the situation the reader faces

---

71. Briend, *Dieu*, 72–73. He also notes that it was common among the nations surrounding Israel to refer to God as Father. R. Mason (*Pictures*, 52–56) discusses the image in both Egyptian and Canaanite belief.

72. Eichrodt, *Theology*, 235.

73. R. Mason, *Pictures*, 50–51.

74. Brueggemann, *Theology*, 244–45.

75. Eichrodt, *Theology*, 236; R. Mason, *Pictures*, 57; cf. Isa 45:9–13.

76. R. Mason, *Pictures*, 24. Albertz (*History*, 552) notes that this imagery is most prominent in the Chronicler's accounts: "Yahweh is said to have been present to the Israelites in both South and North as the family friend."

77. R. Mason, *Pictures*, 58–59.

78. Ibid., 62–64.

"in the real world" would seem to deny that the kingdom is restored or even that God is in control. Luke, therefore, must lead the reader to see that God acts in keeping with these expectations or risk the reader denying that the OT God has truly been active in these events.

God in Second-Temple Judaism

While it is reasonably certain that the reader (given the repeated LXX citations in Acts) is familiar with the beliefs about God expressed in the OT, there is much less certainty about the Second-Temple literature. These writings come from a range of locations (spatial, temporal, and social), indicating that Judaism was represented in several varieties during this period. Any analysis must be careful not to homogenize, so this discussion will attempt to note divergences in this literature where they may impact the reader's expectations. The following is not exhaustive, but sketches the general way(s) the OT concepts were developed during this period and suggests how this might affect the reader. Again, it is not maintained that the reader is familiar with these texts, but that, through sympathy with Judaism, the reader could know the general conceptions about God expressed by them.

God as a Character/Personal. The trend toward less direct-narration of divine action continues, but there is great diversity. God remains indirectly involved (using both human and supernatural agents) and divine control over events is generally affirmed. While, typically, Josephus de-emphasizes direct divine involvement, God can appear (*Ant.* 17:41–45)[79] and there is a sense that divine delivering power (sometimes termed manifestations—ἐπιφάνεια, cf. *Ant.* 33:10; 9:58) makes God present (cf. *Ant.* 8:282; 12:300).[80] Artapanus places emphasis on human action even where the biblical account attributes the action to God,[81] but *Jubilees* includes direct divine involvement where Genesis does not (cf. 10:23 with Gen 11:5).[82] God speaks and appears (directly and in dreams) in the *Jubilees* account.

Many writers use human-like language with reference to God. The apocalyptists picture God seated on a throne surrounded by courtiers (e.g. *As. Mos.* 10:3; *1 En.* 47:3; *2 En.* 66:3). Allusions are made to God's face, hand, arm, foot, ear, and mouth (e.g. *Sib. Or.* 3:549, 672; *Pss. Sol.* 13:1; 18:3; Wis 5:16; *As. Mos.* 10:3; 12:9; *1 En.* 1:3; 14:24; 25:3). God is characterized as showing emotions such as wrath (Sir 5:6; 45:19; *Jub.* 3:23; 1 Macc 1:64; 3:8; *1 En.* 91:4; Bar 2:13) and love (Sir 2:11; 4:10; Tob 13:6, 10; *T. Iss.* 1:1; *T. Naph.* 8:4, 10; *T. Jos.* 1:4; Wis 3:9).[83] Thus, God can be presented in relational ways. As Cohen comments,

79. Gnuse (*Dreams*, 16–17) argues that an actual appearance by God cannot be ruled out here since Josephus' terminology is in keeping with the biblical canon.

80. Betz, "Miracles," 214; von Schlatter, *Theologie*, 53–54.

81. Collins, *Between*, 43. Denis (*Introduction*, 258) notes something similar in Aristeas, who deletes all non-earthly scenes.

82. Both works retell biblical accounts, although they are different kinds of writing (Artapanus is a Hellenistic-Jewish historian, *Jubilees* a biblical midrash).

83. Wicks (*Doctrine*, 30–122) discusses anthropomorphic/anthropopathic language at length. When using Wicks, care has been taken to avoid his conclusions (particularly where they address trends in the data) since

"Popular piety does not need or want an immutable and shapeless Prime Mover; it wants a God who reveals himself to people, listens to prayer, and can be grasped in human terms. . . . This is the God of practically all the Hebrew and Aramaic, and some of the Greek, Jewish literature of antiquity."[84]

Regardless, most authors show restraint in using anthropomorphic(-pathic) language so as to acknowledge divine transcendence. Philo sometimes even removes such language from biblical passages.[85] Tobit's author also seems reluctant to use language that likens God to man.[86] Baruch follows the OT "vacillating" between divine immanence and transcendence.[87] Sirach avoids mentioning that God was ever seen (even in dreams).[88] *Jubilees* employs anthropomorphic language but never describes a divine form.

Divine transcendence often seems to be portrayed by placing mediators between God and man. For Philo, God's *Logos* (speech or reason) is the divine means for contact with the world (God being "far removed").[89] Angels, for Philo, become intermediaries between man and God, a concept found also in the way they are pictured as bearing human prayers to God (*T. Levi* 3:5–7).[90] But angels are also envisioned as God's governing regents (cf. *1, 2 Enoch*), bearing messages to men (*1 En.* 93:2; *2 En.* 1:8; *Jubilees 91*), and as agents for punishment or aid (*1 En.* 100:4; *2 Maccabees*). Transcendence, however, does not appear to have affected God's ability and willingness to hear and respond to prayers, or to be involved in defending the people since the literature presents people calling out to God in prayer and God responding. Cohen concludes, "Whatever feelings the Jews had about God's elusiveness and ineffectiveness were caused not by his transcendence or remoteness but by the incomprehensibility of his actions."[92]

The Acts reader, then, would still think about God in a personal manner. The reader anticipates some anthropomorphic(-pathic) language, although transcendent imagery and concepts are more likely. Since intermediaries were prominent in the literature, the reader could be familiar with divine activity being seen through actions by angels or other divinely connected figures. Thus, the reader may expect to see less direct divine involvement, but be able to attribute both direct and indirect actions to God. The portrayal of God would still have to be consistent with the OT since the Second-Temple conceptions seem to develop from the OT images.

---

his work pre-dates the discovery of the DSS and the re-dating prompted by those finds. His work also tends towards homogenizing the works (in part because he uses systematic-theological categories), failing to give enough weight to the individual differences. However, he provides extensive citations that are helpful for comparison.

84. Cohen, *Maccabees*, 87.

85. Ibid.

86. Wicks, *Doctrine*, 35.

87. deSilva, *Introducing*, 211.

88. Wicks, *Doctrine*, 30.

89. Cohen, *Maccabees*, 82.

90. See deSilva, *Introducing*, 9.

91. See Schürer, *History*, 309–10.

92. Cohen, *Maccabees*, 86.

God as King. The image reflecting God seated on a throne amidst the angelic court expresses divine cosmic majesty[93] founded in God creating all things (Sir 42:15—43:33). The title 'king' emphasizes God's greatness (cf. Sir 50:15; Tob 13; 1 *En.* 84:2), and, thus, portrays the transcendent Lord over all creation.[94] The temple is interpreted as God's dwelling place even if this is only a future hope (cf. *Sib. Or.* 3.767–84).[95] However, the Enochic ascents present the divine throne-room using temple imagery from Daniel 7, Isaiah 6, and Ezekiel 1–2 and 40–48, emphasizing that God's dwelling place is transcendent.[96] Similarly, 4Q403–5 pictures the heavenly tabernacle as God's throne-room using imagery from Ezekiel.[97] Since the Jerusalem temple (alongside the heavenly temple) continues as a divine throne-room (cf. 1 *En.* 91:11–17; 93:1–10), Jerusalem, nevertheless, remains the center for divine rule over Israel and the gentiles.

The divine descents in *1 En.* 83–90, *Jubilees,* and *The Testaments of the Twelve Patriarchs* (books which picture God as a king on the exalted throne), "simply enshrine the idea that God will in the future judge the wicked and bless the righteous."[98] Thus, the kingly God is the present and future judge over God's people and the world. God also defends the people (seen most clearly in 1–2 Maccabees). In *As. Mos.* (chs. 4, 10), God, as Israel's King, is in covenant relationship with the people (God is the God of their fathers). Obedience to the covenant will lead God to defend them, removing the persecutors.[99] In the *War Scroll,* God is portrayed as the king who enables his faithful to win the war between the "sons of light" and the "sons of darkness."[100] Divine kingship (just as in the OT), therefore, appears to have spurred hopes for a time marked by rest and peace, where the divine social order would be re-established (1QM 12:7–16; 17:6–7; cf. also 1 *En.* 25:3–7; 1QSb 3:5; 5:21). Indeed, *Pss. Sol.* 17 pictures God's reign as a time when foreign oppressors are removed and the dispersed are gathered, restoring God's inheritance.[101]

Finally, while in the OT Israel's king was presented as modeling divine rule, foreign domination leads to God repeatedly being presented as the King over kings. This image encapsulates the belief that gentile kings do not have the power that God does (Jdt 10:14; 3

93. Ibid., 84.

94. Camponovo, *Königtum,* 134, 140; Wicks, *Doctrine,* 40. Russell, *Disclosure,* 86: "Here, then, we have a picture of a wholly transcendent God, whose great glory is blinding in its magnificence and whose presence is portrayed in flames of fire."

95. Grelot, *L'Espérance,* 109; Camponovo, *Königtum,* 330–31.

96. See Knibb, "Ethiopic Book," 40; Nickelsburg, 53.

97. So Schürer, *History,* 463; cf. Schwemer, "Gott," 45–118.

98. Wicks, *Doctrine,* 38. Collins ("Kingdom," 95) suggests that the belief that God would overthrow Israel's enemies was common to the varied understandings concerning God's kingdom in Second-Temple thought.

99. Camponovo, *Königtum,* 173–74. For a similar thought in the *Letter of Aristeas* see Fischer, *Eschatologie,* 118; also discussion of 2 Maccabees below.

100. Camponovo, *Königtum,* 305–6. He (*Königtum,* 176) also finds this eschatological hope in the way God is presented as king in *Judith,* the additions to Esther and Daniel, 2 Maccabees, and *3 Ezra.* See also the eschatological hymn in *As. Mos.* 10.

101. See Nickelsburg, *Jewish,* 208. Grelot (*L'Espérance,* 100) notes that the restored messianic kingdom pictured in *Pss. Sol.* 17 is oriented on social justice and conformity to the Torah.

Macc 2:1–20).[102] In 2 Maccabees, God is the sole good King (1:24–28) who will act to show who truly is God. This presents a contrast to the earthly kings (7:16–17; 9:8–10; 13:4–8), who think themselves powerful (even godlike, 9:8–10), but are really just mortal.[103] Thus, the conception that God is King provides hope to the oppressed people—they do not need to fear the gentile rulers; those rulers need to fear God if they go beyond the authority God grants them.[104]

The Acts reader should still expect to see God as the ultimate power since God is the transcendent Lord of Heaven. The expectation that the "kingdom of God" would be established remains present, although the emphasis may be eschatological. The reader also would continue to understand divine kingship as pertaining to God dispensing justice and defending the people. Thus, references to the kingdom cause the reader to reflect on how important covenantal faithfulness is. One striking factor is that the concentration on God's heavenly temple may lead the reader to be less focused on the physical temple as the divine dwelling place, although the latter idea does appear.

God over History/Time. Divine control over history/time continues to be connected with God leading Israel. *First Enoch* 83–90 retells Israel's history and the divine providential control over it, expressing a belief that God is responsible for its fortunes (cf. *Jub.*; *4 Ezra* 11–12).[105] In *Judith*, Israel's past, present, and future are presented as divinely ordained (cf. 9:5). Current events, therefore, could demonstrate divine direction, as Philo appears to see in the solution to the crises in Alexandria and Jerusalem (*Legat.*).[106] First and Second Maccabees also illustrate this belief, seeing God controlling Israel's defense (and punishment).[107]

For some writers, divine control over history involved direct interventions (Artapanus often uses miracles to note God directing history).[108] Nickelsburg observes that the way the plot in Tobit (which includes angelic involvement) is so intricately woven emphasizes how carefully God orchestrates events in history.[109] Second Maccabees recounts angelic manifestations that defend the temple (3:39; 5:18) and indicates that God even controls the

---

102. Camponovo (*Königtum*, 142) finds that this concept features particularly in writings during the Seleucid period. Concerning 3 Macc 2 he writes (199), "Es stellt sich so die Frage, wer der wirkliche König ist. Die beiden Gebete geben deutlich ihrem Glauben Ausdruck, dass Gott der wahre König ist." Cf. Wolter, "Reich," 546.

103. Nickelsburg, *Resurrection*, 94–95; van Henten, *Martyrs*, 113–14, 164–65; Enermalm-Ogawa, *Langage*, 66–67.

104. Josephus rarely refers to God as king. He may have seen the need to de-emphasize ideas about God's kingdom because they had become too closely related to messianic revolts. Alternatively, Josephus could be concerned with treating the Torah as a political constitution overseen by priests (a theocracy rather than a kingdom—see S. Mason, *Josephus*, 105–9). However, Josephus relates two sons of Herod comparing Caesar with God in a positive light (*Ant.* 16:106; 17:103); this would intimate that Josephus may have refrained from referring to God as king due to deference for the Emperor.

105. See Rowland, *Open*, 136–43; Wicks, *Doctrine*, 41.

106. Collins, *Between*, 132.

107. See Wicks (*Doctrine*, 62–63) and below on 2 Maccabees.

108. See Denis, *Introduction*, 256.

109. Nickelsburg, *Jewish*, 32; cf. Wicks, *Doctrine*, 36.

details: the sun suddenly appearing on a cloudy day (1:19–22);[110] Antiochus being thrown from his chariot the moment he calls for it to speed up so he can crush Jerusalem (9:3–7); and the temple purification taking place on the same date as its profanation (10:1–8).[111] In contrast, 1 Maccabees affirms divine control over events (prayers and echoes/recitations from Scripture imply the author saw God's sacred history unfolding in Israel's history),[112] but direct intervention is not narrated. Likewise, the deliverance in Judith is attributed to God, although it is played out through her activism. Miracles in the absolute sense do not occur, but the author does express belief that God acts in history.[113]

References to stages in history and to the rise of empire after empire place the focus on divine control over all nations (as in Daniel).[114] It is "part of the genius of the apocalyptic visionaries" that they saw the transcendent God controlling the details of world history.[115] Even a relatively late apocalypse like *4 Ezra* (ca. 100 C.E.) expresses the conviction that God has determined the succession of kings. But, the belief that God ordered history and apportioned rule over nations was not limited to apocalyptic literature: it can be found in the additions to Esther, and Wisdom (6:3).[116] Authors make reference to God controlling the timing of events—*Pss. Sol.* 17:23 suggests that only God knows the time (prohibiting speculation about it) when the kingdom of God would be established.[117] God sets the time for the events of the last days (*Apoc. Bar.* 27:11). God is the "Head of Days" (*1 En.* 39:11), who has appointed days for all things (*1 En.* 92:2). God arranges "times and seasons" (*Apoc. Bar.* 48:2; *4 Ezra* 4:36). In *Ant.* 15:373–79 God gives Manaemus foreknowledge about how long Herod will reign as king, suggesting that God determines the king's appointed (προθεσμίας) times (15:378; cf. 17:41–45, 345–48, prophecies about reigns coming to an end).[118] Thus, God is pictured as controlling history/time, whether in relation to kings and kingdoms or to any element of human affairs.[119]

Luke's reader, then, would expect to observe God directing not only the events, but also their timing. The reference to "times or periods" in combination with the "kingdom of God" could lead the reader to forgo speculation (as *Pss. Sol.* 17), but the phrase is also associated with God determining kingly succession so that hopes for a restoration would not necessarily be overcome. Regarding how the events are narrated, the reader would

110. So van Henten, *Maccabean*, 44.

111. Collins (*Daniel*, 325) notes here the epitomator's interest in ironies, providence, and correspondences.

112. Bickerman, *God*, 17; DeSilva, *Introducing*, 256; cf. Nickelsburg, *Jewish*, 116: "Our author believes that through Judas 'the savior of Israel' (9:21) God 'the savior of Israel' (4:30) delivered his people."

113. DeSilva, *Introducing*, 103; Nickelsburg, *Jewish*, 107. Wisdom 10–19 also suggests this non-interventionist view; see Nickelsburg, *Jewish*, 181–82.

114. Cohen, *Maccabees*, 100–101.

115. Russell, *Divine*, 86–87.

116. DeSilva, *Introducing*, 333, 121, 138.

117. See Grelot, *L'Espérance*, 100; Nickelsburg, *Jewish*, 209.

118. Josephus appears to be influenced by Daniel, thus this motif is not surprising (see S. Mason, *Josephus*, 49, 120–21). Josephus also seems to view prophecy as a means for revealing divine providence (see Squires, *Plan*, 136–37).

119. See also Strauss, *Messiah*, 46–47.

expect to see divine control over history whether the recitation included direct intervention or not.

God's Will/Plan. The divine will/plan is seen as operative in the course of events. Judith (9:5) expresses the belief that whatever happens after she has prayed is God's will. In Sirach God's will is evident not just when there is no other thing to attribute the outcome to, but in every outcome (11:12, 33). First Maccabees seems to express that God's purpose is worked out through the Hasmonean family.[120] The divine plan is also revealed in how history unfolds (*1 En.* 83–90, 93:1–10 + 91:11–17 + 93:11–14). Indeed, for the apocalyptists, divine control over everything provided an order to the world, meaning the divine will could be known and obeyed.[121]

All creation works to fulfill God's desire to punish the guilty and reward the righteous (*Sir* 39:28–31; 40:8–10).[122] The apparently intentional relation to Israel's OT past in 1 Maccabees suggests that God's current action develops from the divine plan to fulfill promises to Israel.[123] Among the apocalyptists, the divine purpose takes on an eschatological dimension since God has given a second age where the righteous receive their reward.[124] This last age will "bring to perfection" what has gone wrong, finally establishing the divine plan for creation.[125]

It is not surprising, then, to see an emphasis on being obedient to the divine will. In Tobit, ultimately, conformity to God's will brings favor. The emphasis on *Halakah* in *Jubilees* speaks to the growing concern about obedience to the revealed divine will—the Torah.[126] While the divine will can be seen as enigmatic (Jdt 8:14; 1 Macc 4:10; Sir 11:21, 25–28), the people are to trust that God intends to preserve the righteous and punish the wicked.[127] This belief seems to have arisen from expectations that the divine plan includes a properly ordered society. For instance, *Pss. Sol.* 17 pictures the messianic age as a time for "restoration of religious faith," where sin, injustice, and oppression are to be wiped out (cf. also 1QS 4:15–18a/18b–23a; 4:23b–25a/25b–26).[128] Thus, the hope for a properly ordered society continues to be understood as integral to God's purpose.

Luke's reader would likely expect the divine plan to be worked out in the narrative flow. *Psalms of Solomon's* emphasis on the messianic (seen as a Davidic figure) age as the time when the divine purpose will be fulfilled, combined with other views that see this as the period for Israel's restoration, suggests the reader might associate references to the di-

---

120. Nickelsburg, *Jewish*, 117.

121. Russell, *Divine*, 84.

122. deSilva, *Introducing*, 189–90.

123. Ibid., 259.

124. Ibid., 344; cf. Grelot, *L'Espérance*, 50–51.

125. Russell, *Divine*, 91–92. Grelot (*L'Espérance*, 47–48) comments that *1 En.* 83–90 pictures the end as a return to the beginning; creation is restored as it was in Adam's time.

126. Nickelsburg, *Jewish*, 80.

127. Desilva, *Introducing*, 102, 189, 198; Wicks, *Doctrine*, 174, 190.

128. Grelot, *L'Espérance*, 100–1; cf. Nickelsburg, *Jewish*, 136. Grelot, *L'Espérance*, 101: "L'exclusion de tout péché, de toute injustice, de toute oppression, constitue un objectif essentiel assigné au peuple et au Messie lui-même."

vine plan with similar hopes. The belief that the divine will can be enigmatic remains and the emphasis on obedience to that will suggests the reader would be intent on discerning what it truly is.

God of Promises/Covenant. The web of beliefs in Second-Temple Judaism stresses that "God has a covenant with his people and the covenant must be fulfilled."[129] The promises to David, the dispersed people being gathered, indeed all the prophetic promises are expected to be fulfilled because God is faithful to the covenant. This led to traditional beliefs about the land being holy, the people being obligated to God for deliverance, and covenantal blessings and curses providing motivation for pious behavior.[130] With regard to the land, nationalistic hopes are expressed in Sirach (36:1–22)[131] and in 2 Maccabees Israel is called the "holy land" (1:7–8) and Jerusalem is God's "holy place" (1:29). Tobit 14:4 expresses a desire for the people to be returned to the "good land." Finally, Baruch (2:27–35; 3:1–8) suggests that repentance will bring about this return. *Fourth Ezra* redefines the covenant relationship, limiting it to those who are faithful[132] and viewing the Abrahamic promise as something that belongs to the "unseen life" (cf. 3:15).[133]

Psalms of Solomon 17 presents the most striking belief about how God would fulfill the promise to David, viewing the messiah as a Davidic king who will restore the people to the land and rule over them in righteousness, assuming many divine attributes and responsibilities.[134] At the same time, the royal Psalms (47, 93, 94, 96–100) become the

---

129. Cohen, *Maccabees*, 100.

130. Collins, *Between*, 22. While Josephus sees a special relationship between God and Israel (cf. *Ant.* 4:114; 3:313; 7:380) and notes the unique benefits that Israel receives from God, he does not use covenantal language. Spilsbury ("God," 182–84, 191) suggests Josephus uses patron-client imagery, which made the covenant understandable to Josephus' readers. Attridge (*Interpretation*, 78, 83), instead, argues that the benefactor/ally imagery replaces covenantal ideas with those about divine providential justice. Motifs reflecting piety and punishment coincide with the Deuteronomistic ideals (so Attridge, *Interpretation*, 86–87; Betz, "Miracles," 218; Collins, *Between*, 62), but Josephus presents the Law as resembling a political constitution, with piety a virtue and justice the basis for punishment (see S. Mason, *Josephus*, 105–8). Further, in Josephus, statements about the 'land' and Davidic promises seem to be systematically deleted (see Halpern Amaru, "Land," 206–8, 227–28; Feldman, "Portrayal," 153; Feldman, *Studies*, 554). Josephus may have had some messianic expectations given the importance he places on the prophecies by Balaam and Daniel (Bilde, *Josephus*, 186–87; Bilde, "Jewish Apocalypticism," 51–55; S. Mason, *Josephus*, 121; Volz, *Eschatologie*, 53), but, whatever shape this hope takes in his thought, Josephus does not relate a Davidide ruling over this period. Jackson (*Josephus*, 90) suggested that Josephus would have been inclined to see Vespasian as the messiah.

131. See DeSilva, *Introducing*, 191–92. Fischer (*Eschatologie*, 13–35, 256) concludes that an expectation for national end-time deliverance via a political messiah plays no role in the western Diaspora writings, although he recognizes that it is mentioned in Philo, the Septuagint, and the sibylline oracles. Given these exceptions, especially the influential Septuagint, and the difficulty in determining the location for many writings, Fischer's conclusions should be seen only as a caution against a thoroughgoing Second-Temple nationalistic fervor, and not as denying that such beliefs were held in the Diaspora.

132. The covenant people are also narrowed in *Jub.* 30:22 (see Wicks, *Doctrine*, 151–52) and Qumran literature (see Nickelsburg, *Jewish*, 123–28, 133–34).

133. Wicks, *Doctrine*, 224.

134. Camponovo, *Königtum*, 222–26; Nickelsburg, *Jewish*, 207–8; Nickelsburg and Stone, *Faith*, 162–68; Strauss, *Davidic*, 40–43. Grelot (*L'Espérance*, 110) questions whether the non-(Christian) interpolated text sees the Messiah or God as the final ruling king. Regardless, divine promises to David would be fulfilled.

basis for eschatological hope, and the LXX seems to place more emphasis on the terms βασιλεία and χριστός than the original.[135] In the Qumran literature messianic figures are mixed (kingly and priestly), but 4QFlor presents a midrash on several texts (2 Sam 7:10–14; Pss 1:1; 2:1–2) affirming that the Davidic messiah was to be the leader during the holy war which would liberate Israel from the enemy nations.[136] Thus, some continued to hope for the Davidic kingdom, even if the hopes were "postponed to an indefinite future."[137]

A great emphasis is placed on the covenant relationship. Israel is repeatedly called on to recognize its sin (i.e., *As. Mos.* 3:5–7; 3 Macc 6:10; Bar 1:1—3:8) and keep the law (*Sib. Or.* 3; Philo's *Praem.*; Sir; Bar, 2 Macc). The idea that covenantal obedience directly affected rewards and punishment had a prominent place. God rewards the faithful, pious Jew, punishes the wicked (Jew and gentile), and defends the righteous (cf. Tob 4:5–11, *Pss. Sol.* 3:3–12; Jdt 5:17–21; 2 Macc).[138] The divine response to this piety defended the divine name and honor before the gentiles, showing that God is the one true God (cf. 3 Macc 6:10; Bar 2:10–18; Pr Azar 22).[139]

Luke's reader then would continue to anticipate that divine promises to Israel are about to be fulfilled. Hopes for a Davidic king remain an element in at least some Second-Temple thought. Since covenantal faithfulness themes are prominent, the reader would presume that obedience is necessary in order to receive divine blessings and avoid divine punishments. Thus, the reader expects pious characters and evidence that people are faithful to God's Law in order to be sure that God is acting in keeping with what is already known.

God and the Nations. The tension in the OT between God as exclusively Israel's God and the promise to bless all nations through Israel continues. On the latter side, there are citations reflecting divine promises to bless all nations (*Jub.* 19:17; 21:25). *Sibylline Oracles* 3[140] and Tobit (13:6) look for gentiles to be converted to Judaism. Judith acknowledges that God accepts the gentile convert.[141] *First Enoch* even pictures the distinction between gentile and Jew being obliterated in the coming age (10:21; 90:30–33).

On the other hand, 1 Maccabees sets God's people on one side and the nations on the other.[142] The *Assumption of Moses* seems to require membership in the Jewish people

---

135. So Grelot, *L'Espérance*, 32.

136. Ibid., 64–75; Strauss, *Davidic*, 43–45.

137. Strauss, *Davidic*, 39.

138. Nickelsburg and Stone, *Faith*, 139–42. Collins, *Between*, 79: in 2 Maccabees, "The covenantal relationship between the people and God provides the underpinning for the political and geographical factors in Jewish identity." Also DeSilva, *Introducing*, 266. The role played by the martyrs and the emphasis on God protecting the temple, city and people continue ideas about covenantal faithfulness and the promise of land.

139. Camponovo, *Königtum*, 199; DeSilva, *Introducing*, 205–11, 229, 321.

140. Grelot (*L'Espérance*, 109) argues that nationalism still persists in this work despite universalistic statements.

141. DeSilva, *Introducing*, 102. *Joseph and Asenath* also seems to emphasize this possibility; see Nickelsburg, *Jewish*, 262.

142. Bickerman, *God*, 18–19.

for salvation,[143] while the additions to Esther emphasize the different lots apportioned to Israel and the nations. Yet, even here, the tension has not evaporated since addition E pictures the gentile leaders acknowledging "positive contributions" by the Jews,[144] and portions in 1 Maccabees portray the gentiles positively. Jubilees 23:29 (unlike 19:17 and 21:25) is particularistic (God's people are removed to heaven and the nations are punished on earth),[145] as are elements in *Sib. Or. 3* (46–61).[146] Thus, Second-Temple thought appears genuinely uncertain about the fate of the gentiles.

For the Acts reader the option remains open to see the witness to all nations as punishment or as blessings. If anything, the reader is likely to be more aware of this tension and more interested in determining which option is developed.

God as Father. Psalms of Solomon 18 (cf. 3:4; 7:8; 13:8; 17:47) pictures Israel as the first-born, only-begotten, "son of God." The suffering that Israel is presently undergoing is that which a father allows in order to instruct his child and not the punishment reserved for those outside the covenant.[147] Third Maccabees 2:11 (cf. 6:8–10) indicates that it is as father (the divine kinsman) that God has delivered Israel and is called on to do so again. As for God's specific relationship to the king, the emphasis on the royal Psalms and the Davidic messiah attest to this belief continuing in Second-Temple thought. For Luke's reader, therefore, the divine concern for Israel seems to remain central in this image and the link to the Davidic king continues to be a possibility.

Overall, then, Second-Temple Jewish theology carries on the majority of the ideas noted in the OT. There are some alterations: 1) emphasis on transcendence; 2) divine action is increasingly portrayed through intermediaries; 3) the physical temple is de-emphasized by some; and 4) covenantal-faithfulness themes become prominent. These factors may influence how the reader expects God to "appear" in the narrative and how the reader values piety. Beliefs about divine control over events and people and expectations about the kingdom being restored to Israel, nevertheless, remain.

Results

OT and Second-Temple authors present God as a personal being who is involved in the events and enters into relationships with other characters. There is a decided trend, however, toward not directly narrating divine action. Intermediaries are involved, or divine action is realized as the narrative progresses. Also, there appears to be a desire to portray God in ways that are consistent with earlier portraits. God should appear as the God already known or else the reader may reject the presentation.

---

143. Collins, "Moses," 147.

144. DeSilva, *Introducing*, 121–22, 125.

145. Nickelsburg, *Jewish*, 82.

146. Camponovo, *Königtum*, 352–56. Despite the probability that these verses are from a different author, they show the tension that exists within the same complete work.

147. Nickelsburg, *Jewish*, 209.

A strong emphasis on divine control is evident. God is the transcendent Lord who orders the world and redeems the people. The divine will is the driving force behind events, working out God's purpose and causing people to respond to divine wishes. God controls history, raising up rulers and nations, determining their limits. Beliefs about the father suggest benevolent, redeeming action, and even conceptions about the God of promises imply that God is powerful enough (and has shown this to be so) to fulfill those promises. Therefore, when these images converge in Acts 1:1–8, the reader would expect that God will be controlling everything that follows.

God's promises/covenant suggests an emphasis on piety and hope for the land and the messianic kingdom to be restored. The special relationship implied by God as father gives the Jews a unique sense that God is interested in them over against other nations. Yet, there is tension here since there is evidence for a belief that God is interested in restoring and blessing all creation as at the beginning. Drawing all seven conceptions together, it seems that Luke builds his implied reader's expectations toward the hope that God will fulfill promises to Israel, especially those associated with God's kingdom and the messiah, and toward anticipating that God will control the events.

Similar Presentations

Literature evokes expectations in readers partly through the reader's beliefs about what type of literature it is. Therefore, analyzing the portrayal of God in works that seem similar to Acts should suggest some expectations the reader might have about such portrayals. This discussion provides material for comparison with Acts while indicating that the reader would expect the portrayal of God to support claims made in the narrative.

Like Acts, both 2 Maccabees and Josephus' *Antiquities* contain prefaces and quote official documents (cf. Acts 23:26–30). Balch notes similarities between the focus in 2 Maccabees on God defending the temple and the emphasis in Acts on the 'growth of the word' when crises in the early community are resolved.[148] Kurz identified correspondences between Acts, Josephus, and 2 Maccabees in the use of Hellenistic style and themes (providence) as well as interest in continuity with Israel.[149] Sterling categorized Josephus' *Antiquities* and Luke-Acts in the same Hellenistic-Jewish writing tradition.[150] Even though Sterling does not place 2 Maccabees in the same tradition,[151] he thinks it "might prove to be an important work to compare with Luke-Acts" because it "shares a number of historiographical concerns."[152] Thus, these Jewish-Hellenistic histories[153] seem to represent works sufficiently similar to Acts to allow comparison.

148. Balch, "Comments," 358–59.

149. Kurz, "Promise," 158–70.

150. Sterling, *Historiography*, 19.

151. Ibid., 141, note 19.

152. Ibid., 387, with note 380.

153. Acts is typically classified in one of four genres: 1) historical novel (see Praeder, "Luke-Acts," 269–92; Pervo, *Profit* (1987); cf. critiques by Alexander, "Fact," 380–99; Aune, *Literary*, 8–84; Bauckham, "Acts of Paul," 105–52; Sterling, *Historiography*, 185, 320); 2) ancient biography (see Talbert, *Patterns* (1974); Talbert, *Gospel?*

God in 2 Maccabees

Second Maccabees contains two letters prefixed to an abbreviation of a longer history, which relates events involving the Maccabees during the period ca. 180–160 BCE. The abbreviator (epitomator) is unknown, and the work which he shortens (from Jason of Cyrene; cf. 2:19) is no longer extant. Most scholars date the epitome between 161 and 63 BCE, with many believing it belongs to the time around 124 BCE (the date given in the first prefixed letter).[154] The epitomator appears to advocate Palestinian Judaism,[155] even though the work is composed in Greek with no evidence for a Hebrew/Aramaic original.[156] It is considered a history in its own right since the writer appears familiar with Hellenistic historiographical and rhetorical techniques,[157] selects the material for presentation, and includes his own theological and moral analysis (cf. 6:12–17).[158] There are, then, certain similarities to Acts, a work also written within the forty years following the last events recorded, with Hellenistic-Jewish interests and style, written in Greek, and probably shaped from generally un-recoverable sources.

The portrayal of God in 2 Maccabees follows three strands.[159] The first two (God as protector and rewarder/punisher) are relatively easy to discern. The last one (God

---

(1977); cf. critiques in Aune, *Literary*, 79; Sterling, *Historiography*, 319–20); 3) scientific/professional treatise (see Alexander, *Preface* (1993); cf. responses by Sterling, *Historiography*, 340–41; Palmer, "Acts," 21–26; Schmidt, "Rhetorical," 27–60); and 4) historiography.

Historiography is the most common choice with various sub-types: general or political history (Balch, "Comments," 343–61; Donelson, "Cult," 1–21); historical monograph (among others, Conzelmann, *Acts*, xl; Plümacher, "Monographie," 457–66; Plümacher, "Cicero," 759–75; Palmer, "Acts," 1–21; Hengel, *Acts*, 36); popular history (Barrett, *Acts*, xxxv; Aune, *Literary*, 77); and 'apologetic historiography' (Sterling, *Historiography* (1992)).

Schmidt ("Rhetorical," 51) notes, "The consensus among historiographers seems to be that 'history' was not a narrowly defined genre in ancient Greek writing, but rather was on a wide spectrum of prose writing styles." This leads him to doubt that, "attempts to settle once and for all whether Luke and/or Acts are really 'history' or 'biography,' or something else, can be successful." While there is some truth to this determination, most scholars (Alexander, *Preface*, 15–16, 166–67; Aune, *Literary*, 140; Balch, "Comments," 343; Holladay, "Acts," 197–98; Kurz, "Promise," 169; Schmidt, "Rhetorical," 59–60; Sterling, *Historiography* [1992]) recognize that Acts finds its origin in biblical history and has strong affinities with Hellenistic-Jewish historiography. Thus, even though historiography is a broad classification, this category seems to provide the best hope for comparison models.

154. Abel, *Livres*, xliii; DeSilva, *Introducing*, 269–70; Moffatt, "Second," 129; van Henten, *Maccabean*, 51–52. Goldstein (*II Maccabees*, 83) dates it to 78–63 B.C.E.; Stemberger (*Leib*, 6) to the mid-first century B.C.E. Zeitlin and Tedesche (*Second*, 28) suggest 41–44 C.E. This date is unlikely since the Romans are portrayed positively, improbable after 63 B.C.E.

155. Stemberger, *Leib*, 6–7.

156. DeSilva, *Introducing*, 268.

157. See Aune, *Literary*, 105–6; Doran, *Propaganda*, 42–44, 46. The work is often considered "tragic" history (Stermberger, *Leib*, 6-7) because it seems to stir up emotions and responses from the reader. However, most Hellenistic historiography did this to some extent (see Doran, *Propaganda*, 97, 104).

158. DeSilva, *Introducing*, 269; Doran, *Propaganda*, 54–55; Goldstein, *II Maccabees*, 6.

159. Second Maccabees will be treated as a whole since that is how it would be received in the reader's period. While debates exist concerning the relationship between the letters and the epitome, there are similarities between them (Doran, *Propaganda*, 5, 10–12; van Henten, *Maccabean*, 45). Goldstein (*II Maccabees*, 25–26) suggests that the contradictions between the letters and the epitome would not have been noticed at

supporting the claims) is a background theme. This *God who controls the events* image in 2 Maccabees suggests possible analogies for the role played by the portrayal of God in Acts.

Protector of People. Second Maccabees is constructed around three temple defenses,[160] so Doran considered it to be temple "propaganda."[161] Initially, God is concerned with preserving the temple's holy fire (1:19–22);[162] the book closes with the temple as God's house and habitation among men (14:35; 15:31–36); and the prologue emphasizes the divine role in purifying the temple (2:19–22). However, a careful examination shows that the temple is defended only because the people are important: "the Lord did not choose the nation for the sake of the holy place, but the place for the sake of the nation" (5:19).[163] While protecting the temple is important (3:12–31; 5:17; 8:2–4, 16–18; 10:1–8; 13:9–17; 14:35; 15:31–36), God defends or delivers much more—the people (3:12–31;[164] 5:19; 8:2–4; 13:9–17; 14:15–18; 14:35); the city (3:38–39; 8:16–18; 10:1–8); the Torah (8:16–18;[165] 13:9–17); the land (13:9–17); and the Sabbath (15:1–5). If the narrative were simply about protecting the temple, then it would be unnecessary to retell Judas' battles since they do not directly contribute to defending it.

Divine actions and interventions on behalf of the people are intrinsic to the work. In the letters God acted to turn away those warring against God's city (1:11–12); Antiochus dies by divine action (1:17; cf. 2:19–22; 9:3–7); and God is pictured as delivering the people (2:17–18). The preface highlights how important divine interventions (ἐπιφανεία) were for the events that transpired (2:19–22) as well as for the victories by Judas' army. When Heliodorus attempts to violate the temple deposits, God causes terror in Heliodorus as angelic riders and two men with whips appear and punish him (3:24–29). Similar apparitions occur (5:1–4,[166] 10:24–31; 11:7–12) and are prayed for (11:1–6) as God defends the people or aids the army. The epitomator mentions another intervention but does not describe it (12:22),[167] and God directly strikes Antiochus (9:3–7). Judas' dream (15:11–16) also appears to reflect a divine intervention that assures a victory will follow.

Divine power is acknowledged by the people and by defeated foes. Note the contrast in Lysias—before the fight he does not consider God's power (11:1–6), afterwards he must acknowledge it (11:13–15). God is ally to the people (8:21–27), watching over the city (3:38–39). Victory is attributed to God (8:5–7; 12:11), and the password (13:15—"God's

first, and Zeitlin and Tedesche (*Second*, 31–40) thought that the common interests meant the epitomator was responsible for editing and attaching the letters.

160. DeSilva, *Introducing*, 268.

161. Doran, *Propaganda*, 47; cf. Attridge, "Historiography," 322.

162. DeSilva (*Introducing*, 271–72) and Koester (*Dwelling*, 51) suggest this incident emphasizes that the temple is important for hopes about a restored Jewish community.

163. Collins, *Daniel*, 264: "the Jewish people is of primary importance. The temple . . . shares in the misfortunes and glories of the people."

164. By protecting the deposits in the temple God protects the people who made the deposits.

165. "By 'ancestral constitution' Jason again means the Torah" (Goldstein, *II Maccabees*, 331).

166. This apparition seems to anticipate God's role in the crisis that follows (see Bartlett, *Maccabees*, 257).

167. For possibilities, see Bartlett, *Maccabees*, 315; Goldstein, *II Maccabees*, 442.

victory") emphasizes this role.[168] When God's past action is recalled (8:19–20; 12:15–16; 15:6–11, 22–23), it reminds and encourages the people that victory comes by God's decision (15:22–23).

Prayer, thanksgiving, and the martyrs all factor in this divine protection. God responds to prayers by the pious (3:15–23; 8:2–4, 14–15, 28–29; 10:1–8,16–31; 11:1–16; 12:5–7, 15–16, 28, 36–37; 13:9–17; 14:15–18, 35; 15:22–23; 18:23–36). After victory, thanks is given to God for what God has done (1:17; 3:30–31; 8:24–27; 10:38; 11:7–12; 12:39–42; 15:25–30, 31–36). Since such practice was uniform among ancient peoples and because 1 Maccabees only provides a selection of such instances, the epitomator's choice to relate so many suggests this theme is significant.[169] The prayers seem to function as a support for the epitomator's argument that God defends the people when the people are pious.[170] The martyrs' piety has a similar effect since they suffer because the people have sinned (7:18–19) and pray that their deaths would turn away the wrath incurred by that sin (7:30–38). Indeed, the narrative appears to present the martyrs' deaths effecting Judas' first victory (8:5–7), and Razi's death may have brought about the victory over Nicanor (chapters 14–15).[171] Thus, 2 Maccabees emphasizes that divine protection results from piety and obedience to God.

Rewarder/Punisher. This last point leads into the second way God is presented in 2 Maccabees—God rewards the righteous and punishes the wicked. Commentators note that this Deuteronomistic theology is featured throughout the work.[172] The epitomator states (5:17–20) that God had neglected the holy place due to anger at the sins of the people. God punishes unfaithfulness and would never delay to defend the place unless the people had sinned. Moreover, God chastises the people in order to teach them and the swift punishment experienced by ungodly Jews is said to signify how good God is (6:12–17). Meanwhile, God allows the sins by the other nations to fill up until they reach their maximum. Even calamity brought upon the Jews is seen as marking divine presence with the people since the worst possible state is to be left alone by God.[173] God will use the gentiles to punish Israel (4:16–17), but any attempt by gentiles to go beyond God's mandate leads to their destruction, and God will restore Israel when it is faithful.[174]

This theology is emphasized in different ways: 1) God and the people often need to be reconciled (1:1–5; 5:17–20; 8:28–29) and piety (particularly by the martyrs) helps to bring about this restoration.[175] 2) A pattern is established when, under the pious Onias, God protects the temple, but, under the wicked Jason, Antiochus is able to profane it.[176]

---

168. Abel, *Livres*, 454.

169. Goldstein, *II Maccabees*, 6.

170. Enermalm-Ogawa, *Langage*, 102–4.

171. Van Henten, *Maccabean*, 144, 155.

172. DeSilva, *Introducing*, 271; Collins, *Daniel*, 266; Zeitlin and Tedesche, *Second*, 54.

173. Moffatt, "Second," 131.

174. Doran, *Propaganda*, 54–55; Goldstein, *II Maccabees*, 12–13; Harrington, *Revolt*, 45.

175. van Henten, *Maccabean*, 142.

176. DeSilva, *Introducing*, 274–75.

3) Covenantal faithfulness is at issue in the actions by the martyrs (6:26, 30; 7:30–38) and their deaths play a role in the restoration. 4) During Judas'[177] campaigns piety is stressed—the Torah is read (8:21–23); the Sabbath kept (8:24–27); widows are cared for (8:28–29); following commandments leads to invulnerability (8:33–36); some soldiers die because they are impious (12:39–42); and prayer occurs during battle (15:25–30). One striking factor 5) is the vivid just-desert *topos*[178] often portrayed through ironic emphases. Heliodorus had thought his weapons powerful enough to protect him, but discovers how powerful God is (3:24–29). Andronicus receives a "deserved" punishment (4:38). With Jason (5:8–10), the one who had expelled is expelled; the one who had left dead unburied is left unburied and unmourned. Antiochus (9:37),[179] Nicanor (8:33–36; 15:31–36), and Menelaus (13:4–8) suffer similarly ironic fates. Positively, this *topos* may be seen in the martyrs' belief that offering up their body now will bring about its restoration in future (7:11, 22–23, 27–29; 14:46).[180] It, therefore, appears that the epitomator believed divine justice was always appropriate (God would always reward faithfulness and punish disobedience).

Supporting the Claims. If God controls the events, protecting the people and rewarding/punishing as appropriate, then the claims made about persons and events seem to receive their support from divine action. Thus, these actions indicate how events or people are to be evaluated.[181] Persecution shows that God is displeased (even for the martyrs since they suffer for the nation). Victories demonstrate that God is pleased. The epitomator's statement (4:17) that the events would bear out that sins against God bring punishment emphasizes such beliefs.

In this light, the portrayal of God supports claims about Jewish freedom. Given all that takes place up through 11:15, the letters from the kings and officials (11:16–38) would imply that God has acted to restore to the Jews the freedom to pursue proper worship. Likewise, Judas' success in battle sanctions the rebellion and, in effect, supports Judas' claim to leadership. This success shows that God has recognized the martyrs' deaths, ending the divine wrath. The martyrs see resurrection as the demonstration of vindication,[182] but the epitomator portrays victory as the more tangible example of it. These aspects also support the epitomator's belief that adherence to the proper Jewish way of life (covenantal faithfulness)[183] is appropriate and, therefore, that God agrees that the Jews should have the freedom to practice their ancestral polity ("way of life"—8:17).

Divine action also appears to provide sanction to the temple and the Hanukkah and Nicanor's Day festivals. The providential temple purification on the same date as its profa-

---

177. Kampen (*Hasideans*, 145–47) notes emphasis placed on Judas' piety in 2 Maccabees.

178. See Doran, *Propaganda*, 95.

179. Doran, *Propaganda*, 63: "How fitting that God's providential disposal of him should occur as he is on his way to destroy Jerusalem once for all."

180. Stemberger, *Leib*, 16.

181. Abel (*Livres*, xxxxiv) notes that divine sanction is central to the epitomator's outlook.

182. Nickelsburg, *Resurrection*, 94.

183. DeSilva, *Introducing*, 266.

nation "underscores" that God accomplishes this re-dedication.[184] Likewise, the second letter suggests God is concerned for and accepts the temple. The letters urge the recipients to participate in the purification festival (1:9; 2:16) and, since the narrative relates both festivals being celebrated (10:1–8; 15:36), divine action is used to support the call to participate.

Summary. Second Maccabees' portrayal of God focuses on God protecting the people, rewarding faithfulness/punishing unfaithfulness, and supporting claims made about people and events. These features intertwine to present a God in complete control, active in the narrative events, concerned with obedience to the covenant, and with the people's welfare. There are similarities to Acts in the way that God intervenes (miraculous wonders, dreams, angels, direct involvement) and in how God responds to prayer and piety/impiety (or how people respond to divine action). Most importantly, since the 2 Maccabees portrayal of God seems to do so, the reader may expect the portrayal of God in Acts to support claims made in the narrative. If this is the case, it would help the reader recognize the apologetic purposes in the work.

God in Josephus

Josephus' *Antiquities* recounts the history of the Jewish people from creation until around 70 CE. It contains twenty books, the first ten covering the biblical material, the remainder focusing on the Hasmoneans (12–13), Herod (14–17), and his descendants (18–20). Josephus, who was a Jew from priestly lines writing under the general patronage of some figures among the Roman elite, completed the *Antiquities* around 93–94 CE.[185] He writes for a gentile audience, which appears to be keenly interested in Judean culture,[186] but he may have expected some Jews would also read his work.[187] As a result, Josephus tends to shape his narrative in a way that is presentable to his elite gentile readership. Dionysius of Halicarnassus is apparently his prime historiographical model,[188] but his Jewishness is also apparent. He is known to have used sources (Nicolaus of Damascus, 1 Maccabees), but his own rhetorical flair is so evident that it is clear he has shaped these sources to his own ends,[189] so that recovering his non-extant sources (Nicolaus) does not seem feasible.

Since *Antiquities* recounts such an extensive historical period, for comparison with Acts it is necessary to narrow the focus. Neither Acts nor 2 Maccabees extensively retells biblical history, so a better comparison can be made to later books in *Antiquities*. Books 18–20 record very few events in Palestine, thus they do not appear appropriate as analo-

---

184. Doran, *Propaganda*, 61.

185. Bilde, *Josephus*, 104; S. Mason, *Josephus*, 99.

186. Attridge, *Interpretation*, 17; Bilde, *Josephus*, 99–101; Jackson, *Josephus*, 66–67; S. Mason, "'Enquire," 80.

187. Bilde (*Josephus*, 102–3) does not rule this out; cf. Feldman, *Studies*, 543; Krieger, *Geschichtsschreibung*, 339.

188. See Attridge, *Interpretation*, 41–57; also Betz, "Miracles," 212–13; Thackeray, *Josephus*, 56–58.

189. See Landau, "Out-Heroding," 30–33.

gies to 2 Maccabees and Acts. To provide some diversity and look at events even more contemporaneous to Acts the Hasmonean section (12–13) can be avoided. Books 15–17, dealing with the reign of Herod the Great, then, seem the best candidates for study. These books cover the period from around 37 BCE—6 CE, roughly a forty-year period (slightly longer than 2 Maccabees and Acts). The time between the events and the writing is longer than with either 2 Maccabees or Acts (90 years versus less than 40). The Herod narratives, however, are organically related to other sections in the *Antiquities*, so the observations from these books will be supplemented with information from the work as a whole.[190]

There are, again, three prominent images in Books 15–17. The first two (God of providence and justice) are relatively easy to discern. The last one (God guaranteeing the constitution) develops from the overall work. Like 2 Maccabees, they present a God controlling the events and supporting claims in the narrative.

God of Providence. Josephus comments that in time (i.e., as history unfolded) God fulfilled the prophecy that Herod would eventually persecute everyone (15:4). Divine control over events, then, is programmatic in these books. Providential direction is characteristic for Josephus' theology,[191] being important to his history's aims (17:354—Glaphyra's dream shows that "God's providence [πρόνοια] embraces the affairs of men").[192] While, generally, providential action does not involve direct intervention in the *Antiquities*,[193] it is ubiquitous nonetheless.

Josephus' providential God is a protector. When Cleopatra is prevented from gaining access to the temple treasures (15:88–91), there may be a suggestion that the unseen God has protected the temple (as in 2 Maccabees). Herod declares that the army is preserved during the earthquake because God is their protector (15:145–46). A flame prevents David and Solomon's tombs from being desecrated (16:181). When the false-Alexander appears, the people attribute his existence to divine protection. These incidents suggest a belief that God's providential help comes in times of need. God may tarry in bringing deliverance, but divine help will mark a real change in fortune since God is the people's ally and leader (cf. 2:334; 3:18–20; 4:114).[194] For the most part, however, such protection takes place behind the scenes.

Hellenistic influences on Josephus' historiography are seen in references to *Fortune*. For the Greeks and Romans (especially the historian, Dionysius), Fortune (τύχη) was responsible for the uncontrollable and inexplicable reversals in political and personal life.[195]

190. The observations about the theology found in *Antiquities* would be little different in whatever part; see Feldman's article ("Hasmoneans," 136–63) comparing 1 Maccabees with Josephus' portrait.

191. So Betz, "Miracles," 216. Attridge (*Interpretation*, 71–74, 76) finds this theme present throughout Josephus' biblical interpretation.

192. Bilde (*Josephus*, 185) suggests that this statement makes God's providence a theological heading over *Antiquities*.

193. Feldman ("Hasmoneans," 159; *Studies*, 568) observes that Josephus systematically de-emphasizes God's direct role in the biblical narratives. Sterling ("Invisible," 116, 129) notes that while Josephus retells Ruth with a stress on divine control, he eliminates direct divine intervention as much as possible.

194. See Attridge, *Interpretation*, 8–79; Betz, "Miracles," 216.

195. S. Mason, *Josephus*, 71; Squires, *Plan*, 43–45.

Fortune causes various ups and downs in life—the change in commoners when they become kings (15:17), the end faced by Hyrcanus (15:165, 179), Herod's favor with Caesar (15:360–61), and the threats to Herod's kingdom (16:300). Yet, Fortune interplays with divine providence. Josephus wavers between attributing certain circumstances to divine wrath or to Fortune taking opportunity to show its capricious hand (15:299–304; 16:188). While Herod's recovery is left to Fortune (15:246), his suffering is likened to a divine punishment. Similarly, divine wrath is responsible for what befalls Antipater (17:60), but Fortune delivers him to his enemies (17:122). Overall, Fortune seems to be a means for expressing divine control over events.[196] This Hellenistic influence implies that although Josephus may have acquired his sense that God controls events from Judaism, he is determined to present it in a way acceptable to his gentile readership.[197]

God of Justice. The way key personalities are depicted emphasizes divine justice.[198] When Herod seeks to stir up the army, he proclaims it a just war because God hates arrogance and injustice (15:130–38).[199] However, justice seems primarily related to the Law—By law the Jews are taught to admire righteousness (16:158); Herod is considered a tyrant for establishing a law contrary to the ancestral customs (16:1–5); yet, Herod defends the justice in allowing the Jews to live by these practices (16:27–57). The way the Law is portrayed implies that Josephus sees it as a Jewish constitution since, "For Jews, as for other nations in his account, the laws are the expression of the constitution."[200] The laws are universal principles because Moses considered how the universe was constructed "before framing his laws precisely so that his laws would be uniquely based on universal truths (*Ant.* 1:18–25)."[201] Since Israel has special knowledge about the Law, it is particularly liable, but the Jewish Law is universally applicable.[202]

This constitution is effective because God maintains justice (rewarding piety and punishing injustice). Thus, Josephus apparently considered piety (like justice) as a virtue. The pious are God's friends and receive reward in kind.[203] Proper worship is worth dying for (15:248) and uprisings occur over concern for obedience to the law (17:149–59). Herod claims that the Arabs lack piety and demonstrates his own by sacrifice (15:130–47).

196. Von Schlatter (*Theologie*, 32–33) maintains that Fortune and fate are in agreement with God's will.

197. So Squires, *Plan*, 18.

198. Feldman, *Studies*, 549. He lists Abraham (1:158), Moses (3:66–67), Samuel (6:36, 294), Saul (6:212), David (6:290, 7:110), Solomon (8:21), Josiah (10:50), Gedaliah (10:155), Daniel (10:246), Ezra (11:121), and Nehemiah (11:183). On the significance given to justice in Josephus, see also Attridge, *Interpretation*, 115; von Schlatter, *Theologie*, 40.

199. According to Feldman (*Studies*, 552–53) the Romans were particularly interested in demonstrating that a war was just. Josephus adopts this emphasis (6:133; 8:399), attempting to establish justification for wars in the biblical account and, later, the Maccabean wars (see Feldman, "Hasmoneans," 144).

200. S. Mason, *Josephus*, 105 (cf. idem, "Aim," 80–87; Attridge, *Interpretation*, 62–66).

201. S. Mason, *Josephus*, 110.

202. Bilde, *Josephus*, 185–86. Josephus systematically removes covenantal limitations so the Law is universally available.

203. For evidence throughout the *Antiquities*, see Attridge, *Interpretation*, 68–69, 116–17; von Schlatter, *Theologie*, 38–39; Spilsbury, "God," 186–87; Sterling, "Presence," 120–29. Jackson (*Josephus*, 80) suggests that Josephus believed Moses's religion was best practiced in absolute personal holiness.

Later, Herod uses his rebuilding the temple to signify his piety (15:382–87; cf. 17:162–63). The real mark on Herod and his early successors, nevertheless, seems to be their impiety. The prophecy about Herod's future reign says that Herod would do best to love justice and be pious, [204] but that he would not do so (15:374–76). When Herod departs from the ancestral customs, conspiracies arise (15:267–83). Finally, Herod's greatest impiety comes when he kills his sons (17:1).

Herod, therefore, becomes a prime example for how divine justice makes the Jewish constitution effective.[205] Herod's distress after Mariamne's execution is likened to divine punishment (15:241–43). His eventual castigation is foreshadowed (15:374–76), and his illness worsens because God was inflicting just sentence on his lawlessness (17:168–70). The disease is similar to that afflicting Antiochus in 2 Maccabees (involving gangrene and worms) and it leads men of God (θειαζόντων) to declare that this was indeed divine punishment. Antipater, likewise, faces retribution for impiety (17:60). Thus, through the link to the Law, the Jewish God is portrayed as the God who administers justice through divine control over events.[206]

Guarantor of Constitution. Steve Mason considers the effectiveness of the Jewish constitution as the primary theme in the *Antiquities*.[207] Josephus comments that his citation of decrees by gentile rulers (16:162–73) is to show that the Greeks have been favorably disposed to the Jewish religion and its way for honoring God (16:174–78). The apologetic rhetoric in *Antiquities* is built around this claim that the Jewish Law and constitution have a greater antiquity and respect than any other law. If Josephus is truly interested in demonstrating that the Jewish constitution is superior, then the ancestral customs must be both just and effective and efficacy can only come from one source—God must be more just than in any other religion so that Judaism appears like no other religion.[208]

This conclusion suggests that God guarantees the constitution. In other words, God authenticates the constitution by providentially controlling history and administering divine justice. The Herod narrative presents a prime example—God shows how great the piety expressed in the Jewish Law is by providential care for the Jews (prospering them under Herod). At the same time, God illustrates the constitution's concern for justice since divine action supports its claims that impiety and injustice will be punished. Thus, the images reflecting the God of providence and the God of justice merge into an overarching conception that God guarantees the Jewish constitution, supporting the claim that it provides the best socio-political structure.

---

204. Landau ("Out-Heroding," 172) notes this is similar to how Herodotus presents virtuous kings.

205. S. Mason, "Aim," 85–86. Landau ("Out-Heroding," 206) identifies the contrast between Herod and Judas and Matthias. The latter two show their piety; Herod simply demonstrates that he is a tyrant. This would imply that the Jewish theocracy is a better model than rule by a single tyrant king.

206. Attridge (*Interpretation*, 60–104) treats justice as serving divine providence. However, it seems more likely that divine control over events is portrayed as serving divine justice and that they are two different categories.

207. S. Mason, "Aim," 85.

208. So Krieger, *Geschichtsschreibung*, 327.

Summary and Results. Josephus sees God controlling history (providence) and being concerned for justice and piety. These features combine to show that God guarantees the Jewish constitution. In other words, the portrayal of God supports claims made in Josephus' narrative. Thus, how the covenant, piety, and divine control over events are presented offer possibilities for comparison with Acts. The most intriguing comparison is the way the portrayal of God is used to support narrative claims.

Both these works of Jewish-Hellenistic historiography are concerned with divine control over events. Second Maccabees emphasizes an interventionist approach; Josephus' God orchestrates events through providence and fortune. Both works show an interest in Deuteronomistic ideals about punishment and reward. While Josephus removes any relation to the covenant, 2 Maccabees strictly maintains the relationship to the covenant, presenting a retributive justice. This suggests that divine control over events and how God is presented in relation to promises/covenant are vital elements in Second-Temple Jewish theology, which confirms earlier conclusions about expectations the reader would have for the Acts narrative.

Both works present the portrayal of God supporting narrative claims. For 2 Maccabees divine protection supports the rededicated temple, the rebellion by Judas, the festivals, and the martyrs. In Josephus, God's providential administration of justice guarantees that the Jewish constitution is the best governmental form. This result suggests that the Acts reader would expect the portrayal of God to function in a similar way.

Findings

This chapter argued that the reader's attention is likely being drawn to two key thoughts about God. First, God controls the events. There are elements in each of the seven conceptions that stress divine action in and control over history. This indicates that Luke's reader expects that the events narrated in Acts are under divine control. However, if the God portrayed does not appear to act consistent with what the reader already knows about God, this expectation will be overturned. Second, the reference to the Father's promise and the kingdom restored to Israel directs the reader's attention to expectations about the fulfillment of divine promises (particularly the kingdom) to Israel. Thus, the reader may require evidence that God has done/is doing so. The reader would also have certain assumptions about how pious the characters should be, making piety and obedience important factors. Finally, the reader should expect the portrayal of God to provide support for narrative claims. This conclusion implies that the portrayal of God would be a primary interest for the reader.

3

Who Acts For God?

It is common among literary critics to claim that God is offstage in Acts.[1] Therefore, as a background character God may be difficult to analyze. Marguerat's claim that Acts is balanced between "poles" reflecting Christology, Pneumatology, and "theology"[2] compounds the problem since discussion about God would be separated from that about Christ and the Spirit. Consequently, Bibb analyzes the characterization of God solely in relation to statements explicitly about God. He includes the Spirit and Jesus only where it is unclear to whom an activity is assigned or where actions by these figures are attributed to God in a later statement.[3] Some limitation should be made, but limitations should not prevent a comprehensive presentation. Thus, this chapter will argue that actions by Jesus and the Spirit also characterize God. First, however, focus is placed on the narrator since his ability to portray divine actions and desires suggests he is an important figure for determining the portrayal of God constructed by the reader.

The Narrator: Access to the Divine

Since the implied author, whose primary voice is the narrator, is considered the one who has arranged the narrative, the narrator would appear to have "access" to (the ability to portray) any character's actions, thoughts, and desires. However, Marguerat suggests that in Luke-Acts the narrator's access and authority is limited by his deference to authoritative eyewitnesses. He writes, "Except for a few rare occasions, the narrator never directly ascribes the action of the narrative to God. . . . only the word of the witness can designate the author of the events that direct history."[4] If Marguerat is correct, then the *witnesses* have more authority and access than does the Acts *narrator*. Such a claim needs to be examined by assessing the narrator's access to the divine and divinely related events/actions. This analysis will demonstrate that the narrator is a primary figure for understanding the Acts presentation of God.

---

1. Darr, *Character*, 51: "God remains offstage, and so the divine perspective . . . is 'external' to the story proper." Shepherd, *Narrative*, 39–40: the Spirit is the "onstage representative of the offstage God." Bibb, "Characterization," 299: "God operates 'offstage' more often in Acts than in the gospel."

2. Marguerat, *First*, 88.

3. Bibb, "Characterization," 45.

4. Marguerat, *First*, 90–91.

Narrators in Literary Theory[5]

The narrator is the "teller of the tale," the "voice" unfolding the textual events.[6] Narrators are different in type, with differing relations to the narrative events, characters, and author/implied author. Because a real author may write a book that embodies ideals with which she or he disagrees, or may write different books which invoke different norms, literary theorists distinguish between the author (the real person who wrote the work) and the implied author (a construct developed by the reader from textual cues suggesting the work's ideological aims—its norms) in whom the author's role is inscribed.[7] The implied author becomes the "principle that invents the narrator," but which also orders the events, develops the images and "stacks the cards" in a certain way.[8] The narrator, then, is the voice that recounts the story, inserts commentary, and manages how the characters are described.[9] It is possible for the narrator to speak or act in a way that does not agree with the implied author's norms,[10] but this unreliable narrator, while not unknown, is not typical among ancient narratives.[11]

Because the narrator manages how the characters are described, the narrator's comments and portrayals are critical in the reader's attempt to construct the character. By controlling the characterization process, the narrator manages the narrative even when he or she allows a character to speak (at such points the narrator hands "over the task of narration to the character").[12] If the narrator has shown the character's trustworthiness, then narration by that individual is considered reliable as well; if the character is untrustworthy, the narration is unreliable.

Although narrators are different from other characters (interacting with the audience outside the story), "the way readers come to know narrators is similar to the means by which they construe *dramatis personae*: through their speech (or 'voice'), choices, actions, interactions with other characters, and so forth."[13] The reader, therefore, comes to know the narrator as the story unfolds, learning to trust or distrust him or her. In this "narrative contract," which the reader enters in the reading process, the reader accepts the narrator as a guide through the story world.[14] This position, however, may change during the narration, depending on whether the narrator adheres to the apparent textual norms.

---

5. This discussion is not exhaustive; rather it provides a methodological foundation for the following study. For more information on narrators see the literature cited.

6. Rimmon-Kenan, *Narrative*, 89.

7. Booth, *Rhetoric*, 71–72; Rimmon-Kenan, *Narrative*, 87–88; Chatman, *Story*, 148.

8. Chatman, *Story*, 148

9. Lee, *Luke's*, 174.

10. Booth, *Rhetoric*, 158–59.

11. See Walworth, "Narrator," 68. Walworth analyzes the Acts narrator as an ultimately reliable (adhering to the text's norms) storyteller. Sheeley (*Narrative*, 157) draws a similar conclusion.

12. Lee, *Luke's*, 175.

13. Darr, "Narrator," 44.

14. Walworth, "Narrator," 20.

Narrators can be above the story (*telling* it) or can be participants within the story itself (*showing* it).[15] Telling narrators are considered as having greater authority—often associated with omniscience or privilege. Showing narrators give up this privilege, but just because a narrator is a character in a story he or she narrates does not mean that the narrator has to give up the omniscient position. It is only when the narrator describes his or her own action, conclusions, etc., that the privileged position is lost.[16] The privilege the showing narrator gives up is offset by involving the reader in the events,[17] helping the reader to identify with the characters, while providing eyewitness testimony.

Thus, in the following analysis of the narrator's ability to authoritatively present God in Acts, one needs to realize how the narrator recounts the story, comments on the events, and characterizes the participants. The narrator's reliability must be assessed. Since the narrator at times "hands" the story over to others, it is necessary to know not only the speech's content, but who speaks and how reliable that speaker is. One must assemble the portrait of the narrator as it develops through the story. Finally, attention must be given to the narrator's involvement in the story and how that might affect reliability.

The Narrator's Access to God

The following analysis is limited to passages where the narrator informs the reader about some event or character that appears to be related to divine activity. This includes references to the Spirit and in some cases to Jesus since these figures can reasonably be assumed to stand in a close relation to God.[18] The following nine attributes illustrate that Luke's narrator has extensive access and authority to portray the divine action and will.

1) Epitomizes teaching in relation to God. The narrator encapsulates Jesus' post-resurrection teaching as "the things concerning the kingdom of God" (1:3; cf. 19:10, 20). In 8:12, 14, he summarizes preaching concerning the "kingdom of God" and the "name of Jesus Christ" as preaching "the word of God" (cf. 18:5, 11; also 17:3, 13).[19] Similarly, the narrator can say (16:31–34) that the jailer, whom Paul and Silas told to "believe on the Lord Jesus," believed in God (πεπιστευκὼς τῷ θεῷ). Thus, the narrator's ability to epitomize leads the reader to conclude that the message about Jesus is a message about God and that belief in Jesus can be seen as belief in God.[20]

---

15. See Rimmon-Kenan, *Narrative*, 95.

16. Ibid., 96–97.

17. Walworth, "Narrator," 41.

18. Hur (*Dynamic*, 98–101) correctly assesses the narrator's ideology as encompassing a theocentric, Christocentric, and "pneumocentric" frame of reference. Hahn (*Theologie*, II, 289–308) suggests there is a triadic or "implicitly Trinitarian" structure to the NT witnesses.

19. In 8:12, the two phrases are united by the same article. Turner (*Power*, 296) suggests the close association here makes the two phrases "partly interchangeable." Similarly, Tannehill, *Narrative*, 14: "These are not two separate topics, for God's reign is established in the world through the rule of Jesus Messiah." Hansen ("Preaching," 298) indicates this relationship between Jesus' message and the "word of God" is maintained throughout Luke-Acts.

20. This suggests only that they stand in a unique relationship, such as belief in one is ultimately belief in the other.

2) Helps the reader relate events to God. Sound (2:1–13) and light (9:1) are said to come "from heaven," presenting these scenes as divine epiphanies.[21] Likewise, the open heavens and items descending from there (10:11) are used to prepare the reader to understand such events as divine interventions.[22] Although it turns out that Jesus speaks to Saul (9:5), the reader so strongly expects God to speak "from heaven" that Jesus and God are linked in the reader's mind (cf. Jesus' place in heaven—2:33).[23] Similarly, the narrator (6:15) notes that the council saw Stephen's face like that "of an angel." Since angels (including the "men in white") are associated with divine commands and information (1:10; 5:19),[24] the narrator prompts the reader to expect Stephen's words (the speech in Acts 7) to have divine authority.

3) Provides access to and interprets visions. The narrator describes the vision before Stephen does (7:55–56; cf. 10:11–16). Thus, the narrator claims access to this divine vision apart from the character who witnessed it. Moreover, the narrator identifies *Jesus* standing at the "right hand of God," while Stephen mentions the *Son of Man*. This substitution suggests that the narrator has the authority to interpret the vision.[25] The narrator, therefore, is not below the eyewitnesses in authority, but fully sanctioned to portray the divine realm.

4) Identifies relationships between characters and divine figures. The narrator indicates a link between Jesus and the Spirit (1:2).[26] Further, while the term Father for God (1:3–4) may be tied to Jesus,[27] it is the narrator who first vocalizes the term (from Jesus' perspective). Thus, the narrator claims the privilege to state that God stands to Jesus as Father. Several characters are called "devout" (2:5; 10:2), a God-fearer (10:2), or a "worshiper of God" (16:14; 18:7). Without providing any further information to support this claim, the narrator defines the positive relationship in which these characters stand to God. Later, the narrator identifies that the believers in Pisidian Antioch held a favored position before God since he (not Paul) states what Paul and Barnabas urged (they were to "continue in the grace of God"—13:43).[28]

21. Barrett, *Acts*, 448–49; Gaventa, *Acts*, 148; Johnson, *Acts*, 162–63; Schille, *Apostelgeschichte*, 220.

22. They are "theophanic" (Pesch, *Apostelgeschichte*, I, 303).

23. Since the theophanic images cause the reader to expect God to speak, it seems incorrect to think that (as Jervell, *Apostelgeschichte*, 280) the reader knows the one appearing to Saul is Jesus. The reader may suspect as much, but does not learn it until Jesus reveals himself in 9:5.

24. So Barrett, *Acts*, 502. Throughout Second-Temple literature angels function as intermediaries, bringing God's words and doing God's actions. See Wicks (*Doctrine*, 122–24) and chapter 2.

25. So Barrett, *Acts*, 383.

26. Διά with the genitive is usually translated "by" or "through." Kilgallen ("Apostles," 414–17) suggests the plausible interpretation that Jesus chose the disciples "because of the promise of the Holy Spirit." The important point is that, whatever the translation, a narrative connection is made between Jesus and the Spirit (cf. Gaventa, Acts, 63).

27. Mowery "Disappearance," 353–58; Mowery "Lord," 82–101. However, Mowery does not note this distinction.

28. *Contra* Schneider (*Apostelgeschichte*, II, 142) these men have believed. While Luke does not make that specific claim, he indicates as much since he implies a continuing state. Grace is used by Luke to indicate divine favor and is often seen as a condition under which the community exists. If these Jews and God-fearers had not already repented and believed, they would need to do so to gain such grace.

The narrator identifies actions by the angel "of the Lord" (5:12–19; 8:26; 12:7, 11, 23).[29] In 10:3, the narrator says an "angel of God" appeared to Cornelius, but Cornelius (10:30) only describes the man as wearing "dazzling clothes." This would imply either that Cornelius is too humble to dare make the connection, or that the narrator is not allowing him to identify this figure's relationship to God. Cornelius' messengers describe the figure as a "holy angel" (10:22), suggesting a divine association but lacking the explicitness expressed by the narrator. Cornelius' version may provide the "first visual impression of the character."[30] However, this does not explain why Cornelius fails to identify the figure as an angel when both the narrator and the messengers do. The vision itself would have given Cornelius sufficient reason to reach this conclusion by the time he reports it to Peter. Thus, it seems that rather than trying to maintain an objective account, it is more likely that the narrative is shaped to maintain the narrator's authority to identify divine figures.[31] Regardless, the narrator claims the authority to interpret the vision as sent by God, something that he does not grant Cornelius.

In Ephesus (18:23—19:7), similarly, the narrator leads the reader to see that Apollos stands in a different relationship to God than the "disciples" of John. The former, like Stephen (6:5) and Philip (8:39), is fervent in spirit ($\zeta\acute{\epsilon}\omega\nu$ $\tau\tilde{\omega}$ $\pi\nu\epsilon\acute{\nu}\mu\alpha\tau\iota$) and speaks out boldly ($\pi\alpha\rho\rho\eta\sigma\iota\acute{\alpha}\zeta\epsilon\sigma\theta\alpha\iota$). The latter are unaware "that there is a Holy Spirit."[32]

5) Demonstrates that God answers prayer. In 4:31–37, the narrator indicates (through the place shaking) that the community's prayer (4:24–30) was heard.[33] The reader is made aware that God has answered the prayer in an even more powerful way than if the narrator had just said "and God answered their prayer." This prayer receives further answers throughout the narrative as allusions are made to items mentioned in it[34]—Paul and Barnabas are emboldened ($\pi\alpha\rho\rho\eta\sigma\iota\alpha\sigma\acute{\alpha}\mu\epsilon\nu o\acute{\iota}$) (13:46; cf. 4:29); "wonders and signs" are performed (6:8; 8:4, 13; cf. 4:30);[35] and Aeneas is healed in Jesus' name (9:34; cf. 4:30).

6) Identifies proper responses to divine actions. When the community, which had witnessed "wonders and signs" (divine actions), is first described it is noted that they were praising God (2:47). After the lame beggar is healed (3:7–12) the narrator draws attention to his

29. $K\upsilon\rho\acute{\iota}o\varsigma$ is used in Acts for both Jesus and God. Even if Jesus is the 'Lord' in these references, Peter's speeches have already suggested Jesus is in a Lordship position "at the right hand of God" (cf. 2:33–36). See below.

30. Kurz, "Effects," 576; also Pesch, *Apostelgeschichte*, I, 337.

31. *Contra* Schneider, *Apostelgeschichte*, II, 74

32. So Haenchen, *Acts*, 553; Lake and Cadbury, *Beginnings*, 237. This translation emphasizes the contrast—Apollos shows evidences related to the Spirit, the disciples know nothing about the Spirit. Jervell's (*Apostelgeschichte*, 475) attempt to connect the Ephesian twelve with Apollos (both know John's baptism) misses how Apollos is positively related to the spirit, but these twelve negatively.

33. Such signs were seen as divine responses to prayer, see Haenchen, *Acts*, 228; van der Horst, "Hellenistic," 44–45; Pesch, *Apostelgeschichte*, I, 179; Schneider, *Apostelgeschichte*, I, 360–61.

34. Tannehill (*Narrative*, 72) counts answers to prayer as one way Luke shows God's active presence in the story. He also identifies (73, 177) this prayer's continued fulfillment in Acts. Additionally, Fitzmyer, *Acts*, 327; Pesch, *Apostelgeschichte*, I, 178.

35. Fitzmyer (*Acts*, 356) identifies the connection to the community prayer.

praising God (3:8, 9). Later (4:21–37), the crowd glorifies God (ἐδόξαζον) for the miracle. The council, which opposes divine activity (4:19), is never said to praise God. This repetition serves to ingrain the idea into the reader's mind, affirming a textual norm—obedient people praise God for divine activity.[36]

The *proper-response* theme can work in reverse (when God is praised an act can be attributed to God).[37] When Peter finishes recounting the Cornelius event (11:18), the narrator notes that everyone there glorified God. Since glorifying God is the proper response to divine activity, it signals to the reader that the granting of repentance to the gentiles is divine action, even before the group states it (cf. also 13:48).

7) Gives evidence of divine favor. The narrator leads the reader to see community growth as a divine action[38]—three thousand people were added (προσετέθησαν)[39] to the community (2:41), which corresponds to the "Lord" adding (προσετίθει) those who were being saved (2:47). Elsewhere, the narrator identifies the large response (17:4, 12) to the "word of God" (17:13). After the Areopagus speech only "some" believed (17:34). This response is not the many (πολλοί) or the great crowd (πλῆθος πολύ), but it is nonetheless a positive response. The reader has been conditioned to see community growth as signifying divine favor (also 19:9, 20) and should do so again. While the subdued narration may cause the reader to wonder what was different about this place, the narrator has led the reader to consider the divine favor on the mission.

In 4:1–8a, by narrating the community's growth after Peter and John's imprisonment and prior to the Council being convened, the narrator may be assuring the reader that Peter and John have done nothing wrong—the church has grown. As before, this would suggest divine favor on their preaching despite opposition from the temple leadership. After the Ananias and Sapphira incident, the narrator (5:12–19) mentions "signs and wonders"[40] (directly fulfilling the community prayer—4:30)[41] and crowds of believers being added (προσετίθεντο—cf. 2:41–47).[42] The "word of God" spreads and the community grows (6:7) after the dispute over the distribution (6:1–6). By stating that the Samaritans

36. Walworth ("Narrator," 165) states that redundancy "allows the narrator to communicate subtly the movement of the text so that the reader is moved toward a discovery of meaning in the interaction with the text." Thus, the narrator uses repetition to draw the reader toward meaning (cf. Tannehill, *Narrative*, 74–76). In 2 Maccabees praise is consistently given in response to divine acts (see chapter 2). Further, praise marked the people's piety and obedience. The presentation in Acts shows similarities since it identifies those who are obedient over against others (4:19).

37. So Johnson, *Acts*, 207.

38. Throughout Acts God is the prime force behind the community's growth (Rosner, "Progress," 223–25). Schneider (*Apostelgeschichte*, I, 279; following Haenchen, *Acts*, 191) sees the ingathering as visibly expressing divine blessing.

39. Fitzmyer, *Acts*, 267: a "theological passive."

40. Acts 14:3 also shows "signs and wonders" signifying divine favor in a difficult situation (Pesch, *Apostelgeschichte*, II, 52).

41. Barrett, *Acts*, 242: Acts 4:31 is intended to "show God's approval of what his people are doing." It would follow that successive fulfillments of the community prayer also demonstrate divine approval (so Bibb, "Characterization," 197).

42. Another theological passive (Fitzmyer, *Acts*, 329).

had received the "word of God" (8:14), the narrator echoes 6:7. Therefore, although perse-cution has scattered the group (8:1), the reader is aware that the new mission is divinely blessed. Similarly, after Saul has escaped, the narrator notes (9:31) that the community increases. Finally, when the narrator describes the preaching to gentiles in Antioch, he states that the "hand of the Lord" (11:21) was with them before he explains that a large number believed; making the divine hand (symbolizing divine approval)[43] evident even before mentioning the growth.

The narrator indicates that Barnabas' action in bringing Saul to Antioch is correct by again mentioning growth (11:26). Here, when concern has been voiced about Cornelius' conversion and suspicion might be registered about bringing Paul to Antioch, the narrator points to divine favor. This theme also appears at 15:35—16:5. Paul and Barnabas split, having disputed over John Mark. Paul goes with Silas, strengthening the churches. The narrator then mentions that the communities Paul and Silas visit increase, emphasizing the divine blessing after this problem.[44]

Why is this significant? For the reader (who might have had doubts about these events), the continued references to divine favor assuage fears. At each crisis point divine favor is indicated, which suggests that the implied author desired to provide assurance to his reader about the narrative events (accomplished by emphasizing divine control). This provides confirmation, therefore, that (just as with 2 Maccabees and Josephus' *Antiquities*) one function for the portrayal of God in Acts is to provide support for narrative claims. To do this, Luke's narrator does not rely on the eyewitnesses but on the narrative's rhetorical structure (repeating specific narrative elements in particular situations).

8) Identifies the Holy Spirit's activity. The narrator is always the one who identifies the *filling* with the Holy Spirit (2:4; 4:8, 31; 6:5, 10; 7:55;[45] 11:24; 13:9; 13:52; 19:6). Likewise, he alone informs the reader that the Samaritans had not received the Spirit (8:15) and that they finally do (8:17). Peter's announcement (10:44–46) that the gentiles "received" the Spirit is delayed until after the narrator has stated that the Spirit "fell," the "gift" had been "poured" on the gentiles also, and that the characters knew this because they were speaking in tongues and magnifying God. It is the narrator who names the speaker in 8:29 as the "Spirit" and describes the "Spirit of the Lord" snatching Philip away (8:39). Later, the narrator identifies the Spirit as the one speaking to Peter (10:19–20), and, thus, implies divine control despite Peter's confusion. The narrator indicates the Spirit is the one speak-ing to the community at Antioch and then emphasizes that the Spirit sent out Saul and Barnabas (13:2–4). Thus, even though the Antioch church sends them away ($\grave{\alpha}\pi\acute{\epsilon}\lambda\upsilon\sigma\alpha\nu$) it is really God (through the Spirit) who sends them out ($\grave{\epsilon}\kappa\pi\epsilon\mu\phi\theta\acute{\epsilon}\nu\tau\epsilon\varsigma$). Therefore, the narrator has unique authority to identify the Spirit's presence and activity.

This narratorial authority counters Marguerat's statement that the narrator is subject to the witnesses.[46] The narrator never hands over the narration to a character that is more

---

43. Haenchen, *Acts*, 366; Johnson, *Acts*, 203; Schneider, *Apostelgeschichte*, II, 90.

44. So Haenchen, *Acts*, 479.

45. The construction suggests this is an already existing condition ($\acute{\upsilon}\pi\acute{\alpha}\rho\chi\omega\nu\ \ldots\ \pi\lambda\acute{\eta}\rho\eta\varsigma$).

46. Marguerat, *First*, 90–91.

inspired or one providing an eyewitness account, but claims the right to recount the Spirit's actions directly. In this way, the narrator gives the reader information that the characters themselves do not have, guiding the reader's responses and beliefs.[47] If the narrator needed eyewitness authority to specify divine activity, the Peter-Cornelius episode would provide the best opportunity. Yet, Peter's account is buried in favor of the narrator's.

9) *Leads reader to draw conclusions about divine action.* The passive ἀνελήμφθη in 1:2 immediately invokes the question: Who took Jesus up? Acts 1:9 offers another passive (ἐπήρθη—"was lifted up") and adds that a cloud received Jesus.[48] By mentioning the cloud (cf. Luke 9:34–35), the narrator answers the first question, suggesting that God has performed this action.[49]

In Acts 5:1–11 the narrator states that Ananias falls down and breathes his last immediately upon hearing that he has not lied to men but to God (similarly Sapphira). The implication is that God has caused this death, but the narrator does not state as much.[50] Rather, by placing the statement about lying to God in close proximity to the announcement about the death, the narrator presents this as divine judgment.[51] Thus, in a way that is less horrific than "and God struck them dead" would be, the narrator guides the reader to the conclusion that God has brought about these deaths.

Simon, the one who is labeled "the power of God that is called Great" and who amazes the people (ἐξεστακέναι), is himself amazed (ἐξίστατο) at the real power of God (8:13). Simon (and the reader) realizes that Simon is nowhere near as great as the God who gives the Spirit to those who believe (cf. 8:20).[52] Divine power is shown to be superior by the narrative interplay.

When Philip and the eunuch suddenly come upon water (8:36), the narrator has already interrupted to insure that the reader is aware that this is wilderness or desert (8:26), where one would not expect to find much water.[53] The narrator does not identify a wadi, brook, oasis, etc., but simply states that they came upon it and this immediately evokes the

47. Kort (*Story*, 41–42) suggests that supplying such information helps the reader make *moral* judgments about characters. There, however, is no reason to limit the reader's judgments to this one category.

48. A third passive (ἀναλημφθείς) is voiced by the two men in white (1:11) rather than the narrator. It, nevertheless, retains the mystery surrounding Jesus' ascension.

49. Fitzmyer (*Acts*, 210) notes the theological passives and identifies the cloud as marking divine presence. See chapter 4.

50. Gaventa, *Acts*, 103: "Even if Luke does not say that these deaths resulted from divine judgment, the sudden deaths and the awe they inspire make that relationship clear." Lake and Cadbury (*Beginnings*, 51) suggest that Luke expects the reader to understand that power goes forth from Peter to strike down Ananias and Sapphira, citing the incidents with Elymas and Simon Magus as similar events. However, these texts do not suggest that Peter and Paul are vehicles for this divine power; instead, the emphasis is on the divine role.

51. Fitzmyer, *Acts*, 324: "It is God who strikes down the guilty."

52. Tannehill (*Narrative*, 105) suggests these features express a contrast between Simon and Philip. Although this conclusion is true, the ultimate comparison is between magic and divine power (see chapter 4).

53. Water could be found in this area, but that does not lessen the reader's sense that providential action has taken place (Barrett, *Acts*, 432; Plümacher, *Lukas*, 91). Sheeley, *Narrative*, 122: "Divine intervention seems to be the point of the passage. . . . The narrator's aside in 8:26 reinforces the reader's perception of divine guidance in the encounter."

question concerning baptism. This helps to emphasize the divine role in this eunuch's salvation and divine control over the situation. Thus, it seems correct to claim, "Luke's rhetoric serves to assure the reader that God, through the Spirit, is in charge of this story."[54]

When Antioch (14:26) is identified by the narrator as the place where Paul and Barnabas were first "commended to the grace of God," the reader is led to realize that all that has happened during their journey was under divine grace. This realization is magnified as the narrator summarizes Paul and Barnabas' report as what "God had done" in opening a "door of faith for the gentiles."[55] The point of view may be that of Paul and Barnabas but the voice is the narrator's and the statement agrees with the conclusions he has been leading the reader to all long. Likewise, with 15:4, 10 (cf. 21:19–20), since their trip found them narrating gentile conversions, combined with gentile circumcision being the point of contention, the reader should conclude that the ministry to the gentiles is to be understood as "what God has done with them."[56] The narrator does not revert to Paul or Barnabas' direct speech to make these assertions, but offers his own summary about what they said. Therefore, the narrator continues to demonstrate the ability to recount divine action apart from the eyewitnesses.

It is the narrator who reveals that the Lord opened (διήνοιξεν) Lydia's heart (16:14) and in 16:15 she mentions her faithfulness. Through these statements, the reader is reminded of the similar phrase in 14:27 where the narrator summarized Paul's report as including God opening (ἤνοιξεν) a "door of faith" to the gentiles. Thus, the narrator again leads the reader to consider divine involvement in her conversion.

The reader encounters several passives in the account of the Philippian earthquake (16:22–30)—the place was shaken (σαλευθῆναι), the doors were opened (ἠνεῴχθησαν), and the chains fell off (ἀνέθη). Previously, the narrator had informed the reader that Paul and Silas were praying and singing praise to God. Given previous swift responses to prayer, the reader would expect God to act. When the earthquake occurs, with these passive constructions, the reader is drawn toward the conclusion that God has acted.[57]

In these accounts the narrator's importance in leading the reader to draw conclusions about God must not be overlooked. The narrator does not rely solely on direct statements about God in order to characterize God. Rather, he uses textual cues to lead the reader in certain directions, shaping the reader's understanding about God and divine control over the narrative world. This evidence runs counter to Maloney's argument that the way divine acts are identified in Acts is through the events being retold to the community.[58] Rather, the reader recognizes divine activity through the narrative construction.

---

54. Shepherd, *Narrative*, 187.

55. So Gaventa, *Acts*, 209; Schneider, *Apostelgeschichte*, II, 167.

56. So Pesch, *Apostelgeschichte*, II, 65.

57. The prayers indicate that the earthquake is God's answer (Haenchen, *Acts*, 497). Pesch (*Apostelgeschichte*, II, 115; also Haenchen, *Acts*, 500) identifies similarities with the community prayer in 4:31 and sees an epiphanic event in the shaking, opening, and falling-off.

58. Maloney, "*All*," 2, 53.

Results

The Acts narrator assumes the right to make connections between characters (Jesus, the Spirit, believers, unbelievers, etc.) and God. Thus, the reader realizes that the narrator claims a unique and authoritative access to divine relationships. The narrator often (Pentecost, growth of the community, community prayer, etc.) leads readers to make connections between events and the active divine presence. Throughout, the narrator emphasizes proper response to God, thus demonstrating an authority to prescribe devotion to God. It is only the narrator's voice that is heard identifying the filling of the Holy Spirit. Further, the narrator has the privilege not only to describe visions prior to those who witnessed them, but also the right to interpret them (cf. 7:54–56a). The narrator is not subject to the witnesses as Marguerat proposed. Rather, the narrator's rhetorical effort is felt throughout the narrative, shaping the reader's reflections about God. Therefore, the narrator appears to be a primary and authoritative voice for God in the narrative and his rhetorical aims must be considered in analyzing the characterization of God.

Jesus: Sharing with God

Despite Moule's statements to the contrary,[59] Jesus, under various titles ("Christ," "Jesus Christ," "Lord," "Lord Jesus," "Lord Jesus Christ"), appears throughout the narrative. Therefore, this section argues that Jesus' presence in the narrative is associated with God through the relationship in which Jesus stands to God in Acts. This analysis will not examine Christological titles (although this can be helpful),[60] but rather investigate how the narrative portrays Jesus in connection with God. As the story develops, Jesus and God share various attributes. When this situation is combined with references to *Lord* that could refer to either figure, the reader is led to identify divine actions and speech in Jesus' deeds and words. Thus, Jesus' actions would seem to characterize God.

Shared Features

For literary theorists the proper name is the factor around which character traits are grouped (the reader moves through the story attaching the actor's characteristics to the name).[61]

59. Moule ("Christology," 159–85) develops an absentee Christology based on Christ's exaltation to the "right of God." Witherington (*Many*, 153–56) and Conzelmann (*Theology*, 202–6) also argue in this manner (for an opposing view see, Buckwalter, *Character*, 175–84; Gaventa, *Acts*, 32; O'Toole, *Unity*, 38–61). This absentee Christology seems to assume transcendent imagery (residence in heaven) results in absence. However, divine transcendence in OT and Second-Temple literature did not suggest that God was unready and unavailable. Instead, divine interventions and direct divine control were anticipated. Thus, residence in heaven does not mean absence. Further, the Spirit's sending does not signify Jesus' absence. Rather, the Spirit provides divine witness to the community and operates as God's agent, as does Jesus (appearing often as "Lord"). Witherington (*Acts*, 152) also seems incorrect to dismiss "Immanuel" theology in Acts. At Corinth, the Lord appears to Paul in a dream giving him encouragement to continue in this place because "I am with you" (18:10). This statement has similar overtones to the end of Matthew.

60. See de Jonge, *Christology*, 102–10; Jones, "Title," 453–63; Moule, "Christology," 159–85.

61. Rimmon-Kenan, *Narrative*, 39; Reinhartz, "Anonymity," 119; Beck, "Narrative Function," 147.

Moreover, some figures are characterized through analogy to others so that, "When two characters are presented in similar circumstances, the similarity or contrast between their behaviour emphasizes traits characteristic of both."[62] In Acts there are distinctive character traits that arise around the name Jesus and the 'name' God,[63] yet throughout Acts, Jesus and God are portrayed in analogous ways. It appears that the reader is to identify these shared features as characterizing both Jesus and God, thus the reader would see Jesus' action as divine action, treating his appearances as divine appearances. The following discussion illustrates how prevalent these shared features are.

In 3:14 (cf. 7:52) Peter characterizes Jesus as the *Holy and Righteous One*. These attributes are associated with the Isaianic servant,[64] but throughout the OT they are also seen as divine characteristics. Brueggemann defines the OT perspective on divine righteousness as God's "ready capacity to be present" and "act decisively" in order to restore or rehabilitate.[65] In Jer 23:6 the title, the "LORD is our righteousness" is applied to the messianic king, emphasizing this figure's role "to endue Israel with the true character of the covenant people both inwardly and outwardly."[66] Holiness in the OT marks that which belongs to God and is used for divine service.[67] It was an attribute, therefore, characterizing both God and God's people.[68] Applied to Jesus, then, these terms would represent Jesus as God's agent acting to rehabilitate or restore the people.

Jesus appears to take on God's position as *origin of life*. Jesus is (3:15) the ἀρχηγόν (author/founder/leader) of life.[69] In the OT all life is attributed to God. God alone created the world and everything in it (Ps 104:27–30). Thus, Jesus' relationship to life seems more typically to characterize God.

Both Jesus and God can be the *recipient of prayer and worship*. In 7:59, Stephen prays that the Lord Jesus would receive his spirit.[70] Yet, "All prayer growing out of the Old Testament faith is definitely limited by the first commandment."[71] The OT does not pres-

---

62. Rimmon-Kenan, *Narrative*, 70.

63. While technically "God" is not a proper name, an epithet, pronoun, or title can function in the same way as a proper name (Chatman, *Story*, 131). Therefore, it is appropriate to treat the word "God" as if it were a proper name.

64. See Witherington, *Acts*, 181.

65. Brueggemann, *Theology*, 130.

66. Eichrodt, *Theology*, 246.

67. Rehm, *Bild*, 39. Johnson, *Acts*, 67: "The title 'Holy One' is properly God's."

68. Baly, *God*, 32–33.

69. Gaventa (*Acts*, 87) notes the "irony of charging the audience with killing the very originator of life." Because the term will appear again in Acts 5:31 (with the meaning 'leader'), it seems likely that Luke (or his source) was playing on the ambiguity in the word. Cf. Witherington, *Acts*, 181; Lake and Cadbury, *Beginnings*, 36.

70. Pesch (*Apostelgeschichte*, I, 265) thinks that the similarity to Jesus' prayer on the cross indicates that Stephen's prayer is addressed to the 'Lord' God. However, the similarity to that prayer in a context where Jesus is clearly presented as Lord (exalted to the right hand) implies that Jesus is being addressed here in the same way as God.

71. Zimmerli, *Theology*, 151.

ent prayer to the angels or to the king.[72] Thus, having Jesus receive prayer closely aligns him with the divine person.[73] Throughout Acts (discussed above), the proper response to divine actions is to praise/glorify/worship God. Therefore, in 19:17, when the beating of the exorcists resulted in people magnifying "the name of the Lord Jesus," Jesus is again aligned with God in receiving praise typically due God.[74]

It would also seem that the *message about Jesus is a message about God*. In 8:12, the narrator links proclamation about the "kingdom of God" with the "name of Jesus Christ." These two items appear together several times in the narrative (cf. 19:4, 8; 20:24–25; 28:17–31). Indeed, the reader's last impression is that the "kingdom of God" is placed alongside the "things concerning the Lord Jesus Christ." This reminds the reader that the message about Jesus is also a message about God.[75]

Jesus' appearances can be portrayed as *theophanies*. In discussing Saul's conversion (9:1–31), the reference to the light from heaven and the voice[76] led the reader to expect God to be the one speaking with Saul[77] since the event is presented as a divine epiphany (discussed above).[78] Due to this expectation, when the Lord[79] addressed here is revealed to be Jesus, the reader associates Jesus with God.[80] Thus, the reader sees that Jesus appears in a role that the OT would use to portray God.

The "Lord" knows Ananias (just as he previously knew Saul, although Saul did not recognize him). The "Lord" also knows the place where Saul is staying; with whom he is staying; where Saul is from and what he is currently doing (praying). Further, the figure

---

72. There are instances in Second-Temple literature where angels receive prayers (*1 En.* 12:12, 15; *T. Levi* 5.5; *T. Dan* 6.2; Tob 3:16–17). These cases, nevertheless, seem to have more to do with the angels being intermediaries for the transcendent God rather than being direct recipients of prayers (Wicks, *Doctrine*, 51, 64). *Contra* Lake and Cadbury (*Beginnings*, 86) who suggest it would be natural to address the "son of man" in prayer.

73. Haenchen, *Acts*, 293: Jesus "takes the place of God."

74. Johnson (*Acts*, 341) implies this when he notes that Luke here brings together three elements typical of his miracle accounts, including "the glorification/praise of God." Jervell (*Apostelgeschichte*, 160–61) emphasizes that God, not Jesus, was praised for the healing in Jesus' name at 3:7–8. Here, God's works (the exorcisms) lead to praise for Jesus' name. Thus, Luke reversed the emphasis.

75. Fitzmyer (*Acts*, 311) claims that Jesus' significance in relation to the "word of God" is seen as early as 4:31.

76. If, as Lake and Cadbury (*Beginnings*, 100–101) suggest, conceptions about the *bat qol* are invoked here, the divine expectation is enhanced.

77. Burchard ("Joseph," 101) and Pesch (*Apostelgeschichte*, I, 304) suggest that Christ's appearance to Saul resembles the appearance by the Commander of the Lord's Army to Aseneth (*Jos. Asen.* 4:1–8). However, only the theophanic elements are shared. Otherwise the Acts descriptions lack the embellishments evident in *Jos. Asen.* (standing by her head, the appeals to being alone).

78. Gaventa, *Acts*, 148: "The language used recalls descriptions of hearing God's voice in the Old Testament (e.g., Num 7:89; Isa 6:8)." On OT theophanies see Fretheim, *Suffering*, 80–95; Patrick, *Rendering*, 91–93.

79. 'Lord,' here, could simply be a term designating respect ('sir'), or it could recognize divinity or supernatural beings. Given the theophanic setting, the latter seem more likely (Johnson, *Acts*, 163; Witherington, *Acts*, 317).

80. Witherington, *Acts*, 316, fn. 47: The theophanic imagery applied to Jesus suggests Luke is "comfortable using the language of divinity of the exalted Christ."

knows what Saul has seen while he is praying (9:12). This Lord, revealed to be Jesus (9:17), is therefore presented as an *omniscient* being.

The "Lord" states that Saul is a chosen vessel (9:15). In Paul's first defense speech (22:1–21) Paul says that God appointed him to this witnessing task, yet in 26:1–23 it is Jesus who has appointed Paul. Rather than a contradiction, because of the portrait already developed, the reader should see the repetition[81] as evidence that God and Jesus share in *choosing* the witnesses (cf. 1:2 with 10:41).

In 15:11 Peter mentions the "grace of the Lord Jesus." Previously, grace was associated with God (11:23; 13:43). Thus, now, both Jesus and God are described in relation to *grace* given to believers. Further, Paul commands the Philippian jailer to believe in the Lord Jesus, but the narrator sums it up as believing in God (16:31, 34). Consequently, the narrator puts *belief in God and belief in Jesus on the same level.*[82]

Jesus' *name* is used in the same way as God's. In the OT, the divine name was used interchangeably with the divine person and presence (cf. Deut 12:5).[83] Thus, if God's name produced a miracle, then God himself did it.[84] In 3:6 Jesus' "name" seems to produce healings (cf. 4:10), so the same miracle power is active in this name.[85] Salvation, which is typically a divine act,[86] is attributed to Jesus' name (4:12). There are Jewish exorcists in Ephesus who are using the "name of the Lord Jesus" when trying to cast out evil spirits (19:13). This recalls Jesus' power over evil spirits, something demonstrated before (5:16; 10:38; 16:18). However, 19:11 considers the miracles, which would include exorcisms, as done by God. This would imply that the exorcists connected Jesus' name with the miracles done (according to the narrator) by God.

81. Clark (*Parallel*, 150–203) discusses the relationship between the three accounts of Paul's Damascus experience, noting the way redundancy impacts the presentation and how these accounts relate to the rest of Acts.

82. Lindsay (*Josephus*, 126, 142) suggests that Josephus refers to belief in Moses (*Ant.* 2:274). However, as Lindsay points out (142), for Josephus this belief in Moses remains indirect, while belief in God is direct. Acts presents belief in Jesus as direct and specifically parallels it with belief in God.

83. Zimmerli, *Theology*, 78: "the presence of Yahweh is expressed . . . as the presence of the divine 'name.'"

84. Eichrodt, *Theology*, 206–7: "Prayers and oaths, blessing and cursing, battles and victories, all were 'in the name of Yahweh' . . . they were accompanied by the utterance of his Name and by the assurance that in this way his presence could be summoned to one's aid." It would follow that invoking the name is a call for the holder of the name to act.

85. Witherington (*Acts*, 175) notes this as a possibility. He denies it (fn. 43) because he assumes that Luke presents an absentee Christology, but see note 59 above. In 9:34 Peter tells Aeneas that Jesus Christ heals him. This more direct statement, which indicates Jesus' active involvement (Gaventa, *Acts*, 162), with the corresponding healing, suggests that Jesus' name can be used to mean that Jesus himself has done the action (so Barrett, *Acts*, 481; Pesch, *Apostelgeschichte*, I, 318–19; missed by Witherington, *Acts*, 327–39). Fitzmyer (*Acts*, 266) suggests that, "For Luke the 'name of Jesus' connotes the real and effective representation of Jesus himself."

86. God, through the Exodus imagery, is uniquely Israel's redeemer and savior (see R. Mason, *Pictures*, 24; Bock, *Proclamation*, 227). Second-Temple literature can refer to other figures as saviors (the Maccabees in 1–2 Maccabees; Caesar in *Antiquities*), but there is no mention that their 'name' is effective for such. Further, those saviors are temporal deliverers, whereas the salvation in Jesus' name goes beyond a mere physical deliverance.

In Acts both Jesus and God *give the Spirit*. Acts 1:4–5 relates the Spirit to the "Father," but in 2:33 Jesus pours out the Spirit. By having Jesus receive this promise from the Father, Jesus' pouring out is linked to God (cf. 11:16–17).[87] Further, the phrase "God declares" (2:17) emphasizes the *I* in "I will pour out my Spirit" (2:18), making the pouring out by Jesus into God's action (cf. also 5:32; 8:20). Acts 16:6–7 places the "Spirit of Jesus" in parallel with the "Holy Spirit." Through the conclusion that God had called them to Macedonia (16:10), the activity by the "Spirit of Jesus" is identified with the divine call. God stands behind and above all—working in and through Jesus, the Spirit, and the mission.[88]

The Pentecost sermon suggests that both Jesus and God are *Lords sitting on the divine throne as judge*. When Jesus is exalted to the "right hand of God" (2:33–34), the implication is that he sits down on the divine throne (cf. 13:33–35). Because of Judaism's monotheistic structure, the divine throne is generally seen as the only one in heaven.[89] This solitary throne provides such a "symbolic function" that finding a figure other than God seated on this throne itself would be "one of Judaism's most potent theological means of including such a figure in the unique divine identity."[90] There are a few instances where other figures sit on the throne (Wisdom, Moses, and the Enochic "son of man"). However, Moses sits on it in a dream and this is interpreted in a non-heavenly way,[91] and Wisdom is an attribute intrinsic to the divine identity[92] and thus not a separate being on the throne.[93] Only the Enochic "son of man" provides a parallel since it appears to have developed from a recognition that the "son of man" in Dan 7:14 participates in the divine rule and thus in God's unique identity as judge.[94] Consequently, when Jesus sits on God's throne he participates in the divine rule and role.

The reference in 7:56 to Jesus at the "right hand of God" echoes Psalm 110 and thus has similarities with Acts 2 and Jesus seated on the throne.[95] However, in Stephen's vision this figure is standing rather than sitting. This difference is difficult to analyze, as demonstrated

---

87. Bock (*Proclamation*, 347, fn. 50) suggests that the exposition in 2:33 means God initiates the pouring out. Jesus becomes the mediator. However, Turner (*Power*, 277–78) states that Jesus does not just mediate God's Spirit, but becomes the "author" of the "specific phenomena" that occur. Either way, the reader identifies pouring out the Spirit as done by both Jesus and God.

88. See Stählin, "Τὸ πνεῦμα," 236. Fitzmyer (*Acts*, 577) notes a "crescendo" here from the Holy Spirit, to the Spirit of Jesus, and finally to God, portraying the evangelizing work entirely under divine guidance.

89. Bauckham, "Throne," 52. His note 19 lists other thrones and the literature in which they appear.

90. Ibid., 53. For more on Second-Temple Jewish monotheism and Christianity see also: Bauckham, *God* (1998); Davila, "Methodology," 3–18; Davis, "Divine," 479–503; Denaux, "Monotheistic," 133–58; Hurtado, "First-Century," 3–26; Hurtado, *One* (1998); Mach, "Concepts," 21–42. Zeller ("Christology," 312–33) offers a return to the classic *religionsgeschichtliche Schule* (viewing Christology from a Hellenistic perspective), but fails to heed Hurtado's warnings to recognize that Jewish/biblical thought remains decisive. There are Hellenistic influences in NT Christology, but this Christology developed from a Jewish framework.

91. Bauckham, "Throne," 55–57.

92. The *divine identity* represents the characteristics that uniquely define God in relation to all other beings and all creation (Bauckham, *God*, 6–9).

93. Bauckham, "Throne," 54–55.

94. Ibid., 58–60. Chapter 2 noted that the divine role as judge is associated with the divine rule and thus important in OT and Second-Temple conceptions about God.

95. Barrett, *Acts*, 384; Bock, *Proclamation*, 222; Fitzmyer, *Acts*, 392; Johnson, *Acts*, 139.

by the numerous solutions offered.[96] Treating Stephen's words in 7:59–60 as his response to the vision, his second statement calls for the "Lord Jesus" not to charge this offense to his persecutors. This portrays Jesus acting as a prosecutor and Stephen asking for leniency. Indeed, Johnson claims that Stephen addresses Jesus as the "judge" who "can assign blame or forgive."[97] The imagery echoes ideas about the son of man participating in judgment:[98] "His [the son of man's] role is to conduct a prosecution to the point of judgment and the execution of judgment. . . . Prosecution of the Jewish people for the sins of their fathers (v. 52), which they have not expiated by repentance, no matter how frequently they were called upon by JHWH to do so."[99] Judges stood to give judgment,[100] just as Jesus/the Son of Man is doing here. Thus, Jesus is acting for God,[101] pronouncing divine judgment on the rebellious Jerusalem leadership who continued their ancestors' ways, killing those sent to them. This does not deny that Jesus will receive Stephen and that his standing facilitates his welcome, but the image primarily seems to reflect Jesus as the eschatological judge.

God's sole rule over all nature and history is an integral feature of the unique divine identity within Jewish Monotheism,[102] yet Peter calls Jesus "Lord of all" (10:36).[103] Is Jesus being included in this unique identity? Cornelius is a gentile and Peter is a Jew. It could be that calling Jesus Lord of all opens up the hope that Jesus is also Lord for Cornelius; a hope seemingly cut off by Jesus' relation to "the people of Israel."[104] Peter's statement, then, could refer simply to Jesus as Lord (a messianic hope) for both Jew and gentile. However, Peter adds that Jesus is the one God has appointed as judge over the "living and the dead" (10:42; cf. 17:31[105]). This reference to Jesus as judge recalls the universal sovereign rule associated with "Lord of all."[106] It also speaks to a special divine role as seen in Pss 9; 96:13; and 98:9,

96. Haenchen (*Acts*, 292, fn. 4) offers three; Fitzmyer (*Acts*, 392) four; Schille (*Apostelgeschichte*, 188) five; Bock (*Proclamation*, 222–24) and Johnson (*Acts*, 139) six; Barrett (*Acts*, 384–85) eleven; while Derrett ("Son," 71–84) lists around a dozen.

97. Johnson, *Acts*, 141.

98. See Munoa, "Jesus," 306–13. Schneider (*Apostelgeschichte*, I, 475 n. 31) thinks that Luke does not emphasize the son of man's role in the judgment. This fails to recognize that the son of man imagery is connected to the exalted Lord and thus the legal role that Lord would have.

99. Derrett, "Son," 83.

100. Ibid., 78.

101. Ibid., 74–75. However, this does not affirm Derrett's claim that Jesus is, for Stephen, "God in another guise" (75). There is a distinction between Jesus and God (Jesus is at the "right"). In Luke's portrait, when Jesus acts God can be said to have acted, but Jesus is not simply God wearing a different hat as Derrett's statement seems to imply.

102. Bauckham, *God*, 10–11, 32; "Throne," 45–46. See also chapter 2.

103. Παντων could be either neuter (referring to things—i.e. creation) or masculine (referring to people). See Fitzmyer, *Acts*, 464; Schneider, *Apostelgeschichte*, II, 75.

104. So Pesch, *Apostelgeschichte*, I, 342; Tannehill, *Narrative*, 139.

105. Fitzmyer, *Acts*, 612: "the risen Christ is seen as sharing in divine judicial activity." The God described in the Athens speech is "Lord of heaven and earth"—i.e., the ruler over everything. Thus, Jesus is included in God's universal lordship there as well.

106. For Dupont ("Seigneur," 233) these images point to Jesus' universal lordship. Dupont puts Jesus as judge only in an eschatological perspective, but in light of the Joel citation the *eschaton* would appear to have begun. Jesus' lordship is both present and future. Dupont notes the present aspect since this lordship is presently connected with sins being forgiven. Such a view would support the conclusion that Jesus stands in Stephen's vision because he operates as judge.

and it agrees with other elements already noted. Jesus appears to be fully associated with the divine "task and position."[107] Therefore, the reader is correct to relate "Lord of all" in Peter's statement to divine sovereign rule.

While there was a tendency to read all the royal Psalms messianically, early Christianity used Ps 110:1 in a unique manner[108]—there is no evidence that this verse was applied to any other figure in the sense used here.[109] By applying this Psalm to Jesus (Acts 2:33–34; 7:56), Luke aligns Jesus with divine cosmic rule.[110] Thus, throughout the narrative, Jesus' exaltation "to the right hand" is used to indicate Jesus is *Lord*. It is not just that this title is given to Jesus, but also that he takes a place with God in heaven—on the throne, judging the world. This idea is furthered in that the quotation from Joel concludes in 2:21 by identifying salvation as coming to those who "call on the name of the *Lord*." At that point the reader is most likely to interpret κυρίος as a reference to God, particularly given 2:17 ("God declares"). Once Jesus has been shown to be the κυρίος in 2:36, an ambiguity is created in relation to who was really referenced at 2:21.[111] Thus, both Jesus and God are called Lord, and combined with the royal aspect it would seem that Jesus and God are being called Lord in the same way.[112]

Ambiguity of "Lord"

As noted, readers attach character traits to proper names or titles. Having more than one name, however, can cause ambiguity, requiring the reader to work out to whom a specific trait is to be applied. Such is especially true in situations where "names (or titles) seem to be interchangeable."[113] In Acts both Jesus and God are called "Lord" in the same way. Although some Lord references are clear, many are not. These ambiguous references lead the reader to see Jesus and God together.

While the direct connection between Jesus and God as Lord is not made until Acts 2, at 1:24 those gathered *pray*, addressing σὺ κύριε. Since the most recent reference to Lord

---

107. Bock, *Proclamation*, 236–37; with some reservation, Barrett, *Acts*, 528.

108. Bauckham, "Throne," 62–63; Hengel, "'Sit,'" 138.

109. It appears in *T. Job* 33:3 but depicts Job's heavenly reward rather than his participation in divine cosmic rule. See Bauckham, "Throne," 62, fn. 37.

110. Fitzmyer (*Acts*, 260) concludes that by using Ps 110:1 in this argument, Lord in 2:36, "implies that Jesus in his risen status has been made the equal of Yahweh of the OT."

111. Gaventa (*Acts*, 77) notes that "a clear distinction" between Luke using Lord for Jesus and for God is "difficult to support." Bock (*Proclamation*, 165) points out that this ambiguity would exist even if a Semitic source was the background. Either the Aramaic *mara* or the Hebrew *adon* would have been read for the divine name *YHWH* in the quotation from Joel 2:21. Fenske ("Aspekte," 54–70; *contra* Haenchen, *Acts*, 185) agrees that the Peter's speech in Acts 2 is not solely dependent on the LXX.

112. Buckwalter, *Character*, 188: "Thus, with good reason we propose that Luke believed Jesus' Lordship to represent 'a status equal to Yahweh.' Jesus appears as 'co-regent' in Acts."

113. Burnett, "Characterization," 20.

is the "Lord Jesus" (1:21),[114] it is possible that Jesus is the Lord addressed here.[115] In 1:2, the reader learned that Jesus had chosen the apostles, thus, choosing the replacement apostle is something Jesus would do.[116] However, since this Lord is addressed in prayer, God is the more likely referent (no groundwork has yet been laid for Jesus to be addressed this way). The "Lord" knows "everyone's heart," which also suggests God is being referenced.[117] Thus, if this is a reference to Jesus, it places him in close parallel with God (being described as one who knows human hearts and who can be addressed in prayer). Hurtado argues that this shows Jesus receiving prayer.[118] If so, it draws Jesus into the unique divine identity at an early stage. The reader, at this point, is likely to assume God is the addressee, but must also consider Jesus. The ambiguity prevents the reader from making a final decision. However, in causing the reader to consider that Jesus could be addressed in prayer in the same way as God, Luke prompts the reader to begin expanding his understanding about how Jesus is characterized.

Similarly, Simon Magus (8:22, 24) is to repent and petition the Lord. Without a strict identifier the reader must reflect on whom Simon should petition. Most fresh in the reader's mind would be that Stephen has petitioned Jesus (7:59). Also, Jesus' name has been associated with forgiveness. Thus, the reader may quickly conclude that Jesus is the Lord mentioned. The reader recognizes that Jesus, like God, receives prayers—affirming conclusions the reader finally reached in the Stephen episode. Thus, in retrospect, the reader is led, almost from the beginning of Acts, to align Jesus and God in prayer.

The people are to call upon "the *name* of the Lord" for their salvation (2:21) and be baptized for the forgiveness in Jesus' name (2:38).[119] Jesus is the "Lord and Messiah" sitting on the divine throne (2:33–36), but the Lord, their God, calls people for salvation (2:39). Since 'to call on the name of the Lord' "is a regular Old Testament formula for worship and prayer offered to God" (Gen 4:26; 13:4; Ps 105:1; Jer 10:25; Joel 2:32),[120] the ambiguity in "the name of the Lord" draws an analogy between Jesus and God.

---

114. Franklin (*Christ*, 43) argued that the assertion that Jesus is Lord in the ascension account confirms the ascension as pivotal for Luke's argument that Jesus is Lord. In 1:6 the disciples use this title for Jesus. The ascension provides the event that allows the disciples to proclaim Jesus' Lordship (see chapter 4), but such 'Lordship' in an exalted sense is not asserted in 1:9–11. At this point the disciples and the reader have begun associating Jesus with God, so a greater significance to κύριος may be observed by the reader who knows that it is used in the LXX for *YHWH*, but since the link is not strong at this point, the reader is likely to decide that Lord simply designates respect, as suggested by the vocative.

115. So Barrett, *Acts*, 103.

116. O'Toole, *Unity*, 40; Lake and Cadbury, *Beginnings*, 15.

117. So Bibb, "Characterization," 172–73 n. 8; Pesch, *Apostelgeschichte*, I, 90. Cf. 1 Sam 16:7 (in a context where David is chosen); 1 Chr 28:9; Jer 17:10. Luke 16:15 has Jesus describing God as the one who knows men's hearts. Luke, nevertheless, also suggests Jesus knows what his opponents were reasoning in their hearts (Luke 5:22), although this reference seems to address their thoughts, not their nature.

118. Hurtado, *One*, 104.

119. Fitzmyer (*Acts*, 253–54) notes the interplay between Jesus and God here, although he draws no implication for the reader's understanding about either Jesus or God. Hurtado (*One*, 108–9) argues that the Christian ritual to baptize in Jesus' name was unique in Second-Temple Judaism.

120. France, "Worship," 30.

Ambiguity also appears in relation to the *Spirit* and *angels*. In 5:9 (cf. 8:39), Peter mentions the "Spirit of the Lord" without an identifying reference for Lord. Since it is a common OT identification and because the Spirit has been portrayed as the Father's promise (1:4) the reader may well consider this a reference to God. The Spirit is linked with God in the preceding verses through Ananias and Sapphira lying to both figures. However, the reader also knows that Jesus is the one who has received the "promise of the Holy Spirit" and now pours out that Spirit (2:33). The actual referent remains unclear because of Jesus' relationship to the Spirit. Similarly, in 5:19 (cf. 8:26; 12:7, 11, 23) an "angel of the Lord" opened the prison doors and led them out. Again, there is no specific identifier and Barrett comments, "Whether by κύριος Luke understood the OT Lord or Jesus it is impossible to determine; probably he would find it unnecessary to make up his mind on the question, if indeed it occurred to him."[121] The reader, however, in assembling a portrait must make some attempt. While Luke has not made any specific connections in Acts between Jesus and the angels,[122] the reader is likely to be familiar with Jewish traditions that God rules over the angels from the divine throne. Therefore, the reader may suppose that Jesus, who is on this throne, also rules over the angels.[123] The ambiguity in the referent for Lord once again causes the reader to reflect on the similarity between the portrayals of God and Jesus.

Acts 5:14 (cf. 9:42[124]; 18:8) states, "believers were added to the Lord." Since those who believed were Jews, they would have already believed in God. Now a new belief is implied, so the Lord here must be Jesus. The ambiguity, nevertheless, would cause the reader to consider the association between Jesus and God. Paul and Barnabas (14:23) commit the elders to the "Lord" in "whom they had come to believe." The most likely reference is to Jesus, but the vagueness in the title and the previous command for the gentiles in Lystra to turn to the "living God" leaves enough room for the reader to again connect Jesus and God—to 'turn to the Lord Jesus' is to 'turn to the Lord God.' Finally, in 16:14–15, the Lord opens the heart of Lydia. Lydia then exhorts them to stay with her if they have judged her "faithful to the Lord." Previously, Paul (14:27) had proclaimed to those in Antioch that God had *opened* a door of *faith* for the gentiles. The linking word *opened* (διήνοιξεν; cf. ἤνοιξεν in 14:27) and Lydia's reference to her faithfulness connect these two passages. Thus the reader should conclude that God has opened her heart and she is faithful to God.

---

121. Barrett, *Acts*, 28.

122. In Luke 4:9, the devil quotes from Ps 91:11 [LXX] concerning God commanding his angels concerning Christ. Thus, in the Gospel also, God controls the angels.

123. Possibly, given the principal angel figure represented in Jewish tradition (for a discussion see Hurtado, *One*, 75–82; Rowland, *Open*, 94–113), the reader may identify Jesus with the angel. One such figure may function as a "grand vizier" who acts for God. However, Bauckham ("Throne," 50) disputes this since even if a "grand vizier" is pictured, that figure never receives worship and is not said to sit on God's throne in the present. Further, Luke nowhere compares Jesus to an angel.

124. Haenchen's comment (*Acts*, 338) that, "Here Jews are the subject; in the case of the Gentiles it would be 'turned to God' (cf. 14.15, 15.19 and 26.20)" merely strengthens this point. Since the phrase "turned to the Lord" (meaning Jesus) can mean the same thing as "turned to God," a close relationship is implied: Jesus and God can be referred to in the same way.

However, *belief* has been connected with Jesus, so once again the reader is struck by the interconnectivity between the possible referents.

Acts 8:25 (cf. 19:10, 20)[125] refers to Peter and John's message as the "*word* of the Lord." The reader would, it appears, naturally have concluded that Jesus is the Lord in 8:22 and 24. Further, Philip's preaching was said to be about Christ. However, the Apostles' message has been previously called the "word of God" (6:2, probably 6:7 also) and here the reader finds reference to two Apostles. Thus, the reader can have no clear-cut answer as to which Lord is meant. This, then, suggests the message is about both Jesus and God.

In 9:31, the community lives in "the *fear* of the Lord." The nearest references to Lord have been to Jesus (9:5–17, 27–28). "Fear of the Lord," nevertheless, echoes the OT "fear of God," which represents a stock biblical image for being God's follower (often in distinction from those who follow other gods).[126] When Cornelius is described (10:1–2) as one who "feared God," the narrator does not use the ambiguous χυρίος but the eminently clear θεός. Thus, those who fear the Lord in 9:31 would seem to identify a group distinct from Cornelius and others like him. The difference seems to come from the vagueness in the term "Lord," which allows the reader to consider both God and Jesus. However, in order to define this gentile God-fearer Luke removes the ambiguity. In 10:33, Cornelius states that they are assembled to hear what Peter was commanded by the Lord,[127] who appears to be God—given Cornelius' characterization as a God-fearer. The reader, however, knows that Peter's vision was delivered by a Lord that is distinct from God (discussed below) and would note that even though Cornelius presently only knows God as Lord, he is about to learn about another Lord. Thus, fearing the Lord applies to both Jesus and God.

When Peter has a *vision* about a sheet descending from heaven and hears a voice (10:13), the voice would seem to be God's. But, the reader would recall that the narrator used the same technique with Saul's vision (9:1–6) and, thus, expect the voice to belong to Jesus. When the voice (called "Lord," 10:14) comes a second time, it refers to God in the third person (different from the baptism and transfiguration scenes in the Gospel), so the reader's expectation appears to be confirmed. In 18:9–10 (cf. 23:11), through a vision the "Lord" commands Paul not to fear. While the Lord here would seem to be Jesus (cf. 18:8), the tie with God is strong given the commands not to fear found in Isa 41:10; 43:5; and Jer 1:8.[128] These OT parallels would again cause the reader to consider Jesus' relationship with God, so that "this scene is no less a theophany than the ones recorded in the OT."[129] In Paul's vision in the temple,[130] the "Lord" (22:19) appears to him and tells him to leave

---

125. Acts 19:10 and 19:20 mention the "word of the Lord." In 19:10 the phrase comes after Paul has proclaimed Jesus as the coming one and Lord (19:4–5) and after his arguments there are said to be about the "kingdom of God." Thus, the "word of the Lord" can be seen to include both Jesus and God as Lord.

126. Ryken *et al*, "Fear," 277.

127. The textual evidence suggests that τοὺ χυρίου is the better reading (see Metzger, *Textual*, 378).

128. Pesch, *Apostelgeschichte*, II, 149. Possibly 1 Kgs 19:18 is echoed too.

129. Witherington, *Acts*, 550, fn. 327 (following Marshall, *Acts*, 296).

130. This event has some similarities to dream incubation—an individual goes to a shrine, engages in a ritual activity and then falls asleep, expecting to receive a dream revelation (Gnuse, *Dreams*, 119). However, Paul does not say he fell asleep or that he went to the temple expecting a revelation.

Jerusalem and go to the gentiles. Because it is Paul's testimony to "him" that the people will not accept, the reader will likely decide on Jesus as the Lord in question.[131] However, since the vision took place in the temple and there can be only one Lord over the temple (the Lord God),[132] the unique relationship between Jesus and God as Lord is emphasized.

Luke notes (11:21) that the "*hand* of the Lord" was with those who preached to the gentiles, causing a number to turn to the Lord.[133] "Lord Jesus Christ" stands in close proximity to the two references to Lord in 11:21. However, since "hand of the LORD" is an OT formula and because hand was used in the community prayer (4:30) to refer to the divine presence and power, the reader must also consider God as the referent. Paul says that Elymas perverts the "straight paths [ways] of the Lord" and tells him that the "hand of the Lord" is against him to bring about blindness (13:10–11). The "Way" has been associated with Jesus (9:2),[134] but the plural here seems to reflect passages like Hos 14:9 and thus God. "Hand" as a reference to miraculous power was associated with God (4:30), but 11:20–21 connects the "hand" with the Lord Jesus. Again, then, the reader finds that both God and Jesus could be referred to by these terms.

The prophets and teachers in Antioch minister to the Lord (13:2). Λειτουργεῖν is associated in the Septuagint with the priestly temple service.[135] Thus, while these men are clearly allied with Jesus and know him as Lord, Luke describes their activity using a term reflecting *worship* offered to God. Once again the reader is prompted to think that worship offered to Jesus as Lord is appropriate.

Finally,[136] in 15:16–18, James quotes from Amos 9:11–12. This passage mentions that David's tent would be rebuilt so that all "other peoples may *seek* the Lord." Because this is a quotation from the OT, the reader would likely identify God as the Lord. This idea is affirmed when James mentions the gentiles turning to God (15:19). However, since Luke uses the ambiguous title Lord, the reader must at least consider Jesus. Indeed, the idea that Jesus fulfills the Davidic promise is echoed with the reference to David's rebuilt tent.[137]

---

131. In Luke 19:45–48 Jesus enters the temple and by cleansing it seems to declare his authority over this place (19:47; cf. 20:2). When Jesus entered the city on the way to the temple he is proclaimed as "king" (19:38), thus it is as the messiah that Jesus takes possession (Chance, *Jerusalem*, 57–58). Since (in Acts) Jesus, the Davidic messiah, has become the exalted Lord (see chapter 4), identifying Jesus as the Lord over the temple is consistent with Luke's Gospel.

132. So Haenchen, *Acts*, 627.

133. Haenchen's comment concerning 9:35 that "turned to God" is the proper phrasing for gentiles (*Acts*, 388) is inaccurate in this instance. However, this strengthens the argument that the two referents are so closely aligned that the reader is prepared to see them as Lord in the same way. Gaventa, *Acts*, 179: "The proximity of this phrase ['the hand of the Lord'] to the phrases 'turned to the Lord' and to 'the Lord Jesus' in v. 20 exemplifies Luke's close association of Jesus and God."

134. The connection between the "sect of the Nazarenes" and the "Way" in 24:1–23 suggests Jesus as the referent there.

135. See Haenchen, *Acts*, 395; Gaventa, *Acts*, 190.

136. There are other ambiguous references regarding boldness (14:3), grace (15:40; cf. 14:26), Paul's ministry (20:19), and whose "will" is involved (21:14).

137. Bock, *Proclamation*, 364, fn. 2.

Thus, within the Acts narrative, Jesus (as Lord) is completely associated with the Davidic promise and can be seen as the Lord that the peoples seek.[138]

Results

The features and actions shared by Jesus and God, as well as the ambiguity created by the unspecified referents for Lord, unite the characterizations of these figures. Jesus and God share attributes like holiness, righteousness, and omniscience. There is a common message, a common grace, and even a similarity in manifestation. Both Jesus and God can be said to send the Spirit and to choose the witnesses. Jesus, like God, receives prayer and worship and is the object of faith. Like God, as well, Jesus judges humanity and is included in the divine rule over all things. This consistent sharing in work, will, and word draws the two figures ever closer in the reader's mind and the analogy drawn between them characterizes both figures.

Since Luke can use the shared title Lord to refer specifically to either Jesus or God, the reader must consider the relationship between Jesus and God where the referent is unspecified. Repeatedly, the reader finds that there are characterizations of the unspecified Lord that could be applied to either Jesus or God. Since many such instances concern themes that Jesus and God shared in (prayer, name, belief, the Spirit, worship, grace), this ambiguity contributes to the analogous portrayals of Jesus and God.

These results have application to Christology (possibly supporting Bauckham's argument that Jesus shares in the unique divine identity). When Paul describes God as creator and ruler in speeches to gentiles (14:15–16; 17:24, 31), the reader's initial impressions made when Jesus is included in these images (10:36, 42; 17:31) is confirmed—Jesus shares in God's unique functions. Through the enthronement Psalms (2:7; 110:1) applied to Jesus and explicit references to Jesus as "Lord of all" and "judge," Jesus is included in this identity. The point here, however, is not to show that Jesus is divine, but simply that the portrayal of Jesus is so similar to that of God that his actions and involvement characterize God. This requires including the actions and attributes associated with Jesus when discussing the portrayal of God.

The Spirit: Witness to God

It is generally agreed that the Spirit presented in Luke-Acts is the OT Spirit of prophecy.[139] Thus, the background for Luke's portrayal of the Spirit is Jewish rather than Greco-Roman. What is not agreed is how extensive that portrait is. Does the Spirit function only to inspire speech?[140] Is the Spirit primarily connected to initiation/conversion?[141] Or is the Spirit's role more complex, involving various aspects from power for witness, to miracles,

---

138. Hoet ("Ἐθνῶν," 404) arrives at the same conclusion. On this passage see also chapter 5.

139. Originally argued in von Baer, *Heilige* (1926).

140. So Menzies, *Empowered* (1994); Shelton, *Mighty* (1991); Stronstad, *Charismatic* (1985); Schweizer, "πνεῦμα κτλ," 396–453.

141. So Dunn, *Baptism* (1975).

salvation, and sustaining the church?[142] While most scholarship has tended toward this latter conclusion, no consensus has been attained. Recently, Hur argued that the portrayal of the Spirit gives "the divine frame of reference," providing reliability to the words and actions performed by other characters.[143] Analyzing this "frame of reference" leads to the conclusion that the Spirit must be included when analyzing the characterization of God, since the Spirit is presented as God's promise and a marker of the divine presence and word, the key witness to the divine will.

God's Promise

The Spirit's presence seems to signify that divine promises have been fulfilled. Jesus mentions the "promise of the Father" in 1:4–5 and in a "this is that" formula Peter defines the Spirit's coming as the fulfillment of God's promises given through Joel (2:14–21).[144] Consequently, in 2:32–33, the Spirit seems to be the content of the Father's promise.[145] The Spirit is twice (2:17, 18) specifically labeled "my Spirit,"[146] which, with the OT quotation, indicates that this promise is the OT Spirit of God.

When the disciples hear about the promise of the Spirit they immediately ask about the restoration of the kingdom. From their response, the reader identifies a connection between the Spirit and God's kingdom. Since the OT prophets saw the Spirit as marking the future kingdom (The Spirit is associated with the restored Israel in Joel 3:1–5; Isa 44:3; and Ezek 11:19; 36:27; 39:29), the Spirit's presence would represent that this kingdom was present/restored.[147] The restored kingdom theme continues when Matthias is chosen to complete the twelve apostles (1:26). The reference to Israel's scriptures draws the new community in relation to Israel and its leadership in relation to Israel's leadership. It is, then, the Spirit (who speaks and is promised in these Scriptures) that now provides for the restoration.[148]

At 2:38, the Spirit is identified as the gift[149] and 2:39 again connects the Spirit with promise. Therefore, the Spirit is both the divine promise and the gift given by God (and

142. Authors arguing for one or all these aspects include Haya-Prats, *L'Esprit* (1975); Keener, *Spirit* (1997); Lampe, "Spirit," 159–72; Lampe, *God* (1977); Turner, *Power*, 1996; Wenk, *Community* (2000).

143. Hur, *Dynamic*, 113–14 (following Shepherd, *Narrative* [1994]).

144. Wenk (*Community*, 252) notes that the Joel text is appropriate since it emphasizes charismatic manifestations of the Spirit.

145. Johnson, *Acts*, 52.

146. Turner (*Power*, 278) argues that when Luke includes ὁ θεός his action is "strictly superfluous" in Jewish thought "because no being other than God could possibly be conceived as 'pouring out' God's Spirit" since "God's *Spirit* (even more strongly than the *Shekinah*) *was a way of speaking of the active* (usually self-revealing) *personal presence of the transcendent God himself*" (emphasis his). Thus, Luke is emphasizing the divine activity and presence in this event.

147. Keener, *Spirit*, 192; cf. Jervell, *Unknown*, 98.

148. Jervell, *Unknown*, 98–99. On restoration see also chapter 4.

149. *Contra* Shepherd (*Narrative*, 161) the word gave (δίδωμι) in 2:4 does not "remind the reader that the Spirit is the promised gift." The Spirit gives rather than 'is given.' Moreover, the Acts reader cannot be reminded that the Father's promise is a gift since it has not been suggested. If the reader knows Luke's Gospel, this connection would be possible, but the gift image plays a more prominent role in Acts—cf. 4:29, the com-

Jesus) to those who repent. In 3:20, God's response to repentance is to send "times of refreshing." The parallel with 2:39 implies that the gift that is the Spirit should be seen as times of refreshing.[150] In 5:32 the Spirit is described as the one "given to those who obey God." Through this repeated association between repentance and obedience,[151] when God gives the "gift" (cf. 10:45) to the gentiles, divine testimony is offered concerning their "repentance to life" (11:15–18; cf. 13:48, 52).[152]

When the Spirit does not "come upon" the Samaritans until Peter and John come from Jerusalem (8:15–17), the gift aspect is emphasized.[153] The Spirit (given Philip's "signs and great miracles") was already active, but God had yet to specifically fulfill this promise for the Samaritans. When Peter rebukes Simon, he emphasizes that the Spirit comes as a "gift" (8:20). In this way, the reader realizes that the Spirit does not come upon the individual as an automatic response, nor is the Spirit gained through human authority, but rather the Spirit is the "gift of God."[154] The narrative emphasizes that the Spirit is bestowed when God (and Jesus, cf. 2:33) chooses and not otherwise.[155] Regardless, when the Spirit comes upon people this gift testifies to the divine will as the fulfillment of promise.

God's Presence

In 1:8 Jesus informs the disciples that they will receive power (for witness) when the "Holy Spirit has come upon" them. In Hellenistic Greek literature, phrases similar to "the Holy Spirit" are uncommon,[156] but the OT (Hebrew Bible or LXX) and Second-Temple Jewish writings (whether originating in Palestine or the Diaspora) offer numerous references to the "Spirit of Holiness"—i.e., the OT "Spirit of God/the Lord."[157] In the OT, the Spirit seems

---

munity's petition was for God to "grant" (δός) them "to speak your word with all boldness," with the divine response involving both the filling of the Spirit and the associated boldness (Johnson, *Acts*, 85).

150. Gaventa (*Acts*, 88) notes that the "times of refreshing" are "in all likelihood synonymous with the 'refreshing' power of the Holy Spirit." This might suggest that rest and recovery are offered to those who are judged for being in the "perverse generation" (2:40), just as after the frog plague in Exod 8:11 (see Fitzmyer, *Acts*, 288 for the link to Exodus).

151. Tannehill (*Narrative*, 30–31) identifies the repeated association of the Spirit with 'gift' as a means to interrelate and emphasize these scenes for the reader.

152. Thus, there are links between piety and God granting promises in Acts. Amaru ("Land," 203–4) notes that the promises concerning land and people were to be understood as "gifts," therefore Luke's terminology is in keeping with biblical thought.

153. So Pesch, *Apostelgeschichte*, I, 275–76. *Contra* Dunn ("'Believed,'" 220; also Schille, *Apostelgeschichte*, 204; Witherington, *Acts*, 285), the Samaritans appear to be believers prior to their receiving the Spirit. Peter and John add nothing to Philip's preaching; rather they simply pray and lay their hands on them (so Turner, *Power*, 364–67; Keener, *Spirit*, 202, fn. 9; Spencer, *Portrait*, 51–52). Further, Simon was not simply impressed by the signs. The participle θεωρῶν is connected to ἐξίστατο rather than ἐπίστευσεν, explaining the cause of the amazement (not the belief).

154. Properly noted by Hur, *Dynamic*, 240; Johnson, *Acts*, 149. Jervell, *Unknown*, 103: "The church does not control the Spirit", but rather the Spirit is a gift "coming down from heaven."

155. Witherington, *Acts*, 288: "The point is that God's gift is in God's control."

156. Chevallier, *Souffle*, 36–39; Keener, *Spirit*, 7: "the Stoics knew πνεῦμα ἱερόν (sacred spirit) but not πνεῦμα ἅγιον."

157. See Chevallier, *Souffle*, 23–64.

to have expressed "God's dynamic presence,"[158] and Second-Temple literature in turn primarily portrays this presence as the Spirit of prophecy. As such, the Spirit inspires speech, provides revelation and wisdom, accomplishes miracles, interprets dreams and provides the source or power to sustain the religio-ethical life of God's people.[159] In this light, the reader would probably see Jesus promising the divine presence among the people.

Also, since the Spirit was with Jesus while Jesus was with the Apostles (1:2), the reader would expect the same Spirit who functioned in Jesus to act in the Apostles.[160] When the reader notes the "wonders and signs" done by the Apostles (2:43), which are connected to the Spirit and God (2:16–22), it is confirmed "that the prophetic Spirit (2:19) that was at work in Jesus (2:22) is also at work in the apostles."[161] Consequently, when in 10:38, Jesus (anointed by the Spirit) does miracles because "God was with him," the implication is that the Spirit marks the powerful divine presence. As Woods notes, "God the Father himself is the one who is acting through Jesus his spirit-anointed agent within the miracles tradition."[162] Whether the reader attributes these signs and wonders to the Spirit or to God, they are divine activities and God's presence is seen with the community.

In 4:8 the narrator notes that Peter is "filled with the Holy Spirit,"[163] while the council identifies the "boldness" with which they speak (4:13). This boldness did not come from any training; rather, the "apostles' speech, inspired by the Holy Spirit (4:8), is beyond their own human capacity."[164] Thus, through the reference to boldness, the reader recognizes that the Spirit is present with the Apostles. Further, the council attributes this bold speech to the Apostles' presence with Jesus. While the reader may not trust the council's opinions (the narrator portrays the council as reactive, annoyed, and accusatory), the reader will probably understand that the Spirit's presence with the disciples now functions in some way like Jesus' presence did previously. In turn, this suggests the Spirit mediates the divine

---

158. Fitzmyer, "Role," 170; cf. Chevallier, *Souffle*, 33–35; Wenk, *Community*, 56; Hur, *Dynamic*, 52; Lampe, "Spirit," 161.

159. Menzies (*Empowered*, 44–80) gives too little weight to the LXX's influence in asserting that the Spirit has no soteriological or miraculous functions. For him (172), the Spirit is distanced from miracles by the way Luke uses δύναμις (Luke 24:49; Acts 1:8). Supposedly, the Spirit mediates power, but is not identified with it, thus the Spirit primarily functions to inspire speech. However, the Spirit is repeatedly associated with power for both inspired speech and miracles, therefore miracles are linked to the Spirit's narrative function. Turner's (*Power*, 82–138; also "Spirit," 103–16) analysis of the literature and criticisms of Menzies are generally accurate. Also, Chevallier (*Souffle*, 23–64), Keener (*Spirit*, 7–27), Hur (*Dynamic*, 41–73) and Wenk (*Community*, 56–115) provide more balanced evaluations of the Spirit's function in Second-Temple literature than does Menzies

160. Hur, *Dynamic*, 222.

161. Johnson, *Acts*, 58.

162. Woods, "Finger," 223.

163. The filling marks Peter and John's reliability and therefore makes their speech authoritative (Shepherd, *Narrative*, 168). Barrett (*Acts*, 226) ignores the way these fillings function in the narrative when he attributes them to different sources. For "filled with"/"full of" the Spirit, see Turner (*Power*, 165–69) and Hui ("Spirit-Fullness," 24–38). Hui agrees with Turner that these phrases refer to empowerment for some activity defined by the co-text, but argues that the difference between them deals with the extent rather than the duration of the empowerment.

164. Tannehill, *Narrative*, 62.

presence that was "with" Jesus. This Spirit-inspired boldness continues to indicate the divine presence right to the narrative's end (cf. 4:31; 13:46; 19:8; 26:26; 28:31).[165]

The Pentecost event is pictured using language from OT theophanies. The sound coming "suddenly from heaven," the rushing wind, and the reference to fire reflect images in OT texts: Exod 19 (the Sinai event);[166] 1 Kgs 19:11–12; and 2 Kgs 2:11 (God speaking with Elijah, taking him up in a chariot by a whirlwind).[167] The reader, therefore, expects the divine presence to be manifested,[168] and the accompanying signs would suggest that expectation is now fulfilled.

In 4:32—5:11, lying to the Spirit and lying to God are placed parallel with each other. This appears to place these figures on par.[169] Thus, if the Spirit can be lied to by the community, then the Spirit's (and God's) presence with the community is implied.[170]

The relationship between the Spirit and the angel of the Lord may also signify the Spirit's manifested presence. Acts 8:26–40 has Philip sent by the "angel of the Lord" to speak to the eunuch. In 8:29, it is the "Spirit," as a direct actor, who tells Philip to approach the chariot. Regardless of which figure speaks, the emphasis is placed on the divine initiative.[171] The alternating addresses (the "angel of the Lord" then the "Spirit") may lead the reader to compare this scene to theophanic appearances in the OT (in Stephen's speech it was an angel that appeared and mediated the Law to Moses—7:30, 35, 38). The association

---

165. These references to boldness contradict Marguerat's (*First*, 112) argument that the Spirit is almost absent from the ending scenes.

166. There is a question as to whether the Sinai event is also important when Peter expounds on Joel's prophecy in Acts 2. Many (among others, Dunn, "Pentecost," 213–14; Hull, *Spirit*, 54–55, Jervell, *Apostelgeschichte*, 132–33; Turner, *Power*, 279–89) answer this in the affirmative (Schreiber ["Aktualisierung," 59–62] discusses recent arguments). In contrast, O'Toole ("Acts," 245–58) argues that Luke has the Davidic covenant in mind, while Menzies (*Empowered*, 189–201) and Chevallier (*Souffle*, 175) also deny any relationship to the Sinai covenant. The best conclusion seems to be that the allusions draw the reader's attention to the extra-text that includes both Mosaic and Davidic themes, the explication then draws from both background ideas.

167. Hull, *Spirit*, 57–58; Hur, *Dynamic*, 159–60; Shepherd, *Narrative*, 160–61. Keener (*Spirit*, 193), sees the wind and fire as simply eschatological images, but misses the spatial reference ("from heaven") that points to the divine presence. In the wider Hellenistic world (see van der Horst, "Hellenistic," 49–50), wind and fire would be familiar signals to the divine presence.

168. Tannehill (*Narrative*, 26) suggests these images will puzzle the reader in the same way as the hearers, "for we are told first of the mysterious sounds and sights and only in v. 4 are these connected with the Holy Spirit." This conclusion misses the sounds' heavenly origin, which answers the reader's expectation for the fulfillment of the Father's promise.

169. Shepherd (*Narrative*, 172) suggests this allows the Spirit to be seen as the narrative presence for God. This conclusion seems likely, but the Lord Jesus also appears in this role. Does Luke view the Spirit as personal or impersonal? Given that the Spirit can be lied to and that in 2:4 the Spirit is the subject for an action verb, personality may be suggested. However, language like "filled with the Spirit" and "coming upon" suggests the opposite. This interplay continues throughout the narrative and thus makes a final decision impossible. For further discussion, see Turner, *Power*, 40–42 (who correctly notes that portraying the Spirit in a personal mode is not the same as saying the Spirit is a person); Jervell, *Unknown*, 115; Fitzmyer, "Role," 177–79; Shepherd, *Narrative*, 3–11. Neither conclusion affects whether the Spirit functions to signify divine presence in the narrative.

170. So Barrett, *Acts*, 266; Jervell, *Apostelgeschichte*, 196.

171. Both the Spirit and the angel "represent the same divine power" (Haenchen, *Acts*, 349). See also Johnson, *Acts*, 155, 157; Shepherd, *Narrative*, 186, 199.

between the angel of the Lord and the Spirit of God in such scenes was known in Second-Temple Judaism—both Philo and Josephus make this connection and in much the same way (the Spirit is suddenly designated the actor when the angel had been previously).[172] In Acts 8, although the link is not explicit, the narrative does appear to draw the angel of the Lord and the Spirit into close relation.[173] The reader could see the angel as a *hypostasis* of the Spirit (or God), or just see the two figures as closely aligned in revealing divine direction.[174] Regardless, there is a sense that the Spirit (and therefore God) is directly present in the narrative. Whether through "signs and wonders," "boldness," or through manifested forms, the Spirit gives evidence to divine action. Consequently, the Spirit becomes a direct witness to divine desires in the narrative world.

God's Word

In 1:16 Peter explains that the Scripture (Pss 69:25, 109:8) had to be fulfilled, which the Holy Spirit "foretold." It is the Spirit that provides authority to the prophetic words (including the Psalms) in Scripture.[175] However, in 2:14–47 it is God who speaks through the prophet Joel. This parallel (both speak through the prophets) makes Scripture the words of both God and the Spirit. This link is made explicit in 4:24–25, where God is said to have spoken through the Spirit.[176] Consequently, the Spirit-inspired, prophetic words, which play such an important role in the arguments for Jesus as "Messiah" and "Lord" (3:18, 22–25; 13:13–52; 26:22), are considered divine words.

The Spirit also appears responsible for inducing words about God in the community. At Pentecost the hearers describe the tongues phenomenon (2:11; cf. 10:46) by relating it to speaking "God's deeds of power ($\mu\varepsilon\gamma\alpha\lambda\varepsilon\tilde{\iota}\alpha$)." In the LXX this phrase was used (Deut 11:2; Pss 70:19; 105:21; Sir 17:8; 18:4; 42:21; 43:15; 2 Macc 3:34; 7:17) to refer to divine actions in Israel's history[177] and was considered a regular feature in Jewish praise.[178] By inspiring these declarations, it is suggested to the reader that the Spirit is responsible for making known divine actions in history.[179] This conclusion, therefore, suggests that,

172. See Levinson, "Debut," 123–38; Levinson, "Prophetic," 189–207.

173. Bruce (*Acts*, 174; also Lake and Cadbury, *Beginnings*, 95) notes that "any real distinction" between these figures is absent. Barrett (*Acts*, 427) responds that Luke puts so much emphasis on the Spirit that he could scarcely put both on the same level. Barrett correctly identifies the emphasis on the Spirit, but Luke does not make an obvious distinction between them here.

174. See Hahn, *Theologie*, II, 271. Witherington (*Acts*, 294 n. 57) correctly notes that Luke makes distinctions between angels and the Spirit. The reader, nevertheless, could see the "angel of the Lord" as manifesting God's Spirit, just as in other Hellenistic-Jewish literature.

175. Pesch (*Apostelgeschichte*, I, 87) refers to the Spirit here as the "Kundgabe des Willens Gottes."

176. Haenchen's (*Acts*, 226) claim that God speaks through the prophets not the Spirit seems to misunderstand the way Second-Temple Judaism portrays the Spirit as God's dynamic presence. Further, this misses the obvious connections the narrative has made in stating that Scripture can be attributed to either the Spirit or God.

177. Fitzmyer, *Acts*, 243; Johnson, *Acts*, 44; Schneider, *Apostelgeschichte*, I, 255.

178. Turner, *Power*, 272; cf. Barrett, *Acts*, 124

179. Pesch (*Apostelgeschichte*, I, 106) connects tongues to the mystery surrounding divine action in creation and salvation history. When the Spirit is poured out in Ephesus, tongues accompany prophecy (19:6), which would again be a speech form induced by the Spirit.

when a character is labeled filled with/full of the Spirit, the speech produced is divinely authorized.[180]

The Spirit marks the proper choice for an office, such as with the distribution problem (6:1–7).[181] When the reader finds μαρτυρουμένους ("having one's character witnessed to")[182] placed in proximity to "full of the Spirit" (6:3), the reader should realize that the Spirit acts as a witness to the men who are fit for solving this problem.[183] The qualification for those who would help here is that they should be "full of the Spirit and wisdom." In turn, Stephen is specifically described as "full of faith and the Holy Spirit" (6:5). Likewise, Barnabas is reintroduced (11:24; cf. 4:36) as someone divinely qualified to be sent as an emissary from Jerusalem to Antioch because he is "full of the Holy Spirit and of faith."[184] For the reader, this characterization gives authority to the exhortation by Barnabas for these gentiles to "remain faithful to the Lord." Consequently, the Spirit acts as a divine identifier—the factor that attests to God's choice.[185]

Similarly, the Spirit's presence testifies to the acceptance of certain groups (the Samaritans—8:16–17).[186] When the Spirit falls upon Cornelius and his household (10:44), divine testimony is provided since the pouring out leads to the conclusion that God is involved (the reader knows it is God's "gift"). The Spirit coming upon these gentiles causes the community to conclude that God has granted "repentance" to the gentiles (11:18), which confirms the idea that the Spirit is given as the divine witness to their inclusion.[187] Later, Peter points out divine action in relation to Cornelius (15:7–8) with the Spirit's outpouring again given as testimony to gentile inclusion. Therefore, Peter considers the

---

180. For instance, Stephen's speech is framed (6:5, 8; 7:55) by markers that the Spirit is present with him.

181. Schneider (*Apostelgeschichte*, I, 224) points out that even the Apostles need the Spirit's outpouring before they qualify as witnesses.

182. Johnson, *Acts*, 106.

183. The Spirit is specifically characterized as a witness in 5:32 (cf. 15:8; 20:23). Shepherd (*Narrative*, 175) sees this as a "literary" prophecy concerning the Spirit's upcoming role. Actually, it makes explicit the role the Spirit has already taken—providing testimony to divine words and actions. Schneider (*Apostelgeschichte*, I, 397) identifies the Spirit's witness as evidence that God has made Jesus "Lord and Messiah." Thus, the Spirit has acted as a witness since Pentecost. Barrett (*Acts*, 291) comments that where the Spirit "is manifestly at work," "it is plain that there is divine action."

184. So Gaventa, *Acts*, 179–180; Tannehill, *Narrative*, 105, 147.

185. Since Luke consistently presents the Spirit as the marker divinely qualifying someone for a task, those (as Walter, "Apostelgeschichte," 370–93) supposing a conflict between some Hellenistic leaders (the seven) and the Apostles seem misguided. The Spirit's presence qualifies the seven for anything God chooses to use them in (just as with the Apostles). Luke has not elaborately constructed a means for subjecting them to the Apostles, but has shown how God has given to the Way leaders appropriate for every necessity.

186. Marguerat, *First*, 126: Through the Spirit, "God 'testifies' to Philip's mission and leads the Jerusalem church to agree with it as well."

187. Hur, *Dynamic*, 247–48: "the coming of the Spirit upon Gentiles alongside notable manifestations is apologetically designed to verify Gentiles, like the Samaritan believers, as members of God's community." So also Shepherd (*Narrative*, 204), although he misses the point by saying that divine actions are "seen in the story through the eyes of faith" (205). Peter is making explicit what the reader already knows to be the case— God has acted. No eyes of faith are involved since the Spirit's action is already identified as divine action.

Spirit to ultimately reflect the divine decision.[188] The Spirit, consequently, is consistently characterized as the witness to the divine choice.

When Saul (Paul) confronts the magician Elymas (Bar-Jesus) in Cyprus, the narrator notes that Paul is "filled with Holy Spirit" as he curses Elymas (13:9). The Spirit's presence provides authority to Paul's words, indicating that God is speaking.[189] Similarly, when James announces that "it seemed good to the Holy Spirit and to us" (15:28),[190] the Spirit divinely sanctions the decision. When Paul passes through Ephesus (18:20–21), he says that he will return to them "if God wills." Before that, "Asia" in 16:6 is likely Asia Minor's capital, Ephesus,[191] which means that the reader is aware that the Spirit has prevented Paul from speaking in this place on a previous occasion. It is only after the outpouring (19:6) that Paul stays in Ephesus to preach (19:8), so this Spirit-outpouring indicates that God has willed that Paul speak here at this time.[192]

The Spirit instructs Philip to join the Ethiopian (8:29) and Peter to go with Cornelius' men (10:19-20)—providing clear direction about the divine will when Peter is confused by the vision.[193] In 13:2 the Spirit calls for the church to set aside Saul and Barnabas to the work to which the Spirit ("I") had called them. At 16:6–10, the reader finds the Spirit giving negative direction to Paul and his companions.[194] The group's determination that God has sent them to Macedonia appears to be made with reference not just to the dream (16:9), but also to the Spirit's negative guidance—this is where God had been leading them all along.[195] Ultimately, therefore, God is behind the action in 16:6–10 and the Spirit is once again presented as an active presence providing divine direction for the missionaries.

However, this direction can appear enigmatic. In 19:21–22, the reader learns that Paul is "resolved in the Spirit" to go to Jerusalem. Previously (17:16), the narrator has referred to Paul's spirit and such could be the case here.[196] However, unlike that situation, 19:21 does not offer a possessive pronoun to identify this spirit. The reader probably concludes (given the δεῖ) that *the* Spirit directs Paul, but there is some ambiguity.[197] Later (20:22), Paul

---

188. So Barrett, *Acts*, 511.

189. Wenk (*Community*, 136) argues that the "filling with the Spirit" not only demonstrates that Paul's words were spoken through the Spirit, but also that the Spirit produced the blindness. By the same token, the Spirit has been portrayed as the divine representative, so ultimately it is God who blinds Elymas. Thus, while Garrett ("Light," 153) claims that the contrast is between Paul and Elymas, the real contrast seems to be between God and Satan.

190. This does not suggest equal partnership between the church and God. The church recognizes what God has already decided (see Johnson, *Acts*, 279).

191. So Fitzmyer, *Acts*, 578; Haenchen, *Acts*, 484 n. 2; Pesch, *Apostelgeschichte*, II, 101; Schneider, *Apostelgeschichte*, II, 205; Witherington, *Acts*, 477.

192. Turner (*Power*, 396) correctly makes these connections.

193. Fitzmyer, *Acts*, 457; Johnson, *Acts*, 185.

194. The "Spirit of Jesus" and the "Holy Spirit" appear to represent the same figure. The reader is already aware that both Jesus and God are connected with the Spirit (similarly Hur, *Dynamic*, 141–43; Shepherd, *Narrative*, 223).

195. Jervell's (*Apostelgeschichte*, 418) comment is appropriate: "Was wir gewöhnlich als Schwierigkeiten und Hindernisse für die Mission bezeichnen, ist für Lukas etwas ganz anderes, nämlich die Führung Gottes."

196. So Barrett, *Acts*, 919.

197. Shepherd (*Narrative*, 232) fails to note the problem facing the reader. Because the reader repeatedly has to choose between Paul's spirit and the Spirit of God, the ambiguity is important to what follows.

mentions that he is going "captive to the Spirit" to Jerusalem. This reference to spirit also lacks an identifier, evoking the same uncertainty.[198] However, since the reference in 20:23 is specified as the "Holy Spirit," the reader will likely conclude that Paul is captive to the Holy Spirit,[199] but the decision remains tenuous. In a formulation previously seen in reference to the prophecy by Agabus (11:28), the believers in Tyre tell Paul "through the Spirit" not to go on to Jerusalem (21:4). The reader would likely assume that "through the Spirit" gives authority to the instructions Paul receives.[200] However, the ambiguity found in 19:21 and 20:22 features here—Paul is "resolved" and "captive" in the spirit to go to Jerusalem, but the spirit seems to be telling him not to go. In Caesarea (21:9–12), Agabus tells Paul that the "Holy" Spirit "says" that Paul will be bound and handed over to the Romans in Jerusalem, but Paul is determined to go on anyway.[201] Luke has left his reader with at least a surface contradiction[202] about how the Spirit's inspiration is to be understood.

While such differences in understanding between a hero or martyr and his friends or relatives may be typical in Hellenistic writing,[203] Luke's emphasis on the Spirit as providing divinely authoritative direction requires the reader to assess how such a conflict could occur. The reader should come to the conclusion (based on 23:11) that it was indeed God's will for Paul to go to Jerusalem.[204] Reflecting on this, the reader must be cautious, recognizing that the divine action and will are often considered enigmatic. Even though the Spirit testifies to events and people, that witness may not always be easy to discern.[205] This does not discount the Spirit's witness, it simply reminds the reader that obedience to the divine will may not be easy since it may be difficult to know. Such analysis can only be made as the reader attempts to construct a coherent character. Throughout, the Spirit remains the one who speaks for God, witnessing to the events to come, but not all attempts to interpret the Spirit's message are to be considered accurate.

Results

There are three prominent features to the portrayal of the Spirit as the divine witness. The Spirit represents God's *promise* spoken by Jesus and given as a gift to those who obey God.

198. Barrett, *Acts*, 970; Fitzmyer, *Acts*, 677; Johnson, *Acts*, 361; Shepherd, *Narrative*, 233 n. 249.

199. So Johnson, *Acts*, 361.

200. Barrett, *Acts*, 562.

201. The reference to Philip's prophetess daughters prepares for Agabus' arrival (Schneider *Apostelgeschichte*, II, 304). It also adds Spiritual weight to the proceedings by drawing the reader's attention to the expected prophetic words. Thus, the reader anticipates that the uncertainty about the Spirit's direction will be resolved here. Luke emphasizes this prophecy as accurate by referring to its fulfillment under Claudius (Schneider, *Apostelgeschichte*, II, 95). Therefore, Agabus is a reliable character.

202. Shepherd, *Narrative*, 236.

203. Bovon, "Saint-Ésprit," 340–51.

204. See chapter 5.

205. *Contra* Bovon ("Saint-Ésprit," 357) and Pesch (*Apostelgeschichte*, II, 211), Luke does not seem to be suggesting that a debate is taking place in which the community takes part in determining what the divine will really is. Rather, God's will is consistent (even if enigmatic); interpretations about the Spirit's direction are not. Only Paul seems to have interpreted it correctly from the beginning.

Consequently, the Spirit is directly related to divine action as God's fulfilled promise. The Spirit also represents divine *power* at work in Jesus and his followers, often seen in "signs and wonder"" as well as inspired speech. The Spirit's theophanic appearance at Pentecost portrays the Spirit as God's *presence*. Thus, the Spirit can be seen as the divine dynamic presence active in the miraculous events in the narrative.

The Spirit spoke authoritatively concerning the divine plan in the OT and continues that role among the people of Way. When the words of Scripture are repeatedly ascribed both to the Spirit and God, the reader's understanding that the Spirit is God's authoritative spokesman is reinforced. Since the tongues at Pentecost are heard in relation to the "God's deeds of power" the Spirit is identified as making known the divine role in Israel's history. At various times, the Spirit acts as *witness* to things—the Samaritans and the gentiles being included; narrative events; and the people, places (not Asia or Bithynia, but Macedonia), and even timings (when Paul should speak in Ephesus) God has chosen. Thus, the Spirit acts as God's witness, providing divine instructions. Consequently, the Spirit is consistently portrayed acting as God's word, revealing God's will, and giving God's instructions. The Spirit, therefore, must be included when analyzing the portrayal of God because the Spirit marks the fulfillment of God's promise, as well as marking God's presence and will.

In summary, in expanding the characterization of God beyond direct references to God, the narrator's direction is important to the reader's conclusions about God. Also Jesus is portrayed in so close a relation to God that his actions can be considered divine actions. Finally, the Spirit is consistently seen marking the divine presence and will. Thus, these characters must be included when assembling the portrayal of God in Acts.[206]

---

206. This agrees with Hahn's (*Theologie*, II, 305) statement that Christology and Pneumatology are integral components of the NT witness to God.

4

The King Who Establishes and Restores Israel's King

IN ACTS LUKE CHARACTERIZES GOD AS THE KING WHO ORDAINS NOT JUST THE TIMES and seasons for the eschatological end, but those for the presently restored (but reinterpreted) kingdom. One strand in this portrayal builds on OT and Second-Temple ideas related to God as the Great King who controls the history of nations. This strand is particularly related to the restoring of Israel's king, Jesus. A second thread, discussed in chapter 5, concerns how this King rules the affairs in the kingdom, determining who enters, what the social order is like, and what requirements are placed on the citizens. This thread relates to God's (re)establishment of God's own people. A final strand, addressed in chapter 6, focuses on the way this Sovereign's will and actions control plot development and, thus, direct human history within the narrative. Ultimately, this characterization is intended to support the author's claims about the events and the message (as in 2 Maccabees and Josephus), providing assurance to the reader about what God has done.

The characterization process is a cumulative one, where the reader builds the portrayal of the character from the various strands as the story advances. The most appropriate way, then, to discuss characterization is to show how each scene adds to the previous one. However, since that process tends to be repetitive and unwieldy due to the volume of characterizing data, this analysis focuses on sequentially developing each strand.

Chapter 2 suggested that in the image reflecting God as King, God was believed to rule over national histories, having responsibility for the establishment and the downfall of kings and kingdoms. This was especially true for Israel since, while God had given them the Davidic line as rulers, God was ultimately their king and would one day manifest that divine rule in an eternal kingdom. This idea is foundational to the first characterization strand—Acts begins with a question about the restored kingdom, portrays Jesus as the Davidic king God exalted to the divine throne, and yet maintains that the kingdom Jesus rules as 'Lord and Christ' is God's kingdom.

Restoration and Coronation

With the reference to the "kingdom of God" in 1:3, Luke prompts the reader to recall beliefs about God's kingdom.[1] Based on these opening verses, the reader, who is sympathetic to Jewish hopes, seems likely to expect the fulfillment of divine promises particularly the

---

1. See pp. 80–81, *Excursus: The Kingdom of God in Luke-Acts.*

restored kingdom (see chapter 2), and thus joins the disciples in questioning the timing for its restoration (1:6). This question appears to be nationalistic ("to Israel"), expressing hopes about a renewed political realm, restored boundaries, and the defeat of Israel's enemies.[2] Johnson suggests that by using ἀποκαθίστημι ("restore") Luke is alluding to Mal 3:23 (LXX) and God restoring the *hearts* of sons and fathers.[3] This may be the case at Luke 1:17 but it is not true here, for the object to be restored (τὴν βασιλείαν) is clearly stated. At this point, however, Luke provides no reason to interpret the kingdom in a spiritual sense (as if it referred to hearts). Further, in the LXX (cf. Ps 16:5; Jer 15:19, 16:15, 23:8; Ezek 16:55; Hos 11:11) ἀποκαθίστημι functions mainly as a "technical term" for Israel's political restoration.[4] Thus, restoration is more likely to refer to re-establishing Israel's former state. At the same time, the reader, whose implicit existence is at a time subsequent to the events presented here, is aware that such nationalistic hopes have not been fulfilled.[5] Thus, the reader experiences dissonance—being reminded about expectations for a restored kingdom, but facing a situation that apparently counters these hopes. The reader will question whether hopes for God to fulfill promises match with the obvious absence of a renewed, self-governing Israel. Has God been faithful to those promises if the land has not been restored?

The Kingdom of God in Luke-Acts

Old Testament and Second-Temple ideas are determinative for understanding the phrase "kingdom of God" at this point since even in Luke's Gospel, "It is taken for granted that the reader will know what is meant" by this reference.[6] While βασιλεία τοῦ θεοῦ and βασιλεία τῷ Ἰσραήλ appear only eight times in Acts, these instances are strategically located:[7] 1) they begin (1:3, 6) and end (28:23, 31) the work. 2) They occur when the message expands beyond Jerusalem (8:12), near the beginning and the end of Paul's missions (14:22; 19:8), and in Paul's only address to believers (20:25).

2. Lohfink (*Himmelfahrt*, 154) suggested three concerns: when will the kingdom be restored (now)?; is it restored to Israel?; and are you (Jesus) the one who restores it? Each issue (*contra* Zwiep *Ascension*, 103, fn. 1) is addressed at various points in Luke's narrative, with the last question answered immediately (No; God is responsible for the restoration). The timing question is focused on here with 'Israel' addressed in chapter 5.

3. Johnson, *Acts*, 26. Sirach 48:9–12 does have Elijah (the figure in Mal 3:23) restoring the "tribes of Jacob" (the covenant community), which may have been the original sense intended for the Malachi passage.

4. Parker, *Apokatastasis*, 4.

5. Fusco ("Point," 1684; also Wolter, "Future," 314–15) correctly notes (although he is thinking about Jesus' return) that the real reader knows these expectations have not been fulfilled. Since Luke's intended real reader and the implied reader would seem to exist at the same time, the same is true for the implied reader. What Fusco does not identify is that, by reminding the reader about previously held expectations, Luke renews the reader's disappointment at this situation.

6. Fitzmyer, *Acts*, 199.

For brief summaries reflecting Luke's presentation of the Kingdom of God see, Barrett, *Acts*, 70–71; Carroll, *Response*, 80–87; Hahn, *Theologie*, I, 559–60; Lindemann "Herrschaft," 211–12; Nolland, "Salvation-History," 68–70; O'Toole, "Kingdom," 147–62.

7. Noted by Prieur, *Verkündigung*, 1–2; Weiser, "'Reich,'" 127–32.

Many follow Conzelmann in identifying Luke's distinctive understanding about the kingdom in its relation to "proclamation" since that is the context in which most kingdom references are found.[8] Such analysis ignores how direct references to the kingdom fit into the larger narrative framework. For example, because 14:22 does not specifically mention the kingdom's proclamation, Prieur argues that he need not consider it.[9] However, 14:22 presents a summarized Pauline exhortation to the community. Therefore, if 20:25, another community exhortation, is connected with Paul's proclamation as Prieur holds, then 14:22 is as well.

Similarly, when Wolter attempts to define the content for Jesus' kingdom preaching (Luke 8:1) by looking at how Jesus explains the "mystery" (Luke 8:10–18),[10] he misses that Luke 8:1 is followed by a reference to the women who had been healed from evil spirits and sicknesses. Previously in Luke 4:43, after two healing and exorcism scenes (4:31–37, 38–41), Jesus claims that also in other cities he has to proclaim the kingdom, yet Luke has not given any content to this proclamation (other than the words from Isaiah (Luke 4:18–19) which also mention healings; cf. also Luke 9:1–2, 6; 10:9). Thus, healings illustrate the content of this kingdom proclamation before Jesus explains the kingdom.[11] Concentrating only on the words spoken by Jesus misses the way the narrative reveals that proclamation's fuller dimensions. This analysis seeks to avoid such and argues that the theme is more prevalent than the scant specific mentions to the kingdom suggest.

Jesus' answer (Acts 1:7) to the disciples makes two claims. The first is that the disciples are not responsible for knowing the kingdom's "times or periods [seasons]." The second is that God controls these times. While Haenchen suggests Jesus' response prohibits speculation about Jesus' return, a return is not at issue here, remaining unmentioned until 1:11. Further, Haenchen misses the role the phrase 'times and seasons' plays in the idea that God controls world kingdoms.[12] Is the reader, then, to take these claims as denying that the kingdom will be restored? The claims do seem to function as a check on the disciples' (and the reader's) kingdom expectations, but which expectations is not clear. Chapter 2 argued that the converging themes in the early verses of Acts were likely to stress for the reader that God was about to fulfill the promises to Israel, with the kingdom being central to this

---

8. Conzelmann, *Theology*, 37, 40, 114. Cf. Grässer, *Problem*, 140–41; "Parusieerwartung," (1979); "Ta peri," (1985).

9. Prieur, *Verkündigung*, 6.

10. Wolter, "'Reich,'" 551–53.

11. Ellis (*Christ*, 115) notes that these healings point to the fulfillment of the age-to-come–the present age receives deliverance from "death-powers."

12. Haenchen (*Acts*, 143; cf. Pesch, *Apostelgeschichte*, I, 68). This failure to explore the relationship between "times and seasons" and divine universal control seems to explain why many scholars (Grässer, *Forschungen* (2001); Haenchen, *Acts*; etc.) equate the kingdom's restoration only with the apocalyptic end. It also seems to be the reason for the assumption by some (Gaventa, "Eschatology," 36; Conzelmann, *Theology*, 121) that Jesus rejects the question "on principle."

fulfillment. Thus, the reader would need the restoration to be emphatically denied in order to overcome Luke's reminder about these hopes.

Is there a denial here? Jesus' claims draw on the reader's extra-textual conceptions concerning God and the kingdom. The first shows similarity to *Pss. Sol.* 17:23, which prohibits speculation about when the messianic kingdom will come.[13] Alternatively, 'times and seasons' could simply be a reference to the time duration and events preceding the end.[14] But, again this misses the way the phrase is related to divine control over nations. The responsibility for the rise and fall of kings and kingdoms is often expressed in OT and Second-Temple thought through references to divine control over "times." For instance, Daniel 2:21 parallels divine responsibility for "times and seasons" with God exalting and removing kings. It is God who directs the course of world events (*Apoc. Bar.* 48:2), raising up kings (Bar 1:11; *Apoc. Bar.* 39), apportioning their rule (Wis 6:3), and judging them (*Pss. Sol.* 2:34).[15] *Four Ezra* 12 specifically notes the divine role in the succession of kingdoms and in determining their allotted times.[16] Further, even *Pss. Sol.* 17:23 implies that God determines the time when the kingdom will be established.[17] With this background, the reader does not see Jesus' claims denying that the kingdom would be established; rather the reader identifies them emphasizing that God ordains the 'times and seasons' for kingdoms. This suggests to the disciples (and the reader) that if the kingdom is going to be restored to Israel, God will be responsible for it.

Such, nevertheless, does not address the disciples' concern about *when* the kingdom would be restored. Since the reader knows that a national Israel has not been restored, there are two options left: 1) the restoration will not happen now; 2) it will take place in an unexpected way. It could be that the disciples are not included in the kingdom since it will be *delayed* for some indefinite time.[18] However, the narrative does not indicate a delay in part because it does not set a time for the kingdom.[19] The kingdom is said to be "proclaimed" in Acts rather than to "come," so it could be inferred that the coming is postponed so that proclamation can occur in the meantime.[20] Nevertheless, the silence about its coming does not necessarily point to delay. If the narrative provides reasons for

13. The denial concerning knowledge about God's eschatological timing is consistent with Luke 12:35–48. This, however, does not indicate an indefinite delay to the *parousia*, but watchfulness because the end will come unpredictably (Carroll, *Response*, 55–60). It is only if one equates the kingdom's establishment with Jesus' return that this would be evidence for denying a present restoration.

14. Bruce, *Acts*, 70.

15. See chapter 2.

16. DeSilva, *Introducing*, 333. The citations by Wicks (*Doctrine*, 127) show how prevalent the view that God controlled the timing of kingdoms apparently was. Philo (*QE* 1:100) uses times and seasons in relation to God controlling man's lifetime. While this citation (*contra* Lucchesi, "Précédents," 537–40) is not a good precedent for 1:6–8 (it makes no reference to kingdoms or nations), it does identify divine control over human affairs, an understanding about this phrase that will be addressed in chapter 6.

17. Nickelsburg, *Jewish*, 209.

18. Lake and Cadbury, *Beginnings*, 6. Also Haenchen, *Acts*, 141 n. 2.

19. So Barrett, "Luke-Acts," 89–90.

20. S. Wilson, *Gentiles*, 78–79 (although he sees both "imminent" and "delayed" strands in Luke's eschatology); also Grässer, *Forschungen*, 298–300. Conzelmann (*Theology*, 114) made the same argument for Luke's Gospel. However, this assumes that the kingdom is not already near in Jesus.

the reader to think the kingdom is present (at least in some form)[21] then its proclaimers would more likely refer to entrance into it (as 14:22) than to its coming. Thus, the possibility that the kingdom has already come would be left open for exploration by the reader. While the witness to the "ends of the earth" suggests to some that a delay occurs before the kingdom's restoration,[22] such witnessing could coincide with, rather than precede, this restoration. Jesus does not indicate that the disciples' witnessing is necessarily prior to, or a condition for the restoration; rather it is presented as their responsibility, while God's responsibility is the re-establishment. It is only if the reader equates the kingdom with the eschatological end that a coinciding restoration is denied.[23] Thus, the phrase could imply a delay in Jesus' return (unmentioned until 1:11), but at this point the reader does not know the relationship between that event and the restoration. Jesus leaves the restored kingdom as a possibility, but the reader does not yet have enough information to determine when it will occur.

The Eschatological Kingdom in Luke-Acts

Like most scholars, Vielhauer maintains that the kingdom of God in Jesus' proclamation is to be understood eschatologically.[24] It does not follow, however, that eschatological means solely relegated to the "end." In Luke's Gospel the kingdom is proclaimed by Jesus and is present in his activity.[25] Grässer disputes this conclusion because the signs of the "Son of Man" (Luke 21:25–28, 31) are future events, which (he supposes) means the kingdom cannot be present with Jesus.[26] This ignores a *present and future* kingdom, an idea many scholars have suggested is evident in Luke-Acts.[27] Evidence for this conception can be seen at Luke 17:21 where Jesus declares that the kingdom is currently present ("among you") before discussing the events concerning the day "of the Son of Man" (17:22–37). Therefore, a present kingdom is set in the same context as a future apocalyptic day. At Luke 21:25–31 the "Son of Man" comes when the kingdom arrives. Elsewhere, however, Jesus speaks about the "least" who have already entered the kingdom (7:28) and the kingdom's nearness in healings (10:9), exorcisms (11:20), and messengers (10:11). On the other hand, he mentions its coming (11:2), eschatological kingdom feasts (13:28–29), and responds negatively to suppositions that the

21. Ellis (*Christ*, 116 and fn. 37) suggests that the early Christian community, "proclaimed the kingdom of God to be a hidden present reality in their midst" (cf. 1 Thess 4:13–18; Phil 1.23; 3:20; Col 1:13; Gal 1:4). As such, Luke's reader would have good reason to look for evidence that the kingdom was in some way present.

22. So Fitzmyer, *Acts*, 205; Witherington, *Acts*, 10.

23. See *Excursus: The Eschatological Kingdom in Luke-Acts.*

24. Vielhauer, "Gottesreich," 55; see also Lindemann, "Herrschaft," 200–201; Merkel, "Gottesherrschaft," 119.

25. So, among others, Hiers, "Problem," 145–55; Merk, "Reich," 201–20; Weiser, "'Reich,'" 127–35; Wolter, "'Reich,'" 541–63.

26. Grässer, *Forschungen*, 294–95 n. 11.

27. See Cullmann, *Christ*, 71–88; Ellis, *Christ*, 112–16; Ernst, *Herr*, 23–27; Carroll, *Response*, 17–20; Hahn, *Theologie*, II, 173–75; Kümmel, *Promise*, 106–24; Kümmel, *Heilsgeschehen*, 48–66; Ladd, *Theology* (1974); Nolland, "Salvation-History," 68–70; E. P. Sanders, *Jesus*, 150–56.

kingdom was to appear immediately (19:11). God's kingdom refers to the blessings that are experienced both presently and at the consummation (6:20; 12:31–32), or things begun in Jesus' ministry that grow and develop toward the *eschaton* (13:18–21). These overlapping images suggest that Luke imagines the kingdom present in Jesus, but also expects a final consummation that can be associated with the Son of Man's coming. Maddox correctly makes a distinction between the day of the Son of Man and the kingdom,[28] but it is unconvincing that the kingdom has become so realized that its consummation is unimportant for Luke (cf. Acts 3:12–26).

Equating the time of the kingdom with Jesus' return is fundamental to Grässer's understanding: "Das Reich selbst tritt erst mit der Parusie in Erscheinung."[29] He suggests that there are two questions behind 1:6: "Is the kingdom restricted to Israel" and "Will the Parousia happen now"?[30] However, the reader would not raise the second question at this point since Jesus' return is not an issue while Jesus is present[31] (the first question will be discussed chapter 5). Moreover, when Grässer argues that the "horizon" in Acts is less concerned with the nearness of the kingdom than the width of the οἰκουμένη,[32] he cites the supposed lack of apocalyptic images as evidence. This reflects a narrow understanding about the kingdom's presence, failing to account for the non-apocalyptic kingdom images that suggest the kingdom is present but in an unexpected and unconsummated form. Grässer's view appears to be a type of kingdom understanding (wholly apocalyptic) that Luke seeks to reinterpret.[33]

Jesus' physical absence in Acts does not remove the kingdom.[34] If the narrative presents images that suggest Jesus is now reigning on the Davidic throne, that he operates as such for the community, that elements of God's kingdom (the Spirit) have broken into the present, and that God (the one who establishes kings and kingdoms) has brought this to pass (all will be argued by Peter in Acts 2), then Jesus' physical presence and the kingdom of God are not co-extensive.[35] This means the "Basileia des Erhöhten" is, for Luke, not simply a heavenly reality,[36] but is manifested in the community, through the Spirit's presence, and in the Lord's continued presence (cf. Acts 18:10) with his people.

---

28. Maddox, *Purpose*, 136–43.

29. Grässer, *Forschungen*, 299.

30. Ibid, 222, following Haenchen, *Acts*, 143. Haenchen's actual second question was, "Is the kingdom coming now?"

31. *Contra* Fusco, "Point," 1678.

32. Grässer, *Forschungen*, 297.

33. Since Luke also seems to reinterpret a wholly nationalistic conception, Weiser ("Reich," 130) is correct to note the issue concerns the kingdom's national limitations. However, he goes too far in calling the question "grundsätzlich unsachgemäß" since Luke redefines but does not reject these features.

34. So Luz, "βασιλεία," 204; O'Toole, "Kingdom," 154.

35. *Contra* Noack (*Gottesreich*, 45–49) who accepts that the kingdom is present in Jesus, but denies its presence while Jesus is in heaven.

36. *Contra* Wolter, "Reich," 550–51.

It could also be that with Jesus' answer the reader is simply to forgo any concerns about the kingdom's re-establishment. However, Jesus (1:8) reaffirms that the Spirit will come (soon—1:5). Since the Spirit's coming was perceived as related to the eschatological period (Joel 3:1–5),[37] the Spirit is not likely to be taken by our reader as the "alternative" to knowledge about the eschaton.[38] Rather, the Spirit was associated in the extra-text with kingdom blessings,[39] which implies that some aspect(s) of this kingdom will be manifested shortly. However, with the ἀλλά, Jesus created a disjunctive: the Spirit was soon to come, *but* (as the reader knows) that has not meant national boundaries were restored. A kingdom aspect is coming soon, but this is to aid a mission that apparently precedes the *eschaton*. Luke seems to be challenging the reader's normal conceptions about the kingdom so as to begin reinterpreting its restoration.[40] In order to understand this reinterpretation, the reader must attend to divine action since God is characterized as the one responsible for it.[41] Therefore, it does seem that, "Luke invites the reader to discover the mystery of 'times and seasons' by the reading of his own narrative."[42]

The reader's question then becomes what does God do and does it have any relation to a king or a kingdom being established? At this point, the narrative shifts to Jesus' ascension (1:9–11). Ἀνάλημφθη in 1:2 brings the ascension to the reader's mind and gives occasion for the reader to recall Luke 24:50–53 from the extra-text. Luke gave that pas-

---

37. See Chance, *Jerusalem*, 50–51; Keener, *Spirit*, 192.

38. *Contra* Grässer, *Forschungen*, 50; cf. Conzelmann, *Theology*, 95.

39. See chapter 3. Further, the Spirit is linked with the messianic "root of Jesse" in Isa 11:1–9. This association is taken up in some Second-Temple literature (*1 En.* 49:2–3; *Pss. Sol.* 17:37, 18:7; *T. Levi* 18:7; 4Q215; 4Q252). Luke apparently follows this line in presenting the Spirit as active in the birth of Jesus, who would sit on David's throne over an everlasting kingdom (Luke 1:31–35) (cf. Strauss, *Davidic*, 263–304; Turner, *Power*, 117–18; Turner, "Spirit," 336–37). Chance (*Jerusalem*, 49–56) argues that Luke viewed the birth narratives as announcing an eschatological event: the Messiah's coming. Thus, in Luke's Gospel the Spirit is associated with the Davidic king in an eschatological context.

40. Parsons (*Departure*, 180–83) calls this literary process "defamiliarisation." A similar awakening and reinterpretation takes place in Luke 1–2. Tiede ("Glory," 22; also Haacker, "Bekenntnis," 441) considers Luke 1–2 critical for understanding Luke's hopes for Israel, expressed in Jesus as the "son of God" who sits on David's throne over the "house of Jacob" in an eternal kingdom (1:32–35). The reliable spokespersons (Gabriel, Mary, Zechariah, Elizabeth, Simeon, and Anna) provide assurances that these hopes will not fail. Moessner ("Ironic," 40–41) cautions, however, that the nationalistic expectations come from Mary, Zechariah, and Elizabeth, who are all seen questioning, doubting, or failing to comprehend what they are told. The other three, meanwhile, are never characterized in this way and do not express nationalistic hopes. Therefore, the reader will consider their view more reliable. Moessner, however, misses that Zechariah and Elizabeth are inspired by the Spirit (1:41, 67), which would restore their credibility. Regardless, as Jewish rejection becomes ever more apparent, the narrative reinterprets this hope (it is more sin forgiveness than deliverance from enemies). Even this, nevertheless, is in line with divine plans for the messiah (cf. Luke 4:16–30). Israel's hopes are not removed (the nationalistic expectations reappear in Luke 24:21 and Acts 1:6), but they are redirected (see Carroll, *Response*, 37–48). Thus Luke is consistent in his attempts to transform the reader's expectations while affirming divine faithfulness to Israel.

41. In Luke's Gospel Jesus denies that the kingdom will come with observable signs (17:20). The point there (consistent with Acts 1:7) seems to be that the kingdom comes at a time determined solely by the divine will (so Carroll, *Response*, 77–78).

42. Johnson, *Acts*, 29.

sage a slightly different context since the blessing Jesus offered presented a priestly image[43] that is absent from Acts 1:1–11 (the reader's attention is currently focused on kingdom images). However, in Luke, Jesus has been shown to take over teaching responsibilities in the temple (19:45—20:8). He did this as "king" (19:38) and, thus, has seemingly claimed lordship over the temple and the priestly duties. Therefore, Jesus' "priestly" action in Luke 24:50–53 is consistent with the emphasis on the kingdom here.

The ascension scene is similar to heavenly "abduction" scenes that were commonplace in Jewish and Hellenistic literature.[44] The emphasis, here, is placed solely on divine action,[45] as evidenced by two "men in white" (angels)[46] suddenly appearing. These two speak with divine authority about Jesus returning in the same way he went. If the intent were to keep the disciples from looking into heaven,[47] the appeal to Jesus' return would be ineffective since it requires the hearers to recall Jesus' ascension into the clouds. Rather, the angels' statement makes emphatic that the "cloud" is the vehicle for this return. In this way, Luke causes the reader to reflect on extra-textual connections between Jesus and the "cloud." The reader, therefore, would remember that Jesus referred to the "Son of Man's" coming "in a cloud" (Luke 21:27; cf. Matt 24:30; Mark 14:26). Recalling these words and because Jesus is known to be the Son of Man,[48] the reader would reflect on another familiar text where

---

43. So Schlier, "Himmelfahrt," 229–30; van Stempvoort, "Interpretation," 35.

44. Greco-Roman literature: Homer *Iliad* 20:233–35; *Odyssey* 4:561–65; Ovid *Metamorphoses* 10:159–61; Hesiod *Erga* 167–73; Philostratus *Vit. Ap* 8:29–30. Jewish literature: Gen 5:21–24 (cf. Sir 44:16; 49:14; *1 En.* 81:6; 87:3–4; *2 En.* 67:1–3; *Jub.* 4:23); 2 Kgs 2:1–18 (cf. 1 Macc 2:58; *1 En.* 89:53; *4 Ezra* 6:26); for references to traditions about Moses' 'rapture' see Meeks, *Prophet-King* (1967); Lohfink, *Himmelfahrt*, 61–69; Zwiep, *Ascension*, 64–71.

Lohfink's conclusion that Luke's account is a "rapture" (*Entrückung*) story (the person's earthly life is ended by being taken up into heaven) has been accepted by most scholars. This, in turn, implied for many that Jesus' ascension is constructed to bring closure to his earthly work (so Benoit, "L'Ascension," 401–5; Ladd, *Theology*, 335; Robinson, *Jesus*, 134–36; Schneider, *Apostelgeschichte*, I, 210–11). However, the reader does not find an end to Jesus' work since Jesus continues to appear as Lord throughout the narrative. This contrasts with the "post-rapture condition" ascribed to most figures in Second-Temple literature, which involves them staying in heaven until the judgment day; only then do they seem to have a continued role. Thus, while Zwiep (*Ascension*, 78–79) maintains that the "Jewish rapture-preservation scheme" provides a "plausible context" for comparing Jesus' ascension-parousia, it is important to realize that Luke has altered this scheme. By recognizing that the ascension is not merely a "rapture," but also looks to the enthronement, the reader can better understand Jesus' continued appearances.

45. Jesus does not ascend, but is taken up (always passive—1:2, 9, 11, 22). Further, a cloud receives Jesus (see chapter 3). Cf. *2 En.* 67:1–3. There, the angels are responsible for Enoch's ascension; here the angels are merely messengers.

46. Any allusion to Moses and Elijah given their description in Luke 9:30 and their traditional (see Zwiep, *Ascension*, 58–71) ascent into heaven is weak (*contra* Johnson, *Acts*, 27, 31). The "bright clothing" is typical for angelic figures (cf. 2 Macc 3:24–39). The commonality with Moses and Elijah here is the cloud, which characterizes Jesus' ascent not the angels. Without clear allusion, then, Johnson's prophetic succession idea remains doubtful. Suggestions (cf. Witherington, *Acts*, 112) that the stress on "seeing" recalls the (Elijah/Elisha) double-portion idea also seem flawed (Paul receives the Spirit, but is not a witness to the ascension). Rather, this stress indicates the importance of witness. The disciples could give effective witness concerning Jesus' exaltation because they had "seen" it (so Chance, *Jerusalem*, 65).

47. As Zwiep, *Ascension*, 107.

48. The reader would know that Jesus is linked with the designation Son of Man throughout the Gospel tradition. Later (7:55–56), Luke will specifically refer to Jesus as the "Son of Man" in heaven.

clouds and son of man appear together—Dan 7:13.[49] There one like a "human being [son of man]" comes with the "clouds of heaven" to the "Ancient One" and receives a kingdom (Dan. 7:14). In this way, the reader links Jesus' ascension with his receiving a kingdom. Zwiep denies that Dan. 7:13 has a "*direct* influence" because that cloud does not move vertically.[50] However, the cloud does not have to move in the same direction in order for the reader to recall this background. All that is needed is sufficient connections (the cloud, the reference to heaven, and the reader identifying Jesus as the Son of Man) to suggest the allusion.

There are two different kingdoms reflected in the Daniel text—a heavenly (angelic) kingdom and an earthly Jewish one.[51] The apocalyptic heavenly kingdom would include the righteous at the resurrection, a conception that would make sense to the reader here. Jesus (the resurrected "Righteous One") ascends to receive his kingdom as the Son of Man. Those who follow him would then also be raised to enter this kingdom.

Is this kingdom established only at Jesus' return?[52] With the promised eschatological Spirit on its way, a presently experienced entrance into this kingdom seems implied. Daniel 7:13–14 does not address when the kingdom comes, although the implication may be that it is an event belonging to the last days. Moreover, since the son of man approaches the Ancient One in the heavens, the kingdom would be received before the return on those clouds.

In Acts 1:9–11, given the angel's question "Why do you stand looking?" in connection with the return, the reader might imagine a delay in it occurring.[53] However, this statement simply directs the disciples' attention to their responsibilities, just as Jesus' answer (1:8) previously.[54] One could suggest that once the Son of Man receives the kingdom there is no reason for a return. A reader of Luke's Gospel, however, would know Jesus' parable about a nobleman who goes away to receive a kingdom and then returns to rule (19:11–27). Historically such situations did take place and would be familiar to Luke's reader since Herod's son, Archelaus, had to entreat the emperor for his kingdom. Carroll thinks Luke 19:11–27 allegorically depicts Jesus' rejection, enthronement (resurrection/ascension), and subsequent return in judgment.[55] If the parable is understood this way, it is possible that it makes the kingdom associated only with Jesus' return.[56] However, the parable only indicates that the rebellious citizens would be judged at the time the nobleman returns. The kingdom has already been granted and the king's rule would have been in force, whether he was present or not. Thus, while Jesus denies that the kingdom will immediately become manifest in Jerusalem (apocalyptically restoring Israel's rule), he does

49. Many commentators make this connection: Barrett, *Acts*, 64; Johnson, *Acts*, 27; Schille, *Apostelgeschichte*, 74; Tannehill, *Narrative*, 19; Witherington, *Acts*, 112.

50. Zwiep, *Ascension*, 105.

51. Collins, "Kingdom," 83–84.

52. As Pesch, *Apostelgeschichte*, I, 74. See pp. 83–84, *Excursus: The Eschatological Kingdom in Luke-Acts.*

53. So Grässer, *Forschungen*, 51–52

54. Gaventa (*Acts*, 67) sees it as a "reliable promise" not an "indefinite delay."

55. Carroll, *Response*, 99.

56. As Wolter, "Israel's," 313–14.

not indicate that the kingdom is only manifest at the end. The nationalistic associations have been removed (just as in Acts 1:8), but kingdom rule remains present. The imagery of Acts 1:9–11, therefore, continues to support the possibility of a restored but reinterpreted kingdom.

Commentators have noted that the ascension illustrates the enthronement of Jesus.[57] Taking his cue from ancient conceptions about kings as "divine beings" and from texts like Ezek 28:40 and Ps 2:7, Lang suggests ancient people viewed the coronation as the king's ascent to the "mountain of the gods" to take his place as a deity, adopted among the gods (as Ps 110:1).[58] It is not clear whether Luke's reader would be aware of this idea.[59] In the mystical tradition, such ascents, nevertheless, were well-known during the Second-Temple period.[60] Von Rad states that Israel never pictured the coronation in a mythical "son of God" manner, yet it did see the king having a special relationship to God that viewed him as God's viceroy ruling from the divine throne (cf. 1 Chr 29:20, 23; 2 Chr 9:8).[61] It would seem, then, that if Pss 2:7 and 110:1 are used in expounding Jesus as king (as will be the case), the reader may well be expected to understand this ascent/coronation imagery. Regardless, the possibility of a restored kingdom is continued for the reader by the allusion to Daniel and placed firmly in the realm of divine action (God caused the ascension; the "Ancient One" grants the kingdom), thus characterizing God as the kingdom's restorer whenever that happens.

As indicated, the final words from the angels (1:11) draw the reader's attention to the disciples' responsibilities (rather than bringing closure to the narrative—the ascension's role in Luke's Gospel).[62] In the following scene, Peter argues from Scripture that replacing

57. Barrett, *Acts*, 83; Johnson, *Acts*, 30; Pesch, *Apostelgeschichte*, I, 73. An important question is whether Luke distinguishes the resurrection from the ascension in describing Jesus' exaltation (being granted sovereign status by God). Benoit ("L'Ascension," 401–2) argued that the resurrection is the primary feature in Christ's exaltation; the ascension being a secondary element completing his earthly appearances. Maile ("Ascension," 44–48) thought that, in depicting the ascension, Luke was doing nothing more than confirming the exaltation which took place at Jesus' resurrection (the majority view elsewhere in the NT). Differently, Lygre ("Exaltation," 196) argued that, although Luke distinguishes resurrection from ascension, both figure in the enthronement-exaltation (also Korn, *Geschichte*, 169).

Because Peter focuses on God exalting (ὑψόω) Jesus "to the right hand" (2:33) and the specification that David did not *ascend* into heaven (2:34) in the same context as Jesus being *resurrected* (ἀνίστημι) so as not to "experience corruption" (2:31), Lygre's conclusion seems proper. While one could assume that Peter believed that the exaltation described here was an invisible event that occurred at the same time as the resurrection, Luke's reader is more likely to think about the visible ascent that has just been described. This factor is missed by Zwiep (*Ascension*, 153–57), who seems to assume that if the reader is familiar with a traditional resurrection-exaltation scheme, this would override the dramatic visual Luke has given his reader. This conclusion relies on the tradition remaining unaffected by the context in which Luke sets it. Once the tradition is brought into the narrative, however, it is made to serve narrative purposes.

58. Lang, *Hebrew*, 20.

59. Lang (*Hebrew*, 41–42) indicates that Deuteronomistic literature de-emphasizes heavenly ascents, indicating that the tradition may not be common in later texts.

60. See Segal "Heavenly," 1334–94.

61. von Rad, *Theology*, 230.

62. So Parsons, *Departure*, 151, 181–82; Tannehill, *Narrative*, 10. As such, Gaventa's ("Eschatology," 36) attempt to identify a pattern in 1:6–11 reflecting an inquiry (1:6, 10), rejection (1:7, 11a), and promise (1:8, 11b) should be rejected for one reflecting inquiry, redirection, responsibility. In neither instance is the inquiry re-

Judas is one such obligation; moreover it is a divine necessity that someone take his office among the twelve (1:21). Both the words concerning Judas' death and those concerning another taking his position must (δεῖ) be fulfilled.[63] With the reference to those who have had a share in Jesus' ministry (1:17; cf. Mt. 19:28—"you who have followed me"), further limited by Matthias' addition to the eleven (1:26), the reader is likely to recall from the extra-text (cf. Luke 22:29–30; Matt 19:28) Jesus' words concerning those who would sit on thrones in his kingdom, judging Israel's twelve tribes.[64] Luke 22:29–30 follows Jesus' announcement about a betrayer (Luke 22:21–22). In Acts, the betrayal has happened and the group who would rule must be restored. Also, for Luke, Judas is specifically one of the number ("the twelve") (Luke 22:3), where the Gospel's ἐκ τοῦ ἀριθμοῦ is echoed in Acts' καταριθμέω.[65] Further, the disciples are to receive the kingdom (Luke 9:27; 12:32; 22:29) and the kingdom is associated with those who follow Jesus (Luke 9:60, 62; 18:29). In the latter cases the context may suggest that entrance has already occurred (they have forsaken everything else and already entered).[66]

Schneider suggests a relationship between the twelve's "full number" and the restored Israel that will be "light to the nations" (Isa 49:6).[67] While this conclusion is dependent on the reader understanding the twelve as *representing* Israel's tribes, it suggests a restored Israel,[68] which would receive a restored kingdom. Lohfink agrees that the twelve represent Israel, but Luke has given up on Israel's reconstitution.[69] However, since Jesus did not deny the restored kingdom, the reader does not have reason to believe that Luke has forsaken the idea. Instead, the reader finds a situation that supports expectations about the kingdom's restoration. Therefore, since Luke seems to relate the twelve to the kingdom's presence, their restoration would be important for identifying a restored kingdom. The implication is that it is now necessary to restore the number who would be judges in this kingdom. Here, again, the reader finds allusions to ideas reflecting the kingdom, Israel, and restoration in a context of divine action.[70]

Through these three introductory scenes, the reader sees God as the one responsible for restoring the kingdom to Israel. Although it remains uncertain when this kingdom is to be restored, the reader has been prepared for its restoration and to view this differently

---

jected on principle, rather a redirection takes place—looking to the divine activity involved (God establishes kingdoms; God took Jesus away on a cloud, suggesting his enthronement). Further, both cases emphasize the disciples' current responsibilities.

63. Barrett, in denying that the twelve's restoration was part of Luke's intention (*Acts*, 93–94), misses the latter necessity.

64. Fitzmyer, *Acts*, 220–21; Jervell, *Unknown*, 98; Jervell, *Apostelgeschichte*, 123–30; Witherington, *Acts*, 126.

65. Jervell, *Apostelgeschichte*, 124.

66. See Wolter, "'Reich,'" 543.

67. Schneider, *Apostelgeschichte*, 229.

68. So Tannehill, *Narrative*, 22: "The Messiah, through the twelve apostles, lays claim to the whole house of Israel."

69. Lohfink, *Sammlung*, 31.

70. Prayer and casting lots indicate a divine choice is involved (so Haenchen, *Acts*, 162, 164; Pesch, *Apostelgeschichte*, I, 91; Witherington, *Acts*, 125).

(in relation to the twelve). Also, in order to determine what, if any, restoration has taken place, the reader will have to look to divine actions.

The Messianic King: Present and Future

Acts 1:1—8:3.[71]

Acts 2:14–36 presents the first proclamation concerning the risen Christ and, thus, concerning Jesus as king.[72] Peter, the reliable spokesman for the community (especially since he recognized the necessity in scriptural fulfillment—1:12–26), notes that Jesus was divinely accredited through "wonders and signs" (2:22; cf. 2:19); a testimony affirmed by God raising him from the dead (2:24). Acts 2:22–24 is a single Greek sentence with all action subordinated to the main subject and verb θεὸς ἀνέστησεν (2:24). Therefore, all the activity in these verses is assigned to God,[73] drawing the reader's attention to divine activity directed toward Jesus.

Peter connects Jesus with the messianic figure presented in Ps 16:8–11. He (2:30) specifically picks up the divine promise concerning the Davidic king (Ps 132:11; cf. Ps 89:3; 2 Sam 7:12) and links it implicitly with Jesus' lineage.[74] Then (2:32–33), Peter unites the

---

71. In order to follow the narrative development of each theme, the portrait will be grouped around three divisions: Acts 1:1—8:3, 8:4—19:20, and 19:21—28:31. The events in 1:1—8:3 are united by their occurring in and around Jerusalem. They are initiatory, establishing foundational elements for the narrative.

Acts 8:4—19:20 is united by the message's expansion beyond Jerusalem and Judea as marked by repeated references to the community's growth (8:14; 9:31, 35, 42; 11:21, 24; 12:24; 13:12, 48–49; 14:1, 21; 16:14, 34; 17:4, 12, 34; 18:7–11; 19:4–5, 8, 10, 20), and by the inclusion of Samaritans (8:4–25) and gentiles (10:1—11:18).

Acts 19:21—28:31 assumes a different focus. The reader finds no further references to community growth. In fact, a climax is reached at 19:20, where the phrase "word of the Lord" marks off the section 19:10–20 and concludes the use of this phrase in the work (Tannehill, *Narrative*, 238). Acts 19:21 begins with a fulfillment statement (suggesting some major activity has been completed) followed by a geographic plan for the remaining narrative—to Jerusalem and then Rome. This implies a change in narrative direction. Most importantly, Paul's speeches and the narrative itself focus on his defense rather than on proclamation. The speeches are repeatedly characterized as defenses (ἀπολογία—22:1; 24:10; 25:16; 26:1, 2), providing the theme for this section. *Contra* Tannehill (*Narrative*, 316; also Haacker, "Bekenntnis," 439), Paul's assertion that he "witnesses" to Agrippa is not a change from defense to missionary witness. Instead, it is in keeping with the statement that Paul's witness to Christ in Rome would be the same as that in Jerusalem (23:11)—a defense (22:1). While this reinterprets the defense as a witness, it does not make it *missionary* witness. Rather, Luke's focus has turned from the growth of the word to Paul's defense, which is ultimately made only with resort to *God's* salvation offer (God has commanded the missionary actions that have led Paul to these present troubles), but it is a defense nonetheless. The two possible exceptions are Paul's addresses in Miletus (20:18–35) and Rome (28:17–28). However, in both cases Paul defends his status before the exhortation or proclamation. Since it is Paul's commission, actions, and piety that come under scrutiny, Luke does not appear to offer a general apology for the church. Haacker ("Bekenntnis," 438; also Jervell, *Apostelgeschichte*, 486, but compare 532) suggests that Paul's defense contributes to Luke's larger apologetic interests. While this is true, the change in the narrative that takes place beginning at 19:21 must be noted—Paul, not Christianity in its entirety, becomes the focus. Christianity benefits from that focus, but its defense should not be taken as the goal for this final section.

72. For a detailed discussion presenting Peter's case for Jesus as the Davidic king see Strauss, *Davidic*, 131–47.

73. Gaventa, *Acts*, 77–78; Tannehill, *Narrative*, 36.

74. See Fitzmyer, *Acts*, 256–58.

resurrection with the ascension (God exalted Jesus to the right hand) as divine actions enthroning Jesus (not David since David did not ascend—2:34).[75] The Spirit[76] being poured forth becomes the testimony that God has made Jesus ruler[77] over Israel (2:36).[78] Given all this divine action, it would seem that God has set the *times and seasons* for this ruler—the time is now, the "last days" (2:17).[79]

With this, Luke implies that the Spirit's outpouring indicates at least the beginning of the *eschaton*.[80] Conzelmann argued that the Spirit is not the "eschatological gift" but its substitute.[81] However, the Spirit's presence was so associated with the eschatological kingdom blessings that the reader would join this conception about the time for the Spirit's outpouring with the reference to the "last days" and see the present as the time for this gift.[82] What the reader finds is that the gift is not the eschatological end, but reflects that the end has begun.[83] Gaventa[84] criticizes Francis[85] for reading the "eschatological" Spirit in 2:17 into the following scenes where the Spirit appears. However, since (as Gaventa notes) Acts 1–2 is foundational for the rest of the work, the reader would carry this initial conception into the later appearances. The eschatological element would not disappear. Here, then, the "last days" do not mark a distinction between the time of Jesus and the church; rather they mark the time when the messianic reign is established,[86] just as the Son of Man

---

75. Zwiep (*Ascension*, 153–57) argues that Luke's terminology (particularly ἀνέβη in 2:34) is "traditional," stemming from a belief that the resurrection involved a "heavenly journey" from which Jesus returned to pour out the Spirit (an event that must precede his "rapture" as an end to his earthly work). However, 1) in Acts the Spirit is not poured out until after the "rapture" has occurred. Consequently, either the ascension does not end Jesus' earthly work or Luke did not understand the resurrection-exaltation scheme in this way. 2) Important to Zwiep's argument is that by using ὑψωθεὶς and ἀνέβη Luke is alluding to ἀναβαίνω εἰς ὕψος (Ps 67:19 LXX) which, in turn, refers to Jesus receiving gifts to pour out (as Eph. 4:8–10). Thus, Jesus would ascend to God's right, receive the Spirit, and return. However, the quote from Ps 110:1 specifies the duration for the sitting—"until I make your enemies your footstool." Unless the resurrection brought about this condition, Jesus could not have returned to pour out the Spirit. Since Satan remains operative (even in the community—5:3), seems to be set in opposition to Jesus (13:10), and currently has dominion over those outside the kingdom (26:18), God's final overthrow of all Jesus' enemies would seem to await the *eschaton*. Thus the sitting would be in effect until Jesus returns. Ἀνέβη, then, alludes to Jesus' "rapture" (not a heavenly journey), but Luke has transformed the genre by not seeing the event as an end to Jesus' earthly work.

76. The promise concerning the Spirit is made in the context of the kingdom's restoration (1:1–8). Therefore, the Spirit being "poured out" by Jesus is at least part of that restoration (Jervell, *Unknown*, 98).

77. Barrett (*Acts*, 151–52) sees an "adoptionistic" Christology expressed here. However, the making of Jesus as "Lord and Messiah" need be nothing more than the movement from king-designate to king-coronate (Witherington, *Acts*, 149).

78. The phrase characterizes this Jewish crowd as the people of God, i.e., Israel (Johnson, *Acts*, 52).

79. *Contra* Haenchen (*Acts*, 179) μετὰ ταῦτα is not the original reading, but the work of a corrector (for discussion see Metzger, *Textual*, 295).

80. So Gaventa, "Eschatology," 37–38; Gaventa, *Acts*, 76; Johnson, *Acts*, 49; Witherington, *Acts*, 140.

81. Conzelmann, *Theology*, 95.

82. See above, notes 37 and 39.

83. So Ellis, *Christ*, 114; Jervell *Apostelgeschichte*, 143; cf. *Excursus: The Eschatological Kingdom in Luke-Acts* and below on Acts 3:12–26.

84. Gaventa, "Eschatology," 38.

85. Francis, "Eschatology," 49–63.

86. *Contra* Fitzmyer, *Acts*, 252; Grässer, *Forschungen*, 52. Pesch (*Apostelgeschichte*, I, 119) notes the connection to the times and seasons in 1:7, but does not draw this conclusion.

was to receive the kingdom in the "last days." Therefore, the reader finds God establishing the eschatological king, the promised Davidic ruler.

Jesus as King?

How appropriate is "king" as a characterization for Jesus? In Acts only those hostile to Paul directly refer to Jesus this way (17:7). This is comparable to Jesus being charged with claiming to be "Messiah, a king" by the Jewish leaders (Luke 23:2), to which Jesus responded with something that is neither a denial nor an admission. A similar response is seen when Jesus is asked by the Council whether he is the "Son of God" (22:69–70).[87] The similarities could suggest that Luke thinks that it is a mistake to attribute kingship to Jesus.

However, there are instances in Luke's Gospel where Jesus apparently accepts the title king. At 19:38 the disciples greet Jesus with the title as he enters Jerusalem. The words from Ps 118:26 are actually modified in order to include βασιλεύς.[88] When the Pharisees wish Jesus to silence the disciples he refuses, implicitly accepting this acclamation. Likewise, the second thief asks for Jesus to remember him when he comes into his "kingdom" (Luke 23:42). Jesus announces that the thief's request will be fulfilled "today," again implicitly accepting kingship. It, therefore, seems that seeing Jesus as king is consistent with Luke's Gospel, yet Luke also apparently wishes to redefine that kingship, not accepting implications supposed by opponents (probably sedition). Further, although direct reference is the strongest form of characterization, it is not the only one. There is much indirect reference to Jesus' kingship throughout Luke-Acts.

Since the return of the Davidic monarch was central to Israel's hopes for restoration,[89] the reader can conclude that the restored Davidic king means that God has been active in restoring Israel. In keeping with the initial reinterpretation, however, this kingdom does not have the nationalistic sense originally associated with it. This is not an earthly king on an earthly throne, throwing off the enemy's yoke. Instead, it is an exalted king on the divine throne—as indicated by the citation from Ps 110:1 (Acts 2:34). Luke could be emphasizing David's, rather than the divine, throne (the nearest antecedent to "his throne" in 2:30 is "his [David's] descendants").[90] However, von Rad argued that Ps 110:1 makes the king sit on Yahweh's throne, which means that it does not refer just to God's favorite sitting in the honored position, but to the king representing divine rule to the people:[91] David's throne is already the divine representative throne.

87. See Marshall, *Luke*, 850–53.

88. The textual witnesses that omit this word seem to be trying to make it align with the LXX reading; so Metzger, *Textual*, 169–70.

89. See Isa 4:2; 7:10–25; 9:1–7; 11:1–16; 16:5; 32:1–8; 55:3–5; Jer 3:15–18; 17:25–26; Ezek 17:22–24; 34:23–31; 37:22–28; Hos 3:4–5; Amos 9:11; Mic 4:8; 5:2; Zech 9:9.

90. Strauss, *Davidic*, 138–39.

91. Von Rad, *Theology*, 320.

As argued in chapter 3, the ambiguity surrounding the title Lord in Acts suggests that Luke had no problem referring to Jesus and God in the same way, so having Jesus sitting on the divine throne is something the reader should find consistent with other narrative developments.[92] Moreover, with the exaltation already in the reader's mind, the ascent to the divine throne is implied in 2:34. This does not lessen the fulfillment of the Davidic promise; rather it stresses the enigmatic way God has fulfilled it.[93] Luke continues to challenge the reader's understanding about the kingdom. The messianic king promised at the time of the kingdom's restoration has begun his reign, but his throne has been transferred to heaven. The messianic reign brings forth eschatological blessings (the promised Spirit), so the divine promises are fulfilled, but the nationalistic element has been removed.[94]

In 4:24–30 the community declares to God its allegiance to the Davidic king through a prayer taken from Ps 2:1–2. For the reader, the community's acknowledgement of David as "ancestor" connects them with divine promises to David, which would include the promised heir. The quotation focuses on the people rejecting God and God's Χριστός (4:26)—the king.[95] This reinforces the reader's belief that Jesus is the king established by God since Jesus is specifically identified as the one God anointed (ἔχρισας—4:27). Further, both David and Jesus are characterized as God's παῖς (servant). Although this term is not exclusively an Christological title,[96] the reader finds it attributed to two figures (David and Jesus) linked by a royal Psalm, suggesting its appropriateness for a king. In this way, the attribution to David prepares the reader for seeing Jesus as the Davidic king, God's servant. Consequently, Peter's proclamation (2:14–36) is affirmed (God has anointed Jesus as king) and God's responsibility (a fulfilled promise) for establishing this king is maintained.

At 5:31 the reader is reminded that God has exalted Jesus to the right hand (cf. 2:33–34; Ps 110:1) but now specifically as leader[97] and savior. These last two terms reinforce the kingship image since the reader would connect them to extra-textual beliefs about a ruler's responsibilities.[98] Further, this kingship is specifically related to *Israel's* repentance. Thus, these three scenes strengthen the reader's conception that God restores the kingdom—God has enthroned God's king (Jesus) on the Davidic throne at the time God set for that event (the "last days") and this king now rules as "Lord and Messiah" (2:36) for *Israel's* deliverance and repentance.

At Acts 1:6–11 the reader did not have enough information to determine the relationship between the kingdom and Jesus' return. Acts 3:12–26 provides the missing informa-

---

92. *Contra* Barrett, *Acts*, 152. See also Pesch, *Apostelgeschichte*, I, 123.

93. An idea familiar to the reader; see chapter 2.

94. While this agrees with Franklin (*Christ*, 24) that the kingdom is established in the heavenly sphere and affects the Christian's present life, it is distinguished from his view by envisioning entrance into the present, although unconsummated, kingdom.

95. See Fitzmyer, *Acts*, 309.

96. See Barrett, *Acts*, 245.

97. Barrett (*Acts*, 290) denies a connection to the "prince of the community" at Qumran (*1QSb* 5:20), who as a Davidic messiah saves Israel (*4QFlor* 1:13), in part because Qumran's salvation is political. However, the lack of a physical realm does not remove all political connotation. It still involves a kingdom, with its own social order (see chapter 5), which stands over against another realm ("this corrupt generation"—2:40).

98. See Fitzmyer, *Acts*, 338; also chapter 2 and below.

tion, recalling kingdom images through references to Jesus as God's messiah (3:18), and to his glorification (3:13)[99] and resurrection by God (3:15). Now, Peter speaks concerning the "time" of the restoration (ἀποκαταστάσεως) of all things (3:21), echoing the disciples' concerns from 1:6. Jesus' necessary reception in heaven[100] reminds the reader about the ascension (1:9–11) and Peter's explication of it (2:14–36). Peter also declares that the one appointed (προκεχειρισμένον—a different word than in 1:7, but a similar idea concerning divine ordination) Christ for them[101] will come at the "time of restoration."

The phrase ἄχρι χρόνων ἀποκαταστάσεως apparently refers to the ultimate restoration as distinct from the "times of refreshing." This conclusion is not necessary for the reader to see a current kingdom restoration in Acts since the phrase could refer to a present restoration that precedes Christ's return.[102] However, it seems more likely that a final restoration is associated with the Son of Man's return in Luke's theology, especially since restoration is so strongly linked to Israel's eschatological hope.[103] Christ's return would, therefore, be associated with the restoration.

This does not appear to be simply a future restoration. In 2:38 the reader saw the Spirit portrayed as the divine response to repentance, now the "times of refreshing" are this response (3:19). The parallel placement suggests to the reader that the Spirit (an eschatological kingdom element brought forward to the present) can be associated with these "refreshings."[104] Thus, the Spirit's presence provides inbreakings of the future restoration into the present.[105] Barrett makes this case, arguing that καιροί here refers to a number of specific points in time and ἀνάψυξις to temporary relief rather than finality. They are distinguished from the χρόνων and ἀποκαταστάσεως. Consequently the "times" here

---

99. Barrett (*Acts*, 195) limits Luke's choice of "glorification" in reference to either the resurrection or the healing but it could also express Jesus' exaltation (so Fitzmyer, *Acts*, 285).

100. Schneider (*Apostelgeschichte*, I, 337–38) argues that the necessity of the ascension requires a delay so that a time for repentance can be offered. However, the text implies only that some time elapses between the ascension and Jesus' return. This does not indicate a delay, for it says nothing about how long this time will be; it is completely consistent with an imminent but not immediate return (see Francis, "Eschatology," 49–63; Mattill, "Naherwartung," 276–93; Mattill, *Luke* (1979)). It does, however, continue the motif that God controls the 'times and seasons' for events related to the kingdom.

101. Barrett (*Acts*, 204–5) correctly denies that Peter's words imply Jesus is not now the Christ (also Schneider, *Apostelgeschichte*, I, 325). The perfect tense used in reference to the appointment shows only that Jesus became the Christ at a time (unspecified here) prior to Peter's statement.

102. As Carroll, *Response*, 145–47.

103. See Parker, *Apokatastasis*, 4–5.

104. Gaventa (*Acts*, 88) makes this connection to the Spirit. Because Fitzmyer misses this parallel (*Acts*, 283), he is troubled by the lack of reference to the Spirit in Peter's speech (suggesting it does not fit Lukan theology).

105. Carroll (*Response*, 144) claims that the "times of refreshing" lack an eschatological element unless Jesus' return is used to determine its meaning. However, ἀνάψυξις is found in eschatological contexts, referring to the rest and "breath" received at the end (4 Ezra 11:46). Parker (*Apokatastasis*, 30–31), therefore, sees the "times of refreshing" as completely eschatological (supposedly the καὶ locates these refreshings at the time Christ is "sent"). Grässer (*Forschungen*, 54–58) makes no allowance for a present and future aspect because he misses the relationship between the refreshing and the restoration; they both result from repentance. In each case the parallel made between the Spirit and the "times of refreshing" (eschatological elements brought forward) is missed.

represent "individual realizations" of the *eschaton*.[106] A final restoration remains for the future, much as the "great and glorious" day referred to in the Joel quotation (Acts 2:20).

The implication is that, although the messianic king is on the throne and Israel receives his kingship blessings, there is another dimension remaining to God's *times and seasons* for the kingdom. The relationship between the restoration here and in 1:7 may evoke nationalistic hopes, but the implication is that these will not be fulfilled outside of a final restoration. Perhaps, though, Luke envisions the kingdom coming only to the select group of disciples, denying any national hope.[107] However, the offer to those who repent does not rule out an ultimate nationalistic restoration, it just emphasizes the kingdom's current pneumatic element.[108] Regardless, because the time for Jesus' return and the pneumatic "times of refreshing" are divinely controlled, the reader identifies God as the one restoring the kingdom. Yet, once again, Luke's God is enigmatically portrayed through a now/not yet restoration.[109]

Finally, although little of the Davidic aspect is mentioned, the comparison between Joseph, Moses, and Jesus in Stephen's[110] speech furthers the reader's impressions about a kingly Jesus. God makes Joseph governor over Egypt (7:10), and God sent Moses to Israel as "ruler and liberator" (7:35). For the reader already familiar with the presentation that Jesus is a king, these statements further the portrait that Jesus is the ruler sent and established by God.[111]

Acts 8:4—19:20

When Philip (a reliable spokesperson since he was introduced as one of the seven "full of the Spirit"—Acts 6:3–5) reaches Samaria he brings the good news concerning "the Messiah" to the Samaritans. The reader knows the title messiah is linked to the Davidic

---

106. Barrett, *Acts*, 205; cf. Gaventa, *Acts*, 88; Tannehill, *Narrative*, 55–56; and Witherington, *Acts*, 185–86. Fitzmyer (*Acts*, 283) denies that these phrases fit Lukan eschatology. However, if (as Fitzmyer admits) Jesus' return is a part of Lukan eschatology, Christ's coming at the "time of restoration" does fit. Part of Fitzmyer's problem is seeing the καιροί and the χρόνων as being ways to say the same thing (288–89). But, the καὶ that separates the clauses allows them to refer to two different periods. Since a difference between the refreshing and Jesus' return can also be identified (Lake and Cadbury, *Beginnings*, 37), the two phrases are not necessarily two ways to express the same thought.

107. Barrett, *Acts*, 206–8.

108. Oepke, "ἀποκαθίστημι, ἀποκατάστασις," 389. His assertion that 3:20 emphasizes that the final restoration is more about establishing the divine order than restoring Israel ignores the narrative links to the hopes expressed by the Apostles in 1:6. It also overlooks that Israel's eschatological hopes are already connected to the re-established divine order (see Parker's [*Apokatastasis*, 5–14] survey of OT texts that relate Israel's restoration to the cosmic eschatological restoration).

109. Preparation for such a view was made in Luke's Gospel, see *Excursus: The Eschatological Kingdom in Luke-Acts*.

110. As "full of faith and the Holy Spirit" (6:5), "grace and power" (6:8), "doing great wonders and signs" (6:8), speaking with the Spirit and wisdom (6:10), and appearing as an angelic figure (6:15), Stephen is characterized as a reliable spokesperson.

111. Cf. Barrett, *Acts*, 357–58; Johnson, *Acts*, 121; Neudorfer, "Speech," 286–88; Witherington, *Acts*, 267, 270.

king and through this summary proclamation the reader sees Philip's preaching as identical to Peter's speeches earlier (2:14–36; 4:24–30; 5:31).[112]

After reading about Saul/Paul's conversion experience, the reader learns that Luke's Saul[113] believes that the messiah's suffering and rising were essential to the argument that Jesus is sitting on the divine throne as the Davidic king—the messiah. Saul preaches that Jesus is the "Son of God" (9:20), which the reader equates to Jesus being the "messiah" by its replacement in a parallel statement about Saul's teaching (9:22).[114] While the terms "Son of God" and "messiah" are not identical in background or use and, therefore, should not be conflated,[115] the terms' parallel positions suggest the reader should see them as similar. In the OT only the king is specifically referred to as God's son,[116] so this title's application to Jesus would seem to point to Jesus as a king and thus as Davidic messiah. Conzelmann, however, claimed that Luke used "Son of God" in order to distinguish Jesus from the political messiah. In turn, the interpretation of the title was to be "deduced" from Christological statements in Luke's work, rather than from background ideas in the Jewish or Hellenistic world.[117] However, the phrase cannot be separated from the images it conjures for the reader. Its appearance will evoke certain beliefs that link it specifically to Israel's king—a political image. At the same time, the parallel placement with "messiah" suggests Luke's reader is to connect the Son of God with the messiah—a figure already identified with the Davidic king.

Yet, Luke's usage is not "merely" the adoptive sense applied to any Davidic king.[118] The reader has already seen that Jesus is portrayed as the Davidic king *par excellence* by his seat on the divine throne.[119] Later, the reader will find that when Paul retells Israel's history (13:14–25) he emphasizes the time of the kings, beginning with Saul, Israel's desired king.[120] The reader would not see the request for a king evaluated negatively, for no criticism is offered against the request or Saul; indeed, God "gave" Saul to Israel.[121] However, the reader finds a contrast between Israel's desires and God's—Saul is Israel's requested king; David is the divinely-favored one. God *raised* David to the throne (13:22), which prepares the reader for the announcement that God has *raised* Jesus from the dead (13:30). The parallel implies that Jesus is the divinely-favored, promised, Davidic seed (the people's

---

112. So Gaventa, *Acts*, 135.

113. The Damascus road experience, particularly the divine commission (9:15), turns Saul/Paul into a reliable spokesperson.

114. The parallel is noted by (among others) Barrett, *Acts*, 465; Haenchen, *Acts*, 331; Pesch, *Apostelgeschichte*, I, 308.

115. Fitzmyer, *Acts*, 435.

116. See chapter 2. Therefore, it is false to assume (as Schille, *Apostelgeschichte*, 227) that Saul takes up a Hellenistic (rather than a Jewish) predicate for the Christ.

117. Conzelmann, *Theology*, 85.

118. Rightly, Fitzmyer, *Acts*, 435.

119. So Neyrey, *Render*, 83–84.

120. Johnson, *Acts*, 237; Pesch, *Apostelgeschichte*, I, 30; Strauss, *Davidic*, 157–58. For a detailed discussion of Paul's argument for Jesus as the Davidic messiah see Strauss, *Davidic*, 148–78.

121. 13:22a does suggest a problem with Saul since God "removed" him, but this does not imply the original request or Saul's kingship were negatively valued.

deliverer—13:23) and, thus, the fulfillment of the promised king.[122] Additional support for this conclusion is drawn from the reader's extra-text. Duling argued that a "promise tradition" developed within Judaism based on 2 Sam 7:5–16. It consisted in three elements: 1) a Davidic descendent would 2) have a "filial" relationship with God and 3) his kingdom would be eternal. This Davidide became the focal point for Jewish eschatological hopes as the one God would raise up to fulfill the promise.[123] All three elements appear in Paul's speech here (cf. Luke 1:32–33), so it is likely the reader would recognize the eschatological fulfillment that has taken place.[124]

Jesus is also identified as the begotten "Son" (13:33). While Haenchen argued that ἀναστήσας Ἰησοῦν in 13:33 refers to Jesus being raised from the dead,[125] Wendt was correct to note that ἐκ νεκρῶν is absent there, but present in 13:30 and 34.[126] Peter's speech at 2:33–34 emphasized the ascension (exaltation to God's right; David did not ascend) in Jesus' enthronement, so, similarly, the reader is likely to see ἀναστήσας here referencing the ascension since the begotten son imagery also suggests enthronement.[127] Strauss argues that the raising of Jesus refers to his whole life, not just to his resurrection and enthronement. The begetting took place at birth (Luke 1:35) and this sonship status is then confirmed throughout Jesus' life, culminating in the resurrection and ascension.[128] While this conclusion seems correct in the context of Luke-Acts, the begotten image is primarily used at 13:33 to indicate that Jesus is the Davidic king. Therefore, Jesus is portrayed as the messianic king and God's kingdom has come to the people of Israel since, in Jesus and through the forgiveness of sins, God is offering entrance into that kingdom.

Jesus's status as king is also related to Paul proclaiming from Scripture that Jesus is the messiah who had to suffer and rise again (17:3). After these words, the ensuing conflict, stirred up by disobedient Jews, concerns which king they will serve—Caesar or Jesus (17:7). The "Jews" here are unreliable characters, so the reader would be suspicious about their negative assertions. However, the reader is already aware that Jesus has been portrayed as king, accounting their unreliability to their misrepresenting this kingdom. This reminds the reader that Luke has reinterpreted the restored kingdom—God has restored the Davidic king on the divine throne, ruling over those who repent and obey God,[129] but it is not presently a nationalistic kingdom that presents a seditious threat to Rome.

Finally, the reader finds indications reflecting Jesus' kingship in the references to Jesus as judge. Peter's declaration that God has appointed Jesus as judge over the living and the dead (10:42) paints Jesus as a royal figure[130] who sits on the divine throne as

---

122. So Fitzmyer, "Role," 175; Goldsmith, "Acts 13:33–37," 321–24; Jervell *Apostelgeschichte*, 359–60; Lake and Cadbury, *Beginnings*, 154; Tannehill, *Narrative*, 170.

123. Duling, "Promises," 55–77; also Hayes, "Resurrection," 333–45.

124. Cf. Chance, *Jerusalem*, 89–90.

125. Haenchen, *Acts*, 411; also Loisy, *Actes*, 532; Lohfink, *Himmelfahrt*, 234.

126. Wendt, *Apostelgeschichte*, 212.

127. Tannehill (*Narrative*, 170) correctly equates divine sonship with enthronement.

128. Strauss, *Davidic*, 164–66.

129. See chapter 5.

130. See chapter 3. Possibly, the description of Jesus as "doing good" (10:38) adds to this portrait. Εὐεργέτης was a title for Hellenistic kings (Lake and Cadbury, *Beginnings*, 121; Schille, *Apostelgeschichte*, 249).

"Lord of all" (10:36).[131] Likewise, Paul speaks about the "man" (Jesus) whom God has appointed to judge the world (17:31). Here again, the reader finds Jesus included in the divine Ruler's role since it is the "Lord of heaven and earth" (17:24) who will judge "by a man."[132] Consequently, the reader perceives Jesus, as the messianic king, assuming ruling functions in God's Kingdom.

Acts 19:21—28:31

In Acts' final section, the reader does not encounter any long speeches detailing scriptural arguments for Jesus as the messianic king. However, Paul indicates that Ananias said he was appointed to see the "Righteous One" (22:14). Twice before (3:14; 7:52), the reader has seen Jesus described this way. In Stephen's speech, the *Righteous One* was seen as the culmination of the rejected saviors that God had sent to Israel.[133] The reader also identifies him with the "Son of Man" who stands in *heaven* (cf. 22:6—the light comes "from heaven") at the "right hand of God" (7:55–56). Therefore, given the portrait traits developed so far, Luke's reader would believe that Paul has seen Israel's rejected leader whom God has given the exalted throne. Further, since in 7:55–56 the reader was likely to think that Jesus' standing in heaven indicated his royal role as judge,[134] the reference to Paul speaking to Felix and Drusilla about "justice," "self-control," and "the coming judgment" (24:25) would reinforce Jesus' royal stature—justice (righteousness) is associated with judgment, just as the Righteous One is the judge.

The emphasis on the resurrection in the presentation that Jesus is the messianic king is again affirmed. The resurrection represents the messianic "hope of Israel"—28:20.[135] How does this relate to the kingdom? Haenchen sees this as a purely messianic hope, having no relation to Israel's restoration.[136] By contrast, Weder thinks the resurrection hope, Israel's hope, and messianic expectations are drawn together by Luke in such a way that Israel's hope is almost exclusively an eschatological messianic one.[137] Völkel argued that Luke has reduced the Jewish hope to the resurrection and, thus, defined it solely in relation to Jesus' resurrection.[138] Each author seems to have missed that Jesus' resurrection has been shown as the means for the kingdom being restored to Luke's redefined Israel (see chapter 5). As such, the resurrection of the king benefits Israel and Israel can receive such blessings now in a foretaste of the eschatological hopes. Mayer correctly points out that Luke understands this hope as not simply a Christian feature, but belonging to part or all

131. Connected to the messiah through the reference to being "anointed" by God (so Haenchen, *Acts*, 352; Pesch, *Apostelgeschichte*, I, 343).

132. Neyrey (*Render*, 85) suggests Jesus mediates divine benefaction, but also notes that, with the references to Jesus' involvement in judging, he has been linked closely with the divine role.

133. See further in chapter 5.

134. See chapter 3.

135. Barrett, *Acts*, 1240; Schille, *Apostelgeschichte*, 478; Schneider, *Apostelgeschichte*, II, 415.

136. Haenchen, *Acts*, 638, and his fn. 7.

137. Weder, "Hoffnung," 485.

138. Völkel, "Deutung," 9–27.

Israel.[139] Indeed, Luke's Paul claims that this is the same hope for which the Jews currently worship night and day (26:7). Since Paul is in line with earlier proclamations concerning Jesus as the resurrected and exalted Davidic king, the reader would also see him as in line with Israel's hopes that have been expressed repeatedly (even if they are reinterpreted) throughout Luke's two volumes.[140]

When Paul stands before the Council, the reader finds him claiming to be on trial "for the hope of the resurrection of the dead" (23:6).[141] The Greek phrase is a *hendiadys*[142] indicating at the minimum that the hope is closely connected to the resurrection. The reader has some reason to connect Israel's hope and the resurrection, since in some OT texts (Hos 6:1; Ezek 37:1–14) Israel's restoration was pictured as a resurrection.[143] More specifically, the reader earlier heard about Israel's hoped for restoration (1:6; cf. Luke 24:21), which Luke has presented as at least partially fulfilled in the Davidic king's restoration to Israel. The resurrection featured prominently in this argument and its appearance here would cause the reader to recall previous speeches in Acts that have presented Scriptural evidence for Jesus as the Davidic king, whose resurrection/exaltation assures Israel's reinterpreted restoration.[144] The reader finds this relation to Israel's hope reinforced when Paul mentions Moses (i.e., the Law) and the Prophets (26:22–23; 28:23). Paul claims he is on trial for a promise God made to Israel (to "our ancestors," to the "twelve tribes"—26:6–7).[145] Also, the reference to the "kingdom of God" (28:23) draws the reader's attention to the connection between Jesus, the kingdom, and Israel's hope (28:20). Thus, Jesus is presented as the promised (and rejected) king who fulfills this hope.

At 24:15 the reader finds Paul mentioning the "resurrection of both the righteous and the unrighteous"—the judgment of all. Since God, through the resurrection, has designated Jesus as the judge over the whole world (17:31), the reader associates this resur-

---

139. Mayer, "ἐλπίς κτλ," 438.

140. See Haacker, "Bekenntnis," 442.

141. The Council is already known to include Sadducees, who are opposed to the resurrection (4:1). Luke's aside about theirs and the Pharisees' beliefs serves to emphasize this point. Thus, when Paul appears before this Council, the reader is prepared for Paul's reference to the resurrection, associating that resurrection with Jesus' since that was the issue at 4:1 (so Prieur, *Verkündigung*, 35).

142. So Gaventa, *Acts*, 314; Schille, *Apostelgeschichte*, 426.

143. Some other texts seem to picture an actual resurrection, but even these are related to Israel's future (cf. Dan 12:2; *T. Jud.* 25; *T. Benj.* 10:6–11). See Haacker, "Bekenntnis," 444–47.

144. Tannehill (*Narrative*, 290) suggests Luke's reason for not including an argument from Scripture in Acts 22 and 26 is in order to portray Paul as exemplifying effective witness to a hostile Jewish audience. However, Luke has not given a Christological exposition from Scripture since Acts 13. With Bock (*Proclamation* (1987)), it seems correct to maintain that Luke finished such expositions at that point—afterwards he only alludes to these earlier arguments. By 19:21—28:31 the importance of the resurrection for the presentation that Jesus is "Lord and Messiah" is so familiar that the reader assumes it. Further, missionary proclamation would detract from Paul's defense, the predominant aim in 19:21—28:31.

145. Since Luke has already equated the hope and the resurrection, the reader finds no difficulty in Paul introducing the resurrection (26:8) after mentioning the hoped for promise in 26:7. This reference prepares the reader for Paul to indicate Scripture's promise concerning Christ's suffering and rising (26:23). Fitzmyer (*Acts*, 756–57, 793; also Lake and Cadbury, *Beginnings*, 289) denies any messianic element to the hope here, but this misses the way Luke has offered the resurrection as evidence that Jesus is "Lord and Messiah." Jesus, the resurrected one, fulfills Israel's hope—the restored king and kingdom.

rection to judgment with the messiah and his kingdom.[146] That Jesus' resurrection is in mind throughout 19:21—28:31 is indicated when Festus summarizes the dispute as having dealt with a "certain Jesus, who had died, but whom Paul asserted to be alive" (25:19). Since Festus can make this assertion without a specific reference to Jesus' resurrection appearing in the preceding narrative, it seems that the reader was to interpret Paul's earlier resurrection appeals as focused on this point.[147] Consequently, while often the reader only finds references to the resurrection of the dead as a general event, the "Christological element" would not be factored out[148] since it is Jesus, as the "first to rise" (26:23), that is primarily meant[149] and through this Israel's restored hope. In this way, Israel's hope, the messianic kingdom, is presented as a current reality (restored in the resurrected Christ) and as something that can still be hoped for (the ultimate restoration—cf. 3:21).

Luke also reminds his reader that, although Jesus is the messianic king, his followers are not military zealots.[150] The Roman tribune, by reference to the Egyptian and the Sicarii (21:38), indicates that he thinks Paul is simply another zealot antagonizing the people against Rome. Paul denies any link to Egypt, declaring, instead, that he is a good citizen from an honorable city. Thus, even though Paul's speech will indicate that the messiah is now Lord (a term applied to Caesar) in heaven, Paul is not leading a revolt. Also, Tertullus attempts to charge Paul with sedition by indicating that he is the sects' "ringleader."[151] Since Paul is found innocent of such charges, the reader is reminded that being a citizen of God's kingdom does not mean being in sedition against earthly kingdoms. Overall, then, the reader finds that throughout the three major sections of Acts Jesus is portrayed as the divinely-established, present and future, messianic king.

146. Prieur (*Verkündigung*, 36–37) correctly makes the link between the ones judged and the judge. In both 10:42 and 17:31, Christ is the judge, with 17:31 given an eschatological element through the reference to "day." That Paul is thinking about judgment is implied by his good conscience (24:16), which suggests he anticipates a favorable decision. When Paul again mentions the resurrection to the Council (24:21), the reader already understands it in relation to Jesus' resurrection.

147. *Contra* Tannehill, *Narrative*, 287–90. Tannehill argues that Luke's "Christological reticence" (he supposedly downplays messianic elements in Paul's defense speeches) counters the claim that the emphasis on Jewish roots is designed simply to assure gentile Christians that they are valid heirs to Israel's promises. Since Luke's reader cannot dissociate Jesus' resurrection from his enthronement as king, this argument is flawed. However, there are other reasons (the overall Jewish context, ongoing offer of deliverance in the face of persecution) for rejecting the claim Tannehill attempts to counter. Luke is interested in a mission to Jews and not just to gentiles (see chapter 5).

148. *Contra* Schneider, *Apostelgeschichte*, II, 348. Prieur (*Verkündigung*, 34) correctly notes that neither in Peter's nor Paul's speeches is a general dead-resurrection proclaimed. They always focus on Christ's resurrection. While both 4:2 and 17:32 may hint at a more general resurrection, it is tied directly to Jesus.

149. So Haenchen, *Acts*, 638; Schneider, *Apostelgeschichte*, II, 363 n. 17.

150. So Haenchen, *Acts*, 621–22.

151. See Barrett, *Acts*, 1097; Haenchen, *Acts*, 653.

It Remains God's Kingdom

Acts 1:1—8:3

When Luke calls the reader's attention to the kingdom of God at 1:3 and then has the disciples mention the kingdom being restored to Israel, the reader may wonder if the same kingdom is being referenced. Divine kingship certainly covered more than just Israel's national hopes, involving (eschatologically) overturning the present world order and re-establishing the glory not just of the Davidic monarchy but of creation.[152] However, the Chronicler (1 Chr 28:5; 2 Chr 13:8) calls David's kingdom the "kingdom of the LORD." Thus, the divine kingdom was thought to be directly related to (although not completely identified with) Israel's kingship. Luke is not substituting one idea for another in relating these terms; instead he appears to desire the reader to explore their relationship.[153] Therefore, although God restores the kingdom to Israel by enthroning Jesus, the reader should not forget that it remains God's kingdom.

In the prayer at 4:24–30 (which affirms the kingdom's restoration), God is addressed as Δέσποτα, the transcendent Sovereign.[154] This image is reinforced by the reference to the Creator God. The Sovereign God controls creation, demonstrated by the place being shaken (4:31).[155] Earthly kings can do nothing apart from the divine will (4:28), becoming "mere puppets" controlled by the real King.[156] Luke's reader would be familiar with such contrasts since this is consistent with the motif identified in Second-Temple literature that compared kings to God.[157] Further, the community prays for God to demonstrate sovereign power by stretching out the divine "hand" (4:30), the same "hand" that controlled the actions of the rulers (4:28). Consequently, God remains the Great King, although Jesus is now the messianic king.

Stephen's speech starts with a reference to the "God of glory" (7:2) and after its conclusion Stephen sees Jesus at the right of the "glory of God" (7:55).[158] "God of glory" occurs

---

152. See Parker, *Apokatastasis*, 4–14; Wolter, "'Reich,'" 545–47; also chapter 2. Viviano ("Kingdom," 97) acknowledged that expressions about divine universal kingship, while related to Israel's kingdom, are not completely consumed by the latter notion. The ideas are not mutually exclusive either (Collins, "Kingdom," 84).

153. O'Toole ("Kingdom," 151) correctly suggests that Luke does not express "two different realities" when connecting the kingdom of God and Jesus, but simply repeats one idea with another. His remarks need to be tempered by the preceding cautions. Nevertheless, it seems unnecessary to separate (as does Lindemann, "Herrschaft," 196–218) references to Christ's kingdom from those to God's (especially in Luke-Acts).

154. Δέσποτα "connotes one with great power and control of circumstances" (Witherington, *Acts*, 201). According to Enermalm-Ogawa (*Un langage*, 126–27) the usage in the prayers in 2 Maccabees comes close to that of a proper name for God, but, elsewhere in the narrative it refers to divine punitive action. Here, the title does appear like a proper name and there is a sense in which the community calls for punitive actions against the rulers. Ironically, the punishment is actually continued demonstrations of divine power for the believers' benefit.

155. Schneider, *Apostelgeschichte*, I, 357; Tannehill, *Narrative*, 72.

156. Barrett, *Acts*, 241.

157. See chapter 2. Barrett (*Acts*, 241–42) is incorrect to assign a late origin to this prayer on the basis that it uses Scripture to "minimize the role of earthly rulers" since much Second-Temple literature did the same.

158. Jervell (*Apostelgeschichte*, 232) comments that the phrase "God of glory" is not merely ornamental because it is set in a context where Stephen's face (6:15) and vision (7:55) emphasize the divine glory.

in the OT at Ps 29:3 in a context where God is said to sit as "king forever" (Ps 29:10). Although there may be no direct reference to the Psalm here,[159] the reference to glory in Acts 7:55 and in the Psalm implies a relationship to throne-room imagery. Thus, the speech is framed by references to transcendent sovereignty.[160] This concept is taken up explicitly in 7:47–50—the "Most High" does not dwell in buildings made with human hands, but sits on the heavenly throne with the earth as a footstool. No building can contain God, for God created everything. This transcendent imagery is directly related to the temple, which in some Second-Temple literature becomes less important than the heavenly, throne-room temple. The emphasis focuses attention on the transcendent God who must be worshiped appropriately.[161] Here, again, the reader finds a reference to God as the Great King arrayed next to an image that reflects Jesus' status as the messianic king ("at the right hand"). Thus, although God has restored the kingdom through King Messiah, God continues to be characterized as the Sovereign who controls everything, especially the restoration.

Acts 8:4—19:20

In this middle section, Jesus' participation in divine rule reminds the reader that it remains God's Kingdom and two brief references to the kingdom of God[162] provide the reader with further reminders. Paul encourages the believers by saying that entrance into the "kingdom of God" requires suffering (14:22). Since the reader has already come to see the reinterpreted kingdom as restored in Jesus, Paul's words are likely to be taken as referring to present entrance.[163] Paul's statement, however, may also suggest that some aspect of this entrance has not happened yet and awaits fulfillment at a later time, just as the ultimate "persecutions" await the end.[164] This would fit with Luke's portrait in 1:1—8:3, reflecting a now/not yet kingdom. Here, because the reader has read Paul proclaiming that Jesus is the Davidic king (13:31–41), calling this a work of God that must not be rejected (13:40–41)[165] implies that Paul's message about Jesus is really about entrance into God's kingdom. Therefore, just as elsewhere, the "forgiveness of sins" offered by the messianic king

159. Barrett, *Acts*, 341. See, however, Fitzmyer (*Acts*, 369).

160. Witherington, *Acts*, 264; Johnson, *Acts*, 114. Munoa ("Jesus," 305–14) points to the scene as one in the *merkavah* (throne-room) vision tradition.

161. Tannehill, *Narrative*, 92–93; Witherington, *Acts*, 263. The issue here is any attempt to confine or manipulate God (see chapter 5).

162. While Tannehill (*Narrative*, 115) correctly identifies the references to kingdom of God as linking Philip and Saul/Paul, these references also indicate that the same kingdom is offered throughout the work.

163. *Contra* Haenchen, *Acts*, 436. *Contra* Lindemann ("Herrschaft," 211) neither 1:6 nor 14:22 deny the kingdom's nearness. In both cases, the kingdom has been reinterpreted through Jesus' ascension to the divine throne. The kingdom is present in an ethical/spiritual manner that includes eschatological elements (such as the Spirit's presence), but awaits a final consummation; people now enter into the kingdom, rather than await its coming.

164. So Barrett, *Acts*, 686; Mattill, "Way," 531–46.

165. *Contra* Haenchen (*Acts*, 413) the "work" is not God rejecting the Jews, but the divine eschatological action in joining Jew and gentile as God's people (Pesch, *Apostelgeschichte*, I, 43).

(13:38) is ultimately aimed at entrance into the kingdom of God.[166] Likewise, at Ephesus, while Paul has previously presented Jesus as the Davidic-messiah king, the reader finds this preaching paralleled with arguing persuasively about the "kingdom of God" (19:8). In Paul's proclamation, the message concerning the messianic king is ultimately the message about the Great King.[167]

As previously (Δέσποτα in 4:24), God is considered the Creator who is Lord over heaven and earth (14:15; 17:24).[168] Luke's reader knows that, in the OT, Israel was itself God's creative "work," but now the redefined people of God (Jew and gentile)[169] receive this designation (13:40–41;[170] 15:16–18[171]). This continues the motif that God is the heavenly Creator King.

No other king can stand in God's way, an idea vividly portrayed to the reader in Acts 12.[172] Herod (specifically called "king"—12:1) acts against the church's leaders (12:1–3). The reader, therefore, classifies him as a θεομάχος—a God-fighter, given Gamaliel's warning (5:38–39).[173] To the reader, all kings are supposed to be obedient to the divine will, but this one opposes it. In so doing, Herod has gone beyond the role that God has given him and God intervenes to show who is truly in control.[174] Peter's rescue (12:6–11), then, can be seen as a divine action directed against Herod—a warning that he opposes a greater power. When the prisoner cannot be found, all the king (showing himself to be a tyrant)[175] can do is kill the guards who the reader knows are without blame in this case.[176] While killing

166. This is not just the proleptic entrance by the church into the kingdom (*contra* Pesch, *Apostelgeschichte*, I, 64), but because Paul's speech confirms the kingdom images seen in 1:1—8:3, entrance into the kingdom becomes the proclamation's goal.

167. Grässer (*Forschungen*, 300–301) assumes that, since the kingdom of God is something that the Ephesians need persuasion about, it is not a present experience. However, if the issue is properly interpreting the kingdom and its relationship to Jesus as the Christ, then this is exactly what one would expect.

168. So Bibb, "Characterization," 243. See also chapter 6. Peter's vision of the animals (10:10–15) relies on the creator image since the Creator has the right to determine which animal is unclean or clean (Pesch, *Apostelgeschichte*, I, 339).

169. See chapter 5.

170. Fitzmyer ("Role," 519) correctly sees "work" here as referring to the "word of salvation" being presented in Jesus. *Contra* Hansen ("Preaching," 305–6) the immediate context (13:38–39, 47) points to salvation (entrance into God's kingdom), rather than the resurrection, as the divine work. Certainly Jesus' resurrection is a key element in this salvation, but Hansen's conclusion narrows the focus too much. Ultimately, however, Paul's warning anticipates the rejection prompted by the gentiles' response to this saving "word". Thus, God's "work" is the united (Jew-gentile) people of God.

171. So Bechard, *Paul*, 113–18; Gaventa, *Acts*, 218; also see chapter 5.

172. *Contra* Haenchen (*Acts*, 388) the adversaries are God and Herod not Peter and Herod.

173. Morton, "Acts 12:1–19," 69; Schneider, *Apostelgeschichte*, II, 105. This notion is enhanced by the references to Passover, which link the event to the actions taken against Jesus and associate Herod with the Pharaoh in Exodus (Gaventa, *Acts*, 183; Tannehill, *Narrative*, 153–54).

174. See chapter 2. *Second Maccabees* refers to this motif in suggesting that the king should not think that his freedom to punish the Jews will continue forever or go unpunished (7:16–17).

175. As a tyrant, Herod invokes a seemingly arbitrary persecution against the church and is only interested in stirring up good favor with the "Jews" during Passover (cf. Haenchen, *Acts*, 388; Pesch, *Apostelgeschichte*, I, 363–64). On tyrants and death-of-tyrant scenes, see Allen, *Death* (1997).

176. The text may only indicate the guards' imprisonment, but there is a strong implication that execution took place since Herod has previously executed James (so Johnson, *Acts*, 214).

the guards is a *topos* in rescue miracles, and may well have been the expected punishment for their failure, this does not absolve Herod.[177] The tyrant did not allow for divine action, therefore, he reacted without regard for his responsibility to act justly. God is shown to be the true King, embarrassing and countermanding the tyrant.

Herod, however, does not learn his lesson and the conflict between divine and earthly kings continues. The reader's expectations for the king involve his pursuing and maintaining peace,[178] yet it is Herod's unexplained (and, therefore perceived by the reader as unwarranted) anger that requires the people of Tyre and Sidon to make peace with him (12:20). The king is also thought responsible for the people's physical needs, but they remain unfed because Herod is angry (12:20). Even though Tyre and Sidon are not Herod's territories, he would have an obligation to honor treaties, especially with regard to sustenance. By contrast, God has been portrayed as concerned with royal responsibilities—the church enjoys "peace" after God has intervened (9:31) and Jesus was sent to preach it to Israel (10:36).[179] Also, God's warning, through Agabus, concerning a famine (11:28) illustrates the divine interest in providing food for God's people. Thus, Herod pales in comparison with God, but, nonetheless, accepts adulation due a god. Such acclamation was common during the Hellenistic period, but was strongly rejected by the Jews out of faithfulness to God.[180] Herod's failure immediately brings punishment—the "angel of the Lord" strikes him, he is eaten by worms and dies (12:23). Similar scenes are found in the reader's extra-text (2 Macc 9:8–10 and *Ant.* 17:168–70).[181] In both cases, the punishment is that considered appropriate to a tyrant, especially one who sets himself up in opposition to God.[182] This suggests that Luke is relating this event in the form of a familiar *topos* concerning judgment on wicked rulers. The reader would recognize that Herod has tried to fight God by attacking God's people and accepting divine status. However, God has intervened to defend his people, demonstrating that God is the true God and the true King.

Acts 19:21—28:31

In the final section, the reader again encounters teaching concerning the Lord Jesus Christ (20:20; 28:23, 31) placed parallel with proclaiming the "kingdom of God" (20:25; 28:23, 31), continuing the emphasis on the connection between the messianic king and the Great

177. *Contra* Pesch, *Apostelgeschichte*, I, 367.

178. On the expectations of God as King see chapter 2.

179. A peace is offered between God and humanity (Haenchen, *Acts*, 352), just as the people here seek a peace between king and humanity.

180. Schille, *Apostelgeschichte*, 275.

181. Barrett (*Acts*, 591) lists other literature reflecting this divine punishment. The 2 Maccabees incident is closer to Luke's account than the Josephus one since it includes the tyrant accepting divine status. Josephus (*Ant.* 19:338) does attribute Herod Agrippa's death to divine punishment for accepting god-like status, however in this case he does not mention "worms."

182. Strom ("Background," 289–92) argues that this passage relates to the judgment against the king of Tyre in Ezek 27–28. However, Herod is not truly Tyre's king and there are closer parallels with 2 Maccabees and Josephus than with Ezekiel.

King.[183] Luke reminds the reader not only that these kingdoms do not conflict, but also that hearing about the restored Davidic king is necessary for understanding the reinterpreted kingdom of God.

The reader finds other allusions to God's kingdom in this section. While speaking to the Ephesian elders, Paul calls the believers an assembly acquired (περιεποιήσατο) by God (20:28).[184] Encountering this Greek word, the reader should recall how God described that faithful Israel would be "my treasured possession (περιποίησιν)" (Exod 19:5–6 [23:21–22 LXX]). The allusion suggests that this new community is supposed to stand in relation to God in the same way that Israel was supposed to in the OT.[185] Patrick comments that the Exodus text pictures Israel as a "political entity" with God as their King. They were to enter into a constitutional arrangement with their King by obedience to their Sovereign's commands.[186] This parallel suggests the new community is to stand as God's covenant people, God's kingdom people. The image is reinforced to the reader when Paul mentions the "inheritance" among the sanctified given by divine grace (20:32).[187] Again, the allusion to faithful Israel seems intended since Deut 4:20–21 calls the Promised Land the inheritance of the people, just after referring to the people as the divine possession. Further emphasizing the connection to Israel, Deut 33:3 refers to obedient Israel as God's "holy ones"—the sanctified.[188] Paul will later refer to the inheritance the gentiles receive when they have transferred from Satan's dominion to God's (26:18). Thus, Luke seems to understand the "inheritance" to be a place in the kingdom. The obedient covenant people have a place in the Promised Land, now reinterpreted (at least for the present) as the restored kingdom.

Finally, the reader is likely to pick up on another allusion to God's kingdom—Paul tells the council that he has "lived" before God with a good conscience (23:1). "Lived" here is a form of πολιτεύομαι, which, while referring to the conduct of life, also connotes one's citizenship.[189] In 2 Maccabees (6:1; 11:25) it is used for the Jews conducting their lives

---

183. Prieur (*Verkündigung*, 45–46) sought to determine what "Scripture proofs" Paul offers concerning Jesus and how this relates to proclaiming God's kingdom by looking at the speeches Paul gives. However, he leaves out elements (the "Son of God" references) that portray Jesus as the Davidic king. He misses, therefore, that this proclamation attempts to persuade that Jesus is the king and through him God has restored the reinterpreted kingdom. There is a greater flaw in Prieur's work—he only examines evidence offered by *Paul*. When Philip related preaching about Jesus and the kingdom (8:12), the summary nature of the preaching suggested the reader was to rely on the presentation in 1:1—8:3 for understanding the reference. Here as well, the reader would be dependent on all previous arguments regarding this, not just Paul's. This failure to follow narrative developments seems to be characteristic in Prieur's work since he begins his analysis from the last reference to kingdom proclamation (28:23, 31), rather than the first.

184. While the reference to "his own blood" is striking and has engendered various interpretations (see Brown, "Does," 552–53; Fitzmyer, *Acts*, 680; Witherington, *Acts*, 623), it should not be allowed to detract from the main point—the community is a divine possession.

185. Tannehill, *Narrative*, 258–59.

186. Patrick, "Kingdom," 75.

187. *Contra* Barrett (*Acts*, 981) the "inheritance," the place among the sanctified, is also a present event. While some elements may remain for the future, its blessings are lived currently (cf. Luke 15:31—the older brother already has his inheritance blessings).

188. See also 1QS 11:7, 8.

189. BAGD, 686; Schille, *Apostelgeschichte*, 425.

in accordance with the divine, royal law. Given this extra-text, then, it would appear to indicate that Paul has lived in accordance with God's kingdom rule.[190]

Luke also reaffirms the divine role as Creator. The reference to idols and the world-wide Artemis worship in Demetrius' speech (19:25–27) should reminds the reader how Paul argued about God and idols in Athens.[191] Since idols are created things, and God has created everything, divine superiority to idols (and other 'gods' like Artemis) is affirmed. God remains the Sovereign Creator.

The reader finds other rulers (just as with Herod in Acts 12) portrayed in a less-than-flattering light when compared with God. When the High Priest commands that Paul be struck, Paul declares divine judgment on him. While the reader might remain uncertain about whether or not Paul did realize that the High Priest was the one he was speaking about,[192] the reader is likely to perceive the irony in calling Ananias, the "leader of the people" (23:2–5). It is the divine law, just as it is God's High Priest, so, ultimately, God is the leader of the people. Even as God's representative leader, Ananias fails to live up to the proper standard, acting toward Paul in "violation of the Law"; the irony being heightened by the contrast with Paul who acknowledges the law's demands.[193]

The Roman governor Felix is attributed with achieving "peace" and showing "foresight [providence]" (24:2). The reader has previously seen these features characterizing the Divine King. Consequently, Felix is receiving high praise. However, because the words come from the rhetor Tertullus, the reader may see them as mere flattery. Initially, the reader, familiar with rhetorical practices and, thus, knowing that it is good form to begin a speech with a *captatio benevolentiae*, may understand that Tertullus' *captatio* (24:2–4) is lengthy because the *exordium* was necessary to build the case in legal proceedings.[194] When the reader observes that Paul's *captatio* is shorter and more direct (24:10), the assessment is likely to change, being considered effusive.[195] Further, since Luke's reader may well be aware (it is noted in Tacitus' *Annals* 12:54; Josephus' *Ant.* 20:8, *War* 2:13) that Felix's rule was marked by serious uprisings that had to be violently quelled, the praise would seem ill fitting. Thus, simply classifying "peace" and "providence" as "stock phrases" misses the irony employed by Luke.[196] For the reader, it is not the Romans, but God, who has achieved peace and acted providentially. As such, when Tertullus charges sedition, the reader may well consider it ironic that the Jewish leaders are commending a Roman's ruling qualities, an act that some Jews might understand as sedition against their true King, God (and God's messiah).

---

190. Barrett, *Acts*, 1057–58; Witherington, *Acts*, 687.

191. Witherington, *Acts*, 591. Demetrius is an unreliable character as is seen by his desire for profit (19:24–25; Tannehill, *Narrative*, 243). Thus, while the reader should identify the similarity to the Athens speech, Demetrius' interpretation will not be valued by the reader (*contra* Johnson, *Acts*, 347). Tannehill (*Narrative*, 243) correctly recognizes the similarities to the Athens speech, but fails to follow through with his earlier observation about Demetrius' unreliability, calling Demetrius' claims "justified."

192. Cf. Barrett, *Acts*, 1061–62; Haenchen, *Acts*, 638.

193. So Johnson, *Acts*, 397; Pesch, *Apostelgeschichte*, II, 243; Tannehill, *Narrative*, 286.

194. Winter, "Official," 320–321; Witherington, *Acts*, 705.

195. So Pesch, *Apostelgeschichte*, II, 257; Schneider, *Apostelgeschichte*, II, 347; Tannehill, *Narrative*, 297.

196. *Contra* Witherington *Acts*, 705–6.

The only ruler (besides Jesus) who gets a generally favorable treatment is Agrippa II. He is repeatedly referred to as "king" (25:13–14, 24, 26; 26:2, 7, 13, 19, 26–27, 30), thus the reader sees royalty as his chief characteristic. Paul considers him worthy to judge the issues (26:2–3), yet even Agrippa fails to live up to the standard for God's kings because he refuses to express his allegiance to the Christ (26:28). Caesar (called "Imperial Majesty"—25:26) also pales in comparison since the reader finds Paul continuing to proclaim the "kingdom of God" in the seat of Caesar's power (28:31).[197] God remains superior to those styled king, leader, or majesty by the world.

Finally, the reader learns about the ruler (Satan) that ultimately opposes God.[198] Paul explains his commission to turn the gentiles from "darkness to light" and from the "power of Satan to God" (26:18). Just as in the Ananias and Sapphira story (5:1–11)[199] and the account concerning Bar-Jesus,[200] the devil opposes the divine will. The reader has seen this conflict elsewhere in the way magic is associated with those who oppose God (8:4–13; 13:4–12),[201] in the opposition offered by the pythonic spirit in Philippi (16:16–18), and in references to exorcisms (19:11–20). The conflict between Jesus and the devil (as well as Jesus' supremacy) is apparent in Peter characterizing Jesus as healing those "oppressed by the devil" (10:38). Thus, throughout Acts, the reader can sense that an ultimate opponent exists, yet remains inferior. Here, Luke's Paul restates both the enmity and the inferiority— Satan stands opposed to God as darkness is to light, yet God transfers those in darkness to light and those under Satan's power into God's kingdom. God remains the Great King and no ruler, human or otherwise, can stand against God's kingdom.

Summary Portrait

The divine restoration of the kingdom is a theme integral to Acts. It is initially prepared for in the question asked by the disciples, in Jesus' response, in the ascension, and in the replacement of Judas. Peter's speech (2:14–36) climaxes with the statement that Jesus is "Lord and Messiah," arguing that Jesus has ascended to the Davidic throne—now the divine throne. David's throne continues to play a prominent role in the proclamation (4:24–30; 5:31) and its restoration is found to be both a present and future event (3:12–26). Acts 8:4—19:20 maintains the characterization that God restores the kingdom through Jesus as the Davidic descendant, who has been made king by God raising him to the throne. As king, Jesus participates in ruling functions over God's Kingdom (10:36, 42; 17:24, 31). This

197. So Pesch, *Apostelgeschichte*, II, 311.

198. Moessner ("Ironic," 43) notes that Satan is first portrayed as Israel's primary enemy in the temptation scene (Luke 4:1–12). Jesus, who would sit on David's throne over the "house of Jacob" (Luke 1:32–33) does battle with Satan, not nationalistic foes. Also, Satan filled Judas' heart, leading him to betray Jesus (Luke 22:3). Luke, therefore, is consistent in redefining Israel's enemies and in portraying Satan as the primary foe.

199. Jervell (*Apostelgeschichte*, 196) correctly points out that the real combatants here were Satan and the Spirit (4:3), rather than the human actors.

200. Analogies between Bar-Jesus and Ananias and Sapphira, however, should not be pressed beyond the general opposition from Satan (*contra* Johnson, *Acts*, 224) since the latter incident did not involve magic and reflected justice being rendered within the community, rather than an external conflict.

201. Johnson, *Acts*, 224; Gaventa, *Acts*, 135–36, 194–95.

Kingdom remains the focus as preaching about Jesus ultimately refers to God's kingdom (14:22; 19:8). In Acts 19:21—28:31, Jesus is the "Righteous One" who will judge with "justice," and the resurrected messiah who sits on the Davidic throne, which is now the Divine throne, giving hope to Israel.

Throughout, the kingdom of God remains God's kingdom even though Jesus is now messianic king. The manner by which the kingdom is restored, however, is reinterpreted. Nationalistic hopes have been removed (although 3:12–26 may allow for such hopes to be fulfilled at Jesus' return), but the eschatological kingdom blessings (the Spirit) have been poured out by the ascended Davidic king. God, the one who establishes kings, has given Israel its promised king, although his throne is heavenly rather than earthly.

God is portrayed as the heavenly Sovereign through references to divine action in creation (14:15; 17:24) and in creating the community (13:40–41; 15:16–18). Herod's humiliation and death demonstrate that God is the true God and true King. Thus, God is the Great King who restores the Davidic one. Because God is sovereign, God has the power to raise Jesus to the throne and offer deliverance through him to the people. Consequently, the core of the "good news" presented by messengers like Philip and Paul continues to be supported by sovereign authority—an authority that is crucial as the kingdom is expanded to include Samaritans and gentiles.

In Acts 19:21—28:31 God has restored the Davidic king and thus the "hope of Israel" through the resurrection. In so doing, God has acquired the kingdom as a possession, giving the (reinterpreted) covenant people of God an inheritance in that nation. As with Herod Antipas, other rulers, human (the High Priest, Felix, and Agrippa) and otherwise (Satan), cannot hope to stand in comparison to the Great King. God remains responsible for the restored kingdom and superior to all pretenders. As such, God is the sole factor supporting the proclamation of the restored kingdom and the sole source for the hope, peace, and providence offered in it. Additionally, allegiance to God's kingdom does not mean seditious activity toward earthly rulers, a factor supporting Paul's claim to innocence.

Johnson notes that the disciples' question about the kingdom's restoration in Acts 1:6 raises an issue concerning whether Jesus' claim to messiahship is justified.[202] Given the reader's conception that the kingdom is restored (in a reinterpreted way) it becomes clear that God is portrayed as the King who restores that kingdom. As such, God is responsible for authenticating Jesus' messianic claim—God has raised and exalted him, making him "Lord and Messiah." Moreover, God restores this kingdom to Israel and God alone sets the *times and seasons* for its restoration. Through miracles and the Spirit's outpouring God provides evidence for the claims concerning Jesus.[203] It is the divine hand that controls rulers' actions and acts for the benefit of the kingdom's messengers. In this way, the presentation that God is the Great King supports the message about the restored kingdom since God has crowned Jesus as the messianic king and offered evidence on his behalf.

---

202. Johnson, *Acts*, 29.

203. Schneider (*Apostelgeschichte*, I, 266) suggests that, while the crowd in Jerusalem could not have been witnesses to the ascension, they were witnesses to the Spirit being poured out at Pentecost (2:1–12). Thus, Luke's Peter uses this pouring out as evidence (2:33). In essence, then, God authorizes the message through the Spirit's witness, a function of the Spirit identified in chapter 3.

5

The King Who Establishes His People

Building on one factor in characterization—the relationships between the character and other characters in the narrative—this chapter examines the way God relates to the restored kingdom's citizens. Indications about who are those citizens, what is characteristic of or required from them, and what God offers them, help the reader fill in the characterization. The reader discovers God in sovereign control over and responding appropriately to the kingdom's citizens, which supports the claim that God has restored the kingdom, although in a different way than expected. Parker,[1] borrowing the term from Gross,[2] argues that *Motivtransposition*, the transforming of nationalistic ideas to a spiritual and ethical plane, was a recurring feature in Jewish thought and that Luke uses this idea. This chapter, then, argues that the reader sees the kingdom presently restored on a different plane, although a culminating eschatological event seems expected. The "spiritual" element is not simply internal to the person, but marked by the Spirit's dynamic presence. Since both the restoration and the kingdom are reinterpreted by Luke, this chapter identifies how these elements have been transformed (at least for the present) into a pneumatic/ethical framework.

Who are God's People?

The first element for examination is identifying those who are marked as God's people, the true kingdom citizens. Initially, the kingdom is for the Jews (Israel), but there is a hint of *more* to come. That becomes evident in the middle portions of Acts, as Jews, Samaritans, and gentiles are all included. Finally, this more-than-Jewish kingdom is affirmed in the final portions of the narrative.

God of the Jews and More?

The reference to the Father's promise (1:4) may provide one reason for the disciples' question concerning the kingdom being restored *to Israel*. As the Father's promise, the Spirit's coming indicates the blessings bestowed by a father.[3] Luke's reader knows (see chapter

1. Parker, *Apokatastasis*, 38–39.
2. Gross, "Motivtransposition," 325–34.
3. Tannehill, *Narrative*, 13.

2) that the metaphor reflecting God as Father indicates a particularly close relationship between God and Israel, established by God creating Israel through the Exodus (cf. Exod 4:22; Deut 32:6; Hos 1:1). It is telling, therefore, that in Acts 2 the reader finds Peter addressing the "Men of Judea" (2:14), beginning the proclamation about Jesus with reference to "You that are Israelites" (2:22) and ending it by referencing the whole "house of Israel" (2:36). These addresses *to Israel* are repeated throughout 1:1—8:3,[4] and, while providing common ground between speaker and hearer, they even more so emphasize that the message is important *for Israel*. However, Israel is to be understood in reference to the people rather than the nation.

Allusions to the covenant reinforce this. In 3:12–26 the reader finds God described as the God of Abraham, Isaac, and Jacob (3:13)—i.e., the God in covenant with Israel.[5] The people are the "descendants" of the prophets and of the covenant made with the fathers (specifically the Abrahamic one—3:25) and it is for them "first" that God has raised up Jesus as a blessing (implying the Abrahamic blessing is fulfilled).[6] Barrett suggests this is an invitation "to take their place in the New Covenant."[7] However, Luke seems to be emphasizing the fulfillment of the Abrahamic covenant rather than offering an invitation to something new. Although emphasis is placed on the Abrahamic covenant, its fulfillment is in keeping with other divine promises (about the Spirit and the Davidic king). Peter's reference to the "God of our ancestors" while addressing the council (5:30) continues this motif.[8] Therefore, *Israel* is those expected to receive the promised blessings as God's covenant people.

Luke's Use of the Title "Israel"

In Luke's work the term "Israel" always refers to the historic people of God and is never used specifically to refer to the Christians, even the Jewish-Christian section.[9] It does not follow, however, that Luke thinks these Jewish-Christians did not represent Israel's fulfillment. By avoiding the specific designation, Luke evades the national and religious limitations such a label conveys (while leaving open the possibility for an ultimate national fulfillment for Israel). Luke portrays Israel's promises as fulfilled in the kingdom, thus making those who enter into the kingdom the true Israel (having responded obediently they are God's covenant people).

---

4. Acts 3:12; 4:8, 10; 5:31. Gamaliel speaks to the "Fellow Israelites" (5:35). Ellingworth ("'Men,'" 153–55; also Jervell, *Apostelgeschichte*, 123) argues that even the address "Friends" (1:16) points to the audience's Jewishness.

5. Pesch, *Apostelgeschichte* , I, 152–53; Gaventa, *Acts*, 86.

6. Tannehill, *Narrative*, 55. Dunn (*Baptism*, 47) argues similarly concerning the Pentecost narrative. The Spirit's outpouring would recall the New Covenant expressed in Ezek 36:27 and Jer 31:33. Thus, conceivably, Luke was expecting the reader to see the call to repentance as an invitation to enter into the New Covenant, where blessings promised Israel would be restored.

7. Barrett, *Acts*, 212.

8. See Bibb, "Characterization ," 200; Witherington, *Acts*, 232.

9. See Hauser, *Strukturen*, 91; Jervell, "Israel," 76.

This conclusion is not altered by the gentiles being called a "people for his name" (15:14) rather than Israel.[10] In the context (discussed below) the gentiles are included in the kingdom under the Davidic ruler. This unites them with the Jews as one covenant people under divine rule, receiving a portion in Israel's blessings. Wolter makes a substantially similar argument—Luke uses Israel in a *denotative* sense to refer to the Jewish people, but in a *connotative* sense (what it signifies) it is applied to those who have responded obediently.[11] Thus, Jew and gentile receive the blessings promised Israel.

Wolter also argued that the disciples' original question in 1:6 implied that Israel, because it was the special heir to God's kingdom, was to be installed in a ruling position over the world.[12] For Wolter, what Luke presents instead is that Israel has been divided and Rome, rather than Jerusalem, has become the "Zentrum einer universalen Basileia." While Luke does present a divided Israel, Jerusalem remains the center for church leadership throughout Acts (see below). Further, since Luke offers no reason to forsake the Jerusalem leadership and does not relate any community decision being made in Rome, it seems mistaken to claim that Rome has become the new center. God has not forsaken Israel's hopes for universal rule; instead those hopes (at least presently) are reinterpreted in relation to the redefined Israel that participates in God's kingdom.

In Stephen's speech God is characterized as the covenant God (of "our ancestor Abraham"—7:2). However, this speech is viewed as treating covenant related issues (Law and temple) negatively. Since this reflects on Jewish identity (Israel's faithfulness),[13] it is necessary to determine if Luke's reader would agree with such an interpretation. The reader finds an initial guide in the testimony being described as suborned and the witnesses explicitly labeled false (6:11, 13). This causes the reader to consider the charges against Stephen as unreliable.[14] Commentators object that, while the charges about Jesus (6:14) are false (because Jesus never made such a statement), Stephen remains a temple and Law critic.[15] However, Luke has informed his reader that the charges and the witnesses are untrustworthy. Therefore, even the statements about Jesus destroying the temple and altering the Mosaic customs (6:14) are to be understood as false.[16] As the reader moves

---

10. *Contra* Dahl, "'People,'" 319–27; Jervell, "Gottes," 15–19; Prieur, *Verkündigung*, 32.

11. Wolter, "Israel's," 320–24.

12. Wolter, "'Reich,'" 548.

13. Jervell (*Apostelgeschichte*, 225–26) stresses how important the charge against Stephen was: "eine lästerliche Rede gegen Mose ist eine Rede gegen Israel als Gottesvolk, weil das Gesetz Israel als Volk Gottes kennzeichnet." Thus, if Stephen is anti-Law, he is anti-Israel.

14. This factor is noted by numerous commentators, see especially Larsson, "Temple-Criticism," 382; Tannehill, *Narrative*, 243; Witherington, *Acts*, 257–58.

15. Pesch, *Apostelgeschichte*, I, 238; Schille, *Apostelgeschichte*, 176–77, 185; Schneider, *Apostelgeschichte*, I, 438.

16. *Contra* Barrett, *Acts*, 319–20, 328.

through the speech, then, the inclination will be towards interpreting it as not violating these issues.

The reader is aware of various views about the temple during this period. Some (cf. 2 Maccabees) saw the second temple continuing as the dwelling place for God (in line with OT conceptions), even if it was not as glorious as the former temple (cf. Hag 2:9) or the heavenly throne-room temple (cf. *1 En.* 90:28–29). Others rejected this temple because it or the service done it had become impure (cf. *1 En.* 89:72–73; 93:9; *T. Levi* 17:10; *Jub.* 23:21), or because the proper design was given to Moses, not David (cf. *Apoc. Bar.* 4:2–6; 11QT). It, nevertheless, remains unclear whether any group (even the Qumran sectarians) believed the temple was obsolete (1QS never makes an explicit statement in this regard, and the Damascus Document [col. 6] envisions some cultic participation). The temple (and Jerusalem in general) also figured in eschatological views during this period, with many expecting that it would be restored, functioning for their salvation.[17] In this case, the reader is informed by the false charges and the previous positive evaluations of the temple (2:46; 3:1; 5:12, 20, 25, 42)[18] that whatever Stephen says, he is not anti-"the holy place."

The reader may note that in Stephen's speech worship takes place outside Jerusalem.[19] This could imply that the holy place is not the temple, but it seems doubtful since the repetition of and focus on γῆ in 7:3–5 connects the promise concerning 'land' to worship in "this place." Where the original (Exod 3:12) specifically mentions the mountain (Horeb), Luke's Stephen has inserted "place" so as to recall 6:13 and the reference to "this holy place."[20] Thus, the reader sees the worship occurring in the Promised Land, in Jerusalem, and specifically at the temple.[21]

The Land, the Temple, and Jerusalem in Acts

While "land" features prominently in 7:1–7, the reader finds few other direct affirmations concerning this promise. Since the "land" seems so closely tied to nationalistic hopes, it appears to have faded into "universal restoration" (3:21) that awaits the end. Still, OT and Second-Temple perspectives on the land ultimately focused on Jerusalem (Zion). This was where Israel would be restored (Isa 26:1–2; 52:1; Joel 3:17; Zech 8:8; *1 En.* 90:28–36; *Jub.* 1:28–29; *Pss. Sol.* 11) and God would rule over the nations (Isa 60:14; Jer 3:17; Ezek 38–39; *Pss. Sol.* 17:23–27; Tob 13:11–12). Therefore, the emphasis on the "place" in Jerusalem is in keeping with Jewish perspectives on Israel's restoration and divine rule.[22]

---

17. See Chance, *Jerusalem*, 7–10.

18. Luke evaluates the temple favorably throughout his work (for discussion see Weinert, "Meaning," 85–89).

19. So Fitzmyer, *Acts*, 366.

20. Schneider, *Apostelgeschichte*, I, 455; Tannehill, *Narrative*, 92. This replacement is missed by Fitzmyer, *Acts*, 372; Johnson, *Acts*, 116; Pesch, *Apostelgeschichte*, I, 249; Witherington, *Acts*, 266. Barrett (*Acts*, 345) correctly notes the replacement, but incorrectly identifies the OT context as making the land of Israel the place the worship occurs.

21. See Larsson, "Temple-Criticism," 386–88.

22. Cf. Chance, *Jerusalem*, 10–14.

Indeed, Jerusalem plays an important role throughout Acts. Various scholars note how Jerusalem remains the center for the church even as it expands—there is a consistent "outward-and-return" pattern.[23] Wolter, however, claims that in Luke's formulation Jerusalem is not the "Mittelpunkt, sondern der Ausgangspunkt" removing Jerusalem (and Israel) as the capital for the universal kingdom.[24] Similarly, Parsons argues that Jerusalem is the "pivot" between Jesus and the mission to the gentiles rather than the center for the church.[25] However, being the *Ausgangspunkt* (or the pivot) does not remove Jerusalem from being the *Mittelpunkt* since the story continuously returns here and it remains the locus for decision making throughout Acts (argued below). Jerusalem is important for Israel's restoration and is never abandoned; it is in Jerusalem that God has brought together "devout Jews" from every nation (Acts 2:5); and it is these who continue to lead the church from Jerusalem.

While Chance argues that Jerusalem and the temple are significant for the gentile mission,[26] he misses the impact (described later) of the temple's Lord commanding this mission (Acts 22:19–21). Bachmann noted that, in both Luke's Gospel and Acts, Jerusalem and the temple are the places where divine universal salvation is announced.[27] In Luke 24:47 Jesus commanded the disciples to preach "repentance and forgiveness" to "all nations, beginning from Jerusalem." At Acts 1:8 the disciples are commanded to stay *in Jerusalem* in order to receive the Spirit that becomes the power for their mission. Thus, the reader is familiar with seeing the center for Jewish life (Jerusalem, the temple) as consistent with the gentile mission.

Some argue that the temple gates being shut after Paul's removal (21:30) dramatically ends the temple's importance for the reader (and the church).[28] This, however, would require an open denunciation, yet Paul's defense speeches confirm the temple as the location for divine visions and worship. Instead, the gate-closing should be understood as these Jews demonstrating concern to prevent any further defilement.[29] Chance's argument that this passage parallels the veil being rent at Jesus' death[30] is tenuous at best. Even if one were to interpret the rent veil as signaling Jerusalem's destruction,[31] the parallel between the veil and the gate fails because the gate closing is not presented as a divine act, where the divine activity is signaled in Luke 23:45 by the accompanying darkness. Jerusalem and the temple, therefore, remain significant for the mission (and the reader) throughout Acts.

---

23. See Alexander, "Reading," 426; also Chance, *Jerusalem*, 101; Hill, "Acts 6:1—8:4," 137; O'Neill, *Theology*, 63 (although he believes Jerusalem is rejected and left behind); Scott, "Acts 2:9–22," 101.

24. Wolter, "'Reich,'" 558.

25. Parsons, "Place," 167–68; also Giblin, *Destruction* (1985).

26. Chance, *Jerusalem*, 99–112.

27. Bachmann, *Jerusalem*, 132–70.

28. Fitzmyer, *Acts*, 697; Moessner, "'Completed,'" 215.

29. So Barrett, *Acts*, 1021.

30. Chance, *Jerusalem*, 121–22; following Talbert, *Literary*, 17–18.

31. As Allison, *End*, 31–32.

Would the reader think the temple was being de-emphasized by the reference to worship at the "tent of the testimony" in the wilderness?[32] Although God gave the tabernacle pattern to Moses (7:44), indicating its divinely ordained status, the people misused it (treating it as the "tent of Moloch"—7:43). Consequently, they did not offer sacrifices to God (7:42) but to Moloch. For Luke, the "tent of testimony" is considered the divinely ordained place for worship, but he also implies that this is the one in which Moloch was being served, suggesting both true and false worship going on at the same time.[33] While this tabernacle initially fulfilled God's promise concerning worship (7:7), it was misused. The reader, therefore, finds that the tabernacle worship is tainted. The same pattern is then depicted for the temple—Israel treated the tabernacle in an idolatrous manner, just as the reader now sees Stephen (through the linking words concerning "hands"—7:41, 48)[34] arguing his contemporaries are treating the temple,[35] which also was built with divine favor (7:46). Therefore, both the temple and the tabernacle were built with divine approval; however, both have become victims of corrupt use. Both the tabernacle and the temple, nevertheless, continued to be places for divine worship in their respective times. The reader, as a result, finds Stephen condemning the temple's misuse, not the temple itself. It, therefore, is not a temple critique, but a critique of Jewish practice.[36]

Should the reader see a contrast between David and Solomon that suggests the latter did something wrong in building the temple? This is not likely since: 1) δέ on its own is not a strong enough contrastive to force such a view.[37] Instead, the contrast occurs in 7:48 with ἀλλά, the stronger adversative.[38] 2) The reader would assume David *intended* to build a place of worship for Israel (the "house of Jacob") because the σκήνωμα in 7:46 would echo the cognate σκηνή used in reference to the tabernacles (7:43, 44). 3) The Greek in 7:48 does not mention a 'house.' Moreover, the reader does not set the house *against* the tent since both are made with hands.[39] Rather, the reader identifies the action toward the temple as akin to that toward the tent—both were treated as idols (things made with hands), ways to manipulate, localize, and control gods.[40] That Luke's Stephen sees the people rather than the temple as the issue is confirmed for the reader when, at the point where Stephen could

---

32. This suggestion is offered by several commentators (Barrett, *Acts*, 371; Johnson, *Acts*, 132; Koester, *Dwelling*, 83; Lake and Cadbury, *Beginnings*, 70; Richard, *Acts 6:1—8:4*, 326–30), claiming that Luke's Stephen builds a contrast between the non-localized tabernacle and the localized temple.

33. Jervell, *Apostelgeschichte*, 243.

34. Schwarz's ("End," 265–74) argument that Stephen is emphasizing divine transcendence here does not explain the parallel between idols and the temple as made with hands. At this point, Stephen is not simply stating divine transcendence, but also Israel's consistent resistance to the Spirit—refusing prophetic warnings about their misuse of the temple.

35. So Gaventa, *Acts*, 128; Pesch, *Apostelgeschichte*, I, 257.

36. So Tannehill, *Narrative*, 93; *contra* Jervell, *Unknown*, 14.

37. See the arguments in Kilgallen, *Stephen*, 89; Larsson, "Temple-Criticism," 390.

38. BDF, 233; Witherington, *Acts*, 262–63.

39. Rightly Sylva, "Meaning," 264. *Contra* Fitzmyer, *Acts*, 382–83; Kilgallen, "Function," 77–181 (although he correctly notes that the issue is about wrongly worshipping God).

40. Gaventa (*Acts*, 128–29), Schneider (*Apostelgeschichte*, I, 486), and Witherington (*Acts*, 262–63, 273–74) correctly note the use of "made with hands" missed by Barrett (*Acts*, 375), Koester (*Dwelling*, 80–81).

have attacked the temple (after the quotation from Isa 66:1), he instead aims at those present. So, throughout the speech, the reader would not see Stephen as anti-temple.

What about the other charges?[41] Stephen does not seek to alter Jewish customs (6:14) because he affirms that God gave them (circumcision—7:8). God also gives the Law's "living oracles" (through the angel—7:38, 53).[42] As such Stephen does not reject the Law or the importance in keeping it (7:53). The reader also associates divine deliverance with covenant promises being fulfilled. Thus, when Luke's Stephen presents God as with Joseph in Egypt and through Joseph providing an avenue for Israel's preservation during the famine (7:9–15), the reader is reminded that God has previously fulfilled promises to Abraham. The reader can then anticipate that God is doing the same now. Furthermore, God (as promised—7:6–7, 17), raised up Moses to be a deliverer (7:25, 27, 35) for the people. Thus, the charge concerning blasphemies against Moses (6:11) is answered because Moses, as a deliverer, is presented to the reader as a completely positive figure.[43] Moreover, since circumcision is later considered a Mosaic custom (15:1; 21:21), the repeated emphasis on the patriarchs being circumcised (7:8) prepares the reader to see this custom as important for God's covenant people. In Stephen's speech, the connection between circumcision and Moses is made through God being revealed to Moses as the God "of Abraham, Isaac, and Jacob" (7:32), the same ones who were circumcised.[44] So, again the reader would absolve Stephen of the charges, finding continual positive affirmation of the Jewish Law, Moses, and customs.

What does the reader conclude about God's relationship to Israel based on the opening section? The addresses *to Israel* and the concern for the covenant demonstrate Luke's interest in the kingdom's relationship to Israel, providing two benefits for the reader. First, they connect the message to what has gone before. This is the God that the reader has always known—the "God of our ancestors," who is acting in keeping with what is already known about God (God is faithful to the covenant and fulfills promises made). Second, they demonstrate that those who are kingdom citizens act in keeping with the covenant God. Peter repeatedly affirms his relationship to Israel's God and Stephen's speech answers (however obliquely) charges that would deny this relationship. Consequently, the reader finds that those who enter into the kingdom are entering into the people of God, the covenant people.[45] The kingdom's God continues to be Israel's God, the covenant God.

41. Stephen's speech is not a direct answer to any of these charges (so Lake and Cadbury, *Beginnings*, 69), but along the way provides counter-evidence (Fitzmyer, *Acts*, 363; Gaventa, *Acts*, 119–20; Tannehill, *Narrative*, 85).

42. The reader would find reasons in both the text and the extra-text to assume that the use of an intermediary in giving the Law does not represent a decrease in its authority. First, calling the Law "living oracles" suggests its ongoing validity and presents "a high evaluation of the law" (Schwarz, "End," 269; also Ravens, *Luke*, 59; Salo, *Luke's*, 181). Second, the reader is likely familiar with the tendency in the Second-Temple period to portray divine transcendence by means of intermediaries (see chapters 2 and 3). Since the appearance of intermediaries emphasizes the divine Lawgiver's transcendent sovereignty, the authority level is increased.

43. So Barrett, *Acts*, 362–63; Fitzmyer, *Acts*, 378; Witherington, *Acts*, 261.

44. Jervell, *Apostelgeschichte*, 239.

45. Johnson, *Acts*, 73–74. Barrett (*Acts*, 35, 289) emphasizes that, for Luke, Judaism is the foundation for the Gospel, and thus Christianity is its fulfillment not its contradiction.

At the same time, the reader will note criticism aimed at the Jewish people. This will create dissonance for the reader—Israel is to receive the promised blessings, but Israel has shown its repeated resistance to God's Spirit (7:51–53). Here, then, the reader is being forced to dissociate the Israel in covenant with God from the Jewish people as a whole.[46] This will require the reader to seek for characteristics (discussed below) that distinguish these groups.

But first, the reader finds hints that the covenant God is interested in more than just the Jews. Jesus refers to the disciples' witness in Jerusalem, Judea, Samaria, and the "ends of the earth" (1:8).[47] The latter two areas suggest an expansion beyond Israel's ethnic and geographic boundaries. It is possible that γη here is better rendered as "land," narrowing the reader's vision to the land of Israel,[48] and emphasizing the mission to the Jews. However, it is precisely the ambiguity accompanying this word that causes the reader to question the kingdom's extent, if not at present, at least when later confronted with Luke's emphasis on the Diaspora Jews and the promise to "far away" people in Acts 2. The reader remains uncertain at this point whether those who will receive the witness will be non-Jews. If the reader is to recognize an allusion to Isa 49:6,[49] this would anticipate a witness to gentiles. The allusion, however, is not assured since the phrase occurs elsewhere in the LXX (Deut 28:49; Ps 134:6–7; Isa 8:9; 14:21–22; 48:20; 62:11; Jer 10:12; 16:19; 1 Macc 3:9). Even if the reader does assume gentiles as the referent, there is no assurance that the witness will be anything more than the proclamation of judgment (see chapter 2). The reader, nevertheless, is left with the sense that the kingdom could be important for those outside Israel proper.

The "Ends of the Earth" in Acts

Many commentators take the "ends of the earth" to be an allusion to Rome, the setting for the end of the book.[50] There are three problems with this conclusion. 1) This idea would not be in the reader's mind at this point since even the Jews were more likely to consider Rome the earth's center rather than its end. The allusion in *Pss. Sol.* 8:15 to Pompey coming from the "end of the earth" is almost solitary in its reference to Rome. Further, affinities to Isa 49:6 and salvation being brought to the "end of the earth" (i.e., among the gentiles) are far stronger (cf. Acts 13:47; where the phrase seems to be used that way).[51]

2) If Rome is the "ends of the earth" then the apostles do not fulfill Jesus' command since they do not witness there in Acts. It would thus be impossible for Jesus'

---

46. Tiede ("'Glory,'" 22) points out that various groups within Judaism at this time considered themselves true Israel. Therefore, the reader would be familiar with such a distinction.

47. See below, *Excursus: The "Ends of the Earth" in Acts*.

48. Schwarz, "End," 669–76.

49. As Pesch, *Apostelgeschichte*, I, 68; Tannehill, *Narrative*, 17–18.

50. Barrett, *Acts*, 80–81; Fitzmyer, *Acts*, 206–7; Fusco, "'Point,'" 1695; Moessner, "'Completed,'" 220–21; Schneider, *Apostelgeschichte*, I, 203.

51. See Green, "Salvation," 85, fn. 5.

return to ever come if that event were contingent on the apostolic witness reaching Rome.[52] Schneider thinks this problem can be solved by seeing a difference between the witness in (ἐν) Jerusalem, Judea, and Samaria, which would involve the Apostles, and a witness unto (ἕως) the "ends of the earth," which is apostolically guaranteed.[53] This places too much weight on the difference between *in* and *unto*, especially since ἕως is simply part of the phrase as it appears in Isa 49:6 (LXX) and other places. A more likely conclusion (given the emphasis on the diverse peoples present) is that the Pentecost proclamation fulfills this aspect of the Apostles' witness.[54]

Finally, 3) Johnson is correct that one's determination concerning the meaning of "ends of the earth" depends more on how one understands the narrative's "ground-plan."[55] Since, as argued later, the necessity in Paul's witness in Rome (19:21; 23:11) is less related to the mission than to demonstrating Paul's innocence,[56] arguments that depend on the ending in Rome do not seem compelling for understanding Luke's usage here. Because there are already Christians in Rome (28:15), Paul is not responsible for the witness reaching there. Prieur argues that the Roman Jews are portrayed as ignorant about Christianity so Paul would be seen as the missionary to Rome.[57] However, this reference need only mean that the Jewish leaders knew about the Christian message's opposition, rather than that the message had not reached Rome.

At Pentecost, the reader notes the diverse peoples present. The similarity to *table of nations* lists (Gen 10)[58] may suggest all peoples are being united under divine rule—as at the beginning (the creative order restored). Such lists feature prominently in Second-Temple literature suggesting this is an Israel-centric world-view.[59] Further, the list in Isa 66:18–20 receives an eschatological interpretation picturing all "nations and tongues" gathered to Israel at the time for its restoration. Although the nations listed are not identical to those in Acts, the parallels may suggest this idea to the reader.[60] People from different places, speaking different languages hear the same thing (divine deeds praised).[61] These

52. As Barrett, *Acts*, 81.

53. Schneider, *Apostelgeschichte*, I, 225–26.

54. Jervell (*Apostelgeschichte*, 136) thinks this is the case because the people that are present come from Judaism in its world-wide context.

55. Johnson, *Acts*, 27.

56. *Contra* Barrett, *Acts*, 80.

57. Prieur, *Verkündigung*, 40.

58. The list's origin is the subject of much inconclusive discussion (see Barrett, *Acts*, 122; Gaventa, *Acts*, 75; Gilbert, "List," 497–529; Lake and Cadbury, *Beginnings*, 19; Witherington, *Acts*, 135).

59. See Bechard, *Paul*, 173–209; Scott, "Luke's," 507–20; "Acts 2:9–22," 87–123.

60. *Contra* Gilbert ("List," 507) extra-text such as this does not have to be pointed out by narrator or character. Commonly known information is assumed by both author and reader. Further, Gilbert (519) misses Luke's interest in Israel's restoration. Thus, the associations with Jewish exclusiveness (rejected by Gilbert) are not necessarily a problem.

61. Even if this does not present the Babel story reversed (see Barrett, *Acts*, 112, 119; Witherington, *Acts*, 131, 136), it suggests the motif that all humanity is united under divine control. This supports Gilbert's ("List," 497–529) claim that Luke wishes to present God, rather than Rome, ruling the world.

people, however, are "devout" *Jews* (2:5); so, while the narrative may hint at something more, it remains squarely focused on the presentation to Israel.[62] Peter's statement that the promise is for the hearers, their children, and all that are "far away" (2:39) provides a similar intimation.[63] The statement is not specific; those "far away" could just as easily be distant in time as in space or ethnicity, but a further audience is implied (cf. 3:26—"first to you").[64] Luke seems to anticipate salvation for the gentiles by ending the Joel quote at 3:5a with the notion that salvation is not restricted to Jews.[65] Pesch tries to solidify the allusion to the gentiles by indicating that the restoration at 3:21 is to be interpreted as gentile inclusion.[66] While 3:25 does mention the Abrahamic blessings spreading to all the earth's families, at this point the reader would remain uncertain how (are they to be forced to become Jews?) or what blessings (full citizenship?) would come to them. The reader needs information, not revealed until 8:4—19:20, to determine how the gentiles fit into the restoration.[67] Nevertheless, the reader increasingly anticipates a further audience (especially knowing that gentiles have received the message) as the opposition in Jerusalem grows. Thus, when in 8:1 the reader finds the church scattered throughout Judea and *Samaria*, the reader now expects to discover this "other" audience.[68]

God of Jews, Samaritans, and Gentiles

As the second section (8:4—19:20) begins, the reader finds a portion of the message's extended audience revealed. Philip preaches Christ to Samaritans (8:5), who believe, are baptized (8:12), and (as an act confirming their status)[69] receive the divine "gift" (8:20), the Spirit (8:17). When Philip preaches Jesus (8:35) to an Ethiopian eunuch, this event could recount the inclusion of the first gentile. The reader would be aware that gentiles came to the Jerusalem temple to worship, as this eunuch had done (8:27). Indeed, many gentiles who were completely uninterested in attaching themselves to the Jewish religion offered

---

62. *Contra* Barrett (*Acts*, 118) Luke does not envision two groups—"Jews" and "pious men;" rather ἄνδρες εὐλαβεῖς is an appositive to Ἰουδαῖοι (so Fitzmyer, *Acts*, 239; Schille, *Apostelgeschichte*, 99).

63. Fitzmyer (*Acts*, 252) thinks that the reference to the "last days" in the Joel quotation suggests the time for the launching out of the message from Jerusalem is at hand. However, Luke does not link this phrase to the expansion beyond Jerusalem. Instead, he ties it to the Spirit's outpouring and the establishment of the king.

64. Tannehill (*Narrative*, 56–57) notes the *implication* of a "progressive mission" (no outright statement is made).

65. Carroll, *Response*, 131; following Rese, *Altestamentliche*, 50. Dupont (*Salvation*, 22–23, 58) consistently overstates the appearance of gentile salvation themes in the Pentecost speech.

66. Pesch, *Apostelgeschichte*, I, 29; also Mussner, "Idee," 293–306; Lohfink, *Himmelfahrt*, 154.

67. Jervell (*Apostelgeschichte*, 170–71) interprets "families" as a reference to the entire people of Israel spread out over the world. This seems forced since, even though Luke does not use the LXX's ἔθνη, the reader is likely to assume that meaning and Jervell's interpretation does not make sense of πρῶτον in 3:26 (a further audience is assumed other than just Israel).

68. Neudorfer ("Speech," 279) notes that Stephen's speech utilizes vocabulary (ἐξέρχομαι, ἐξαποστέλλω, ἐξάγω, ἔλευσις) that suggests movement "away from a given point." While, by itself, little weight would be given to this occurrence, along with the increasing opposition it would confirm the reader's impression that the expanded audience will soon be revealed.

69. See chapter 3.

sacrifices at the temple.[70] The reader, nevertheless, will have some uncertainty about label-ing him a gentile since Luke never specifically calls him such.[71] This uncertainty may only arise in retrospect when the reader realizes that Cornelius is unambiguously described as a gentile (10:28, 45). The argument that the Ethiopian should be seen as the real first gentile convert,[72] then, misses that Luke does not specifically characterize the man as a gentile, something he does repeatedly with Cornelius. The similarities between the two events are not intended to reconfirm gentile inclusion (as supposed), but to assure the reader that both inclusions are divinely ordained. Luke's emphasis on the subsequent Cornelius narrative suggests he did not envision this as a competing narrative about a gentile conversion.[73]

More important to the reader may be the reference to Ethiopia, which in Isa 11:11 is one place from which Israel's scattered people would be gathered. Coming so closely after the witness in Samaria, and because Greek and Jewish maps that placed Ethiopia at one end of the earth were common,[74] the reader would be able to identify Jesus' command (1:8) being at least partially fulfilled and through it Israel restored. Thus, this Ethiopian, whatever else he may represent, prefigures the "ends of the earth" being reached.

When Cornelius and his household hear the message that has been sent to the "people of Israel" (10:36—i.e., to the "Jew first") concerning Jesus, they too receive the "gift of the Holy Spirit" (10:45).[75] This divine action provides the evidence that all gentiles are included in the kingdom when they fear God (10:35) and repent (11:18), demonstrating that "membership in a particular nation"[76] is not a prerequisite for membership in the kingdom. Later, the reader finds James declaring that in this act God began to take from the gentiles "a people for His name" (15:14), including them in God's people. The reader will note an interplay between τὰ ἔθνη and λαός (the Lukan designation for God's people, Israel), suggesting that the nations have now been chosen as God's people—an astonishing

---

70. See Schürer, *History*, 309–13.

71. Because the reader would know non-Jews and non-proselytes worshiped in Jerusalem, Jervell's (*Apostelgeschichte*, 270–71) argument that Luke has to be narrating the conversion of a proselyte seems unfounded. There is no reason to narrate the inclusion of a proselyte since Luke has already noted that a proselyte was included in the church (6:5).

72. Tannehill, *Narrative*, 110–11.

73. Haenchen, *Acts*, 314; Johnson, *Acts*, 159; Pesch, *Apostelgeschichte*, I, 289. Many commentators (see Haenchen, *Acts*, 314; Pesch, *Apostelgeschichte*, I, 287–95; Schneider, *Apostelgeschichte*, I, 498) indicate to vary-ing degrees the possibility that the man was either Jewish or a proselyte. Barrett (*Acts*, 420, 424–26) argues that neither conclusion is possible given Luke's characterization that he is Ethiopian and a eunuch.

74. Esth 1:1; 8:9; Ezek 29:10; Zeph 3:10; Diodorus Siculus 3:1–37; Pliny, *Natural History* 6:35; Dio Cassius 54:5.3. See Tannehill, *Narrative*, 108–9; Thornton, "End," 374–75; Romm, *Edges* (1992); Spencer, *Portrait*, 150; van Unnik, "Ausdruck," 400.

75. Conzelmann (*Theology*, 95, 214) and S. G. Wilson (*Gentiles*, 59–87) suggested that, for Luke, the gentile mission and the Spirit are not eschatological elements. The latter issue was argued in chapter 4. In turn, then, since the gentiles (and the Samaritans) receive the eschatological Spirit, they are included in the eschatologi-cal people (so Chance, *Jerusalem*, 98–99). The expanded community remains the eschatological people even though the end has not come yet.

76. Johnson, *Acts*, 194.

emphasis on the divine choice in their inclusion.[77] S. G. Wilson suggests Luke simply may have been careless in using λαός here,[78] so attributing any conscious motive is difficult. The reader, nevertheless, will see the interchange in terms and be forced to consider the relationship between the gentiles and the people of God. Since the reader finds only one kingdom being presented and because repentance and obedience to God are the only conditions for entrance, the reader finds Jew and gentile brought together in one restored kingdom. The portrait assures the reader regarding the validity of this, since only divine action could convince Jews concerning its reality.

The image is not that Jew is *replaced* by gentile, but that gentiles have been *joined with* Jews in David's restored "dwelling" (15:16–18)—an occurrence the reader has seen in the Antioch church.[79] From the OT (Amos) extra-text for this quotation, the reader knows that the rebuilt "dwelling of David" refers to the restored kingdom under the Davidic king after Jerusalem's fall in 587–86 BCE. Chance argues that the tent here is to be understood in relation to the "dwelling place" in Acts 7:46.[80] However, 1) the dwelling which David *wished* to build is never referred to by Luke as David's σκηνή (neither is the temple David's temple), while Jesus does sit on *David's* throne as heir to the Davidic promise (13:34; cf. Luke 1:32). 2) Σκήνωμα (7:46) comes from Ps 132(LXX 131):5, relating to background conceptions about the temple. In contrast, the σκηνή in Amos 9:11 reflects conceptions about the kingdom. Bauckham identifies σκηνή here as a reference to the temple, but correctly argues that Luke's text is developed from several conflated passages (Amos 9:10–11; Hos 3:5; Jer 12:15) that stress that the eschatological temple would be restored at the time when Davidic rule was restored to Israel.[81] This temple would be the place that gentiles would meet and worship God. The extra-text, therefore, suggests to the reader images reflecting both the restored kingdom and gentiles joined with Jews to worship God in it.

This kingdom in the Amos text was to include Edom and all the peoples formerly aligned under the Davidic dynasty.[82] In Luke's quotation (following the LXX), however, Edom is replaced with "all other peoples," giving the Davidic kingdom a global sense. Because the reader now associates Jesus with the Davidic king,[83] the allusion suggests a restored kingdom consisting of everyone who has now come under the Davidic messiah's rule—Jew, Samaritan, and gentile.[84] James' words could refer merely to the Davidic dy-

77. See Schneider, *Apostelgeschichte*, II, 182.

78. S. G. Wilson, *Gentiles*, 225.

79. See Pesch, *Apostelgeschichte*, I, 354–55.

80. Chance, *Jerusalem*, 39–40; following Richard, "Divine," 188–209.

81. Bauckham, "James," 154–84.

82. Cf. Hoet, "Εθνῶν," 404–5; also Barrett, *Acts*, 725–26; Johnson, *Acts*, 265; Strauss, *Davidic*, 187.

Edom could also represent people hostile to God's kingdom (Num 20:14; Amos 1:11). Thus, if Edom is subdued, God will have restored peace and returned Israel to its former boundaries under David, the only Israelite king to conquer and rule Edom (2 Sam 8:14) (see Parker, *Apokatastasis*, 83–84, who follows Motyer, *Day*, 202–4).

83. Haenchen (*Acts*, 448) and Schneider (*Apostelgeschichte*, II, 182–83) see no connection to the Davidic king, but this ignores the background to the Amos quotation.

84. So Barrett, "Luke-Acts," 95; Johnson, *Acts*, 268; Tannehill, *Narrative*, 188–89.

nasty being restored in Jesus,[85] but the restored king implies the restored kingdom. Indeed, the "dwelling" imagery, combined with the references to "all other peoples" and "all the Gentiles" (15:17), implies that a people (not just a king) is being restored.

When Paul first turns to the gentiles (13:47), the reader encounters a quotation from Isa 49:6 (cf. Acts 1:8) that envisions the "ends of the earth" receiving divine salvation, suggesting that God planned for the gentiles to be included.[86] The gentiles who believe are then directly characterized as those "destined for eternal life" (13:48)—a phrase that may express the Jewish designation for being the chosen people.[87] If it is not a specifically Jewish designation, it at least indicates that God has chosen them. The reader has already seen Paul begin his speech by mentioning God's past choice of Israel (13:17). Thus, the reader finds both gentiles and Jews characterized as being among *God's* chosen people, reaffirming their status in God's kingdom.

That in 8:4—19:20 the kingdom never ceases to include Jews can also be gleaned from Paul's synagogue sermon.[88] The reader finds the message addressed to "You Israelites" (13:16) and others who "fear God."[89] God is characterized as the covenant God—the "God of this people Israel" (13:17) to whom God has given a deliverer, Jesus (13:23), and to whom God has faithfully sent prophets preaching repentance (13:24).[90] The hearers are covenant people ("descendants of Abraham's family"—13:26) and thus heirs to the Abrahamic covenant concerning land (13:19) and seed. The latter promise seems to extend to God raising David and establishing a kingdom, whose ultimate fulfillment comes in the promised Davidic seed, Jesus (13:23).[91] Therefore, Israel, God's covenant people, is intended to receive divine blessings. Certainly some Jews rejected this message, prompting

---

85. Strauss, *Davidic*, 190–92. Chance (*Jerusalem*, 38; also Jervell, *Luke*, 51–69) suggests that the Jewish-Christians are the restored element here. The "dwelling" was to be restored so that the gentiles could seek the Lord. Thus, the dwelling did not include the gentiles; it allowed them to find the Lord. While Israel does seem the primary entity restored through the Davidic king, this does not indicate that gentiles are not being included with Jews. The gentiles who find the Lord through the restored kingdom are included in the λαός, for they receive the Lord's name (15:14, 17). Bauckham ("James," 168–69) points out that in receiving this name the gentiles become God's possession. Further, Amos 9:12 pictures the Davidic rule spread to the surrounding nations. Thus, the gentiles come under Davidic rule as God's possession—participants in Israel's covenant blessings and obligations.

86. Tiede (*Prophecy*, 5, 122; "Glory," 27–33) ties gentile inclusion to God punishing Israel for their disobedience, but this does not fit with the way Isa 49:6 is used here. Further, divine action, not persecution (cf. 8:1—no apostolic persecution; 9:31—the church had peace), is responsible for Peter speaking to Cornelius. After Paul's first turn Peter says that the divine *choice*, not Jewish rejection, led to gentile inclusion (15:7).

87. Pesch, *Apostelgeschichte*, II, 46.

88. Jervell (*Unknown*, 16) suggests that preaching in a synagogue itself indicates "Christianity is the religion of Israel."

89. It is unclear whether this reference and the similar one in 13:26 addresses Jews, proselytes, or gentile god-fearers. Any of the three could be addressed in this way (see Barrett, *Acts*, 629–31, 639).

90. Pesch (*Apostelgeschichte*, II, 36) suggests John represented the last in the line of prophets who spoke concerning Jesus' coming. Paul's speech resembles Deuteronomistic historiography (Schneider, *Apostelgeschichte*, II, 130), emphasizing divine action in Israel's history, just as in Stephen's speech (Haenchen, *Acts*, 408; Pesch, *Apostelgeschichte*, II, 30, 34).

91. Τούτου is brought forward to emphasize the fulfillment of the promise in Jesus (Haenchen, *Acts*, 409).

Paul's turn. However, when Paul moves on to Iconium the reader finds him back in the synagogue, preaching to Jews (14:1). Just as in 3:26 the reader sees the message coming to Jews first, but now "first to you" is called a necessity (13:46). Consequently, in these turns it is the proclamation to the Jews first that is programmatic (necessitated), not the witness to gentiles.[92] Indeed, Paul had been divinely commissioned (9:15) to be involved in the inclusive gathering of the "people of Israel."[93] As the narrative continues Paul will be seen and treated as a Jew with Jewish customs being a point of contention with gentiles (16:20–21). Even after a second turn, Gallio considers the charges against Paul an intra-Jewish issue (18:14–15). Thus, for Luke's reader, God remains the God of the Jews, but the secondary subjects have now become evident—Samaritans, gentiles, and the "ends of the earth."

God of the Jews and More

In Acts' final section (19:21—28:31) the reader receives confirmation that gentiles are citizens in God's kingdom. When Paul arrives in Jerusalem, the announcement concerning what God has done among the gentiles (21:19) is received readily by the Jewish believers. Likewise, Paul confirms to the Jews in Jerusalem that God has commissioned him as a witness to "all the world" (22:15). The announcement that this means going "far away to the Gentiles" (22:21) makes the previously referenced "all" so abundantly clear that the mob protests Paul's very existence.[94] Further, this witness is not to proclaim judgment, but to "turn" the gentiles so that they receive an "place" in the kingdom (26:18). God's kingdom is now to be populated by gentiles.

However, the reader will note a decidedly Jewish interest. When the mob realizes Alexander is a Jew (19:33–34) and shout him down with the same cry that they invoked in relation to Paul (19:28), the reader finds Christian proclamation portrayed as allied with Jewish monotheism.[95] At two places the reader encounters time measured in relation to Jewish feasts, despite the events not taking place in or near Jerusalem (20:6—"Unleavened Bread"; 27:9—"the Fast," i.e., the Day of Atonement). While there was no "Christian" calendar which Luke could use, there was a Roman calendar. Luke's choice of the Jewish calendar suggests that a Jewish view of the world is being maintained for the reader. The Jewish dating is odd in what some commentators consider a "Hellenistic work,"[96] offering more reason (such dating appears significant) for thinking the reader is to be sympathetic towards Judaism. These references remind the reader about Paul's (and, it would seem, the narrator's) Jewish context. Consequently, the Jewish God is seen as responsible for

---

92. Pesch, *Apostelgeschichte*, II, 45–46, 148; Strauss, *Davidic*, 176–77; Tannehill, *Narrative*, 173–74, 223.

93. Johnson, *Acts*, 165; Schille, *Apostelgeschichte*, 223; Tannehill, *Narrative*, 119.

94. So Barrett, *Acts*, 1042. *Contra* Bibb ("Characterization," 254) divine action is not being used to signal a change in mission focus. The mission has been aimed to Jew first and also to gentiles throughout the narrative.

95. While Johnson (*Acts*, 349) agrees with this conclusion, he wonders if Luke holds this view—all evidence suggests he does.

96. Lake and Cadbury, *Beginnings*, 254.

determining the timing for narrative events (they can be recorded on the divine calendar), assuring the reader about the narrative events.

When James and the church rejoice in what "God had done" among the gentiles, the numerous believing Jews who are obedient to the Law (21:20) are emphasized. This, in turn, suggests that zealousness for the Law marks those (Jew and gentile) who make up true Israel.[97] Paul confirms for the reader the importance of this group by agreeing (both financially and practically) to participate in a vow. Later, Paul affirms that it is Israel's God ("of our ancestors") who has sent him to the gentiles (22:14) and whom he serves in accordance with the Law and the Prophets (24:14). Paul also affirms non-Christian Jewish worship by claiming his hope is identical with that expressed by those from the "twelve tribes" who "worship day and night" (26:6–7).[98] Objecting to the divine declaration that the Jews would not hear him (22:18–19), Paul even claims unwillingness to depart from Jerusalem. Likewise, being "well spoken of by all the Jews" is a seen as one characteristic that qualifies Ananias for his role as God's representative to Paul (22:12). Therefore, Jewishness and hope offered to Israel appear important for this prominent kingdom spokesperson.

Luke, consistent with the Jews first motif seen previously, arranges the word order so that "Jews" precede "gentiles" or "Greeks" (20:21; 26:23) in mission contexts. Specifically, even though Paul announced to Agrippa his divine commission to the gentiles (26:18–20), the reader finds Paul narrating his preaching in Jerusalem and Judea before mentioning similar action with the gentiles. Even the final turn (28:23–28) confirms the Jew first mission since it takes place only after the proclamation has been made to the Jews[99] and Paul has attempted to convince the Jewish leaders in Rome from the Law and the Prophets. Paul models this mission procedure which is not altered by the turn here anymore than it was altered previously.[100] That the message is important for Jews is stressed through the address ("Brothers"), which the reader has seen emphasizing that the audience is Jewish and that Paul identifies with them.[101] Thus, despite Luke illustrating the Gospel's advance among the gentiles, the reader is assured all the way to the narrative's end that the Jewish citizens have not now become second-rate,[102] and that promises to Israel are indeed being fulfilled.

God of Justice and Order

The OT theologian, Walter Brueggemann, argued that the metaphor concerning God as King is connected with images that suggest divine concerns for justice (fairness and pro-

---

97. Pesch, *Apostelgeschichte*, II, 221. The way Paul's piety is presented continues this idea, see below.

98. Cf. Chance, *Jerusalem*, 37. Haacker ("Bekenntnis," 441) claims that this shows a "deep solidarity" with Jewish concerns about their existence before God.

99. *Contra* Pesch, *Apostelgeschichte*, II, 307.

100. *Contra* Moessner, "'Completed,'" 219.

101. So Jervell, "Israel," 78.

102. So Tannehill, *Narrative*, 272, 282. This casts serious doubt on any claims (as Schneider, *Apostelgeschichte*, II, 420) that the church in Luke's period is entirely gentile.

tection) and social order (the life and health of God's people).[103] To be assured that the kingdom is restored to Israel, the reader would expect evidence that the society created exhibits an order and a concern for justice that agrees with what is known about God.[104] The second element of this characterizing strand, therefore, looks at four attributes (*leadership, inclusion, welfare, and order*) expected of God and now characterizing God's people in Acts, assuring the reader that the kingdom has been restored.

Why These Four Attributes?

At 2:41–47 the reader finds the new community demonstrating a commonality that is worked out in the selling of property and possessions for the benefit of everyone who had need. This picture would be familiar to the reader since the famed philosopher Plato saw such actions as representing the perfect state.[105] Acts 4:32–37 offers a second summary; this time focusing on the community's unity and social concern—property is shared and the needy are non-existent due to their commonality. The absence of any needy recalls another text familiar to Luke's reader—Deut 15:4 where this was to be the situation in the Promised Land.[106] Thus, whether from a Greek or Jewish perspective, the reader is led to think about conditions in a perfect society/kingdom.[107] There are, then, repeated concerns about social *order*: 1) The group has *leaders* (the apostles are responsible for teaching—2:42—and the distribution—4:35). 2) The group maintains unity and commonality (themes that unite 2:41–47; 4:32–37; 5:1–11; 6:1–7),[108] suggesting *inclusiveness* through a lessening in social class distinctions. 3) They are concerned for the *welfare* of the disadvantaged among them (selling property to meet any need that arises).[109] Thus, the first citizens in this restored kingdom demonstrate that they are concerned with issues involving fairness and order, in keeping with their Divine King.

---

103. Brueggemann, *Theology*, 241–47. See chapter 2.

104. Further, it provides evidence against Grässer's ("Parusieerwartung," 110) claim that when Luke "spricht vom Reich" he means "die christliche Botschaft." The evidence for God's kingdom being present is both the *message* and the *community* created.

105. *Republic* 420C–422B; 462B–464A; *Laws* 679B–C; 684C–D; 744B–746C; 757A. So Johnson, *Acts*, 61–62; Plümacher, *Lukas*, 16–18; Tannehill, *Narrative*, 45. With the *restored kingdom* theme, the "ideal state" *topos* seems a better interpretive option than friendship (cf. Mitchell, "Social," 255–72) or the foundation story for a "religious-philosophical group" (cf. Sterling, "'Athletes,'" 688–96).

106. So Barrett, *Acts*, 314; Haenchen, *Acts*, 231; Tannehill, *Narrative*, 45. Capper ("Palestinian," 336–37) claims that the reference to "together" sets the first summary against a Jewish background (the Essene community), while the second shows more "idealising" through references to Greek commonplaces. However, the allusion to Deut 15:4 suggests that here too the focus is on the Jewish background.

107. Pesch (*Apostelgeschichte*, I, 132–33) identifies here a new "society," presented in Jewish and Greek terms.

108. Tannehill, *Narrative*, 43–44.

109. The community appears to have considered property something whose disposal provided benefits to the community on an as-needed basis (so Barrett, *Acts*, 314; Gaventa, *Acts*, 100; Schneider, *Apostelgeschichte*, I, 291).

Idyllic Portrait of the Community?

It appears incorrect to label these community summaries as "idyllic."[110] Capper argues persuasively that the "community of goods" presented in these early summaries rests on solid historical grounds.[111] Coupling his argument with the argument made here that such scenes portray the community living according to divine demands, leads to the conclusion that the portrait is not so much to be seen *as ideal,* but *as evidence* that God's kingdom is present.

Elsewhere, Capper argues that in the Hellenistic world the reader would associate the community of goods motif with a distant Golden Age.[112] He considers this likely in Acts since he believes references to the community's sharing stops after 6:1–6 and is replaced with "alms-giving." However, community members were already engaged in alms-giving, although what they gave was not money but health (3:5–6), a holistic concern for the person's welfare. This holistic concern becomes the model, particularly since the community of goods itself is presented as being directed toward a common social order. It is not a new activity prescribed for Luke's reader, or one that belongs to the distant past, but one that provides for community needs in a variety of ways.

If an *idyllic* portrait were intended, one would expect that the early community would not have difficulties. Instead, both 5:1–11 and 6:1–6 depict disruptions to the community's order.[113] These disruptions give further support to the conclusion that Luke is not presenting a golden-age church, but demonstrating the divine order evident in it. It had difficulties (then as now), but for Luke's reader God is active in ordering the community.

The emphasis on these four attributes continues throughout 1:1—8:3 as, in contrast to Joseph Barnabas (4:36–37), Ananias and Sapphira fail to appreciate the divine order. Their conspiracy (5:2, 9) to lie (5:3, 4) about the sale amount suggests that they do not share the group's commonality,[114] or its interest in the disadvantaged, and their willingness to withhold part of the funds indicates that their concern is mere pretense.[115] Capper suggests they are pretending to undergo the same process that Joseph Barnabas and others (2:45; 4:34–36) did.[116] Instead, the couple through their deception does not maintain the community's concern for interdependence. Since it is God who addresses the problem,[117]

---

110. As Fitzmyer, *Acts*, 268.

111. Capper, "Palestinian," 323–56.

112. Capper, "Reciprocity," 504–9. Cf. Mealand, "Community," 96–99.

113. *Contra* Esler (*Community*, 136) the reader is not surprised to find the church's unity and commonality disrupted at 6:1 because it has happened already at 5:1–11.

114. Fitzmyer, *Acts*, 323; Pesch, *Apostelgeschichte*, I, 197–98; Witherington, *Acts*, 215.

115. It is an attempt to appear as something they are not (Fitzmyer, *Acts*, 316; Witherington, *Acts*, 208).

116. Capper, "Interpretation," 120–22. When the sum was laid before the Apostles' feet it was expected to be the full amount, even if the couple had full authority over it up to that point. However, Capper goes beyond the evidence in suggesting there was a financial norm expected of the community members.

117. Barrett (*Acts*, 267) notes the "coincidence" that ἐξέψυξεν is used for Ananias, Sapphira, and Herod (12:23). It may be not so coincidental—it seems to characterize all three as divinely caused deaths.

it is implied that they have violated the divine social order and God took action to restore justice by removing "evil and deception."[118]

A similar concern for justice can be identified in the dispute involving the Hellenist[119] widows (6:1–7). Because one group of widows, who were typically disadvantaged anyway,[120] are suffering an injustice in the food distribution, the commonality[121] (and order) is upset. Concern for widows was a key element in OT "justice" (Exod 22:24; Deut 14:28–29; 24:17–21; Isa 10:1–2; Zech 7:10–12), thus the situation again shows a violation of divine social order. This circumstance is resolved when men whom God has qualified ("full of the Spirit and of wisdom"—6:3) are selected and committed to resolving this issue. Once again, God is seen as concerned with and responsible for maintaining fairness in kingdom life.

The reader also finds that God cares about the welfare of all people. God heals the lame beggar, whose leaping may recall the restoration of Zion as described in Isa 35:6 ("the lame shall leap like a dear").[122] If so, then God's re-established social order restores both the needy and the sick (cf. Deut 7:15).[123] Likewise, the "believers" were bringing the sick into the streets to be healed (5:14–15). There is no indication that either these sick people or those from the surrounding cities who were healed from sickness and evil spirits (5:16) were believers. Therefore, the reader sees God showing concern for the physical wellbeing of everyone, not just those in the kingdom.[124] Indeed, the believers request such merciful interest, replacing the imprecatory[125] or petitioning[126] portion of their prayer in 4:24–30 with a call for God to "heal." Pesch indicates that the healings would make the community the orientation point for those around them.[127] In this way, they would be seen by others as the model for the divine social order, further establishing the image that this is the

118. Fitzmyer, *Acts*, 320. Havelaar ("Hellenistic," 77–82) seems correct in concluding that this story can be understood as an excommunication. God has removed those who have offended the community's order. She (68–73) points out a parallel in Herodotus 6:86, where lying about money was taken as an offense against God. While this punishment's drastic nature is only paralleled once elsewhere, a reader familiar with popular Hellenistic literature would recognize divine punishment in such cases.

119. The reference is to the group's predominant language (see Fitzmyer, *Acts*, 347; Gaventa, *Acts*, 112; Johnson, *Acts*, 105). Because one of the seven is a proselyte, an adoption (rather than a repudiation) of Jewish culture is assumed (Barrett, *Acts*, 304). Hill (*Hellenists* (1992)) has argued conclusively that there is no evidence in Luke's account for theological difference between these groups.

120. Cf. Johnson, *Acts*, 105; Witherington, *Acts*, 248.

121. Fitzmyer, *Acts*, 343–44; Tannehill, *Narrative*, 80.

122. Fitzmyer, *Acts*, 279; Witherington, *Acts*, 176. In Luke's Gospel the nearness of the kingdom is also expressed in healing (10:9) and exorcisms (11:20) (see Carroll, *Response*, 84–86; Nolland, "Salvation-History," 68).

123. Pesch, *Apostelgeschichte*, I, 140.

124. Johnson, *Acts*, 72.

125. Haenchen (*Acts*, 229) treats this as if it were imprecatory: God is to "look on their threats" and respond as God desires. However, the prayer does not stop with the call on God to "look," but specifically mentions what the community desires.

126. Witherington (*Acts*, 203) identifies the key difference between 4:24–30 and Isa 37:16–20 as the petition for deliverance being replaced by a request for signs and boldness. He ignores the specific reference to healing.

127. Pesch, *Apostelgeschichte*, I, 208.

restored kingdom. This analysis, then, suggests a value in examining each attribute as it is developed in the remaining narrative.

Leadership

Throughout Acts 8:4—19:20 the Apostles maintain a leadership role in the social order—engaged in confirming new groups and decision making (8:14;[128] 9:27; 11:1; 15:2, 4, 6, 22). However, Luke expands the leadership (although it remains centered in Jerusalem), to including the "believers" from Judea (11:1; 12:17), James (12:17; 15:13), and the elders (15:2, 4, 6, 22). Pesch argues that the other James' death and Peter's departure causes James (Jesus' brother) and the Jerusalem elders to take over as the "managing committee" for the church.[129] However, since Luke broadened the leadership references before these events are narrated (11:1), this should not be the reader's conclusion. Instead, it would reflect the group's growth coupled with Jerusalem's importance (it is the "Zentrum des Verbandes" for the new community)[130]. It is not until 19:21—28:31 that the Apostles disappear from mention, but by then the reader is aware of the expanded Jerusalem leadership.

When those in Antioch begin preaching to Greeks, Luke says simply that the "church in Jerusalem"[131] heard this. The "church" there is also listed among the authorities agreeing to the Apostolic Decree (15:22). It, therefore, appears correct that "Luke regarded the church at Jerusalem as having some authority over younger communities."[132]

Further, the reader finds Paul maintaining loyalty to the Jerusalem church. When his second journey ends, he "went up" (the classic phrase for a trip to Jerusalem)[133] to greet the "church" before returning to Antioch. Antioch may be pictured as the center for Paul's missionary work, but the narrative subordinates this mission center to that in Jerusalem (Paul goes to Jerusalem after his conversion—9:26–30; Barnabas, a Jewish-Christian associated with the earliest Jerusalem community defends and retrieves Paul—9:26–30, 11:22–23; Paul takes part in the Antioch relief mission to Jerusalem—11:27–30; conflict resolution must be achieved in Jerusalem—Acts 15), even as it indicates Paul's autonomy in making decisions about his missions.[134] This subordination has suggested to some that Paul receives his authority from the Jerusalem Apostles.[135] However, the emphasis on Jerusalem seems less intended to subordinate Paul to the Apostles than, given the larger portrait, to

---

128. The apostolic visit here connects the Samaritan community with Jerusalem, the center for God's people (rightly Jervell, *Apostelgeschichte*, 263).

129. Pesch, *Apostelgeschichte*, I, 357.

130. As Pesch (*Apostelgeschichte*, I, 352) states.

131. The expanding leadership may explain why Barnabas, rather than an Apostle, is sent to Antioch. For Samaria the Jerusalem leadership listed by Luke was limited to Apostles, but by Acts 11 this narrative circumstance has changed.

132. Lake and Cadbury, *Beginnings*, 170.

133. Haenchen, *Acts*, 354, 544; Pesch, *Apostelgeschichte*, I, 156; *contra* Lake and Cadbury, *Beginnings*, 230. Going "down" from Jerusalem is mentioned at 8:5; 9:32; 11:27; 12:19; 15:1; 21:10. Going "up" is also found at 9:30.

134. See Chance, *Jerusalem*, 108–12.

135. Cf. Grässer, *Forschungen*, 206–10.

show that as the community grows it maintains a God-initiated social structure. This does not lessen Paul's status as a divinely authorized witness (made clear at 9:15). Jerusalem was the expected place for leadership since it was the place from which God was to rule over the nations (see *Excursus: The Land, Jerusalem, and the Temple in Acts*). Consequently, the kingdom maintains a social order with agreed upon leaders even as that leadership expands in 8:4—19:20.

In the final section the reader finds that the church in Jerusalem continues to be led by James and the elders (21:18), suggesting continuity in leadership order. In keeping with previous presentations, the reader encounters these leaders providing a means to alleviate a potential problem among the believers (21:21–24),[136] showing their concern for maintaining divine order.[137] Paul seems to demonstrate his respect for that leadership (as well as his own concern for order) by agreeing to their proposition (21:26). Differently, Paul tells the Ephesian elders that God has appointed overseers to "shepherd" God's assembly (20:28). This apparently exemplifies God actively providing those who can tend and watch over the people,[138] not only in Jerusalem, but in all locations.

Inclusion

The Samaritans, disdained as half-breeds and for their improper worship,[139] and gentiles, considered unclean and unworthy of fellowship (10:28), are brought into the kingdom by divine action (both receive the "gift" of the Spirit—8:17; 10:47; 11:17), showing that "no one can be excluded."[140] If the reader perceives gentile uncleanness (an inferior socio-religious status) as the obstacle that must be overcome for an inclusive mission to begin, the *Holy Spirit* coming upon those previously thought un-*holy* represents the ultimate reversal.[141] Further, Peter's former notions about divine partiality are overcome by divine intervention (10:34), destroying any exclusivity he might have believed the Jews held.[142]

The reader finds the eunuch's[143] conversion implying the inclusiveness of this new social order. Although εὐνοῦχος could be a title, referring to either emasculated or non-

---

136. Haenchen (*Acts*, 614) is correct to identify an attempt here to preserve the church's unity. This conclusion is apparent, however, without recourse to hypothetical reconstructions concerning the (unmentioned by Luke) Pauline collection.

137. Tannehill (*Narrative*, 268) and Johnson (*Acts*, 379) identify parallels with 11:1–18 and 15:1–31. Additionally, the leaders' actions are in keeping with solutions to other difficulties such as 5:1–11 and 6:1–8 (discussed below).

138. So Barrett, *Acts*, 974.

139. See Gaventa, *Acts*, 134–35; Handy, "Acts 8:14–25," 290; Ravens, *Luke*, 75–76.

140. Gaventa, *Acts*, 174; cf. Erwin, "Acts 10:34–43," 179–82; Tiede, "Acts 11:1–18," 179.

141. Tannehill, *Narrative*, 135–36.

142. So Bond, "Acts 10:34–43," 80–83.

143. The reference to the man as an Ethiopian indicates that he had to be 'black' (see Snowden, *Blacks*, 5) and, therefore, this text could be used to address modern issues concerning racial inclusiveness. However, denigrating people because of their skin color seems to be little evidenced in antiquity (Snowden, *Before*, (1983); Witherington, *Acts*, 295).

emasculated high officials,[144] the combination with δυνάστης (which in LXX Jer 41:19 translates the Hebrew word for eunuch) points to a "sexually mutilated" individual.[145] The compounded terms emphasize for the reader the man's exclusion from Israel.[146] Indeed, according to Deut 23:1 a eunuch could not partake in the assembly.[147] However, Isa 56:3–5 prophesies divine salvation coming to the eunuchs, giving them a place in the covenant. This event was seen as an act of justice (Isa 56:1). Given this extra-text, the reader is likely to understand this situation as illustrating this promised inclusion and justice.[148] Likewise, Tabitha's doing "acts of charity" (9:36), a way to do "justice,"[149] suggests this justice characteristic is prized by the church.

The emphasis on Tabitha and the widows may indicate another aspect in kingdom inclusiveness since here a woman is portrayed as having prominent role among the disciples[150] and the welfare of women is a community concern. Additionally, the reader finds repeated references to prominent women throughout 8:4—19:20 (Mary, 12:12; leading women in cities, 13:40; 17:4, 12; Lydia, 16:14–15,40; Damaris, 17:34; Priscilla, 18:2, 18, 26). Although this is not among the major themes in Acts, it does suggest an interest in the significant role women played in the early church.[151]

It was indicated previously that the reader finds gentile inclusion into the people of God affirmed in 19:21–28:31. Additionally, the provisions in the decree from Acts 15 are reiterated (21:25), reminding the reader how God provided for peace between Jew and gentile in the kingdom (inclusion by faith not circumcision, yet piety is maintained—argued below)

Welfare

Tabitha, like Jesus (10:38), is characterized as a doer of "good" (9:36); one concerned about community welfare. Her 'resurrection' demonstrates divine interest[152] in this welfare since it is obvious that she has been a great help to the saints in Joppa (particularly the widows, cf. 6:1–6). This interest, also demonstrated by healings and exorcisms (8:7; 9:34, 40; 14:10; 16:18; 19:12), characterizes the divine social order for the community since God's power is at work restoring wholeness and order. Further, Agabus' Spirit-inspired famine prediction

144. Haenchen, *Acts*, 310; Pesch, *Apostelgeschichte*, I, 289.

145. Johnson, *Acts*, 155; Schille, *Apostelgeschichte*, 210; Spencer, *Portrait*, 166–67; *contra* Pesch, *Apostelgeschichte*, I, 289.

146. So Schneider, *Apostelgeschichte*, I, 498.

147. Jews were not alone in ostracizing the emasculated; see Spencer, *Portrait*, 167–71.

148. Spencer, *Portrait*, 172; Tannehill, *Narrative*, 109; *contra* Pesch, *Apostelgeschichte*, I, 289.

149. Johnson, *Acts*, 64–65.

150. So Witherington, *Acts*, 328; Witherington, *Women*, 150.

151. Witherington, *Women*, 156–57. Luke's portrayal, nevertheless, is not always positive since Rhoda (12:13–16) seems generally a comedic figure, disrespected by the characters in the story (see Harrill, "Dramatic," 150–57). Also, many feminists see problems with the Tabitha account (see Anderson, "Reading," 128–33).

152. The prayer indicates this is a divine act (Pesch, *Apostelgeschichte*, I, 324; Schille, *Apostelgeschichte*, 240; Schneider, *Apostelgeschichte*, II, 49).

indicates the divine interest in the community's physical need—through it the church in Antioch is encouraged to provide for others (11:28–29), just as the Jerusalem church itself had been doing in 1:1—8:4. The new Jew-gentile society shows its unity with its foundational core by providing for its spiritual ancestor.[153]

In 20:1–2 the repeated references to exhortation/comfort (παρακαλέσας) draw the reader's attention to Paul's concern for strengthening the believers, a concern for their welfare. Trémel argued that the ensuing Eutychus narrative focuses on Paul's "witness," with the community receiving comfort (παρεκλήθησαν—20:12) from such.[154] However, the reader does not here find comfort mentioned when Paul preaches. Rather, comfort appears after the assembly receives the living Eutychus. Lake and Cadbury rightly noted that 20:12 seems misplaced (the boy is long since healed, Paul's speech is over, and everyone has left).[155] By interrupting the narrative Luke focuses the reader's attention on the comfort and its source in the boy's resurrection. The reader already knows that miracles done through Paul are divine acts. This notion is enhanced by the similarities between this account and the Elijah/Elisha stories (1 Kgs 17:21; 2 Kgs 4:34). Ultimately, then, the divine action (not Paul's witness) provides the comfort, with God again demonstrating care for the kingdom people.

Further, when Paul warns about "wolves" that would destroy the flock, the reader does not find him entrusting the community to the elders' power, but to a greater power, God—the One who builds them up and gives them an "inheritance" before such enemies (20:29–32). Paul's prophetic warnings indicate that God is aware that some would arise within the church seeking to lead it away from divine care (20:30). Therefore, the reader concludes that God acts to protect the people, establishing their leaders and preparing them for the difficulties to come. It is divinely willed (δεῖ) that believers help the weak, and the Lord Jesus is the source for the requirement (emphasized throughout Acts) concerning shared goods (20:35). Therefore, God is portrayed as concerned about the community's welfare, its order, and its care for one another.

God is also shown caring for those outside the community. God heals many inhabitants of Malta even though there is no indication that any become believers (28:7–10).[156] Further, in the shipwreck account, the reader repeatedly finds σώζω forms used to indicate the hope of (or in one case its lack—27:20) the passengers and crew, and what is to be accomplished at its end (27:31, 34, 43–44; 28:1). For Luke's reader, salvation has been the divine province from the beginning and is no less so here, for the "angel of God" assures Paul that God will preserve everyone on the ship (27:23–24). From that point on, no "method of escape is acceptable that doesn't include all."[157] Thus, the divine concern for

153. Haenchen, *Acts*, 375; also Pesch, *Apostelgeschichte*, I, 355, 357; Tannehill, *Narrative*, 148.

154. Trémel, "A propos," 361–62; also Schneider, *Apostelgeschichte*, II, 284–85.

155. So Lake and Cadbury, *Beginnings*, 257.

156. Johnson (*Acts*, 465–66) suggests this scene shows the Gospel message conquering another new territory. However, there is no proclamation here (correctly Schneider, *Apostelgeschichte*, II, 401; Tannehill, *Narrative*, 340).

157. Tannehill, *Narrative*, 333.

deliverance extends beyond the kingdom's borders.[158] There is, however, no hint at universal salvation.[159] Incidents that provide healing, exorcism, or deliverance from dangerous situations for those outside the kingdom seem intended to show God's universal sovereign concern for all humanity. Those who will be saved in Luke's ultimate sense are only those who repent and, turning to God, enter the kingdom (argued below). Throughout Acts, then, God repeatedly demonstrates divine providence whether through deliverance or in caring for the community's psyche and welfare.

Order

The divine interest in the kingdom's social order is demonstrated to the reader in God producing peace (i.e., order, harmony, and security).[160] Acts 8:4—19:20 begins in persecuting turmoil, but God acts directly on its key source—Saul. The Lord Jesus confronts the murderous Saul on the road to Damascus, turning this disobedient rejecter of the divine will into an obedient chosen vessel (9:15). The reader finds that Saul's divinely worked transformation[161] results in the church in Judea, Galilee, and Samaria having "peace" (9:31).[162] Pesch helpfully identifies this initial account concerning Saul's conversion experience as focusing less on Saul's call than on his transformation from being a persecutor.[163] This implies that the reader's attention is focused (just as Luke summarizes) on the peace produced for the community. A cynical understanding[164] about the reason for this peace would be Saul being sent away to Tarsus (9:30). However, Luke does not characterize the trouble facing Saul (9:29) as affecting the whole church. The reader's only hint about such a broad persecution came at 8:1–3. Thus, the reader understands this peace coming through the removal of the chief threat by a divine transformation, not from this figure being removed from the community he has now joined.

Later, the reader learns that peace is the reason God sent Jesus to the "people of Israel" (10:36). This is not just friendship between Jew and gentile, but takes on cosmic (the "devil" is defeated) and political dimensions (Jesus is "Lord of all"—a term often used for the Emperor).[165] Therefore, peace (as expected given the king's responsibility for it) appears to be a value important for God's kingdom.

---

158. So Pesch, *Apostelgeschichte*, II, 295.

159. Witherington, *Acts*, 767; *contra* Tannehill, *Narrative*, 337–38.

160. See Fitzmyer, *Acts*, 463.

161. It is an overstatement to claim (as Pesch, *Apostelgeschichte*, I, 308; Roloff, *Apostelgeschichte*, 146) that the Lord's transformation of Saul makes the church impregnable, but Luke does indicate that it collapses the persecution against it (Schille, *Apostelgeschichte*, 229).

162. Noted by Pesch, *Apostelgeschichte*, I, 311; Schneider, *Apostelgeschichte*, II, 18, 33; Tannehill, *Narrative*, 124. Although peace is not mentioned in Acts 12, the persecutor's (Herod) death is followed by a notice concerning the church's growth (like 9:31—so Johnson, *Acts*, 216; Schneider, *Apostelgeschichte*, II, 109). It would appear that God produces proper conditions (including peace) for the kingdom's growth.

163. Pesch, *Apostelgeschichte*, I, 308–9.

164. See Lake and Cadbury, *Beginnings*, 107; cf. Gaventa, *Acts*, 157; Johnson, *Acts*, 176.

165. See Gaventa, *Acts*, 170–71.

The reader also finds God involved in creating peace through dispute settlement. In both Acts 11 and 15, the opponents' challenges (going into the house of the uncircumcised; requirement of circumcision for gentiles) focus the reader's attention, such that 11:1–18 centers around table fellowship, while 15:1–33 is concerned with circumcision.[166] Since the troublers in Antioch assert that gentiles cannot be saved unless they are circumcised according to the custom of Moses (15:1), not "unless they are circumcised and obey Moses,"[167] the reader does not put greater weight on Law in reading Acts 15.[168] When the Pharisaic party demands obedience to the Law of Moses (15:5), circumcision is emphasized by appearing near the front of the clause and Law-obedience is made a separate requirement from circumcision. The reader's attention, then, is drawn to *circumcision* as a means for identifying those who are among God's true people.

In the following debate, there is no immediate emphasis put on Moses/Law-obedience, leaving its relevance unclear to the reader. Even when the term "yoke" appears (15:10), the reader's thoughts would not necessarily turn to the Law since other yokes were known.[169] As S. G. Wilson noted, even if the yoke is seen as a reference to the Law, it is not necessarily a negative characterization (it can be a gladly undertaken obligation).[170] The reader, therefore, determines its referent and connotation by context—it includes the Law, but emphasis is on circumcision as a boundary marker for God's people. The reader understands this from the extra-text—during the Second-Temple period circumcision is seen by both Jew and gentile as a mark that distinguishes Jews from gentiles and not simply as a Law-concern.[171] A Jew who failed to circumcise his male child or sought to reverse the procedure was considered an apostate.[172] In this light, the reader sees the opponents presenting circumcision and Law obedience as the authentic markers for identifying who is included in the people of God. They contend that gentiles must undergo circumcision in order to be included.[173]

When the four conditions (15:20) are added to the decree *because Moses is read* in every synagogue (15:21), the reader finally sees Moses and the Law addressed. However, neither Moses nor the Law is denigrated since they continue to affect God's people—the divine Law has already made provisions for gentiles (discussed below).

---

166. Lake and Cadbury, *Beginnings*, 125. *Contra* Haenchen (*Acts*, 359) gentile baptism is solved at 10:47. Although gentile baptism and gentile fellowship may be "two sides of the same thing" (Schneider, *Apostelgeschichte*, II, 83), this narrative focuses on fellowship. Barrett (*Acts*, 534–35; also Blue, "Influence," 480–94) confuses the issues because he thinks the common appeal to divine action and prohibition against hindering it indicates only one argument is addressed in both cases. Jervell (*Apostelgeschichte*, 388–402) seems uncertain as to what is the issue in Acts 15— it is variously the Law, circumcision, and gentile purity. While the first two are addressed in Acts 15, the last is taken up in 11:1–18 and the decree provisions seem to have little to do with this issue.

167. This is the WT's reading, but does not show strong support elsewhere.

168. As do Haenchen, *Acts*, 442–55; Schneider, *Apostelgeschichte*, II, 174.

169. See Lake and Cadbury, *Beginnings*, 174.

170. S. G. Wilson, *Luke*, 60; following Nolland, "Fresh," 105–15.

171. So Dunn, *Theology*, 356; Gaventa, *Acts*, 213.

172. Hengel and Schwemer, *Paul*, 71–73.

173. So Barrett, *Acts*, 696; Johnson, *Acts*, 261; Plunkett, "Ethnocentricity," 476.

Returning then to the main issues in these pericopae, the reader identifies both 11:1–18 and 15:1–33 as disruptions to the social order—one attributes to gentiles an inferior socio-religious status (they are unclean and, therefore, unequal kingdom participants).[174] The second addresses the proper markers for inclusion in the kingdom. The great "debate" (15:7) has brought the community to a crisis point that must be resolved if the community's values are to be maintained. In both cases the reader finds continuing the dispute identified as rejecting the divine will—an idea made pointedly in the second instance as Peter equates burdening the gentiles with circumcision to testing the Lord (15:10).[175] The reader has seen this sin, and the corresponding disruption to the social order, attributed to Ananias and Sapphira (5:9),[176] and so considers this one a disruption as well. Moreover, the reader's sense that the divine will is at issue is enhanced by the Pharisaic party's belief that circumcision is necessary ($\delta\epsilon\tilde{\iota}$) for gentiles to be included in God's people (15:5).

To resolve these issues the reader finds three identical arguments in both pericopae: 1) God initiated the action on both sides—so Peter's fellowship with gentiles was ordained by God (11:5–9, 13–14)[177] and God chose the gentiles to hear and believe (15:7), grounding the circumcision-free gospel in *divine action* toward Cornelius.[178] 2) God testified to the divine will by giving the Spirit (11:17; 15:8).[179] 3) God did not distinguish between Jew and gentile—Peter was to go with Cornelius' men without making distinction (11:12)[180] and God cleansed both peoples through faith (15:9; cf. 10:15, 28),[181] and abolished any distinction.[182] Consequently, "repentance that leads to life" comes to gentiles in the same way as to Jews (11:18) and both peoples are cleansed by the faith that marks them as kingdom citizens apart from (not in contradiction to) circumcision and the Law.

In both cases, the reader sees divine benefaction (11:17—"the same gift"; 15:11—the "grace of the Lord Jesus") overcoming the impediments and resolving the difficulty.[183] In Acts 15 even greater stress is placed on divine action since Luke focuses the reader's attention on it from the beginning by repeating references to "what God had done" (15:4; cf. 14:27). After Peter's speech, Paul and Barnabas recount the confirmatory signs and wonders *God had done* among the gentiles (15:12). James notes *divine action* in taking a people from among the gentiles (15:14), confirmed by Scriptural fulfillment (15:16–18; Amos 9:11–12), and, therefore, gentiles should not be troubled because this is what *God*

---

174. See Haenchen, *Acts*, 354; Pesch, *Apostelgeschichte*, I, 346. Plunkett ("Ethnocentricity," 474–75) rightly points to this as an ethnocentric status, rather than one related simply to purity.

175. Peter's refusal to "hinder God" (11:17) functions identically (so Tannehill, *Narrative*, 185).

176. Gaventa (*Acts*, 216) and Johnson (*Acts*, 262) also identify the parallel.

177. Soards (*Speeches*, 77) notes that the rhetoric transfers responsibility for the event from Peter to God.

178. Gaventa, *Acts*, 215; Haenchen, *Acts*, 445; Pesch, *Apostelgeschichte*, II, 77.

179. See chapter 3.

180. While the phrase could refer to Peter going without misgiving, the previous scene has illustrated Peter realizing the true extent to divine impartiality (10:34–35) (so Barrett, *Acts*, 540; Johnson, *Acts*, 185).

181. If both *believe* to be saved, then both *believe* to be cleansed.

182. Pesch, *Apostelgeschichte*, II, 78.

183. See Kieffer, "Linguistic," 83.

has chosen to do.[184] Consequently, the reader finds that divine action has led to the joy (15:31) and most importantly, the reconciling peace (15:33) engendered by the decree being read. While the latter phrase could refer to the well-being wished for the traveler, in this dispute context it seems to take on a deeper sense reflecting the community—they are all brothers.[185] Peace here, then, is understood as restoring social order to the community. Thus, divine actions and will, whether directly (as with Paul) or in retrospect (as with table-fellowship and circumcision), are portrayed as the key factors in maintaining peace in the kingdom, confirming its status as the true kingdom of God.

A Saving God Who Requires Obedience[186]

The final element in this characterizing strand involves four themes (piety, obedience, acceptance/rejection, salvation) that differentiate the community in Acts, assuring the reader that these are truly God's Kingdom people. The importance of these characteristics can be seen in Peter's Pentecost speech. At 2:12, some in the crowd respond to what has happened by asking what the Pentecost event signifies (τί θέλει τοῦτο εἶναι). While, as an idiom, such a phrase was common, the use of a θελ root word may cause the reader to anticipate that the event 'desires' a response. A requirement *is* emphasized by the crowd's second question—"what should we do" (2:37). The people (and the reader) perceive from the event and Peter's explanation that they are required to perform some sort of pious action. That obligation is repentance and baptism, which is summed up as being saved from "this corrupt generation" (2:40). Some will accept and others will reject this summons. Here, then, the reader finds four themes that characterize God in relation to the kingdom's citizens—*God saves* and God requires *pious obedience*; some will *accept but others reject* the kingdom requirements. Tracing out these themes will show their significance and interrelation.

Piety

Initially, the reader finds a stress on the disciples' responsibility to respond to directions from Jesus and the angels (1:6–8; 1:9–11; see chapter 4). Immediately after the latter statement, the narrator shows the group obeying Jesus' command (they return to Jerusalem—1:12, cf. 1:4). At the same time, stress is placed on their piety by the reference to Olivet as a Sabbath day's journey away. Through this aside Luke could simply be giving information the reader lacks—the distance from Olivet to Jerusalem.[187] Narrative asides, however, do more than supply new information; they also provide emphasis.[188] Luke's reader, familiar with the

---

184. Likewise, in Acts 11 it is the divine decision that provides the answer to the objectors (Pesch, *Apostelgeschichte*, I, 339).

185. So Johnson, *Acts*, 278; Roloff, *Apostelgeschichte*, 234.

186. Ὑπακόη and ὑπακούω are used infrequently in Luke-Acts (Luke 8:25; 17:26; Acts 6:7; 7:39), but (as will be illustrated) obedience is a frequent theme.

187. Gaventa, *Acts*, 67.

188. See Sheeley, *Narrative*, 37–38.

Gospel accounts, already knows that Jerusalem and Olivet were a distance apart that could be traveled on a holy day (Matt 26:30; Mark 14:26; Luke 22:39). Thus, the reference to the Sabbath focuses Luke's reader's attention on the disciples' piety, not the distance. Whether or not this event took place on a Sabbath,[189] its mention portrays the disciples as concerned with Jewish legal prescriptions.[190] Such indications reflecting devout Jewish piety among the believers[191] are repeated throughout 1:1—8:3. There are persistent references to their prayer (1:14, 24; 2:42; 3:1; 4:24, 31; 6:4, 6; 7:59, 60). The community, also demonstrates interest in the temple (2:46; 5:20–21, 42; 6:7[192]), and consistently engages in praise to God (2:11, 47; 3:8, 9; 4:21; 5:41). In particular, 3:1–11 presents three features indicating Jewish piety centered around the temple: 1) They go to the temple,[193] 2) at the time for the evening prayer and sacrifice,[194] and are requested to (3) give alms—a way of "doing justice."[195] With regard to the latter, it is possible that the reader could see in the healing that takes place here the giving of a new justice, a new social order which includes complete wholeness. Therefore, the preceding discussion about the social order, fairness, and justice evident in the community would also reflect the group's piety. Such actions were seen as fulfilling Mosaic Law (Deut 15:4). Thus, Capper correctly point out how important alms-giving was for the community ethic.[196]

Chapter 2 noted that in 2 Maccabees such piety marked the people's appropriate action in relation to God, ensuring that God would hear and respond to their oppression and continue to act as deliverer. Thus, piety had a prominent place in our reader's extra-textual world. Further, the reference to "piety" (3:12) in relation to the miracle suggests that Second-Temple ideas concerning piety as a necessary condition for divine action are influencing the presentation. However, the reader's expectations concerning piety are altered because, in contrast to 2 Maccabees, Peter expressly denies that piety engenders

---

189. See Barrett, *Acts*, 86; Haenchen, *Acts*, 150–51.

190. Fitzmyer, *Acts*, 213; Johnson, *Acts*, 33.

191. Christians are portrayed as devout Jews (Barrett, *Acts*, 177–78). Carras ("Observant," 693–708) compared the Jewish piety presented by Luke (for "Christian" and "non-Christian" Jews) with that presented by Josephus, concluding that Luke's portrait compares favorably with Josephus. Since Josephus was trying to present the Jews positively, it follows that Luke was as well.

192. The reference to priests who have become obedient implies the Way is accepted among those associated with the temple cult.

193. While Blue ("Influence," 473–97; also Blomberg, "Christian," 401–2) correctly identifies the impact that Jewish worship, particularly in the household setting, had on Luke's presentation, his attempt to de-emphasize the temple's importance seems misguided. Luke does not make the temple the setting for the event simply because there was a crowd there; rather Luke consistently presents the temple as a place the community goes to for worship. Blomberg ("Christian," 397–416) relies on what is left unsaid (no direct reference to Sinai; no mention of sacrifices (though this is incorrect here)) to make a case that Luke is leading his reader away from valuing the Law and the temple positively. This seems to demonstrate a problem in his approach—it focuses on omissions rather than on what is actually said. Thus, Blomberg misses the way Luke's emphasis on piety presents Law and temple positively for the reader.

194. So Schneider, *Apostelgeschichte*, I, 299 (but strangely he thinks they arrive after the sacrifice—something not apparent from the text); Fitzmyer, *Acts*, 277; Witherington, *Acts*, 173).

195. See Johnson, *Acts*, 64–65.

196. Capper, "Reciprocity," 499–518.

divine action ("as though by our own power or piety").[197] Peter's words, therefore, disallow piety from controlling or manipulating God. The reader is expected to identify piety as demonstrating that reverence is the norm for God's people (cf. also the "great fear," 5:5, 11, 13; 2:43).[198] God is therefore characterized in this opening section as possessing a majesty that elicits respect and honor from the people.

In Acts 8:4—19:20 the kingdom's citizens pray (8:15; 9:40; 10:9; 12:5, 12;[199] 13:4; 14:23; 16:13, 16, 25) or are entreated to pray (8:22, 24); fear the Lord (9:31; 10:2;[200] 19:17); do good works and alms (9:36; 11:24[201]); are described as holy (9:32, 41); refrain from receiving worship (10:25–26; 14:14–18) and despise idolatry (17:16); are circumcised (10:45; 11:2; 16:3); fast (13:2, 4; 14:23); attend synagogues (13:5, 14; 14:1; 17:1; 18:4, 8, 19, 26; 19:8); respect the Sabbath (13:14, 42, 44; 16:13; 17:2; 18:4); glorify the Lord (13:48; 16:25; 19:17); and keep vows (18:18).[202]

The reader also discovers other Jewish customs represented as important for the community, even if they create difficulty and requirements about them must be relaxed.[203] Concerns for purity in relation to gentiles (10:28; 11:3) are mitigated by a divine cleansing act (10:15, 28; 11:9, 17). Circumcision (15:2, 5), while still practiced by Jews (10:45; 11:2; 16:3[204]), is made non-obligatory for gentiles by God giving the Spirit apart from circumci-

---

197. Barrett (*Acts*, 188) tries to refute notions of divine-men with this passage. He (193) comes closer to the point in discussing Honi and Hanina ben Dosa, whose piety and power could "compel" God to action. Witherington (*Acts*, 179) ignores piety's importance in Second-Temple thought, defining it only from a non-Jewish perspective.

198. These references incorporate both religious awe (see Fitzmyer, *Acts*, 271; Haenchen, *Acts*, 192; Schneider, *Apostelgeschichte*, I, 287, fn. 25) and fear of supernatural punishment (Barrett, *Acts*, 268).

199. The reader may wonder if the unbelief about Peter's release suggests a failure to believe in God's readiness to intervene. For the narrative community such doubt seems possible since God did not intervene with James. It is precisely the contrast between James' inexplicable death and Peter's deliverance (*contra* Haenchen, *Acts*, 388) that would prompt the reader's doubts and the need to reconcile the narrative features. However, because they pray fervently in a seemingly hopeless situation (Haenchen, *Acts*, 383), it seems that they at least believed God could act. Since the reader could assume that James' death and Peter's imprisonment would cause despair, the command to tell the other James and the brethren could be taken as intended to provide encouragement (aligning with divine concerns for the community's welfare).

200. Chapter 3 indicated a distinction between the groups in 9:31 and 10:2 based on the object of the fear (Lord, God). However, the fear attributed to the first group does prepare for Cornelius being portrayed as properly responsive to God (so Gaventa, *Acts*, 157).

201. Barnabas is a "good" man and the reader knows him to have shown his reverence for God by offering his property.

202. The emphasis is on Paul's faithfulness and piety (Haenchen, *Acts*, 543; Tannehill, *Narrative*, 227).

203. *Contra* Pesch (*Apostelgeschichte*, I, 338–39) Luke does not apply Peter's vision (10:1–15) to Jewish food restrictions. Since Peter puzzles over the vision's application from the start, the reader does not find the characters entertaining this interpretation. Instead, Peter realizes he has done the same thing with gentiles as he had with the food offered to him—declare them all impure (Gaventa, *Acts*, 165–66; Plunkett, "Ethnocentricity," 468). Barrett (*Acts*, 509; Jervell, *Luke*, 138; Schille, *Apostelgeschichte*, 245) adds that Luke does not include anything parallel to Mark 7:19, which explicitly labels all foods are pure.

204. Whether or not later Jewish law, which traces Jewish lineage from the mother's side (*m. Qidd.* 3:12), was practiced in the first century (see Cohen, "Was," 251–68; cf. critiques by Bryan, "Further," 292–94; Witherington, *Acts*, 474–76), Luke appears to present Timothy as if others would assume he were a Jew (Barrett, *Acts*, 762; Gaventa, *Acts*, 232; Johnson, *Acts*, 284). Thus, Paul, it seems, has Timothy circumcised because he would be considered Jewish, making him more acceptable to Jews. This does not mean that Luke considered circumcision a condition of salvation for Jews (so Pesch, *Apostelgeschichte*, II, 97; Schneider, *Apostelgeschichte*,

sion (15:8). The reader discovers no animosity directed toward circumcision as a practice, only toward it as necessary for being included in the kingdom.[205] Also, while Jewish customs maintained by Christians are considered a problem for the Roman citizens in Philippi (16:20–21), the reader finds this problem remedied by God physically delivering Paul and Silas and 'spiritually' delivering the jailer (16:30–31). Since Paul and Silas were engaged in prayer and praise to God prior to this divine action, Jewish piety would be identified as a help rather than a hindrance to rescue. Moreover, neither Paul nor Silas is described denying their Jewishness and Paul's Roman citizenship is not revealed until after these deliverances.[206]

Further, the reader identifies regard for the Mosaic Law maintained. In response to concerns about obedience to that Law (15:5) and because (γὰρ) Moses is preached and read in the synagogue (15:21),[207] the Apostolic Decree includes four clauses that in their OT context related to prescriptions for both Jews and aliens living among them (15:20; cf. Lev 17–18).[208] Some argue that the fit to Lev 17–18 is inexact and that it is not clear that these Leviticus texts are to be applied to resident aliens. Instead, Luke's aim is to prevent idolatry.[209] However, the reader has been given no reason from the context to think idolatry is a problem, but some (cf. 15:1, 5) to think that concern for the Mosaic Law is. The allusion to Lev 17–18 is strong enough to cause the reader to recall this extra-text since, in that text, the phrase "aliens who reside among them" is associated five times with prohibitions that correspond to the ones listed here: sacrifice (17:8); blood (17:10); strangled (hunted/torn—17:13–15); and fornication (18:26). This suggests that there were certain things already expected from non-Jews who were living among God's covenant people.[210] Therefore, in applying these prescriptions to those among the gentiles who have turned to God (15:19), the implication seems to be that no more burden should be placed on the gentiles than God had determined should be placed on the alien living among the Israelite people.[211] Already, the kingdom has been redefined on an ethical/spiritual plane, so the borders for God's covenant people would no longer be geographic. Jew and gentile, upon

II, 200) since that issue was resolved in Acts 15. It, however, does suggest an interest in maintaining Jewish piety. Haenchen's (*Acts*, 480–82) objections that the "historical" Paul would never have allowed this miss the point that Luke wants his reader to assume such actions by Jews to be customary piety offered to God, not conditions for salvation.

205. Johnson, *Acts*, 259.

206. Conzelmann (*Theology*, 141) thought Paul's Roman citizenship allowed Roman law to act as a "savior." The narrative does not suggest that Roman law has saved him from anything. God did the delivering.

207 Γὰρ gives the grounds for a previous statement but commentators are unclear as to which (15:19—Williams, *Acts*, 184; 15:15–18—Dibelius, *Studies*, 92). The most natural reading takes it with 15:20 since this is the nearest statement (so Haenchen, *Acts*, 450; Johnson, *Acts*, 267; S. G. Wilson, *Luke*, 83–84).

208. This view is accepted by many scholars, Haenchen, *Acts*, 469; Pesch, *Apostelgeschichte*, II, 81; Schille, *Apostelgeschichte*, 321-22; Schneider, *Apostelgeschichte*, II, 184.

209. So Gaventa, *Acts*, 222; Witherington, *Acts*, 461–65.

210. See Bauckham, "James," 171–75.

211. *Contra* Jervell (*Unknown*, 30; *Luke*, 143–45, 190–93) Luke does not present this as a greater restriction than already existed, but what God expected all along. Jervell (*Apostelgeschichte*, 398) attempts to correct this judgment, saying that while no part of the Law was originally imposed, the God-fearing gentiles were keeping these commands anyway. However, this requires the reader to accept Jervell's unsubstantiated thesis that only God-fearers have been converted from among the gentiles.

entering the kingdom through faith not circumcision or law obedience, live within the boundaries defining God's people.[212] Now, both peoples (maintaining divinely prescribed piety) live together. Therefore, throughout 8:4—19:20 the kingdom's citizens retain customary piety, as would be expected from those claiming to be God's people.

The reader also finds piety presented as a qualifying characteristic for converts. The eunuch has been to Jerusalem to worship (8:27) and is reading Scripture (8:28, 32). Cornelius' immediate direct characterization by the narrator (he is devout, fears God, gives alms, and petitions for the people, 10:2) marks him for special attention. When these features are repeated by the angel (prayers and alms—10:4),[213] Cornelius' messengers (God-fearing, well spoken of by the Jews—10:22), and in Cornelius' retelling (prayer and alms—10:30), the reader's attention is focused squarely on this man's devotion. He appears as the perfect candidate for God's kingdom since he illustrates the actions associated with one who reveres God.[214]

The reader's conceptions about piety as a qualifying characteristic are confirmed through Peter's declaration that God receives everyone who "fears him" and "does what is right" (10:35).[215] Such people are characterized as in the proper state to respond with the repentance and faith that mark entrance into the kingdom. The reader should realize, however, that *acceptable to God* and *saved* is not the same thing. Cornelius is *acceptable*, but is not *saved* until he responds with repentance and faith (the reader realizes repentance has taken place from 11:18).[216]

Later, both Lydia (16:14) and Titius Justus (18:7) appear qualified to have their hearts and homes opened by being worshipers of God. Thus, God, consistent with OT and Second-Temple thought, rewards righteousness. However, the reader will also find that God is free to determine who enters the kingdom—the Samaritans are included, but Luke does not characterize them as greatly pious. Instead, they appear gullible and willing to follow a false "god," Simon Magus (8:9–11). Likewise, Paul is a persecutor and violent rejecter, yet God directly intervenes. In this case, the reader sees piety as the result of, not the precursor to, divine action since prior to his conversion he breathes "threats and murder" but afterwards he prays—9:11,[217] and fasts—9:9.[218] Consequently, while reverence

---

212. So Johnson, *Acts*, 267. Thus, *contra* Witherington (*Acts*, 465), these prescriptions make sense in application to gentiles in the Diaspora—this piety would be expected from those who are within the boundary marking God's people.

213. Cornelius is the only gentile to receive an angelic vision in Acts, which further marks his distinct piety (Gaventa, *Acts*, 164; Johnson, *Acts*, 194). Esler (*Community*, 162) may be correct in concluding that God is treating the prayers and alms from a gentile like a sacrifice for a Jew. Luke, nevertheless, does not suggest that it is merely this man's piety that has caused God to break down the barriers. Rather, Luke will focus on divine action making all things clean (see Hamm, "Tamid," 222–23).

214. Bibb, "Characterization," 216–17; Jervell, *Apostelgeschichte*, 310; Johnson, *Acts*, 187; Kieffer, "Linguistic," 85; Tannehill, *Narrative*, 133.

215. Both qualities refer to OT piety (Schneider, *Apostelgeschichte*, II, 75 ns. 141–42). Barrett (*Acts*, 520) suggests that righteousness is to be understood as akin to alms-giving.

216. Kilgallen, "Clean," 301.

217. Evidence that Paul is sincere (Haenchen, *Acts*, 324) and pious (Johnson, *Acts*, 164).

218. Pesch (*Apostelgeschichte*, I, 305; more cautiously, Barrett, *Acts*, 452) sees this as an act of repentance. Gaventa (*Acts*, 150–51) appears to disagree with this assessment. However, her concern to show that Paul does

for God characterizes God's people, it does not constrain divine action. OT texts consistently portrayed God as free to choose God's people (Isaac not Ishmael, Jacob not Esau, etc.).[219] Thus, once again, the reader sees God depicted in keeping with what is already known about God, but the reader's boundaries are stretched as now Samaritans, gentiles, and persecutors have a stake in God's people. God majestically remains in control over the kingdom and its citizens, assuring the reader that God has assembled a kingdom people.

In the final section, believers pray together (20:36; 21:5) and glorify God for divine actions (21:20). Paul characterizes Ananias as pious towards the Law (22:12). Jewish believers are concerned for the Law and Mosaic customs (21:20–24) as well as items that make for proper gentile piety (21:25). However, since the reader encounters a greater array of evidence amassed concerning Paul's piety and obedience than for other figures, it seems that the reader's attention in 19:21—28:31 is being drawn to Paul and his defense.[220] The reader finds Paul desiring to attend Jewish feasts (20:16). He prays with the community (20:36; 21:5), before healings (28:8) and in the temple (22:17). Paul goes up to Jerusalem to worship (24:11), presenting alms and offerings (24:17).[221] He is concerned about being blameless in his actions toward all people (24:16) and toward God (23:1). Paul repeatedly claims to be a Jew (21:38; 22:3; 26:4), even the strictest sort (26:5), a Pharisee (23:6; 26:5)—a statement with which at least some council members agree (23:9).[222] Further, Paul gives thanks to God for divine actions on his behalf (27:35—the promise of deliverance; 28:6—his safe arrival and acceptance by the brethren in Rome). The reader even finds Paul's piety indicated by the reference to Paul staying with Philip and Mnason (21:8, 16). These two figures are associated with the earliest Jewish believers, and their hospitality implies, in turn, that Paul is accepted by these devout Jews.[223]

The reader encounters this emphasis on Paul's character leading up to and directed toward the problems Paul faces in Jerusalem. Such problems occur in two phases—first, Jewish believers fear that Paul was teaching Jews not to observe Mosaic customs, par-

---

not take an active role in his conversion misses the importance the culture placed on demonstrating piety. Paul's prayer and fasting provide the reader with immediate confirmation that God has transformed Paul, and that Paul is now worthy to take up the role assigned to him.

219. See Hoet, "ἐθνῶν," 405–6.

220. Jervell (*Luke*, 163) and Tannehill (*Narrative*, 286) are correct that the defense scenes are cumulative; however, Paul's defense is not simply found in these scenes but also in Paul's piety and obedience. Consequently, Gaventa (*Acts*, 303) misses the point in indicating that Paul's silence in 21:12–26 sharpens the accusations against him—the reader is aware (from how Paul has been characterized so far) that these are false charges.

221. Here (*contra* Fitzmyer, *Acts*, 736; Haenchen, *Acts*, 655), Luke is not alluding to the "collection," but emphasizing Paul's Jewish piety (rightly Tannehill, *Narrative*, 300).

222. The main distinction between the "Nazarenes" and both the Pharisees and Sadducees is that the first believe Jesus to be the messiah (rightly J. T. Sanders, *Jews*, 87). However, Sanders asserts (*Jews*, 100) that Paul's claim to Pharisaism has nothing to do with him actually being a Pharisee. Supposedly, Luke's Paul wishes to identify with certain views held also by Pharisees, thus showing Christianity is in continuity with Judaism. However, Luke has Paul claim to *be* a Pharisee and to *live* as a Pharisee. His self-characterization is that he is both a Christian and a Pharisee. Since the Pharisees accept the possibility that Paul could be speaking the truth, the emphasis is on the Way as aligned with or even identified with (not simply in continuity with) Jewish (Pharisaic) belief (Fitzmyer, *Acts*, 714–15).

223. So Barrett, *Acts*, 1003.

ticularly circumcision (21:21). When the provisions for gentiles are reiterated (21:25), the reader is assured that the problem Paul faces is not with the gentile inclusion but with Jewish piety.[224]

Would the reader then think that the Jerusalem leadership has acceded to Judaizers who want everyone to adhere to Jewish legal standards?[225] For the reader, pious action has been considered normative throughout the work. The reader also knows that Paul is not opposed to Jewish believers being circumcised since he had Timothy circumcised after the decree (16:3). Gaventa's objection that this is because of the Jews and not due to respect for the Law[226] misses the way Luke consistently presents Jewish piety (including Law obedience) as characteristic for believers—concern for Jewish customs is respect for the Law. Further, Luke has pointed out Paul's vow observance (18:18). When this information is coupled with Paul's desire to participate in the Pentecost feast (20:16), the reader finds Luke's Paul not only unwilling to violate Jewish customs, but actively interested in Jewish religious practice. Luke's reader, therefore, would find no problem in Paul's willingness to demonstrate piety by keeping the divine Law (21:24).[227]

From the reader's perspective, a devout Jew like Paul undertaking the prescribed actions could be a reasonable solution to a problem for the community (whether or not it appears as such for those outside the community). Luke does not mention the involvement of Jewish believers in Paul's trials. However, this silence need not be interpreted as their complicity with the Jewish mob;[228] rather, Luke suggests that Paul has done what is necessary to solve the problem in the community, and then picks up another theme—(Asian) Jews have renewed their persecution—one in which Luke has not shown Jewish believers having any role in helping Paul (beyond delivering him from plots). Further, since no letter condemning Paul is received by either Christians or Jews in Rome (28:15, 21) there is no reason to believe the Jerusalem church leaders were active in opposition to Paul.[229]

The second phase comes from outside the group. The reader finds Paul, like Stephen before him, being charged with crimes against the Law and the temple as well as acting against the people (21:28). Given the similarities in the charges, the reader is likely to assume once again that these charges are false (discussed previously), but Luke does not leave it at that—providing responses to each charge. The reader learns that Luke's Paul cannot be acting against the people, for he repeatedly declares his Jewishness (21:38; 22:3; 26:4) and directly denies anti-Jewish charges to the Jewish leaders in Rome (28:17). Paul's speech in Acts 22, designed to address the issues raised at 21:28, portrays Paul as a Jew truly obedient to God.[230] Since Ananias is also characterized as law pious and in good standing

224. Pesch, *Apostelgeschichte*, II, 221; Johnson, *Acts*, 376. Jervell (*Apostelgeschichte*, 527) correctly suggests that mentioning the decree confirms Paul's interest in making sure gentile converts remain pious.

225. As Pesch, *Apostelgeschichte*, II, 222.

226. Gaventa, *Acts*, 299.

227. So Witherington, *Acts*, 648.

228. As Barrett (*Acts*, 1000) who thinks that the Jewish-Christians take part, seeing through the "sham" of James' solution.

229. So Jervell, *Unknown*, 18–19.

230. So Haenchen, *Acts*, 630; Pesch, *Apostelgeschichte*, II, 233.

with the Jews, the reader realizes (if not already assumes) that being a Jewish-Christian is neither a contradiction nor a violation against the people. Therefore, throughout these final chapters any charge against Paul or the Way as anti-Jewish is viewed by Luke's reader as demonstrably false.[231]

Luke has already given the reader sufficient reason to reject the claim that Paul preaches contrary to the Law, but adds that Paul declares himself to be trained in the Law by Gamaliel and thus zealous for God (22:3). Such zeal can be dangerous since it can easily be directed against God; even as Paul's was (he persecuted the Way—22:4). Luke's Paul, nevertheless, sees it as common ground (it appears in a *captatio*) with the crowd and a means to demonstrate that he has not lost his zeal for the Law. When rebuked, Paul appeals to the Law (23:3–5), defining himself as its adherent. Moreover, the Lord's messenger to Paul, Ananias, is characterized as a devout Law-keeper (22:11). This illustrates to the reader that those who are obedient to the Way are no less pious toward the Law. Paul will later affirm this conclusion, saying that as a member of the Way he serves Israel's God according to the Law and the Prophets (24:14). J. T. Sanders claims that Luke does not maintain the theme that the Jewish Christians were "perfectly Torah-observant."[232] However, Luke has Paul remaining Torah-observant even in his last visit to Jerusalem. It is Paul's Torah-observance that indicates to the reader Paul is not violating the temple.

Finally, in response to his supposed temple desecration (cf. 24:6), Paul will first narrate a vision that occurred in the temple (22:17–21). By locating Paul in the temple, Paul's loyalty to it is suggested to the audience (and the reader).[233] More importantly, the reader finds that it is the Lord over the temple Paul has supposedly defiled that has commanded him to go away to the gentiles. If the temple's Lord demands such action, Paul's ministry among the gentiles cannot be anti-temple.[234] Consequently, while Paul's statement may seem ill-advised given the response from the crowd, it fits Paul's defense against these charges.[235] The temple has previously been the scene for an announcement suggesting the inclusion of non-Jews (3:25). Therefore, finding the temple used as a staging area for worldwide mission, the reader can assume Christianity is consistent with, rather than separate from, Judaism and the temple.[236] Further, both the narrator (21:26) and Paul (24:18) will point out that Paul went through ritual purification prior to entering the temple. Therefore, the temple remains undefiled by both Paul and his mission. By answering these charges, Luke maintains the presentation that Paul and all believers are those pious toward God, confirming that these are truly God's kingdom people.

---

231. So Tannehill, "Narrator's," 256-57; Witherington, *Acts*, 659-60.

232. J. T. Sanders, *Jews*, 117.

233. So Haenchen, *Acts*, 627; Johnson, *Acts*, 390.

234. Rightly Jervell, *Apostelgeschichte*, 545.

235. Tannehill (*Narrative*, 277) claims Paul's vision and announcement concerning going away do not fit his defense. However, it is the command from the "Lord" over the temple that authorizes Paul's mission, so the vision would be central to the apology.

236. *Contra* Haenchen, *Acts*, 628; so Tannehill, *Narrative*, 282–83.

Obedience

When the lame beggar is healed (3:1–10), the crowd responds with "wonder and amazement" echoing the amazement and perplexity that marked the Pentecost crowd (cf. 2:12; 3:10),[237] suggesting to the reader that this act too requires a reaction. That response, just as with the Pentecost speech, is repentance (3:19), but here obedience receives even greater importance through the reference to the Prophet like Moses who must be heard (ἀκούσεσθε; ἀκούσῃ) or the crowd faces being cut off from God's people (3:22–23). The OT context (Deut 18:15–19) suggests that this prophet (who Peter identifies as Jesus—3:20) would give divine commands that must be obeyed. Indeed, those who *hear* respond with action, since Luke notes that many who "heard" (ἀκουσάντων) reacted properly by believing (4:4). With the reference to the covenant (διαθήκης) (3:25), the reader notes a further suggestion of obedience as the covenant (which was associated with piety and obedience in Second-Temple literature) obligated proper response to God.[238]

As shown previously, in 1:15–26 the reader identifies the believers' obedience to the divine will in Scripture. Later, when commanded not to speak in Jesus' name, Peter replies in a stock phrase (it appears in various places, including the account of Socrates' trial and 2 Maccabees) expressing the requirement to obey God (4:19).[239] This is reiterated emphatically at a second command to stop (5:29). The repeated interplay of divine and human authority that takes place in these interactions between the apostles and the Jewish council, indicates a rhetorical stress on obedience to God. Thus, the reader's attention is drawn to an obedience contest,[240] in which the reader learns that because the authorities listen to Gamaliel rather than to Peter and John (5:39—"they were convinced by him"), they show themselves obeying human authority not divine.[241] The Apostles, however, demonstrate their obedience by teaching in the temple in accordance with the angel's command (5:19–21).

The repeated references to the temple in 5:17–21 also underscores the conflict over whether the Apostles or the Council better discerns and obeys the will of the Lord over the temple.[242] This may affirm Chance's argument that Luke is replacing the Jewish leadership with the Apostles. The former have rejected Jesus and the latter have now been appointed as leaders over God's true people,[243] demonstrated by their obedience to the divine commands. This does not mean, however, that the temple or the cult is rejected; only that God has given Israel a new leadership. Indeed, Luke emphasizes that the temple belongs to God's people since the angelic command requires these people (represented by the

---

237. Note the similar words ἐξιστάνω and ἐκστάσεως.

238. Fitzmyer, *Acts*, 290–91.

239. Cf. Barrett, *Acts*, 237–38; Johnson, *Acts*, 79; Lake and Cadbury, *Beginnings*, 45; Pesch, *Apostelgeschichte*, I, 169, 216.

240. Tannehill, *Narrative*, 62. Barrett (*Acts*, 218) notes this, but he goes too far in suggesting this makes Christianity not Judaism; rather, for Luke, it makes Christianity the heir to what Judaism is supposed to be.

241. Johnson, *Acts*, 100–101.

242. Gaventa, *Acts*, 106; cf. Barrett, *Acts*, 289.

243. Chance, *Jerusalem*, 66–84

Apostles) to maintain a presence there.[244] Thus, Luke seems to define true leadership in relation to obedience to God rather than social or cultic position.

Peter announces that God gives the Spirit to those who "obey" God (5:32). Through recollection the reader would note that it is only the community that has received (2:1–12), been filled with (4:8, 31),[245] and been related to the Spirit (5:3, 9). This suggests that only the believing community can be said to be obedient to God (only they have received the testifying sign). They have been marked with the pneumatic element that identifies God's people. Consequently, obedience is not only a requirement, but also a characteristic marking the kingdom's citizens. Because obedience is so important to the narrative, the reader will seek to determine what the divine will is so as to heed it. Also, the exclusive connection between the Spirit and those who are obedient would seem to suggest that the reader would be thrown into a crisis (see below) if a prominent figure in the community were thought to be directly disobedient to the Spirit's will.

As the narrative moves into the phase where the community expands outward from Jerusalem (8:4—19:20), prominent characters—Philip (8:26, 29); Cornelius (10:5, 7–8);[246] and Peter (10:19–20)[247]—respond to divine commands. Paul (Saul) is repeatedly characterized by his obedience to divine directives (response to the Lord's commands—9:6, 8; 9:20, cf. 9:15; 18:9–11; response to the Spirit's commands—13:4; 16:6–7, 10) and cognizance of the divine will (13:46; 18:21). The reader finds an entire church (Antioch) branded by its sensitivity to the Spirit's words (11:28–29—the prophecy concerning famine; 13:2–3—the Spirit's call to set Barnabas and Saul apart). Likewise, the Apostolic Council follows the Spirit's wishes (15:28—"it has seemed good to the Holy Spirit").

As this obedience, therefore, continues to characterize God's people, the divine interventions could seem to overwhelm human discovery, make responses automatic and cause faith to lose, as Haenchen states, "its true character of decision."[248] However, for Luke's reader the obedience operational here is based on difficult decisions the characters have to make. Obedience itself was not necessarily easy, but rather they decided to obey God even though information was lacking or the situation was unclear. This, then, illustrates their faithfulness to God, not God overwhelming their reason.[249]

In this second major section of Acts, God's opponents are those who reject and fight the divine will (i.e., are disobedient). The reader finds a perfect example in the pre-conversion Saul. Saul is in full agreement with those who kill Stephen (8:1). Thus, the reader must classify him among the disobedient people of Israel, who as Stephen has declared, always

---

244. Jervell, *Apostelgeschichte*, 205–6.

245. Jervell (*Apostelgeschichte*, 188) notes that the δοῦλος in 4:29 corresponds to δεσπότης in 4:24. This further emphasizes the community as those who are the obedient servants of the Sovereign.

246. Cornelius' servants effectively characterize him as one who complies with the divine will. Cornelius then affirms his obedience to the divine commands (Pesch, *Apostelgeschichte*, I, 340, 342).

247. See Schille, *Apostelgeschichte*, 246. Both Peter and Cornelius act in "blind obedience" to God (Haenchen, *Acts*, 347).

248. Haenchen, *Acts*, 362.

249. For more specific responses to Haenchen's criticism see Cosgrove, "Divine," 189–90; Johnson, *Acts*, 187; Plunkett, "Ethnocentricity," 473–74; Tannehill, *Narrative*, 128–29.

oppose the Holy Spirit (7:51) and reject God's "Righteous One" (7:52).[250] Like Heliodorus, who in 2 Macc 3:24–29 is accosted by a manifestation sent by the "Sovereign of spirits and of all authority" for attempting to violate the temple treasury, Saul is given the punishment due those who oppose God— blindness (9:9). Luke's account, then, while not based on the 2 Maccabees incident, indicates a familiar *topos* that the reader would interpret as picturing those who oppose God.[251] Fitzmyer, however, objects to the idea that the blindness represents punishment.[252] It is true that Luke does not directly mention punishment, but, given the *topos*, it is the blinding in relation to the manifestation of the Lord, which indicates this conclusion.

The same fate befalls Bar-Jesus (13:11),[253] who is shown to be God's enemy by the Spirit-directed (13:9) characterization Paul gives—he is a "son of the devil" rather than a son of Jesus (as, ironically, would be indicated by his name), an "enemy of all righteousness," and, because he perverts "the divine guidance of human beings"[254] (i.e., the Lord's "straight paths"), he is an obstacle to the divine will (preventing them from being obedient to God).

As discussed in chapter 4, Herod suffered a fate reserved for those who fight God. Further, fear about fighting God seems to be behind Peter's concern not to deny baptism to the gentiles (10:47)—since the Spirit has come upon them, it would be fighting God to deny them water baptism. The same fear may be expressed in the eunuch's question in 8:36 ("What is to prevent me from being baptized?"). While this could imply a problem in the nascent church concerning gentile baptism,[255] because the reader has already been warned about fighting God (the scene with Gamaliel), it seems to indicate such an opportunity is rejected by Peter and Philip. The theme also appears in Peter's concern about preventing God from including the gentiles (11:17),[256] which leads him to compare gentile circumcision with testing the Lord (15:10—an act punishable, it seems, by death given the reference to it in the account of Ananias and Sapphira [Acts 5:9]).

In the final section (19:21—28:31), the reader encounters Paul stating that he has served the Lord (20:19; 27:23) and obediently proclaimed all God's will (20:20, 27). This proclamation involved testifying to repentance toward God and faith in Jesus' name (20:21), which the reader has seen as the obedient response required throughout Acts. Paul declares that doing "deeds consistent with repentance" is a key element in his proclamation (26:20), indicating that those who are repentant are not simply sorry, but respond

---

250. So Tannehill, *Narrative*, 114.

251. *Contra* Haenchen, *Acts*, 323. See Haenchen (*Acts*, 321 [fn. 6], 326) and Barrett (*Acts*, 441) for verbal echoes between Acts 9 and 2 Maccabees.

252. Fitzmyer, *Acts*, 426.

253. Johnson, *Acts*, 163; Witherington, *Acts*, 402.

254. Fitzmyer, *Acts*, 503.

255. So Schneider, *Apostelgeschichte*, II, 80–81. Witherington (*Acts*, 299–300) indicates it relates to restrictions the eunuch would have had in Judaism. Thus, unlike Judaism, entrance to the kingdom is not restricted.

256. "Wer den Heiden die Taufe verwehrte, würde sich damit gegen Gott wenden" (Schneider, *Apostelgeschichte*, II, 46).

outwardly through their piety and obedience. Thus, the reader's impression that repentance is something that is demonstrated through pious, obedient actions is reinforced.

Even though declarations of innocence are typical for farewell discourses,[257] Paul's protests during his speech to the Ephesian elders (20:26) that he is not responsible for the blood of his listeners would remind the reader about his obedience. The keywords καθαρός and αἷματος should cause the reader to recall 18:6, where Paul demonstrated that he had fulfilled his duty to proclaim the word using the same terms.[258] The reference to blood may also recall Ezek 33–34 and the prophetic watchman's responsibility to proclaim the divine word ("their blood shall be upon themselves"; "their blood I will require at the sentinel's hand"). Paul, it would appear, is emphasizing his obedience to divine requirements for such prophetic spokespersons.[259] Consequently, Paul is doubly obedient—he obediently proclaims obedience.

Paul's conformity to the divine will is such that it sees him bound to go to Jerusalem despite the Spirit's witness that afflictions await him there (20:22–23). The reader has already seen such willingness in Peter and John, who claimed they must follow the divine will despite the threats they faced (4:19–20; 5:29). Similarly, the reader may well know that martyrs, such as those in 2 Maccabees and Josephus (*Ant.* 17:158–59), were willing to undergo suffering in obedience to God. Therefore, the reader sees Paul portrayed in line with those who are radical in their obedience. It would seem that what Fitzmyer describes as the "first characteristic" of Paul's ministry,[260] his humble service to the Lord (20:19), is really an act of obedience. Such service is also found in his conformity to the heavenly vision (26:19) that charged him to preach in Damascus, Jerusalem, and to the gentiles, and which affirms the "clear conscience" (23:1) he has concerning his actions—he has been obedient to all God's commands.

However, the reader will also note how difficult such obedience is. In 19:21—21:14 there are a number of non-specific references to "spirit." That is, there is no clear modifier, such as my, Paul's, God's, or Holy, to make it absolutely clear to the reader whose spirit is referenced. This ambiguity requires the reader to determine which spirit is being described, since this affects whether Paul is following his own or the divine will.

Paul (19:21) is described as having purposed in the "spirit" (ἔθετο ... ἐν τῷ πνεύματι) to go to Jerusalem. Previously (17:16), the narrator has referred to Paul's spirit and such

---

257. Pesch (*Apostelgeschichte*, II, 199) argues that Paul's speech here contains numerous features found in Testaments (see also Munck, "Discours," 155–70), a genre well known in OT and Second-Temple literature (Gen 49; Josh 23–24; *T. 12 Patr.*; *T. Mos.*; *1 En.* 91–104; *Apoc. Bar.* 57–86; *4 Ezra* 14:28–36) where an OT figure gives a final message as his death or departure nears. However, the Acts narrative contains only an illusory reference to Paul's death, lacking or at least minimizing a component that was a necessary part of the Testamentary genre (Collins ["Testaments," 325] calls the clear anticipation of death, the "most fundamental defining characteristic" of testaments, and Eades ["*Testament*," 796] notes that testaments seem "to presuppose the impending death of the testator"). As such, Acts 20:17–31 is better classified as an example of the Farewell Discourse. See chapter 6—*Excursus: Paul's Impending Death?*

258. So Johnson, *Acts*, 362.

259. So Tannehill, "Rejection," 91–92.

260. Fitzmyer, *Acts*, 676.

could be the case here.[261] However, unlike that situation, 19:21 does not offer a possessive pronoun to identify this spirit. While the reader will likely assume God's Spirit to be the referent (especially given the necessity (δεῖ) in his seeing Rome),[262] as the narrator makes repeated references to Paul's decisions (Paul decides to return through Macedonia—20:3; Paul determines to sail past Ephesus—20:16) and intentions (Paul intends to leave on the next day—20:7; Paul intends to go by land—20:13), the reader has reason to re-evaluate this assumption. Through these references, attention is drawn away from Paul's submission to the Spirit and towards Paul's purposes on this journey, leaving the reader to wonder if the initial conception was wrong and it really was Paul's spirit that had him bound for Jerusalem.

When the narrator joins the group in Philippi (20:6), the reader begins to experience the events through this focalizing participant. The "we" is relatively anonymous so the reader can take part in the narrative, identifying with the events and sensing their urgency.[263] While it is appropriate to be cautious about using modern reading ideas like reader participation,[264] Luke seems to involve the we-narrator at crisis points (discussed below), suggesting some intent to heighten the reader's experience through involvement in the story.

The involvement of both the narrator and the reader becomes important when, in 21:4 the we-narrator says that Paul, "through the Spirit," was told not to go to Jerusalem. As at 19:21, the narrator does not give an identifying marker. The reader previously saw this formulation in reference to the prophecy by Agabus (11:28), indicating that the reader should assume that this phrase gives authority to the instructions Paul receives.[265] Further, because Paul informed the Ephesian elders that the "Holy Spirit" testifies in every city concerning the afflictions that await him in Jerusalem (20:23), the reader would expect that what is now occurring exemplifies such action.[266] The implication is that the Holy Spirit has been telling Paul not to go to Jerusalem. However, this conclusion disagrees with Paul's declaration (20:22; echoing 19:21) that he is "captive to the Spirit" (suggesting the divine will) to go to Jerusalem. The reader must resolve a dilemma—Is going to Jerusalem God's will or Paul's? When Agabus, whom the reader already knows as an accurate prophetic voice (11:28), declares the Holy Spirit's witness that Paul will be delivered in chains to the Romans at Jerusalem (21:11), Luke reinforces the question—Is Paul going to Jerusalem

---

261. So Barrett, *Acts*, 919.

262. Tannehill, *Narrative*, 239. Shepherd, (*Narrative*, 232) fails to note the problem facing the reader. Because the reader repeatedly has to choose between Paul's spirit and the God's Spirit, the ambiguity is important to what follows.

263. Gaventa, *Acts*, 230; Tannehill, *Narrative*, 246–47. Whether or not the historical Luke is the we-narrator (i.e., Paul's companion), the reader has no reason to assume that a different narrator is involved. Robbins ("By Land," 216) claimed that first-person narration was characteristic in sea voyage narratives, but that has been effectively countered by Porter ("'We' Passages," 554–58). Thus, this is not merely a literary convention.

264. As Witherington, *Acts*, 605 n. 188.

265. Barrett, *Acts*, 562.

266. This is commonly recognized (Cf. Haenchen, *Acts*, 600; Pesch, *Apostelgeschichte*, II, 203; Schille, *Apostelgeschichte*, 407; Shepherd, *Narrative*, 236; Tannehill, *Narrative*, 254).

despite the divine witness that he should not, or is Paul following the divine will despite the difficulties that await him?

The reader might resolve this dilemma by assuming that the narrator's participation lessens his ability to present the divine will.[267] While narratorial participation ordinarily works this way, with a lessening in authority,[268] the reader has already been given evidence that the we-narrator is a reliable in such matters. After Paul and Barnabas were separated, the narrator indicated that divine favor rested on Paul and Silas through the growth in the churches they visited (16:1–4).[269] However, at this point, the narrator's authoritative voice indicates that the Spirit was inhibiting the missionaries' progress (16:6–8) or at least denying Paul the right to choose his own path. Gaventa suggests that at 16:6–8 the Spirit already prevented Paul from choosing his own path, so the spirit in 19:21 cannot be Paul's. However, this parallel (Paul is making decisions and plans about his journeys) is another reason for suspecting that Luke's we-narrator is playing an important role. He has shown up in the other place where Paul's plans seem to conflict with the Spirit's.[270] In Acts 16, then, Paul's group appears uncertain, lacking any positive direction.[271] This little 'hiccough' would have the reader questioning the initial determination that God favored the mission, much like the situation in 19:21—21:14 where the reader is questioning the assumption that the Spirit is guiding Paul.

In Acts 16, the narrator (as a participant in the story) comes to the reader's aid when he proclaims the conclusion that God had called the group to preach in Macedonia (16:10—"*we* immediately tried to cross over to Macedonia, being convinced that God had called *us*"). Despite, then, the narrator's direct involvement and the supposed corresponding loss in omniscient privilege, his utter reliability concerning the divine will works to convince the reader that the initial conclusion was appropriate. Consequently, the reader implicitly trusts the we-narrator to interpret the divine will.

In Acts 21 the reader apparently receives help from the narrator. He joins those in Caesarea who beg Paul not to go to Jerusalem (21:12), thus suggesting that God wants to stop Paul from making the journey (just as in 21:4). When Paul announces his continued intention to go up to Jerusalem, all the narrator can do is unite with the group in a prayer that "the Lord's will be done" (21:14). One might suggest that the crowd declares, 'This is the divine will and we accept it,'[272] but because the attempts at persuasion have failed (21:14) and because Luke has built tension both for the reader and for the community about what awaits Paul, the crowd instead seems to leave Paul's fate in God's hands.[273] The reader, then,

---

267. As do Tannehill, *Narrative*, 264, fn. 5; Witherington, *Acts*, 628 n. 277.

268. See chapter 3.

269. For this signifying divine favor see chapter 3.

270. See Gaventa, *Acts*, 268. Pesch (*Apostelgeschichte*, II, 203) suggests a parallel between 16:6–10 and 19:21—21:11 in the Spirit's leading, but does not reach this conclusion.

271. So Dunn, *Acts*, 217; Munck, *Acts*, 158.

272. As Barrett, *Acts*, 997–98; Tannehill, *Narrative*, 264.

273. Fitzmyer, *Acts*, 690. The attempt (Tannehill, *Narrative*, 264) to find a parallel with Jesus' Gethsemane prayer (Luke 22:42) is suspect. It is not Paul, but the narrator, the reader, and the community who resign themselves to the divine will. Paul apparently committed himself to that end long before.

would note the resignation in this statement.[274] At the same time the statement functions something like a community prayer, which, since God has previously given immediate answers to such prayer (4:31—the shaking of the place; the description of events that follows in 5:12–17), leaves the reader expecting that the events that follow will bear out the divine will. Further, the reader has been given repeated assurances that what is going on throughout the narrative is in accordance with God's plan (see chapter 6).

What, then, is the reader to do as Paul goes to Jerusalem, is bound, and imprisoned? By leading the reader to a dilemma through using ambiguous references to the Spirit, the narrator has required the reader to turn to the narrator for help in the issue. The help comes, then, in an unexpected way—for by involving the reader in the narrative through the narrator's participation, the we-narrator has resigned the reader to agree with the community prayer and to believe that the divine will is being done. The reader is to trust that God is in control even here and respond obediently. The reader's trust is confirmed when in 23:11 Paul receives another vision assuring him that he must ($\delta\epsilon\hat{\iota}$) witness to the Lord in Rome as he has in Jerusalem (cf. 27:24). The implication is that Paul's witness in Jerusalem was just as necessary as his witness in Rome is and, therefore, that Paul has been obedient to the divine will all along.[275]

While the narrator *appears* to have led the reader astray, he has, in reality, subtly focused the reader's attention on this motif concerning obedience to the divine will. The dilemma draws the reader into commitment to the divine will. Moreover, by showing the narrator's own distance from fully comprehending the divine plan, the narrator leads his reader to understand that even if the reader is unsure *how*, he still knows *that* God is active and God's will is being done. In a narrative where signs, wonders, visions, and the Spirit's voice consistently direct events, it would be easy for Luke's reader to assume that following the divine will is simple—God manifests His will clearly and the believer is to follow it. However, in these texts where warnings come "through the Spirit" to Paul—warnings that include seeming commands not to go to Jerusalem and that draw even the narrator into the action—the reader sees that sometimes it is not even easy to understand what the divine will is, let alone follow it. The reader has already learned that facing suffering, trials, and death, are not valid reasons for being disobedient. Now the reader learns that the divine will's enigmatic nature cannot be raised as an excuse either. For the reader, then, the warnings are not given to turn Paul from the path to Jerusalem. Rather, they seem to lead the reader to obediently commit to the divine will as it is being worked out.[276] This obedience to the divine will, emphasized throughout the narrative, remains supremely important for the reader, despite the difficulty of such obedience. Obedience, then, is a characteristic expected not only from the community, but from the reader and such obedience continues to demonstrate that the community is God's true people.

---

274. So Lake and Cadbury, *Beginnings*, 269; *contra* Schneider, *Apostelgeschichte*, II, 305.

275. So Barrett, *Acts*, 1068; Pesch, *Apostelgeschichte*, II, 245.

276. Thus, Haenchen's (*Acts*, 602 n. 1) claim that Luke does not see the difficulty seems mistaken. Luke has repeatedly made the point that obedience is important; he now draws his readers into a commitment to obedience even when facing dangers.

Acceptance/Rejection

The obedience theme is emphasized by being presented side-by-side with rejection. While some in the crowd wondered what the Pentecost event meant, others mocked (2:13), suggesting from the outset that the reader would find a divided response to what God is doing. Luke consistently links rejection and acceptance throughout Luke-Acts. Carroll notes that in Luke's Gospel kingdom language is often "surrounded by an atmosphere of division and rejection."[277] Tiede[278] and Brawley[279] see this division and rejection theme prefigured in Simeon's oracle about Jesus causing "falling" and "rising" in Israel (Luke 2:34)—Jesus was to be Israel's hope but also to bring division. The reader, therefore, expects both positive and negative responses to Jesus. On the other hand, Koet argues that Simeon's words refer to consecutive stages in Israel's history.[280] Thus, Israel would first fall (rejecting Jesus) and then be restored (its hope remains). These two interpretations need not be set against each other[281] since Luke gives reasons to believe both that Jesus brought division and that Israel's hope remains.

Cook remarks, however, that the positive response by many Jews (including the "thousands" of Jews in Acts 21:20) is purely a literary pattern building the readers expectations and thus showing the great failure that is the Jewish response when (as he thinks) Paul declares that God rejects them (28:26–28).[282] He, however, misses the two real literary patterns: 1) rejection/acceptance are displayed side-by-side and 2) salvation is offered in the face of rejection. Luke's reader finds 1) a distinction made within Israel, so that *true Israel accepts, false Israel rejects*; and 2) *in God's mercy, hope remains.*[283] This distinction has roots in Luke's Gospel—the Baptist's ministry epitomizes Israel's culling since an axe is taken to the unfruitful trees (Luke 3:19); the converse being that the fruitful trees remain (cf. Luke 3:17—wheat gathered, chaff burned). Such a division, a *remnant*, is known from the OT, thus, when only some in Israel believe this is unsurprising to the reader.[284] It also agrees with Peter's words that only those who call "on the name of the Lord" will be saved (2:21).

This acceptance/rejection theme is found in the aftermath to Peter and John's sermon at Solomon's Portico (4:1–7), where many in the crowd "heard," but, in a deliberate contrast, their opponents (including the Sadducees) are characterized as *hearing* something else—they are disturbed at the teaching and the proclamation in Jesus about the "resurrection of the dead." The reader is aware from the extra-text (the Gospels, common knowledge[285])

---

277. Carroll, *Response*, 86 (for verse citations see his fn. 191).

278. Tiede, *Prophecy*, 30; Tiede, "'Glory,'" 27.

279. Brawley, *Centering*, 89.

280. Koet, "Simeons," 1157–63.

281. Tiede ("'Glory,'" 28) accepts the consecutive stage idea.

282. Cook, "Mission," 102–23.

283. Contra J. T. Sanders, "Jewish," 52.

284. See Jervell, "Future," 109.

285. Cf. Josephus, *War* 2:8.14.

that the Sadducees deny the resurrection.[286] Since the resurrection plays only a small role in the ensuing trial, it seems likely that this reference is designed to characterize these opponents as unable to hear anything beyond their own prejudices.[287] Peter's "let it be known" (4:10) requires the Council to respond appropriately to divine action. Thus, ignorance and prejudices are no longer an option, only obedience is.[288] Yet, the Council demonstrates their refusal to hear by responding to calls for obedience with further threats (4:19–21). Their obstinate rejection is emphasized to the reader by the Council's deadly intent that can only be assuaged by Gamaliel[289] invoking the fear of theomachy—fighting against the divine will (5:39). The reader knows the consequences belonging to this threat through a *topos* from the extra-text. In 2 Maccabees 7:18–19 Antiochus is a God-fighter because he has tortured the Jewish people. In response, the martyrs announce that he will face a horrendous death—the fate belonging to those who fight against God.[290] Here, despite Gamaliel's invocation of theomachy and its implications, the reader finds the Council acting violently toward the Apostles (5:40). This rejection then grows beyond the religious leaders (now Diaspora Jews, the people, the elders, and the scribes—6:9, 12)[291] and goes beyond disobedience to inducing false testimony and witnesses (6:11, 13–14).

In Acts 8:4—19:20 the acceptance/rejection motif is again found in the proclamation and response to the gospel. Peter (10:39–40) and Paul (13:26–28) announce that Jesus was the savior sent by God but rejected by the people. The reader sees Paul's warning from Scripture (13:41; cf. Hab 1:5) emphasizing that rejection would mark their continued disobedience to the prophets. Some Jews, nevertheless, respond identically to the Jewish Council in Acts 4–5 since in 13:43–45, the reader finds "grace" characterizing those who accept Paul's message and "jealousy" marking the rejecting Jews. The reader previously witnessed such characterization in Acts 4–5 where divine "grace" defined the community (4:33) and the Council responded with jealousy (5:17). This repetition causes the reader to identify this rejection as the same kind the Jewish leaders have consistently demonstrated.[292] Longenecker attempts to explain the jealousy in 13:43–45 and the Jewish rejection in 22:22 by suggesting that the Jews in both cases recognize and reject the "law-free" implication in

---

286. Making them an "ideal foil" (Gaventa, *Acts*, 91; cf. Johnson, *Acts*, 76).

287. Jervell (*Apostelgeschichte*, 175) suggests that the resurrection is behind the dispute over the man's healing since it is the resurrected one's name that has brought about the healing. This underscores the point—the failure to respond to God's messiah is illustrated through the Sadducees' prejudice against resurrection.

288. Witherington, *Acts*, 194.

289. Gamaliel is an ambiguous character (Gaventa, *Acts*, 109–10), as is evident in the conflicting characterization analyses offered by Gowler (*Host*, 277–79) and Darr (*Character*, 116–20) (for a comparison see Lyons, "Words," 30–48). The reader cannot be certain how to take Gamaliel's words, for, while he urges caution towards the disciples so as to avoid fighting God, he lumps Jesus together with Theudas and Judas. This does not mean that Gamaliel reflects "bad faith" (as Johnson, *Acts*, 103); rather Gamaliel is being used (somewhat ironically) to make a point about the divine role in this matter.

290. Throughout 2 Maccabees fear of opposing God is held up as a key virtue for all rulers (see van Henten, *Maccabean*, 30–34). In this case, there may me a telling irony since the Council has already shown itself to be θεομάχοι by killing Jesus (so Schneider, *Apostelgeschichte*, I, 396).

291. Representing all Israel (Pesch, *Apostelgeschichte*, I, 237).

292. Rather than presupposing a religious community in competition with the synagogue (as Haenchen, *Acts*, 414), Luke uses jealousy to indicate a pattern—the synagogue is not the problem, Jewish rejection is.

Paul's teaching.[293] This conclusion seems incorrect since any supposed law-free elements are not evident in these texts, and the jealously in 13:43–45 echoes Acts 4–5, implying that this reaction is an entrenched animosity, demonstrating willful disobedience in response to the message (cf. 13:40–41).

In the next city some Jews and Greeks believe and other Jews reject the message (14:1–2). Likewise, the message receives a divided response in Thessalonica (17:4–5)—with the jealousy motif appearing again—and Athens (17:32–34), which together stand in contrast to the whole hearted acceptance by the Bereans (17:11–12). The narrator, through the direct address to the reader (interrupting the narrative), pointedly identifies the Athenians as only interested in telling and hearing something new (17:21). In contrast, the narrator commends the Bereans for their great eagerness (πάσης προθυμίας) to see if Paul's message was true. Thus, one group is interested in *truth*, one in *hearing*, and the reader is to favor the former. The middle section of Acts ends with two more cities demonstrating a divided response (18:6–8; 19:9–10). Therefore, a clear distinction is made between those who are inside the kingdom (those obedient to God) and those that are outside (those rejecting God).[294]

Salvation

The narrative relationship between obedience and rejection is important to the portrayal of God as savior/deliverer. Although God is not called Savior in Acts, the title is appropriate. The reader would be familiar with such a designation for God from the OT extra-text and Luke relates Mary using this title for God at Luke 1:47 (cf. 2:30). Further, the indirect characterization reflecting God as Savior is quite strong (as will be illustrated), not least in that the initial references to being saved are directly related to God's call (Acts 2:39–40).

From the start, salvation seems to be directly offered to those who reject since the people's dismissal of Jesus is the "supreme sin" needing forgiveness.[295] Jesus is a man attested by God, yet rejected by the people (2:22–23), and glorified by God, but disowned by them (3:13). Moreover, Jesus is the rejected "stone" in whom alone salvation is offered (4:10–12;[296] cf. 5:31). God is requested to act for the continuation of the mission (4:24–30) directly in the face of those who have gathered against God (salvation seems to be offered to those who have rejected). In Stephen's speech with its Deuternomistic flavor (the recall-

---

293. Longenecker, "Moral," 143–48.

294. Acceptance/rejection themes in 19:21—28:31 are discussed in relation to the *salvation-in-the-face-of-rejection theme.*

295. Barrett, *Acts*, 203–4.

296. In 4:9, Luke uses a form of σώζειν to express healing. This usage anticipates how the term is used in 4:12, where it refers to salvation offered in Jesus' name (Barrett, *Acts*, 228; Haenchen, *Acts*, 217; Tannehill, *Narrative*, 61). The parallel between healing and salvation suggests that salvation is a return to order, which agrees with seeing the restored kingdom as re-establishing the divine social order (cf. Fitzmyer, *Acts*, 301–2). Thus, the reader might note that the εὐεργεσία done to the sick man suggests the benefaction offered by the wealthy to the poor (Plato *Laws* 850B; Aristotle, *Politics* 1286B; Wis 16:11; 2 Macc 6:13; 9:26; see Johnson, *Acts*, 77)—God demonstrates proper civic concern.

ing of Israel's disobedience and the need for repentance), [297] Israel's history is characterized by its consistent refusal of God's deliverers—the patriarchs rejected Joseph, who would provide deliverance from the famine (7:9, 14); the Hebrews in Egypt rejected Moses, who would deliver them from bondage (7:25, 27, 35); Israel discarded and became disobedient to the Mosaic law (7:38–39), denying divinely ordained worship in the process (7:40–42), which led to their misuse and misrepresentation of the temple (7:43–50). This speech ends by denouncing the continued rejection—always resisting the Spirit (7:51), betraying and murdering the "Righteous One" sent as a deliverer, and failing to keep the Law.[298] Haenchen incorrectly assumed that only the "radical denunciation" of the temple could prompt the outrage.[299] Instead, the narrative suggests this is caused by the repeated, and now direct, charge concerning the Council's disobedience and rejection, exacerbated by the vision reflecting the rejected one at God's right hand.[300] Regardless, when those present react by rebuffing yet another message, this time with the utmost violence (death), Jesus can still offer forgiveness (7:59–60).

Jewish Responsibility, Repentance, and Ignorance

Conzelmann argued that Luke places the guilt for Jesus' death on the Jews alone.[301] J. T. Sanders used this conclusion to argue that Luke is anti-Jewish.[302] For Sanders, Jesus is committed into the Jews "hands" and the Jews take Jesus away (Luke 23:25–26). He then interprets ἄνομοι in Acts 2:23 as referring to "sinful men" (not the Romans), making the Jews (as the sinful men) solely responsible. However, Luke says Pilate delivered Jesus 'to their will' (τῷ θελήματι αὐτῶν), not into their "hands." This suggests only that he agreed to their demands. The 'they' who led him away could be Romans. That the Jews (particularly their leaders) receive substantial blame for Jesus' death seems clear; that they alone carried it out does not. Even if Conzelmann's argument is accepted (and Acts 4:27 counters the suggestion that Herod and the Romans have been to some extent absolved), Sanders' conclusion does not follow—the message that the Jews can be forgiven for their rejection of God's deliverer and can be included again in God's people continues throughout the work. Hope (not condemnation) is offered to the Jews.

Sanders goes on to deny the possibility of forgiveness because he rejects the notion that forgiveness is offered in Stephen's speech.[303] However, he (in line with the

297. Cf. Schneider, *Apostelgeschichte*, I, 453, 468; Tannehill, *Narrative*, 87; Witherington, *Acts*, 262.

298. See Kilgallen, "Function," 176–82. However, Kilgallen fails to note the reversal motif that is also characteristic in the speech (it is not thoroughly negative towards Stephen's hearers). It is difficult to see how these repeated rejections show a division in Israel (as Ravens, *Luke*, 62–63) since Stephen does not indicate a group of people agreeing with God's deliverers.

299. Haenchen, *Acts*, 286.

300. So Tannehill, *Narrative*, 246.

301. Conzelmann, *Theology*, 90–93.

302. J. T. Sanders, *Jews*, 9–11.

303. Ibid, 55–56; also Jervell, *Apostelgeschichte*, 248.

method he proposes)[304] ignores the narrative context. Luke's speeches are not independent treatises and should be read and understood based on what is revealed in the narrative to that point and the narrative suggests the opportunity for all to repent. Further, in the passion narrative, the opportunity for repentance is not directly offered, but Jesus prays for their forgiveness (Luke 23:34—given an A reading since it appears at least with some modification in most witnesses) and Sanders admits this text offers such an opportunity.[305] Stephen prays in a similar manner (7:60). In both cases repentance/forgiveness is expressed in the following narrative rather than in a speech. Therefore, Israel's tendency to reject God and God's messengers does not in turn mean God has rejected Israel.[306] Consistently throughout Acts, then, forgiveness is offered to those who reject even when they continue to reject.

How, then, does "ignorance" relate to Jewish denial and rejection of Jesus (3:13–17; cf. 13:26–39)? Conzelmann suggested that these themes come from two different sources and that ignorance can really only be applied to gentiles.[307] However, this is not the impression the reader would have—the *Jews* are described as acting in ignorance. Peter seems to suggest that they handed over and killed Jesus without fully realizing what they had done. They were unaware Jesus was the "Holy and Righteous One," ignorantly carrying out what God had determined should happen to their messiah. They are guilty for crucifying Jesus, but they did so without fully understanding how significant this action was. Ignorance, then, is not an excuse, but the way the Jews were able to fulfill the divine plan. In Stephen's speech the same pattern can be found—people acted against Joseph (7:9–10) and Moses (7:35) without realizing they would be God's deliverers, yet God provided the deliverance anyway. Jervell suggests that, by portraying Israel rejecting God's deliverers in the same context as God fulfilling promises, Luke emphasizes that God fulfills promises despite rejection.[308] This would imply, then, that God is restoring Israel despite the negative way some receive this restoration.

This *salvation-in-the-face-of-rejection* theme unpacks what is meant by the offer of salvation and how the reader is to understand the way the kingdom can be restored to an Israel that does not include all (and only) the Jewish people. When divine salvation is first mentioned—the last verse from the Joel quotation (2:21)—the idea that God delivers the people is recalled. The reader's extra-textual expectations for such deliverance include victory over God's enemies and, thus, some form of political intervention. However, when Peter calls for repentance (a turning that leads to breaking with those who reject

304. See J. T. Sanders, *Jews*, 50. Rather than start with the first speech in Acts (Peter's call to re-establish the twelve—1:16–22), Sanders chooses to start with Stephen, ignoring the narrative development.

305. Ibid, 63.

306. *Contra* J. T. Sanders, "Jewish," 61–63.

307. Conzelmann, *Theology*, 92–93.

308. Jervell, *Apostelgeschichte*, 237–38.

the message),[309] the enemies appear to be redefined—the crowd is to be saved from this "corrupt generation" (2:40). At this point, the only clue the reader has for identifying this "generation" is those who crucified Jesus.[310] Deut 32:5 and Ps 78:8, nevertheless, may be the models for this phrase.[311] In both texts disobedience is a factor. As outlined, the rejection/disobedience displayed by those who crucified Jesus is the issue to which salvation is offered. Therefore, God's enemies become those who reject God and divine salvation becomes the reversal of fortune[312] that comes with Jesus' resurrection—a forgiveness of sins that corresponds to entrance into God's kingdom.

Luke here *presents salvation as both a freedom from* punishment due the "corrupt generation" *and an attachment to* God's people.[313] The connection between salvation and entrance into the kingdom is also made in Luke 18:24–26—Jesus' statement about how difficult it is for the rich to enter the kingdom evokes the disciples' question about who can be saved.[314] Green writes that in Luke's Gospel, "To be forgiven . . . is to be (re)admitted into the community from which one has been ostracized on account of sin."[315] Forgiveness can be manifested in healings, exorcisms, or, as here, in restoration to community. The kingdom is already here, so the time to repent and enter is now.[316]

With the accompanied entrance into the kingdom, salvation gains a "political" significance. Gaventa does not identify this, but she does state that the salvation offered by God is not merely "private" or "spiritual."[317] Rather, it concerns the "house of Israel" and later the gentiles (social, if not political, entities). Wolter notes that Luke's conception of God's kingdom revises the "one-sided" view that God opposes foreign rule over Israel.[318] Luke would not be alone in such a perspective (see chapter 2), but, as the narrative moves along, the reader will note features that suggest earthly rulers pale in comparison with God. As such, foreign rule appears to be tolerated for the present, but the consummation is likely to bring a different situation, where a truly 'political' restoration is possible.

As has been the case with many themes, this 'political' kingdom is reinterpreted onto the ethical/spiritual plane—those who reject God represent those who belong to a different people,[319] a people who have shown that they are God's enemies and fighters against God. While this indicates "insiders" as well as "outsiders" are called to repentance,[320] it also

---

309. So Fitzmyer, *Acts*, 267.

310. Pesch, *Apostelgeschichte*, I, 278.

311. Haenchen, *Acts*, 184.

312. Tannehill, *Narrative*, 36: "God's action nullifies and reverses the rejection of Jesus expressed in the passion story." For 'reversal' cf. Fitzmyer, *Acts*, 287, 301, 373; Pesch, *Apostelgeschichte*, I, 166.

313. Barrett, *Acts*, 231.

314. Cf. O'Toole, "Kingdom," 155–57.

315. Green, "Salvation," 90.

316. *Contra* S. G. Wilson (*Gentiles*, 79) since repentance is the means for entering into the kingdom, there is no reason to use the "imminence of the kingdom" as a "motivation" for repentance.

317. Gaventa, *Acts*, 77; also Barrett *Acts*, 203.

318. Wolter, "Israel's," 310–11.

319. So Barrett, *Acts*, 210.

320. Witherington, *Acts*, 155.

suggests that (for Luke's reader) former *insiders* are now *outsiders*; thus *all people need to be moved back into the social group designating the kingdom and out of that designating the corrupt generation.* The kingdom is being restored to Israel, but only those who repent and receive forgiveness in the name of its king (Jesus) will receive the blessings offered.

Chance notes that accepting/rejecting Jesus is the key issue for maintaining citizenship in Israel.[321] Carroll also correctly identifies the division being created as to who are and who are not God's people.[322] However, since all are called to repentance, it is not the case that refusing the message "removes" the person from God's people.[323] Rather, since all are aligned with the corrupt generation responsible for Jesus' death, all have forsaken their place in God's kingdom and need to repent in order to be restored to it. As Jervell comments, to reject the "Prophet like Moses" is to reject Moses and, therefore, to renounce claim to being God's people.[324] This would imply that, by killing Jesus they have already failed to heed the Prophet and are cut-off (3:22–23), but salvation is available for everyone who repents. God has redefined the kingdom and its citizens based on their response to Jesus, the king, yet this maintains the presentation that the kingdom is restored to Israel.

As the message expands outward from Jerusalem, salvation continues to be offered in the face of rejection. Peter (10:39–40) and Paul (13:26–28) set the gospel as divine action in response to Jesus being rejected. God brings deliverance to Paul while he is actively persecuting Jesus (9:1–2, 5). As a result (μὲν οὖν) of the rejection faced in Iconium, Paul stays there longer testifying to the Lord (14:3).[325] While it seems odd that a continued stay should result from rejection, this is apparently the point. Likewise, despite the divided response in Corinth, Paul stays one-and-a-half years in that city (18:11). Even though it is rejected by the synagogue, the mission continues next door (18:7). Thus, the reader finds Paul giving up "as little ground as possible" (both physically and 'spiritually' since God-fearers and synagogue leaders are among Paul's group)[326] as he continues to preach in the face of rejection. In both cases, the continued proclamation is directly attributed to the divine will (Spirit-inspired boldness—14:3; divine vision—18:9–10). Further, the reader knows that the destruction foretold by the prophets (13:40) can be avoided. In this light, the reader realizes that when Paul shakes the dust (13:51; similarly 18:6) from his sandals, this is not an ultimate rejection, even in the local setting,[327] since God has authorized salvation to be offered in the face of such rejection.

Even the Christian 'heroes' must have their opposition overcome by divine action. Both Ananias (9:13–14) and Peter (10:14–16) demonstrate their reluctance to respond

---

321. Chance, *Jerusalem*, 71.

322. Carroll, *Response*, 137–41.

323. *Contra* Carroll, *Response*, 139.

324. Jervell, *Apostelgeschichte*, 240.

325. See Barrett, *Acts*, 669–70; Lake and Cadbury, *Beginnings*, 161. Translating the phrase as an adversative (Sharp, "Meaning," 528) makes little sense because, unlike Acts 28:5, it is difficult to see what Paul's action is supposed to be an adversative to: no one has told him to "get out." It also does not relieve the difficulty; in either reading Paul responds to rejection by continuing the mission in its face.

326. Tannehill, *Narrative*, 222; also Jervell, *Unknown*, 16.

327. *Contra* Johnson, *Acts*, 244.

to God's gracious actions.[328] Hubbard suggests such reluctance is characteristic in commissioning accounts.[329] However, in Acts this reaction only occurs in relation to Paul and Cornelius. Since Luke does not use the theme elsewhere in Acts, it seems to stress how God has overcome all objections to these (controversial?) figures. As before, God is shown to be the merciful God who continues to respond to rejection by overcoming obstacles and offering salvation.

In the final section of Acts, obedience when faced with persecution continues the salvation-in-the-face-of-rejection motif. The reader finds that persecution and chains do not prevent salvation being offered since Paul will continue to hope his hearers join him as Christians (26:29) and Paul remains faithful to proclaim the message despite Jewish conspiracies (20:19–21). Paul is seen modeling this motif when twice (Acts 22, 26; cf. Acts 9) he recounts how God has confronted a persecutor in the midst of his persecution, changing him into a proclaimer of God's Way.[330] In 26:14, the Greek proverb "it hurts you to kick against the goads" underscores for Paul's audience (and for Luke's reader since it was a common Hellenistic expression)[331] the drastic turnaround he faced. Paul assumed he was being obedient to God, but found that he was actually attempting the impossible—fighting God (cf. 5:39).[332] While Schille claims that, because Paul's first defense speech (22:3–22) was rejected by Jews, Luke does not believe that this subject can be heard in a Jewish forum,[333] the reader finds Paul presenting his case before Jewish leaders right to the end (23:6–10; 26:2–29; 28:17–28). Jervell argues that when Paul was sent away from Jerusalem (22:18), God had determined that the mission in Jerusalem was over.[334] This does not seem correct, especially since, as argued previously, the leadership remains in Jerusalem. More likely, the reader will note the emphasis on *Paul's* witness to Jesus (not the witness in general) being rejected there. Regardless, Paul continues to offer his defense, which includes the "hope of Israel," in the face of opposition.

Even at the end, the reader does not find the Roman Jews characterized as rejecting Paul's words; rather they are divided in response (28:25). Paul (28:26–28), nevertheless, declares from Scripture the Spirit's words that Israel has always been hard of hearing and seeing (Isa 6:9–10). Is the reader to join a substantial group of scholars and interpret this final turn as indicating the ultimate rejection of non-believing Jews?[335] Or join with others who believe that there is still hope for these Jews.[336] Wolter observes that the lack in

328. Johnson, *Acts*, 185; Tannehill, *Narrative*, 116–17, 134; Witherington, *Acts*, 351.

329. Hubbard , "Role," 188–89.

330. So Tannehill, *Narrative*, 258.

331. Cf. Euripedes, *Bacchae* 794–95; Aeschylus, *Agamemnon* 1624; Terence, *Phormio* 1:2.27.

332. See Barrett, *Acts*, 1158; Haenchen, *Acts*, 685. On this theme see above. Johnson (*Acts*, 435, 441) blurs the sharp transformation Paul is expressing by suggesting Paul was being pulled toward the "messianists" but resisting. This implies an internal struggle that Luke never hints at. Paul learns that he is fighting God, not that he is resisting the pull of the Way.

333. Schille, *Apostelgeschichte*, 424.

334. Jervell, *Apostelgeschichte*, 545–46.

335. E.g., Cook, "Mission," 106; Eltester, "Israel," 129; Maddox, *Purpose*, 184; Räisänen, "Redemption," 106; J. T. Sanders, "Salvation," 115; Tyson, "Problem," 126.

336. Alexander, "Reading," 434; Fusco, "Luke-Acts," 1–17; Merkel, "Israel," 397; Ravens, *Luke*, 250; Tannehill,

consensus developed in part because the texts about the fate of unbelieving Jews lead different interpreters in different directions.[337] In most cases the negative appraisal misses God's persistent counter to Jewish rejection (the ongoing offer of salvation in its face). An example will illustrate this.

Moessner noted a pattern in Luke's Gospel which saw (A) Israel's history tending toward "stubborn" disobedience; (B) God had sent his messengers to plead for Israel's repentance, with Jesus culminating that process; (C) Israel *en masse* rejected those prophets including Jesus; (D) thus, God will bring "final judgment" on Jesus' generation.[338] This analysis seems convincing enough, pointing to an ultimate judgment on the perverse generation. When Moessner finds tenets A-C present in Acts but D missing from Paul's final turn he argues that the reader would inescapably assume D.[339] This conclusion fails to note that in Acts, 1) salvation is directly offered *to those who rejected Jesus*. And 2) It is directly offered *in the face of such rejection*. Luke has reinterpreted the judgment so that it means the rejecting Jews have been removed from the divinely restored Israel. Therefore, these Jews now face a judgment "Day" (10:46; 17:31) at the hands of the deliverer God sent them. D is missing in Acts because it awaits this Day and, until then, salvation is offered to those who reject.[340]

One could argue that the reader is to see the quotation from Isa 6:9–10 at Acts 28:26–28 like the one from Isa 49:6 at 13:47 (the latter stressing the witness to gentiles and the former the rejection by the Jews),[341] which comes after the Jews there repudiate Paul's message (13:45; cf. 18:6). Prieur claims that ἀντιλέγεται in 28:22 prepares the reader for the resulting rejection by the Roman Jews.[342] However, by repeatedly (cf. 28:19) reminding the reader that Jewish rejection has meant *blaspheming* contradiction, Luke prepares his reader to see a different reaction here. Since no such repudiation precedes the quotation from Isa 6:9–10, the reader should note the break in pattern. Paul's words are not a response to a self-determined unworthiness (as 13:46) and, therefore, the reader is more likely to compare them with the warning from Hab 1:5, which preceded (13:41), rather than followed, Jewish blasphemy. Since the judgment announced there was avoidable through obedience (13:40), it would be here also.[343]

One might object that Luke is placing more emphasis on the quotation from Isa 6:9–10 by referencing the "Holy Spirit" as the author of these words. However, the reader identifies Scripture as words spoken through the Spirit (1:16) and possessing divine au-

"Israel," 83–85; Tiede, "Glory," 34; Wainwright, "Luke," 79.

337. Wolter, "Israel's," 308.

338. Moessner, "Paul," 96–101.

339. Ibid, 101–3.

340. Brawley ("God," 296) correctly notes that, whatever one thinks about whether Paul has condemned the Jews here, it is important not to treat Paul's words to certain Jews in Rome as Christianity's words to Judaism. The situation is no less local here than in the previous turns.

341. Witherington, *Acts*, 800.

342. Prieur, *Verkündigung*, 40.

343. That Luke sees prophecies as conditional can also be noted in how he presents the one in 21:11—the community views the consequences as avoidable if Paul does not go to Jerusalem (see Tannehill, *Narrative*, 265–66).

thority (2:17). The quotation from Isa 6:9–10, then, is not given any greater authority than any other quotation from Scripture. Instead, the reference to the Spirit being "right in saying," in a context where Israel's historic obstinacy is mentioned, should lead the reader to recall similar words by Stephen concerning Israel consistently rejecting the Spirit (7:51).[344] That event preceded the act (stoning Stephen) that illustrated the listeners had repudiated his message. Forgiveness, nevertheless, remained a possibility (7:60). As such, for Luke's reader, 28:26–27 fits into a pattern of warnings (which precede repudiation) against rejecting the divine saving offer. This pattern does not point to a mandatory rejection by the Jews, but warns them against continuing the path their ancestors followed. Therefore, Paul's turn is not a response to repudiation (as 13:45; 18:6),[345] but a warning so as to turn their hearts to obedience. The reader would think that forgiveness is offered since it was after Stephen was killed.

Cook claims that by allowing "never" to characterize the Jew's hearing and seeing this close to the end, Luke seems to discourage any thought that a Jewish mission will be fruitful.[346] While the reader is consistently reminded that Israel's past has shown opposition to the divine will, this portrayal would not translate into a belief that God has rejected the Jews. The reader knows that God has been patient with Israel throughout its history and there is no reason (especially since salvation continues to be offered to everyone) to see this changing now. Further, Moessner points out that the Deuteronomistic view saw the prophet assert mass rebellion "precisely at the point of a mixed or varied response."[347] Even though some were faithful, the whole group could be painted as rebellious. The literary pattern would suggest to the reader that, just as with the prophets of old, Paul was calling Jews to repentance in the face of their mixed response.

Additionally, the reader would note the hope signaled in Isaiah's words—God desires to heal them (28:27), even though they have repeatedly blocked such attempts.[348] The reader would know that Isaiah's words did not mean God completely rejected Israel when originally spoken, so they would not be taken to do so here.[349] Thus, this turn to the gentiles does not end the mission among the Jews, but simply declares Paul's call for a historically obstinate people to become obedient. Although some commentators see the statement that the gentiles "will listen" as indicating the futility in continuing to present the message to the Jews,[350] the καί in 28:28 is not to be read exclusively but inclusively—they "too will hear." Carroll assumes the καί creates a contrast between the responses demonstrated by the Roman Jews and the gentiles.[351] However, some in Paul's audience were persuaded, so they did "hear." Thus, the καί cannot be contrasting their ability to hear; instead, it affirms

344. J. T. Sanders ("Jewish," 58) thinks that by recalling such history Luke portrays the Jewish people as being "congenitally obstreperous and opposed" to God.

345. *Contra* Haenchen, *Acts*, 729.

346. Cook, "Mission," 106.

347. Moessner, *Lord*, 105.

348. Tannehill, "Rejection," 98.

349. Witherington, *Acts*, 802.

350. So Pesch, *Apostelgeschichte*, II, 310.

351. Carroll, *Response*, 160.

that the gentiles are included. Seccombe notes that the "inclusive" translation is in keeping with the Jew first motif that has been featured in Acts (cf. 2:39; 3:26; 13:46). The message must come to Jews and, Paul reaffirms, to gentiles.[352]

Paul continues to speak to "all who came" (28:30), which, since no repudiation took place, implies both Jews and gentiles in the audience.[353] Tannehill argues that references to the "kingdom of God" and the "teaching about the Lord Jesus Christ" reflect Paul's synagogue preaching rather than the way Paul preaches to gentiles (cf. 14:8–20; 17:1–35).[354] These ideas are also found in Paul's farewell speech (20:21, 25), which is not directed to a synagogue audience. The audience there, nevertheless, would not be 'pagan' and would be expected (given 19:10) to include Jews and gentiles. Thus, the terms suggest (but do not require) a Jewish element among the hearers.

Finally, given Luke's portrayal that God mercifully offers salvation in the face of rejection, God rejecting the Jews (not the Jews rejecting divine salvation since Luke has demonstrated such) would be a jarring, unexpected ending to the work. Luke has "proclaimed the triumph of the gospel, not its defeat by a recalcitrant people."[355] For the reader, judgment will ultimately come on those who reject (10:42; 17:31; 24:25), and it is tragic that so many Jews have rejected the message, but it remains God's decision as to when the offer is no longer valid.[356]

The question remains, however, as to Israel's hopes at the consummation. Carroll argues that there is no evidence for a nationalistic Israel, in part because there can be no "'third chance' for unrepentant, unbelieving Israel."[357] However, he ignores how God controls salvation (it is offered in the face of rejection). It is incorrect to claim that there is no "future second chance," as if they were to receive only one opportunity to respond appropriately.[358] Because God continually responds to rejection with the offer of deliverance, there are as many chances as possible until the judgment. Certainly the Jews were expected to respond in the present and were without excuse (3:17; 17:30–31), but the message is directed toward rejection and until the day of judgment arrives God is expected to continue to offer mercy in the face of rejection. Further, Carroll assumes a condemnation (rather than a warning) in the quotation from Isa 6:9–10 and that Acts 3:19–26 refers to a completed restoration taking place prior to Jesus' return. Regarding 3:19–26, Carroll does not take seriously enough the allusions to 1:6 and the nationalistic kingdom expectations present there (see chapter 4). Jesus' reply did not deny such expectations, but began a process for transforming the impression that the kingdom is wholly apocalyptic and na-

---

352. Seccombe, "New," 369; following Nolland, "Luke's" 106.

353. Brawley, "God," 296; Marguerat, "Enigma," 298–99; Tannehill, *Narrative*, 351; *contra* Schille, *Apostelgeschichte*, 479.

354. Tannehill, "Rejection," 100.

355. Barrett, *Acts*, 1237.

356. Thus, while Jervell (*Unknown*, 41–42) is generally correct to recognize that God has fulfilled promises to Israel, and that the people of God includes both Israel and gentiles, his assertion that the synagogue is now rejected and the mission to the Jews unnecessary is contradicted by this motif.

357. Carroll, *Response*, 162–64 (quote on 163).

358. Ibid, 148.

tionalistic. The avenue is open for the eschatological end to bring about all Israel's hopes, but when this occurs it is still only repentant Israel that will receive its blessings. Even so, Luke does not declare that the original kingdom expectations will be fulfilled; he only fails to deny them. It is God's present faithfulness to Israel's hopes that suggests their complete consummation.[359] It is also God's faithfulness to His promises that confirm for the reader the presently restored kingdom.

Summary Portrait

God's interaction with the kingdom citizens furthers the reader's conception that the kingdom has been restored. Indeed, the reader finds that the kingdom is offered *first* to the "people of Israel," yet these ideas are reinterpreted. God, the Great King, is the covenant God and the people who enter into the kingdom are covenant people, but not all Israel has entered the kingdom. A secondary audience is anticipated throughout 1:1—8:3, but the nature of that audience remains unresolved. The reader's initial impression, however, is that, if the witness to them is like that to Israel, they will be included in the covenant people (i.e., in God's kingdom). In 8:4—19:20 the secondary audience is revealed. By direct action, God has given Samaritans, gentiles, even the "ends of the earth" (the Ethiopian) access to the kingdom. Yet, this kingdom is still Israel's as emphasized by the addressees of the speeches and the repeated proclamation *to Jew first*. In the final section, Luke uses the attention on Paul's Jewishness to show his reader that, *although gentiles have received inheritance among the people, God has not allowed Jewish believers to become second-class citizens in this restored kingdom.*

The kingdom's God is known by the reader to exhibit a concern for life, health, fairness, and justice. If this is truly God's kingdom, then the reader expects to see its citizens acting in keeping with God's concerns. The initial community demonstrates this interest through its commonality and willingness to provide for the needs that arise within it. Further, God is seen responding to injustices and disruptions either by removing the offenders (e.g., Ananias and Sapphira) or by providing the means for addressing the imbalance (e.g., men full of the Spirit). Finally the reader sees divine concern for all people through the sick, lame, and oppressed being restored to wholeness. God is characterized as concerned with justice and order in the kingdom and God's people are defined by their adherence to this concern, confirming that they are true kingdom citizens.

With the expansion of the message (Acts 8:4—19:20), the necessity to show that the kingdom's citizens acted in keeping with their Ruler grows, since the inclusion of non-Jews could be seen as a human action that is not in keeping with its restoration. *Luke presents the continuing social order, concern for justice, inclusiveness, and social welfare that marked the original community.* This illustrates divine concerns since ultimately God has brought about this social order. Luke particularly emphasizes the divine role in providing peace—removing persecutors and presenting the means (divine actions provide evidence) for settling disputes, confirming that God has brought these events to pass.

359. Cf. Seccombe, "New," 367.

In the final section, God continues to establish the kingdom's social order—giving comfort, providing overseers, warning against threats, and granting strength to endure them. Further, healing and deliverance extends to those outside the kingdom, illustrating divine concern for the welfare of the whole world. These actions are in keeping with the reader's expectations of God as a benevolent King, confirming that the values of God's kingdom are in force in the community.

A final element in this characterizing strand focuses on what God offers and expects from the kingdom citizens. To be assured that this is what God has done, the reader needs to see that entrance into the kingdom is being granted, and that those who enter respond appropriately. One part of this presentation relates to obedience, for obedience by the citizens suggests that God is majestic and to be revered appropriately. God is powerful enough to demand obedience and God's people show their respect through their obedience. Since God has always required this, the reader finds continuity between Luke's portrayal of God and what is already known about God, suggesting that this fits expectations for the restored kingdom. Different from some other portrayals, however, God cannot be manipulated by piety. *Luke uses the obedience motif to characterize God as Savior, for God is shown as the merciful God who reacts to the rejection (always presented side-by-side with obedience) of the divine will with a continued offer of salvation—deliverance from the consequences reserved for God's enemies.* However, the portrait is enigmatic since God's enemies are redefined—they are no longer Israel's national enemies, but those who reject the divine will as expressed in Jesus. Thus, God is the Savior of God's people, redefined as those obedient to God. By defining the people according to their adherence to divine concerns and obedience to divine commands, Luke has transformed what the reader understands by Israel. It is only those who are marked by the appropriate signs (ethically and pneumatically). The kingdom has been restored to them; to the rest the offer of entrance continues.[360]

In 8:4—19:20, likewise, the piety shown by believers and converts confirms the kingdom's presence—they demonstrate their willingness to bow before the Great King. God, nevertheless, reserves the right to bring salvation to those who show themselves unworthy (Samaritans, the persecuting Saul), which provides hope even for those who maintain their obstinacy. God persists, therefore, in defining the kingdom's enemies, while offering merciful salvation in the face of rejection. Although the kingdom has expanded, the King continues to relate to the citizens in the same way.

In the final section, while Luke again focuses attention on piety and obedience, these images center on Paul's defense. Paul's continued devotion to God, Law, temple, and people, while giving evidence that Paul is not guilty of the charges against him, illustrates the piety that allows kingdom citizens to maintain good consciences before God.[361] Luke encour-

---

360. Moessner ("Ironic," 48–49; *Lord,* 310–12) takes a similar view—the part or remnant of Israel that understood the divine plan has been restored. However, *contra* Moessner, Luke has not given up expectations for Israel's national hopes.

361. Conzelmann (*Theology,* 14–15, 165–66) claims that Luke neither wished to reform his community to the early church's standard, nor to maintain its attitude toward the Law and the temple. However, the consistent way that both social order and Jewish piety is emphasized throughout Acts suggests that Luke saw these attitudes as important, at least in that they represented the community as living under kingdom rule. Thus, if

ages his reader to commit to the obedience Paul demonstrates by involving the reader in Paul's difficult decision to heed the divine will (19:21—21:14). Finally, Luke maintains divine sovereignty in salvation—although the Jews falsely charge Paul, seize him, reject his message, and conspire to kill him, God does not reject the Jews. Luke leaves it to God to decide when the offer of salvation will be rescinded.

The relationship between God and the kingdom citizens provides further support for the offer of the kingdom to Israel. By showing that the kingdom belongs to the Jew first, Luke reinforces that *God has restored the kingdom to Israel*. At the same time, Luke leads his reader to anticipate the kingdom will expand (which will also be a fulfillment of scriptural promises). The community's social order provides evidence that it is indeed *God's promised kingdom that has been established*. God has gathered and maintained a people who share divine concerns for the welfare of others. Finally, the offer of the kingdom is supported by God requiring the kingdom's citizens to maintain piety and obedience. God has always demanded such features, so evidence that God's renewed people act in keeping with these requirements supports the restoration of the kingdom. At the same time, since God reserves the right to determine who God's enemies are, and to offer the kingdom directly in the face of rejection, *God verifies the offer*—God determines the kingdom's subjects and its enemies. Throughout, divine freedom and control remain the key factors supporting the claims.

The narrative also indicates that it is *God who has authorized* the inclusion of Samaritans, eunuchs, and gentiles. God's people, the kingdom citizens, are not bounded by ethnic or social restrictions. The overwhelming references to divine action in the Cornelius account and that event's use in settling social order problems supports the claim that God has authorized gentiles to join in the Kingdom. Gentiles are not obligated by circumcision because God acted apart from, and not in contradiction to, circumcision. Yet, God remains true to what is known about God because all kingdom members, regardless of ethnicity, are called to appropriate pious obedience (radically demonstrated in Saul's transformation), although such piety is not a condition for salvation. Similarly, divine persistence in offering salvation to those who reject supports the continued mission to the unrepentant.

The emphasis on Paul's piety and obedience in Acts' final section seems to be offered as an apologetic for Paul and not simply as an attempt to portray Paul as a heroic figure. It consistently points away from Paul to God—God has commissioned Paul, God has helped him, and God has established leaders for the church, continuing to be its protector. Divine actions are the primary means for supporting the claims that Paul is an obedient Jew. Paul, therefore, can claim not to be "disobedient to the heavenly vision" in proclaiming to Jews and gentiles the kingdom message (26:16–19) because Paul has been compelled by God, the only force that can authorize such a mission,[362] to act as a divine witness. Even Luke's attempt to resign the reader to the working out of the divine will provides a defense for Paul—it helps the reader identify with the difficulty Paul faced in maintaining obedi-

---

Luke has any interest in seeing his church model the kingdom's presence, he would want the people to act in this manner. Certainly changes would be necessary (particularly after the temple's destruction), but the general attitudes would still be encouraged. It is not simply a way to appropriate Israel's history for the church.

362. So Haenchen, *Acts*, 686.

ence and understand that neither imprisonment nor suffering necessarily signals divine disfavor.

Finally, it appears that the reader still sees authorization for a mission to Jews, confirming that the restoration is to all Israel. God has not allowed Jewish believers to become second-class citizens and God continues to offer salvation in the face of rejection. Since God has not rejected the Jews, neither should those who proclaim the Way. It seems incorrect to assert that Paul's final turn has brought "the times of the Gentiles" (Luke 21:24).[363] This was presented in 8:4—19:20 and confirmed in 19:21—28:31. Instead, even Paul's final turn has reiterated a universal hope as the kingdom has been restored to Israel, although in an unexpected way.

363. As Moessner, "Completed," 219.

6

The God Who Directs Everything

HOW A CHARACTER SHAPES OR RESPONDS TO THE CIRCUMSTANCES EXPRESSED AS THE plot develops indirectly characterizes that narrative figure. The final characterization strand, therefore, looks at the way the divine will and actions relate to plot development. Certain events carry a divine necessity requiring responses by the story participants. When the mission expands beyond Judea a new dimension is added to divine involvement—conflicts arise between God and magic or other religious beliefs. These scenes present God's control over the kingdom and its people. Finally, divine actions (particularly in relation to persecutions, removing the messengers from the hands of the authorities, and forging the plot) prompt narrative events or answer questions the narrative raises for the reader. Philo (*QE* 1:100) used the phrase "times and seasons" in relation to God controlling man's lifetime. While this usage, as argued in chapter 4, is not a good precedent for understanding Acts 1:6–8 since it makes no reference to kingdoms or nations, it does identify divine control over human affairs as a factor characterizing God's role as *ordainer of times and seasons*. As the reader might expect, then, divine involvement is intrinsic to the plot in Acts, indicating that these are the events God has ordained and further supporting the claim that the kingdom has been restored to Israel.

Necessity and Fulfillment in God's Plan

Acts begins with the expectation that God is about to fulfill promises and that there is a necessity to the actions that are taking place. The announcement that the disciples will receive the Father's promise (1:4, 8) leads the reader to expect to see God as one who *fulfills*. Peter's words that "scripture had to be fulfilled" concerning Judas' death (1:16) and replacement (1:21) enhance this presentation. A divine (they are the Spirit's words) necessity is attributed to Scripture through the use of δεῖ (1:16, 21), implying that these events are planned by God.[1] The prayer for the Lord to reveal the chosen replacement suggests God will determine Jesus' witnesses and their role. Consequently, these opening scenes leave the reader expecting that, whether through scriptural fulfillment or through revelations, the narrative will unfold according to the divine will.[2]

---

1. So Haenchen, *Acts*, 159, fn. 8. Contra Fitzmyer (*Acts*, 220) Judas being replaced is not merely "providential," but necessary.

2. Schneider (*Apostelgeschichte*, I, 237) considers promise and fulfillment foundational to Luke's narrative.

In Luke's Gospel πληρόω verbs are often connected with a promised event (from Scripture or within the narrative) coming to fulfillment (Luke 1:20; 4:21; 9:31, 51; 21:22, 24; 22:16; 24:44). In Acts, the reader finds a πληρόω compound used in reference to the day when Pentecost arrives (2:1). With the expectations built in the preceding scene, the reader would believe that the moment for fulfillment has come[3] (revealed to be the Father's promise by the Spirit-filling that follows—2:4). Later, the reader notes Stephen using a πληρόω verb to refer to the stages in Moses' life (7:23, 30) that are connected to the time (ἐν ᾧ καιρῷ—7:20, cf. 7:17) for the fulfillment of the divine promise to Abraham. Since ultimately the deliverance effected through Moses points to the Righteous One (7:37, 52), whose exaltation has brought the time for the Father's promise, the poured-out Spirit (2:33, 36), to be completed, the reader finds 1:1—8:3 book-ended by a particular sense for "times and seasons"—God controls human history (the events and their timing).

In the Pentecost speech, therefore, the reader sees a new "time" being established since Pentecost represents the "last days." The reader finds "God declares" (2:17) added to the Joel quotation, emphasizing the divine role in this event. Consequently, this new era is the time for God to fulfill promises made previously (2:17–21; Joel 2:28–32). Since these promises were made to Israel in the past, they suggest to the reader that God had a predetermined plan that God is now putting into effect.[4] Throughout Peter's speech, the reader identifies other indications of this plan—Jesus was delivered over by God's "definite plan" (2:23) and his resurrection was inevitable (οὐκ . . . δυνατὸν—2:24) because Scripture (2:25–28; Ps 16:8–11) made evident that God had determined it.[5] Similarly, Jesus' ascent to the throne is directly willed by God because it fulfills Scripture (2:30/2:34–35; Pss 132:11/110:1). Therefore, Jesus' death, resurrection, and exaltation are to be understood as divinely determined events already revealed in Scripture.

Peter's second sermon (3:12–26) continues this theme—the suffering experienced by God's Christ was preannounced (προκατήγγειλεν) in Scripture, God has fulfilled it (3:18), and Jesus is the Christ pre-appointed (προκεχειρισμένον) for them.[6] The reader then finds that the Prophet like Moses (3:22; Deut 18:15, 18) and the covenant blessings to Abraham (3:25; Gen 22:18), both promised in Scripture, had to be fulfilled. Likewise, to the Council, Peter declares Ps 118:22 (4:11) fulfilled in the rejected Jesus. As Scriptural fulfillment (combined with the δεῖ in 4:12) the reader understands that God has made Jesus' name essential for salvation.[7] The reader also identifies Ps 2:1 (4:25–26) expressed as fulfilled in the community's experience (4:27). Further, the persecuting events mentioned there were divinely ordained (ἡ βουλή [σου] προώρισεν—4:28), indicating that the divine plan extends not just to Jesus' death, resurrection, and ascension, but to the events experi-

---

3. So Barrett, *Acts*, 111; Fitzmyer, *Acts*, 237; Tannehill, *Narrative*, 26. Schneider (*Apostelgeschichte*, I, 248) denies that Luke is indicating a Scriptural fulfillment, but the following Joel quotation suggests as much.

4. So Witherington, *Acts*, 146.

5. Fitzmyer, *Acts*, 256; Pesch, *Apostelgeschichte*, I, 121–22.

6. Conzelmann (*Theology*, 151) identified προ compounds as an important means for expressing the divine plan in Acts.

7. Fitzmyer, *Acts*, 301; Pesch, *Apostelgeschichte*, I, 167.

enced by the community.[8] Finally, 1:1—8:3 ends with Stephen's long recounting of Israel's history (7:2–53). The reader finds here numerous citations from Scripture and references to fulfilled promises, which come to their conclusion in the death of the preannounced (προκαταγγείλαντος) Righteous One (7:52). Throughout Acts' opening section necessity and fulfillment characterize divine control over the narrative events.

The promise-fulfillment motif maintains a strong, but transformed, presence in 8:4—19:20. When the eunuch responds to Philip's question concerning whether the eunuch understands what he is reading from Isa 53:7–8, the reader would assume that the prophecy must be satisfied either in the prophet or someone else (8:34). By beginning with this Scripture and preaching Jesus (8:35), Philip seems to support this belief.[9] However, unlike previously, there is no specific statement that the passage *needed* to be fulfilled. Elsewhere the reader finds Peter alluding to prophetic witness (10:43) rather than giving specific proofs from Scripture.[10] Paul repeatedly cites Scripture (13:27) and the fulfillment of promises (13:23, 32–33), expressing themes similar to those in the speeches in 1:1—8:3. There, nevertheless, is again no specific statement that these events are *necessary*. Likewise, the prophetic words from Amos 9:11–12 (Acts 15:16–18) are fulfilled, but without indication that they were foreordained or necessary. It is only when Luke summarizes Paul's dispute at Thessalonica that the reader again finds reference to Jesus' death and resurrection as necessary according to the Scriptures (17:2–3).

While in 1:1—8:3 the speeches often directly expressed *preordination* in Jesus' suffering and death, Paul only suggests the "words of the prophets" were ignorantly fulfilled (13:27). Although the reader should think these events were destined, representing Scripture's "ironic fulfillment"[11] (particularly because similar statements in 1:1—8:3 were), Paul does not directly indicate foreordination, giving the impression that fulfillment was accidental. Moreover, Paul warns that his audience "beware" that the words of Scripture do not become true (13:40–41). Thus, the reader is aware that at least some divinely inspired (prophetic) words do not require fulfillment (those that seem to describe God's people as determined in their resistance to God).[12]

The reader, however, finds that necessity, fulfillment, and preordination are expanded beyond their relation to Scripture. The witnesses concerning Jesus have been pre-chosen (προκεχειροτονημένος) by God (10:41). Paul, like Jesus (17:2–3), is divinely required to face sufferings (9:16), a constraint Paul applies to all who would enter the kingdom (14:22).[13] Further, Paul identifies the proclamation to the Jews first (13:44) as having a

---

8. So Fitzmyer, *Acts*, 310; Gaventa, *Acts*, 96.

9. So Barrett, *Acts*, 431; Pesch, *Apostelgeschichte*, I, 292.

10. Pesch, *Apostelgeschichte*, I, 333; Schneider, *Apostelgeschichte*, II, 63. While Stanton (*Jesus*, 70–85) showed that there are OT texts behind the speech, Luke does not have Peter quote anything directly.

11. So Tannehill, *Narrative*, 169.

12. *Contra* Schille (*Apostelgeschichte*, 297) Luke does not make the Jewish refusal part of the divine plan. The proclamation to Israel first, not Israel's rejection, is necessitated in 13:46.

13. So Haenchen, *Acts*, 436; Pesch, *Apostelgeschichte*, II, 64 (his reference to Acts 9:26 should be 9:16); Tannehill, *Narrative*, 181. Gaventa (*Acts*, 209) seems correct that the force of δεῖ in these instances is not to make suffering an entrance requirement, but to present suffering as consistent with life in the kingdom.

necessity (ἀναγκαῖον) that, possibly, stems from the message's relation to Israel's history,[14] but remains unexplained by Paul (or Luke). Thus, the reader does not have sufficient reason to identify it with scriptural fulfillment. In 1:1—8:3 Luke used πληρόω verbs on a few occasions to refer to the arrival of the time for a promise (2:1; 7:23, 30). In 8:4—19:20 πληρόω is used just after the promise that Paul's sufferings would be necessary (9:16)[15] and at the very moment that those sufferings begin (9:23). Likewise, the fulfillment expressed in 14:26 relates to the word of the Spirit concerning the work (ἔργον) to which God called Paul and Barnabas (13:2).[16]

In every instance, preordination, necessity, and fulfillment have moved from simply relating to Scripture to relating to divine directives outside Scripture. From this, the reader perceives that it is not just what God has spoken in the past that requires completion, but also what God is doing in the present. James underlines this notion by formulating scriptural fulfillment in 15:15 so that the prophetic words are said to agree with the new divine action. Thus, divine action determines how scriptural fulfillment is understood.[17] God maintains control over the kingdom's affairs, whether past or present.

In 19:21—28:31 the reader finds that, even when it is indicated that the Messiah "must suffer" and die, the customary δεῖ is replaced with a form of μέλλω (26:23).[18] While this would not lessen the reader's sense that God directs the events surrounding Jesus' passion and resurrection (this was firmly established in 1:1—8:3), it would focus attention on those places where δεῖ is used—in relation to the divine necessity in Paul's trip to Jerusalem and Rome (19:21; 23:11; 25:10;[19] 27:24), the major focus in this section. As such, the reader encounters a divine necessity driving the plot throughout 19:21—28:31.

As in 8:4—19:20, references to divine ordaining are not directed toward the events surrounding Jesus' passion. Instead, the reader finds Paul appointed for certain actions (22:10)[20] and for specific purposes (22:14), including his witness to what he has and will see (26:16). In the latter two instances Luke supplies the reader a word with a προ prefix, suggesting the event is foreordained.[21] Thus, Paul's actions would seem to be defended by this divinely predetermined selection. This *choice* works together with the necessity in going to Rome since the final reference (26:16) to Paul's appointment indicates that Paul must testify to the things "in which I will appear to you." The reader knows that the Lord has appeared to Paul concerning his "witness" in Rome (23:11). As such, the reader should

14. So Barrett, *Acts*, 656.

15. Pesch (*Apostelgeschichte*, I, 300) considers this a promise.

16. Bechard (*Paul*, 100–123) considers τὸ ἔργον a "code word" for this missionary journey, thus the divine *work* is emphasized throughout the journey.

17. Johnson, *Acts*, 271.

18. Witherington (*Acts*, 748) glosses over this change.

19. Paul asserts that Caesar's court (therefore Rome) is the necessary place for Paul to be (Schneider, *Apostelgeschichte*, II, 359).

20. In 9:6 this was expressed as a necessity (δεῖ), but now as an appointment. Regardless, Paul is to act under divine ordination (Pesch, *Apostelgeschichte*, II, 234).

21. So Barrett (*Acts*, 1041; *contra* Lake and Cadbury, *Beginnings*, 280) on 22:14. Barrett (*Acts*, 1159) denies a temporal significance for 26:16, but if the first has a temporal significance it seems odd to suggest that the second does not.

conclude that Paul remains a prisoner on his way to Rome because God has appointed him to a task.

Throughout the narrative, then, Luke uses necessity and fulfillment to emphasize divine control over the events. The reader finds, however, that Luke keeps transforming the elements that receive this emphasis. Such transformation does not remove the initial impressions, but leads the reader to greater and greater expectations about the divine influence over each narrative event. If God is directing each event, then the reader receives strong assurance that what has happened is indeed *ordained* by the one who sets *times and seasons*.

God in Conflict

When the mission expands beyond Judea, a new dimension is added to divine involvement. Conflicts arise between God and magic or other religious beliefs. These scenes, like the references to necessity and fulfillment, present God in control over the narrative events, confirming that they are divinely ordained.

Simon Magus (8:9) is characterized as practicing magic. The reader knows magic as a widespread (although despised) practice during the Hellenistic period. It found such popularity because it offered a way to harness supernatural power for protection against evil spirits or fate. Rituals, incantations, formulas, and amulets were used to gain help from gods or spirits, believing that these would guarantee that the "power" would act on the person's behalf. Magic, therefore, was seen as a way to manipulate and control "powers."[22] This label is strongly pejorative and is often used to identify a person or a group as "deviant."[23] This suggests that Luke wishes to portray Simon as an unreliable character. Simon also is characterized as the "power of God that is called Great" (8:10). It is difficult to identify this title's origin,[24] but it seems to express that Simon was at least presenting himself as someone who could manipulate the power of God if not as an actual divine being.[25] The statement, "this man is," does appear to predicate Simon as *the* power of God and not just its bearer. Thus, Simon is perceived by the reader as God's enemy, usurping and manipulating divine power.

The reader finds Simon's fortunes reversed through the narrative interplay—Simon considers himself someone great (μέγας) and the people call him "the great (μεγάλη)" "power (δύναμις) of God," who has astonished (ἐξεστακέναι) them. However, Simon believes the message about God's kingdom, seeing the "great (μεγάλας) miracles (δυνάμεις)," which amaze (ἐξίστατο) him.[26] Simon, however, treats the Spirit's outpouring like one of

---

22. On magic, see Arnold, *Power*, 18–19; Arnold, "Magic," 701; Aune "Magic," 1521; Garrett, *Demise*, 11.

23. Garrett, *Demise*, 4.

24. Fitzmyer (*Acts*, 404) and Witherington (*Acts*, 284) cite a reference in PGM 4:1225–29 about a deity that is less than the supreme god, but manifests that god's power. Fitzmyer (*Acts*, 404) suggests the possibility that it is a play on the Hebrew name for God ('ēl), which means "power" or "mighty one."

25. For more discussion, see Haenchen, *Acts*, 303; Pesch, *Apostelgeschichte*, I, 273–74; Schille, *Apostelgeschichte*, 202–203; Schneider, *Apostelgeschichte*, I, 489–90; Spencer, *Portrait*, 92.

26. See Spencer, *Portrait*, 89, 94–95.

his magic arts (something that can be purchased).[27] The Spirit, the real power of God (cf. 1:8), is viewed by Simon as a greater power than any he had previously known (the reader has not seen him attempt to purchase anything prior to this outpouring).[28] In response, Peter calls the Spirit God's "gift" (8:20; cf. 2:38), stressing that God cannot be overpowered or manipulated. Luke's God is free to bestow the power of the Spirit whenever, wherever, and on whomever God chooses. The reader has already found that the Spirit does not necessarily come simply through baptism (2:1–5; cf. 9:17; 10:44),[29] or through the laying on of hands (2:1–4; cf. 10:44—Simon perceives it as coming in this fashion, but Simon is an unreliable character, so his perception would not be used to infer how the Spirit was received),[30] and now learns that the happening is especially not controllable by practitioners of magic.[31]

Acts 13:4–12 and the encounter with Bar-Jesus begins with an emphasis on God commissioning this mission.[32] In 13:2–4, the Spirit calls them and sends them out. This is paralleled by the church setting them apart and sending them away. In each case divine action is the operative feature.[33] This emphasis suggests that the magician Bar-Jesus is opposing God's will by preventing Sergius Paulus from hearing God's word.[34] This man, who, like Simon Magus, relies on magical power, meets the "hand of the Lord," which strikes him with blindness. The reader has already seen blindness marking those who oppose God (Paul in Acts 9).[35] Further, God's "hand" is understood in the OT (Judg 2:15; 1 Sam 12:15) as the active force God uses against those who oppose the divine will;[36] thus the reader sees divine power being demonstrated, showing the "teaching about the Lord" (13:12) to be superior to the enemy's deceptions. Consequently, the divine will cannot be controlled by those who, like Bar-Jesus, would seek to pervert it.

At 16:16–18 the reader may recognize the truth in the servant girl's proclamation that Paul and his companions are servants of the "Most High God"—at first glance it does

27. Haenchen, *Acts*, 304; Johnson, *Acts*, 148; Witherington, *Acts*, 283–84. Simon is not motivated by hoarding goods (*contra* Witherington, 286) since there is no indication that he wants to keep the authority for himself. He may be motivated by a desire for profit—selling the Spirit to others (so Lake and Cadbury, *Beginnings*, 94)—but not hoarding.

28. Gaventa, *Acts*, 138. Also Schneider (*Apostelgeschichte*, I, 485), but the scene does more than remove miracles from the magical realm, it demonstrates divine supremacy over any other "power."

29. Rightly, Pesch, *Apostelgeschichte*, I, 275–76.

30. So Tannehill, *Narrative*, 106-7; Witherington, *Acts*, 288; *contra* Lake and Cadbury, *Beginnings*, 93.

31. Since this passage relates a conflict between Simon and God, rather than Philip or Peter, attempts (as Koch, "Geistbesitz," 64–82) to explain the passage as based on conflicting accounts about how the church in Samaria was founded miss the point.

32. Gaventa, "Initiatives," 83–84; Johnson, *Acts*, 221.

33. See also Gaventa, *Acts*, 191; Schneider, *Apostelgeschichte*, II, 119–20; Witherington, *Acts*, 394.

34. So Haenchen, *Acts*, 400.

35. See chapter 5. *Contra* Fitzmyer (*Acts*, 503), although Paul does pronounce a curse, he does not appear to be calling upon God to exact punishment; rather he announces the punishment God has already determined (the "hand of the Lord is against you"). Only in this way does the scene parallel 5:1–11 and then just the Sapphira incident (Peter did not announce a curse; rather, based on Ananias' death, he spoke knowing what God had already decided).

36. See Johnson, *Acts*, 224.

appears that a "pagan religious practice is made to acknowledge that salvation comes from the Most High God of Christianity."[37] However, the reader has reason to believe that there is little Jewish influence in the area (cf. 16:13).[38] The "place of prayer" could be a synagogue[39] or an open air meeting-place near a river providing water for ceremonial washing.[40] Since Paul seems only to have spoken to women here, the implication may be that there were not enough men for a full synagogue.[41] Regardless, Luke describes the girl in allusion to the Delphic oracle, characterizing her as pagan. In this pagan context, the reader would recognize that her announcement points the crowd away from the God preached by Paul and toward Zeus or any other god the locals considered as the principal god.[42] If this is allowed to continue there would be no reason for the people to change their allegiance. The announcement from the pythonic spirit, thus, appears as another attempt by a "power" to control God's word (confusing the message).

Alternatively, this event could be understood like the Gospel accounts of Jesus silencing the demonic announcements that he is the "Son of God." Those announcements may have been understood as attempts to seduce people from proper worship offered the one God.[43] Even if, then, the reader believes the demon is speaking the truth, its words would still be seen as attempts to confuse the hearer. Regardless, when Paul casts out the spirit in Jesus' name, God's message remains clear and beyond manipulation by "spirits."

Acts 19:11–20 begins with a reference to God doing "extraordinary" miracles through Paul (healings and casting out evil spirits),[44] preparing the reader for the following scene where wandering Jewish exorcists attempt to use Jesus' name in their practices (suggesting they think it a magically powerful formula).[45] If the exorcists succeed using this formula, then perhaps Paul's miracles are accomplished in the same way since Paul and these ex-

37. Fitzmyer, *Acts*, 583; also Johnson, *Acts*, 294; Witherington, *Acts*, 490. Pesch (*Apostelgeschichte*, II, 113) thinks the girl's words characterize Paul and Silas as Jews, setting up the following scene. In this pagan context it is doubtful that they would be understood as such and this does not explain Paul being annoyed by the words. As Schille suggests (*Apostelgeschichte*, 345–46), exorcism scenes do not require the reference to the exorcist's annoyance (the demon's presence is enough to excite passion). Therefore, something more significant must be involved and Luke gives every reason to believe that Paul would happily accept being labeled a Jew.

38. So Fitzmyer, *Acts*, 585.

39. Hengel, "Proseuche," 175; Lake and Cadbury, *Beginnings*, 191.

40. Pesch, *Apostelgeschichte*, II, 104–5.

41. Schille, *Apostelgeschichte*, 341. This, however, is far from certain; cf. Reimer, *Women*, 90–92.

42. So Trebilco, "Paul," 60; Witherington, *Acts*, 494–95. If Paul (or Luke) thought that these words were great publicity for the mission—i.e., the girl spoke the truth (as Schneider, *Apostelgeschichte*, II, 215)—then there seems little reason for Paul to become annoyed at her words (Trebilco, "Paul," 60).

43. See Guttenberger, *Gottesvorstellung*, 320–27.

44. Fitzmyer, *Acts*, 648: "Luke is careful not to attribute this ability [miracles] to Paul himself; it is God who works through him." The emphasis on divine action also protects against seeing the handkerchiefs as magical (Pesch, *Apostelgeschichte*, II, 171). Bibb ("Characterization," 245) wrongly suggests the *extraordinary* miracles identify an increased display of divine power. Rather, in the conflict setting, the *extraordinary* aspect emphasizes divine superiority to the magical practices used by others.

45. Pesch, *Apostelgeschichte*, II, 172; Schille, *Apostelgeschichte*, 379. Garrett (*Demise*, 92) indicates that the reader is supposed to connect this scene to Acts 8 and other places where Christian miracles are confused with magic.

orcists are portrayed as competitors.[46] Johnson thinks that their attempt to appropriate Paul's power is an acknowledgement that it is superior, drawing the parallel to 16:16–18.[47] However, as argued previously, in 16:16–18 the "spirit" does not acknowledge God as superior, but attempts to subvert the message. Likewise, here the narrative framework (the association with magical practices) suggests that this is an attempt to control divine power and subvert the message.

The consequences of a failure in this conflict would be: 1) Paul could claim no special relationship to God and divine power, 2) God's power can be controlled through formulas,[48] and 3) Paul's message would be no different than whatever these exorcists represent. Thus, when Sceva's[49] sons are beaten and stripped, the reader is assured that Paul's authorization comes from God. The spirit knows Jesus and Paul, suggesting it recognizes their legitimate authority.[50] However, the Jewish exorcists are unknown and have no power since "what is important is not whether the exorcist 'knows' the name of Jesus, but whether the demons 'know' the exorcist as one who has truly been invested with authority to call upon that holy name."[51] This lack of power is dramatically illustrated by the power the "spirit" demonstrates over them (Luke uses κατακυριεύσας and ἴσχυσεν—19:16). Divine power, which worked Paul's exorcisms, is once again shown to be beyond manipulating formulas. At the same time, this power seems to be a direct force in the growth of the word as emphasized by the power-references in 19:20 (κατὰ κράτος τοῦ κυρίου ὁ λόγος ηὔξανεν καὶ ἴσχυεν).[52]

Two further conflict scenes center on God as the Creator. In Lystra (14:8–20) the reader finds the conflict between the city gods ("Zeus whose temple was just outside the city") and the living God set as one where an obstacle to belief has been raised (the "faith" engendered in the saved/healed man).[53] As in Philippi (discussed above), God's message and power is in danger of being attributed to the local gods by identification with Zeus and Hermes. There is substantial evidence for linking these two Greek gods with this area in Anatolia,[54] in part because Ovid's *Metamorphoses* (8:620–724) relates these two appearing in this region. This idea, therefore, was popular enough that the inhabitants, and anyone else familiar with the legend (especially the reader), would have been quick to consider

46. Pesch, *Apostelgeschichte*, II, 172. Schneider (*Apostelgeschichte*, 269) identifies a strong contrast is drawn between 19:12 and 19:13.

47. Johnson, *Acts*, 340.

48. Tannehill, *Narrative*, 237.

49. If (as Lake and Cadbury, *Beginnings*, 241; Witherington, *Acts*, 581) Sceva is identified as a high priest because it was believed the chief priests had better knowledge about the divine names, this would serve to heighten the battle over who has access to divine power. A further heightening is found in the setting in Ephesus, a city known as a haven for magical and demonic activity (see Arnold, *Power*, 14–20; Lake and Cadbury, *Beginnings*, 240).

50. So Garrett, *Demise*, 93; Pesch, *Apostelgeschichte*, II, 173.

51. Garrett, *Demise*, 93.

52. So Gaventa, *Acts*, 268.

53. Pesch (*Apostelgeschichte*, II, 57) identifies the miracle as setting the scene for what follows.

54. See Gill, "Acts," 82–84; Bechard, *Paul*, 280–86, 299–300.

Zeus and Hermes when these miracles occur.[55] Further, it is probable that the names Zeus and Hermes have already been applied to local gods.[56] Thus, the area shows a tendency toward syncretism.

When Paul and Barnabas realize this has happened, they present the two, traditional, Hellenistic-Jewish *topoi*[57] about God: 1) He is the living God, rather than a vain belief. This contrast points to God as the *living* One as in 2 Kgs 19:16 (Isa 37:17; cf. Hos 1:10; 4:15; Isa 37:4; Dan 5:23; 6:26; 2 Macc 7:33) versus the *nothings* (cf. Isa 2:20; 31:7; Jer 2:5, 8)—the non-living gods who should simply be cast away.[58] 2) God is the Creator, who made heaven and earth, the sea, and all creatures.[59] This God has permitted their past beliefs, but has given witness by providing for them (giving rain and harvests, satisfying them with food and gladness) and now demands a "turning."[60] For the reader, divine control over creation means that God controls every nation and its history. Thus, God has the right to demand such a "turning" from creation.[61] Only the God who actually controls all things matters.[62]

When the conflict culminates, the reader's conceptions about the Creator God, particularly in light of the extra-text, continue to play a part.[63] The locals misunderstand the message and are stirred into rejection by Jews from Iconium and Antioch, stoning Paul and leaving him for dead. In 2 Maccabees God's ability to raise the dead is directly associated with creative power. The second (2 Macc 7: 9) and third brother (7:11), as well as their mother (7:22–29), are ready to face death because they believe that God, as the creator of the body, can restore it in the resurrection.[64] In Pss 21:2 and 124:8 the divine role as Creator provides assurance that God will help in difficult times. Likewise, Darius' question (Dan. 6:20) links the Living God to Daniel being delivered. Thus, in the extra-text divine creative power is associated with resurrections and rescues. Here, while Paul may not be

---

55. So Fitzmyer, *Acts*, 531; Gaventa, *Acts*, 207; Witherington, *Acts*, 424–25. Hansen ("Preaching," 307–8; following Martin, "Gods," 152–56) argues that the reader would find an indirect "legitimisation" through the associations with Zeus and Hermes since these gods were seen as guaranteeing veracity. The problem is that any relationship to these gods is immediately denied. Thus, if the reader had such notions to begin with, the denial forces their rejection.

56. So D. Gill, "Acts," 84; Fitzmyer, *Acts*, 531.

57. Schille (*Apostelgeschichte*, 307) identifies the contrast between empty and living, the creator belief, and the call to repentance as *topoi* in Jewish-Hellenistic proclamation (see also Gaventa, *Acts*, 208; Haenchen, *Acts*, 530; Lake and Cadbury, *Beginnings*, 166).

58. See Fitzmyer, *Acts*, 532; Haenchen, *Acts*, 428; Johnson, *Acts*, 249.

59. See chapter 2 for how important the Creator image is for characterizing God.

60. If the local gods are thought to be responsible for the community's agricultural life, then this would be a direct contrast to them.

61. Cf. Schneider, *Apostelgeschichte*, II, 160–61.

62. Johnson's assertion (*Acts*, 251) that these Lystrans are in a position to believe seems incorrect. They do not understand the miracle or Paul's proclamation about God. They react to these events through their own beliefs, rather than coming to new ones. If Luke wanted his reader to think these people were ready, he would at least have suggested a divided response among the people. Instead their response is pure idolatry. Tannehill (*Narrative*, 178–79) correctly characterizes the Lystrans as far from receptive.

63. Schille (*Apostelgeschichte*, 308), Haenchen (*Acts*, 429) and Johnson (*Acts*, 253) see a break in scene at 14:19. However, Schneider (*Apostelgeschichte*, II, 155) correctly notes that the same crowd is involved in both events. Thus, the reader will not envision a change.

64. See Abel, *Livres*, 376, 378; Collins, *Daniel*, 313; Nickelsburg, *Resurrection*, 94–95.

raised from the dead, he is delivered from a deadly situation, implying to the reader that God has demonstrated creative power—the control over all things Paul has proclaimed to the Lystrans.

In response to the idolatry in Athens (17:16), the reader finds Paul presenting the God they attest to unknowingly—the creator God (17:24).[65] This God is the one with all the power—God gives life, breath, and everything to everyone; God created all people from one man, making all humanity equal under God. God also determined the "times" for their existence and the "boundaries" of their inhabitance (17:26).

How would the reader understand the reference to *times* and *boundaries*? Since God created men to "inhabit the *whole* earth," the boundaries do not designate livable zones as opposed to uninhabitable ones.[66] Psalm 74:17, where the "bounds of the earth" and "summer and winter" are found together, presents one possibility from the extra-text. The times, in this case, would refer to seasons just as in Acts 14:17.[67] However, the concern in Jewish apocalyptic and historiographical literature for divine control over history, particularly as it is associated with "times and seasons,"[68] must also be considered (especially in light of Acts 1:6–8). With this background, the reader would see the times referencing periods in history (nations rising and falling).[69] Since rain (which defines the times in 14:17 as seasons) is not mentioned here, the reader is more likely to choose this final option. The decisive factor in this interpretation's favor is the judgment "day" mentioned in 17:31—an appointed *time* drawing a historical period to an end (cf. 3:21), rather than a seasonal period.[70] The times and the boundaries, then, remind the reader about divine control over history. Since God has determined their existence and their history, God can rightly demand their repentance. This control is further emphasized by one (Christ) being appointed as judge.[71] Because this will take place at the time (on the "day") determined by God (17:31),[72] the Creator controls everything.

---

65. Schneider (*Apostelgeschichte*, II, 236–37) appears to be correct that this scene is more about the Athenians' curiosity than an attempt to judge Paul's words (also Gaventa, *Acts*, 250; Haenchen, *Acts*, 520). Paul is not on trial (so Johnson. *Acts*, 314); therefore, this is proclamation not defense. The Athenians, nevertheless, are not "inquiring minds or noble truth seekers" since they call Paul a babbler and seize him—17:18–19; cf. Witherington, *Acts*, 516–17.

66. *Contra* Pesch, *Apostelgeschichte*, II, 137–38.

67. Schille, *Apostelgeschichte*, 357–58; Haenchen, *Acts*, 523.

68. See chapters 2 and 4.

69. So Witherington, *Acts*, 526–27

70. Johnson (*Acts*, 315) claims that the times refer to God applying a creative order to things—separating time in an orderly fashion. This assertion fails to account for the apocalyptic judgment image that also appears in the speech.

71. Note that God's creative power provides the evidence (rightly, Gaventa, *Acts*, 253)—resurrection from the dead (17:31).

72. Schneider (*Apostelgeschichte*, II, 233) correctly notes that the "Day of Judgment" gives urgency to the call for repentance. *Contra* Tannehill (*Narrative*, 213–14) Paul's presentation here relies on the "history of a special group." All ideas are interpreted in a Jewish/Christian, monotheistic framework. The reference to the "Day" centers the presentation on specific Jewish/Christian beliefs about divine rule. Therefore (*contra* Jervell, *Unknown*, 17), even here Luke does not promote a "Gentile Christian universalism."

As promise-fulfillment framed 1:1—8:3, these conflict scenes frame 8:4—19:20 (8:4–25/19:11–20). They also enclose subsections within the narrative. Including the account about Herod's 'divine' adulation, a conflict scene begins and ends the pre-Pauline mission section (8:4–25/12:20–24). Since Luke may well be aware that the famine took place after Herod's death,[73] the Herod narrative seems deliberately positioned. Talbert suggested this transposition enabled Luke to end both halves of Acts with a prominent apostle in prison.[74] While there is no indication that Acts 12 concludes half the book (chapters 14–15 seem more likely for the midpoint), it does conclude the pre-Pauline mission. Because Luke places God-in-conflict scenes at other sub-section beginnings and endings (see below), this framing motif seems the more likely reason for the transposition.

Paul's first mission begins with the narrative about Bar-Jesus (13:4–12) and ends with problems in Lystra (14:8–20). Paul's second mission really begins once it is determined that God wants Paul and his companions in Macedonia (16:6–10). Here, right after Lydia's conversion Luke narrates the pythonic spirit episode (16:16–18). The speech in Athens (17:16–34) is only followed by the short scene in Corinth (18:1–17) that ends the journey. The third mission, because it climaxes at Ephesus, begins and ends with an encounter 19:11–20.[75] This framing sets the inclusion of and mission to the Samaritans and gentiles entirely under divine authority. No other power or religious belief can touch it because God's power completely encompasses it. Again, this assures the reader that what has happened is what God had intended.

Two more God-in-conflict scenes are found in 19:21—28:31. In keeping with Luke's changed focus onto Paul's defense, the reader discovers differences in the way these scenes are used. In 19:21–40, although the scene begins with a conflict between Artemis and God, the reader's focus is shifted to Paul (through the emphatic "this Paul"—19:26). Against Johnson's[76] claim that Paul is "marginal" to the account and Pesch's[77] that this is a story about the Way (not Paul) are the following: 1) Incidents involving Paul have been the focus from 19:1 on. Tannehill suggests that, while Paul is not a major actor in the scene, the scene itself is engendered by the effect Paul has had in Ephesus and the surrounding area.[78] 2) Paul's purpose expression (19:21) points to Paul as the focus. 3) Demetrius specifically names Paul (19:25). 4) Although Paul is absent, Gaius and Aristarchus are characterized in relation to him, and 5) Luke narrates Paul's attempt to go into the crowd.

---

73. See Witherington, *Acts*, 368, 375; Hengel and Schwemer, *Paul*, 243–57.

74. Talbert "Again," 39–40.

75. Johnson (*Acts*, 226) identifies parallels with Peter in Acts 4–5, but misses the larger narrative framing identified here. Witherington (*Acts*, 423) also recognizes parallels between Peter and Paul, suggesting an attempt to show the "divine plan" works out in "an orderly fashion." Certainly Luke sees order in this plan, but citing only parallels with Peter misses the divine order. Tannehill (*Narrative*, 237–38) notes the "ring" that surrounds Paul's missionary work as a whole (13:4–12; 19:11–20), but misses the structure identified here. Miesner's ("Missionary," 199–214) attempt to structure Paul's missionary journeys as a chiasm is unconvincing because it fails to note how divine conflicts are used to frame the work, and because there is nothing missionary after 19:20.

76. Johnson, *Acts*, 352.

77. Pesch, *Apostelgeschichte*, II, 178–79.

78. Tannehill, *Narrative*, 241.

As mentioned, Paul mysteriously cannot be found by the crowd (like 17:6). Haenchen suggests Luke cannot have Paul present either because it would be insensible for Paul to convert all the Ephesians or he would have to speak words that more effectively come from the town clerk. This conclusion misses how Luke systematically removes or silences Paul in scenes where he is brought before gentile authorities (argued below). Luke simply does not portray these assemblies as proper places for Paul's defense.[79] Instead, the town clerk gives a speech[80] in which he confirms that Paul's companions have neither robbed the temple nor blasphemed Artemis. Indeed, the reader would recognize that nowhere does Luke present the messengers giving a direct attack on any one deity, let alone Artemis. The message has always been focused on the One God's positive attributes, not the negative attributes ascribed to any specific other. In contrast to the messengers, the reader finds this crowd repeatedly portrayed as confused, unruly, and unlawful. Additionally, the repeated cry "Great is Artemis of the Ephesians" would likely be read ironically. The "great" goddess Artemis, with her world-renown and lordship over spirits and fate,[81] is defended by an unruly mob. Paul's God, however, has demonstrated true power over spirits (19:11–20).

The reader determines, then, that it is not the messengers who are illegitimate, but those who have gathered. Nevertheless, no official decision about Paul or these men is offered since the clerk repeatedly mentions that this is not the appropriate venue for legal decisions (19:38–40), which seems to demonstrate the divine hand in delivering Paul.[82] During this scene, the reader's attention has shifted from Paul's proclamation to his legal status. Although the reader may not realize how extensive this shift is until Paul is arrested and begins to give his defense (22:1), upon reflection the reader can assume that, since no official decision was given before, the ultimate decision about Paul's status may not end up in the hands of "legal" authorities.

When Paul is bitten by a snake after being saved from the shipwreck, the natives (βάρβαροι—28:2, 4)[83] think Paul is being punished by "Lady Justice." This allusion indicates that the reader is to recall Hellenistic conceptions about the goddess who tracks down the guilty.[84] When Paul does not die (the narrative implication is that God has saved him yet again), they change their view and believe Paul is a god. Similar to 19:21–40 but in

79. Haenchen, *Acts*, 578.

80. A judgment about the reliability of the town clerk is difficult. Schille (*Apostelgeschichte*, 391) thinks he simply expresses naïve views about the "threat" from Christianity. Tannehill (*Narrative*, 244) agrees, but suggests he could also be engaged in "strategic flattery" and, thus, maintains a position like the Asiarchs' (moderately favorable to Christians).

81. See Arnold, *Power*, 20–28; Witherington, *Acts*, 587–88.

82. Witherington (*Acts*, 583) correctly identifies the "divine hand" in keeping Paul from being tried or punished. *Contra* Fitzmyer (*Acts*, 655) Luke does not suggest anything about whether it contravenes city laws—the clerk does not make a legal decision. The only charges addressed concern affronts to local religion.

83. The term is used to refer to those who do not speak the Greek language or follow Greek customs. It can reflect those who are aliens, or those identified as culturally inferior (Johnson, *Acts*, 461). Since it is not used for the Lystrans in 14:8–20, it does not seem just to refer to their speaking a non-Greek language. More likely, it colors their beliefs as primitive (and, thus, unreliable). Tannehill (*Narrative*, 340–41) correctly notes that the Maltans' views are not to be taken as the author's, but as 'pagan' beliefs (also Barrett, *Acts*, 1224; Witherington, *Acts*, 778).

84. See Fitzmyer, *Acts*, 783; Johnson, *Acts*, 462; Witherington, *Acts*, 778–79.

contrast with 14:8–20, Paul does not respond to their false beliefs (although Paul's prayer, offered prior to Publius's father being healed, provides evidence that Paul is not divine).[85] This failure to respond could be because (unlike in Lystra) the Maltans do not attempt to worship Paul.[86] However, there are hints that the reader interprets the event differently. In the scene after Malta, Paul sails in a ship with the Διοσκούροι as its figurehead (28:11). The reader is likely familiar with common Hellenistic beliefs that Castor and Pollux were protectors of ships and saviors for those facing danger at sea.[87] Here, Luke does not need to respond to such beliefs because the narrative has already shown that God is the one who protected Paul (27:24). Likewise, then, at 28:1–10 Luke allows the narrative rather than Paul to counter any claim that gods like "Justice" provide justification for Paul. Commonly, shipwreck survivors were thought to be judged innocent by the gods,[88] but the reader already knows that Paul is a prisoner due to the divine will (cf. 19:21; 21:11, 14; 23:11; 27:24) not due to any guilt. Thus, 19:21—28:31, in contrast to the middle section, systematically leaves out responses in these conflict scenes, allowing the reader to identify from the narrative that divine action supports Paul's innocence.

The reader, therefore, finds these two passages characterizing Paul's "legal" status rather than his missionary role. They are united by silence about implied suggestions regarding this status. Gaventa identifies the "startling" silence by believers in the Ephesus scene and on Malta, interpreting it as demonstrating the implacable resistance facing the gospel (Ephesus) and the lack of any need to reply (Malta).[89] However, she fails to note that while in 8:4—19:20 each God-in-conflict scene was countered through speech or direct action, in 19:21—28:31 Luke has changed tactics along with his changed focus. Legal authorities and Hellenistic religious conceptions about "Justice" ultimately add nothing to Paul's defense.

Like 8:4–19:20, conflict scenes frame the final section (19:22–40/28:1–10). Overall then, where the mission began expanding beyond Jerusalem (8:4–25) and just prior to Paul's arrival in Rome (28:1–10) the narrative is framed by encounters with other religious beliefs. Therefore, the reader sees divine authority completely encompassing not only the gentile and Samaritan inclusion, but also Paul's defense. In both cases, this assures the reader that God controls these events maintaining divine authority over the kingdom, its messengers, and everything else.

God Involved Everywhere

Throughout Acts it is impossible for the reader to miss divine involvement, assuring the reader concerning what has happened. This particularly plays out in how God directs the

---

85. Pesch, *Apostelgeschichte*, II, 299; Schille, *Apostelgeschichte*, 472; Schneider, *Apostelgeschichte*, II, 404.

86. Witherington, *Acts*, 779.

87. See Fitzmyer, *Acts*, 786; Johnson, *Acts*, 463; Ladouceur, "Hellenistic," 446; Witherington, *Acts*, 781.

88. See Miles and Trompf, "Luke," 264; Tannehill, *Narrative*, 341. Rapske ("Acts," 44) correctly notes that the readers "are quite definitely being encouraged" not to view Paul as being justified by the shipwreck.

89. Gaventa, *Acts*, 270, 274–76, 358.

results of persecution, removes the messengers from the hands of "legal" authorities, and forges the plot. Acts 1:1—8:3 sets up these themes.

As Acts begins, the reader notes God involved in and directing the events—the ascension is a divine action; Pentecost is pictured as a theophany; the filling and boldness associated with God's Spirit indicate divine involvement; roles are filled by divine selection; the community grows by divine power; and deliverances from prison occur by supernatural action.[90] God also directs plot development. Divine commands prompt action (1:8) and divine necessity provokes others (1:21). The theophanic appearance at Pentecost (2:1–4) requires explanation (2:14–36). God (3:13) heals, which leads to a proclamation that provokes a conflict with the Jerusalem leaders (4:1–2). Peter and John's Spirit-inspired boldness in response (cf. 4:8, 13) triggers a narrative dilemma: who will the Apostles obey—the temple leadership or God?[91] The answer is given by Peter and John's adamant refusal to do anything but what they had "seen and heard" from God (4:19–20), indicating that they are merely responding to divine promptings.

Because the temple leadership has arrested the Apostles, the reader may be concerned about whether their message is correct. If the religious leaders objected to it, does God? Bibb points out that these figures were expected to know the divine will. If they object to this message, God must also.[92] However, Luke's reader also knows that the temple leadership was active in opposition to Jesus. Thus, the concern is somewhat muted and a dilemma is posed: on whom does divine favor rest—the Apostles or the religious leadership? God responds to the implied question by answering a petition for action by demonstrating divine power (the shaking) and providing more Spirit-inspired boldness (4:31). The narrator then emphasizes this point by describing the community as under divine grace (4:33),[93] receiving answers to the prayer (5:12; cf. 4:30), and growing (5:14).[94]

Luke uses an intensifying series of conflicts to keep the reader's attention and advance the plot from 4:1—8:3.[95] The reader finds that the previous divine demonstration of favor causes another conflict, where the temple leadership "jealously" responds to this favor by arresting all the Apostles (5:18). However, this time God does not appear content to let the issue wait for the trial, but intercedes, delivering them from the prison. Incidents expressing divine deliverance in 2 Maccabees indicated divine favor on the recipients. This extra-textual conception suggests that Luke's reader interprets the Apostles' escape similarly. It also implies that it is incorrect to claim[96] that the deliverance plays no part in the remaining account. Although the Council does not address the miracle, the reader can

---

90. These issues were all discussed in chapter 3.

91. So Barrett, *Acts*, 218; Fitzmyer, *Acts*, 304.

92. Bibb, "Characterization," 199.

93. So Barrett, *Acts*, 254. Gaventa (*Acts*, 100) thinks the grace comes from the community's neighbors because God is not specifically mentioned. But, since μεγάλη is repeated in such proximity with references to "power" and "grace," the reader is likely to see a common source for both. Obviously, the power did not come from the neighbors (so Jervell, *Apostelgeschichte*, 192; Witherington, *Acts*, 207).

94. On these elements expressing divine favor see chapter 3.

95. See Parsons, *Departure*, 165–67; Tannehill, *Narrative*, 64–65; Witherington, *Acts*, 199.

96. As Fitzmyer, *Acts*, 333.

already identify which group truly knows the divine will—divine favor has supported the Apostles rather than the Council.

Next, the reader would note indications that Stephen's trial originates in divine activity. The widow-crisis occurs at a time when the community is growing (6:1). Stephen is qualified to provide help in this crisis by God filling him with the Spirit and wisdom (6:3, 5).[97] Since the reader finds that Stephen's wisdom and Spirit (6:3) is identical to the futility faced by his opponents (6:10), the reader realizes that it is his God-given "grace and power" (6:8) that leads to the dispute with the Diaspora Jews. As the Council is about to question Stephen, he is described as appearing with a face like that of an angel—a divine messenger (6:15). With all these indications reflecting divine involvement, the reader cannot help but assume that God has brought Stephen to the appropriate point for performing a divinely chosen task. That task becomes clear when the speech concludes and Stephen, under divine control (filled with the Spirit—7:55), sees the opened heavens (7:56). While Stephen's speech produced anger, violence comes only after the vision. Thus, it is God who provides the proverbial "straw" since it is God who, through the divinely qualified spokesman, reveals the point of contention—the Righteous One at God's right hand. God provokes the persecution that will scatter the church.[98]

Throughout the opening section of Acts God is involved in every narrative development. This pattern continues throughout Acts as God continues to forge the plot. Before focusing on that aspect, however, there are two additional sub-themes to investigate—Divine involvement in the results of persecution and in the removal of the messengers from "pagan" authorities.

Results of Persecution

As Acts 1:1—8:3 closes, the reader must consider how the persecution that has begun will affect the kingdom. The reader initially finds clues to answer this through the various references to divine reversal of certain persons' fortunes. In 2:23–24, 3:13–15, 4:10–12, and 5:30–31 Luke notes how God, through the resurrection, has reversed the actions done against Jesus (a motif that continues in the proclamation found in Acts' second section; cf. 10:38–40; 13:29–30). This presentation seems modeled on Gen 50:20 (where God turned for good what was meant for evil)[99] given the way Joseph and Moses appear in Stephen's speech.[100] God provides deliverance through Joseph by being with him despite his brothers' treachery (7:9–10). Moses is the one rejected as ruler and judge, but made ruler and deliverer by God (7:35). These portraits then lead to a reference to the rejected "Righteous

97. On the Spirit as witness to God's choice and favor see chapter 3.

98. Stephen's speech emphasizes divine control over God's people from the outset. With the appearance to Abraham (7:2), the speech sets Israel's history as beginning with divine revelation and command (so Jervell, *Apostelgeschichte*, 232–33). Thus, Luke affirms that God has been guiding God's covenant people from the start, just as God continues to do in the present.

99. So Barrett, *Acts*, 143, 198, 228, 357–58. For the reversal motif, see also Fitzmyer, *Acts*, 287; Gaventa, *Acts*, 86; Neudorfer, "Speech," 284, 288–89.

100. See Barrett (*Acts*, 362–63) and Fitzmyer (*Acts*, 366–67, 373–74) for further discussion concerning Joseph and Moses and their relationship to "Righteous One" in this speech.

One" (7:52), recalling the reversal motif that Luke has developed. Thus, the reader is aware that God uses negative situations for divine purposes. This portrayal reflecting a God who reverses fortunes prepares the reader to expect that the persecution will produce greater gains for God's kingdom since God maintains control over the events narrated.[101]

Acts 8:4 begins, then, with those, like Philip, who were dispersed ($\delta\iota\alpha\sigma\pi\alpha\rho\acute{\epsilon}\nu\tau\epsilon\varsigma$)[102] proclaiming the word. Consequently, the Samaritans are included in the kingdom because God used the persecution directed towards God's people for God's advantage.[103] Since the obedient ones are dispersed, God also reverses the trend in Israel's history that dispersions resulted from disobedience.[104] Further, because 9:1 makes Saul's ravaging the church (cf. 8:3) the setting for his Damascus road experience, Stephen's murder and the subsequent persecution are used by God to reverse the fortunes of Saul (from God's enemy to chosen vessel; from one who causes suffering to one who must suffer—9:15) and the church (peace and growth follow—9:31). Tannehill notes that the similarities between the converted Saul and Stephen are such that Saul seems to step into the latter's role.[105] These similarities enhance the reversal that God has performed, replacing a lost messenger.

At 11:19–30 the reader encounters the Stephen episode used in this way one final time.[106] Those who were scattered make their way to Antioch (11:19), where they begin to speak to Greeks (gentiles)[107] (11:20). This event results in the establishment of the Antioch church (the base which Paul will go out from and return to for the rest of 8:4—19:20). By linking these events back to the Stephen episode, Luke reminds his reader that God maintains control even over the difficulties God's people face. At the same time, divine control over the mission plan is emphasized, for the leadership in Jerusalem does not plan for either Samaria or Antioch; rather, they respond to divine action.[108]

The conflicts between Paul and both Jews and Greeks also fit this model. The opposition from Bar-Jesus leads the proconsul to belief (13:12). Hostility by Jews means rejoicing for gentiles (13:48). Repeatedly, conflicts in one city are precursors to mission successes in the next (13:51, cf. 14:1, 5–7; 16:39, cf. 17:1–4; 17:5–8, cf. 17:10–12; 17:13, cf. 17:34). God turns Paul and Silas' arrest into an opportunity to display theophanic power (16:26) and provide salvation for the jailer (16:31–34). Thus, such incidents as Paul arriving in Athens are not mere accidents.[109] Paul arrived there because God has turned persecution into opportunity. From this, the reader learns that Luke's narrative world does not have

101. So Schneider, *Apostelgeschichte*, I, 479.

102. Cf. 8:1 and 11:19.

103. Tannehill (*Narrative*, 102) mistakenly thinks that Hellenists become the initiators and the Apostles the verifiers. Both roles belong to God. Tannehill, nevertheless, does think the "real initiative" is in divine hands (103).

104. See Spencer, *Portrait*, 33–35.

105. Tannehill, *Narrative*, 114.

106. This connection is noted by Gaventa, *Acts*, 176–77; Schille, *Apostelgeschichte*, 262; Tannehill, *Narrative*, 146.

107. On "Greeks" as a reference to gentiles, see Barrett, *Acts*, 550–51; Pesch, *Apostelgeschichte*, I, 352; Schneider, *Apostelgeschichte*, II, 89 n. 22.

108. So Gaventa, *Acts*, 181.

109. *Contra* Johnson, *Acts*, 312.

accidents—God controls everything in it. Consequently, the reader comes to understand that God changes difficulty, opposition, and setback into further growth for the kingdom. God orders the world, demonstrating divine control over human affairs.

Where previously the reader had seen the way God reversed persecutions centering on actions *by* Paul, in Acts' final portion it concerns those actions directed *toward* Paul. At 9:15 the Lord said that Paul would witness before "gentiles and kings and before the people of Israel." While the first and last members of this triad were evidenced in 8:4—19:20, the middle term remained unfulfilled. Also, 19:21—28:31 begins with arrival in Rome seemingly a divine necessity (19:21), a belief confirmed as the narrative unfolds. Thus, the reader has two narrative expectations for this section—a speech before a king and a trip to Rome. Luke's reader finds these plot aims achieved through persecution—Paul becomes a captive because a crowd is falsely stirred up against him (21:27–28). Coincidently, this results from Paul's attempt to show his loyalty to the Law and Jewish customs. Even though the solution suggested by the Jerusalem church appears to have ended in defeat, the reader finds that it allowed for Paul's necessary advancement toward Rome (God has again reversed a negative outcome).[110] Then, the reader learns that immediately after Paul received assurance concerning this necessity (23:11), a Jewish conspiracy to kill Paul is revealed (23:12–15). The providential discovery leads to Paul being moved to Caesarea, where, to avoid a second conspiracy (25:3), Paul has to appeal to Caesar (cf. 28:19). The reader assumes that persecution has constrained Paul's options—the Jewish conspiracies make Jerusalem a dangerous place for Paul.[111] Even acquittal in Caesarea poses dangers since it would release Paul to the whims of his local Jewish opponents.[112] Paul's appeal, then, secures the trip to Rome (25:12; 26:32).[113]

While this persecution fulfills one narrative expectation, the reader also finds the process leading to an opportunity for Paul to speak to King Agrippa (26:1–29), completing the remaining expectation from 9:15.[114] Ultimately however, Paul will declare that divine help (26:22) has brought him before the king. Consequently, God has turned persecution into plot achievement.

The motif concerning Paul's own reversal from persecutor to proclaimer continues as well. When Paul twice recounts his experience on the Damascus road (22:3–11; 26:9–17), he presents himself as one who believed that zeal for the Law meant persecuting the Way. The encounter with the exalted Lord changes this *blind* zeal (illustrated by his own blind-

---

110. See Tannehill, *Narrative*, 271; Zumstein, "L'apôtre," 387.

111. So Pesch, *Apostelgeschichte*, II, 266; Schille, *Apostelgeschichte*, 442.

112. Barrett, *Acts*, 1121, 1239.

113. *Contra* Pesch (*Apostelgeschichte*, II, 267) Paul's appeal to Caesar is due to his witness in Rome being necessary and the way persecution has forced his hand. It is not a symbol that the church is divorced from Judaism.

114. So Fitzmyer, *Acts*, 748; Pesch, *Apostelgeschichte*, II, 273; Schneider, *Apostelgeschichte*, II, 361–62; Witherington, *Acts*, 734. While Luke (*contra* Schille, *Apostelgeschichte*, 445; so Barrett, *Acts*, 1122–23) does not consciously use parallels between Jesus' passion and the events in chapters 25–26, the repeated references to Agrippa as "king" (see chapter 4) suggest Luke is emphasizing the fulfillment of 9:15.

ness) into a *directed* zeal for the divine will.[115] Thus, the divine ability to turn persecution into proclamation is emphasized anew.

Removal from Authorities

Beginning in Acts' second section, Luke portrays the message and the messengers as consistently removed from the hands of pagan authorities. This is seen first in Thessalonica, where the reader encounters disobedient Jews who stir the crowd into a conflict over which king they serve (17:5–7). When the mob makes its way to the magistrates (17:8), there is only one problem—Paul and his companions are nowhere to be found (17:6). The implication may be that while the Thessalonians worry about who is king, God demonstrates it—God has removed the messengers from their control, denying thereby that God's people are "seditious."[116]

In Corinth, the Jews bring Paul before Gallio, charging Paul with teaching unlawful worship (18:12–13). Before Paul can speak in his defense, Gallio refuses to hear this case since it is not within his purview, nothing compels him to hear the case, and, most importantly given Luke's emphases, it concerns Jewish law and customs (18:14–15).[117] Through Gallio's unwillingness to judge this matter, God protects Paul from the Jews. The following event emphasizes this point for the reader since it turns out that Gallio is not a great defender of either law or order. He simply takes no interest in Jewish affairs; ignoring the Jew, Sosthenes, being beaten, just as he previously ignored Jewish legal issues.[118] In a narrative that has repeatedly focused on divine authority over Scripture (the Law) and Israel (God's people) the reader finds that such matters do not belong to Rome but to God. It is God (not Rome) that cares about God's people and Law.[119] In neither incident discussed here does the authority give a legal decree, thus divine authority is maintained by the message and the messengers being removed from the control of the authorities.

Turning to Acts 19:21—28:31, the God-in-conflict scenes discussed earlier imply that God removed Paul from all other authorities. This might seem an odd implication since Paul is a prisoner for much of this section. However, the reader consistently finds that Paul's circumstances as a prisoner are not as they appear, for no one is ever certain about what to do with him—the crowd shouts contradictory things (21:34); guards fear putting him in chains (22:29); tribunals intended to discover charges find only more confusion (23:10); no one can determine a charge against him as worthy of death or imprisonment

115. See Pesch, *Apostelgeschichte*, II, 233–34.

116. Schille (*Apostelgeschichte*, 351–52) thinks the believers are being charged as revolutionaries.

117. Pesch (*Apostelgeschichte*, II, 151) considers this the real factor in Gallio's refusal. *Contra* Schille (*Apostelgeschichte*, 366) this fits within the Lukan view since Luke consistently interprets the Christian mission in a Jewish framework.

118. See Cassidy, *Society*, 92–93; Tannehill, *Narrative*, 227. Thus, (*contra* Conzelmann, *Theology*, 142) this is not presented to show Rome's "ideal conduct." Gallio is uninterested in anything Jewish.

119. It is argued below that Rome is consistently prevented from making legal decisions about the message and the messengers. To this extent, Conzelmann (*Theology*, 143) was correct that Rome is deliberately excluded from deciding the relationship between Judaism and Christianity. What Conzelmann failed to realize is that this moves the argument into God's 'courtroom.' Rome has no ability to justify either group.

(23:29; 25:25–26; 26:31); authorities knowledgeable concerning the Way put off making decisions (24:22);[120] accusers are missing (24:19); other authorities do not even know how to investigate the issue (25:20); and Festus shows Rome's inability to comprehend, let alone decide, theological issues by considering Paul's teaching madness.

While the reader finds Roman authorities convinced concerning Paul's legal innocence, the reader considers their continued willingness to keep Paul a prisoner as indicating their utter confusion concerning his status. Tannehill, nevertheless, suggests that, through "the education" of the Roman commander, Lysias, the reader is expected to see that Romans can learn to understand who Paul is. Supposedly, Lysias comes to understand the truth, moving from assuming that Paul is guilty (21:38) to realizing that he is innocent (23:29).[121] While Lysias does express a different position from when he started, his conclusions provide no change in Paul's status. This underscores the Roman confusion, not their enlightenment, since even realizing the truth they do not act on it. Such utter mismanagement suggests that the reader should not see that Roman rule "employed correctly" is a help to the church;[122] rather, the only help comes from God. In the reader's extra-text, when Jesus is brought before Pilate and Herod (Luke 23:1–25) a similar Roman failure is pictured. Neither Pilate nor Herod condemns Jesus, yet the request from the Jews to kill him is granted. Thus, Luke consistently shows Roman rulers (and their vassal kings) unable to act appropriately in relation to Jesus and his followers. The reader forms the impression that Paul was being sent to Rome for (from the human perspective) insensible reasons.[123] Even when Paul gets to Rome, the charges against him are unknown to the Roman Jews and the book ends without Paul's appeal to Caesar being heard—no Roman legal authority makes a final decision about Paul. Thus, Luke consistently places the message and the messenger beyond Roman judgment.

Why, then, is Paul a prisoner? Luke's answer can be found in Acts 20:22–23. Paul tells the Ephesian elders that he is bound (δεδεμένος) in Spirit to go to Jerusalem before he informs them that bonds (δεσμὰ) await him there. In other words, Paul is a God's prisoner before he is Rome's prisoner.[124]

Paul's Impending Death?

Should the reader assume that Paul's *bonds* and *afflictions* (Acts 20) imply a veiled announcement concerning his death?[125] In light of this removal-from-authorities motif they seem only to prefigure plot action, heightening expectations that Paul will suffer for his witness to Christ. Likewise, references to Paul's departure (20:25,

120. Commentators offer various explanations for this delay (see Johnson, *Acts*, 414), but it seems like the reader identifies it as another uncertain Roman action toward Paul (cf. Jervell, *Apostelgeschichte*, 572).

121. See Tannehill, *Narrative*, 273–74.

122. *Contra* Schille, *Apostelgeschichte*, 437.

123. So Haenchen, *Acts*, 690; Pesch, *Apostelgeschichte*, II, 275; although their assessment that these events show Luke unclear concerning what brought Paul to Rome appears incorrect.

124. So Gaventa, *Acts*, 297.

125. As Pesch, *Apostelgeschichte*, II, 203; also Haenchen, *Acts*, 592.

38) focus on the bonds which make his imprisonment (not his death) the reason they will not see him.[126]

Paul mentions the possibility that he will die. After Agabus announces what awaits Paul in Jerusalem, Paul tells the crowd trying to persuade him not to go there, that he is willing "even to die in Jerusalem for the name of the Lord Jesus" (21:13). This statement adds to an ambiguous announcement Paul made previously during the Miletus speech. There, he claimed that he did not consider his "life of any value" in comparison to finishing the work to which the Lord Jesus had called him (20:24). This statement is not necessarily an allusion to Paul's death, but when the reader encounters the clearer statement at 21:13, the reader may reassess the former in this way.

Such statements are common in martyrological accounts familiar to the reader in the extra-text. In both 2 Maccabees 6–7 and in Josephus' *Antiquities* (17:158–59), those who are about to be martyred claim that death is preferable to disobedience to God. Likewise, Paul seems to think death better than disobedience to the Lord Jesus' call. Does this mean that the reader was to see Paul's death as imminent? The problem with answering this question affirmatively is that Peter and John have already made similar martyrological-type statements (5:29—"we must obey God rather than any human authorities"; cf. 4:19), yet neither of those two die in Acts. Indeed, Peter and John's statements are closer to the martyrological model, for they are made before a body that has the power to bring about their death. In addition, Stephen makes no such statement, yet *he does die.* Thus, Luke uses the language of martyr's to stress the obedience of his protagonists without committing those same characters to martyrdom.

Some argue that Paul's Miletus speech fits into a literary genre known as Testaments. Typically, in this genre, a figure announces his impending death, recalls his past, predicts some future problem to be faced, and gives final words of exhortation.[127] A brief look at Acts 20:18–35 reveals that these elements seem to be present— Paul reviews his past (20:18–21),[128] predicts a future problem (20:29–30),[129] and gives some final words of exhortation (20:32–35). What is not as clear is the reference to

---

126. *Contra* Schneider, *Apostelgeschichte*, II, 30; so Barrett, *Acts*, 978. Jervell (*Apostelgeschichte*, 511; also Lohfink, *Sammlung*, 89) who elsewhere champions Paul's turns as local, sees the address to the Ephesian elders as global—it represents his departure from all the churches through death. However, such a conclusion ignores the context described above and the role the scene plays in prefiguring narrative action.

127. See Collins, "Testaments," 325–55; Eades, "Testament," 796–97; Lambrecht, "Paul's," 332–33.

128. Harrelson ("Significance," 210) notes that there was a tendency to focus ethics on the individual. Thus the review of the past often (as in *T. 12 Patr.*) focused on the individual's past sins. Luke, in contrast, has Paul citing the things he has done well.

129. Some (Lambrecht, "Paul's," 335) would suggest that Paul's reference to the future coming of these "wolves" is a *vaticinium ex eventu*—i.e., Luke is writing this account with the benefit of hindsight, referring to the events that have already occurred in Ephesus. The problem with this argument is that predicting a future problem, particularly one that referred to some potentially "falling away," simply fits the *sin-exile-return* pattern often found in the testamentary predictions (see Collins, "Testaments," 338). This pattern can be seen from *T. Iss.* 6: "I know, my children that in the last times your sons will abandon simplicity and cleave to insatiableness . . . and abandoning the commandments of the Lord, they will cleave to Beliar . . . You therefore tell your children, so that if they sin they may turn the more quickly to the Lord, for he is merciful and will deliver them to bring them to their land" (cited by Collins). In Paul's case, there is no reference to the land's restoration, but this is simply in keeping with a reinterpreted kingdom restoration.

Paul's death since,[130] as noted above, when first read the statement that seems to allude to Paul's death (20:24) is ambiguous at best. Further, as argued, in the context of Acts such statements are not followed by the speaker's death. Thus, the speech lacks an obvious reference to Paul's impending death. The announcement or imminent expectation of death is a key feature in determining the Testamentary genre. Collins notes, "The most fundamental defining characteristic of a testament is that it is a discourse delivered in anticipation of imminent death. . . . The testament begins by describing in the third person the situation in which the discourse is delivered and ends with an account of the speaker's death."[131] Obviously, there is no account of Paul's death given, either in Acts 20 or elsewhere in Luke's narrative. Without it, the speech can only be considered to belong in a related genre, the Farewell Discourse.[132] This genre shares all features with the Testament except the announcement-expectation of death.

Thus, even if the reader recognizes this scene as testamentary, this type of literature, as Gaventa notes, can be related as much to departures as to deaths[133] and, as Witherington claims, this speech lacks the "'last will and testament' character" reflecting someone at "death's door."[134] The reader knows that Paul's freedom to continue his strengthening of the churches is threatened, but his death is but one possible outcome—one that the narrative does not take up.[135]

There are other places where the possibility of Paul's death is brought up—at two points it is noted that he has done nothing worthy of death or imprisonment (23:29; 26:31). Paul, himself, mentions that he is willing to die if he is found to have done something worthy of death (25:11). However, Paul's final statement about the possibility of his death is that he was not found to have done anything worthy of it (28:18).

---

130. *Contra* Dibelius, *Studies*, 157–58. Lambrecht ("Paul's," 326) argues that the parallels between Paul's speech and Jesus' final discourse in Luke 22 (a look back at the past—Luke 22:35; warnings and exhortations—Luke 22:24–27; a difficult period after departure—Luke 22:35–38; blessings and prayers—Luke 22:32) are intended to convey a similarity in these figures' death. These, however, are simply generic features and should not be used to show a conscious parallel in fate.

131. Collins, "Testaments," 325; cf. Eades, "Testament," 796: "The testament, however, seems to presuppose the impending death of the testator, which lends a heightened sense of urgency to the message." De Jonge (*Testaments*, 113), in discussing *T. 12 Patr.*, notes that "all testaments, with the exception of that of Joseph, mention the age at which the patriarch concerned died." It could be noted (as Kolenkow, "Genre," 130) that in *Jub.* 20–22 Abraham gives a testamentary address, even though he does not know when he is going to die. Still, the motif of death is apparent; whereas, Paul's possible reference to his death is allusory at best. Indeed, Collins ("Testaments," 327) questions whether *T. Sol.* can be considered a Testament because it does not narrate Solomon's death.

132. Collins ("Testaments," 331) identifies Acts 20:17–31 as an example of a Farewell Discourse (cf. Michel, *Abschiedsrede*, 70). He further notes that with the great number of testaments "embedded" in other literary works (Tob 14; 1 Macc 2:49–70; *Jub.* 21, 36; *L.A.B.* 19, 23–24; 33; *2 En.* 14–18; *2 Apoc. Bar.* 43–47 [lacks a death scene]), this form of writing would be familiar to readers. At the same time it also shows that there is "only a thin line between the genre 'testament' and the broader category of 'last words' where the distinctive testamentary framework is lacking."

133. So Gaventa, *Acts*, 283.

134. Witherington, *Acts*, 612.

135. *Contra* Gaventa, *Acts*, 286.

There are plots to kill Paul (23:12–22; 25:2–3), but these are consistently thwarted by what seems to be divine providence. Paul's life is threatened, but his death is not impending in Acts.

Overall, the reader finds Paul left as God's prisoner, ready to die if need be (21:13), but free from condemnation (28:30–31), unworthy of death. This is not a person living under a "veiled" death sentence.[136] Paul can enjoy such remarkable freedom during his Roman imprisonment[137] because Roman authorities have no real control over Paul. Paul remains unhindered (28:31), because, paradoxically, he is bound by what the reader knows to be the real power in Luke's world—God. Therefore, Luke's reader does not see Christianity protected by Roman legal authority since Luke ultimately does not seem to present any authority but God mattering.[138]

Forging the Plot

Just after Acts' second section starts, the reader encounters God managing the plot in directing Philip to go down the road to Gaza and to join the Ethiopian (8:26–40). Then, the Spirit removes Philip after the baptism, demonstrating that the conversion was "gottgeführt und gottgewollt."[139] In this account there are various aspects (the eunuch's reading choice; Philip's arrival at the exact time he is reading it; and finding water on the desert road) the reader is likely to find providential.[140] If $\kappa\alpha\tau\grave{\alpha}\ \mu\epsilon\sigma\eta\mu\beta\rho\acute{\iota}\alpha\nu$ is translated as a reference to "midday" the providential aspect is deepened—it would suggest the eunuch's journey was an emergency since travel would not normally be done during this hotter period.[141] The angel's command would be seen as aimed directly at Philip meeting this

---

136. Thus, it seems mistaken (as Schille, *Apostelgeschichte*, 418; Haenchen, *Acts*, 731–32) to assume that the reader is to conclude that Paul's trial ended in death (see Witherington, *Acts*, 618–20).

137. Haenchen (*Acts*, 719) and Schille (*Apostelgeschichte*, 429) emphasize this seemingly incongruous freedom, but it simply fits Luke's emphasis on Paul as God's prisoner.

138. *Contra* Pesch, *Apostelgeschichte*, II, 182–83. Haenchen ("Judentum," 155–87; *Acts*, 630; similarly Conzelmann, *Theology*, 138; Roloff, *Apostelgeschichte*, 337) claimed that Paul's appeal to the "hope of Israel" in his defense speeches was an attempt to claim continuity with Judaism and thus allow for Christianity to be treated by Rome in the same way as Judaism (as a *religio lecita*). For Haenchen, therefore, it should not be thought that Christianity actually maintained the same hope as Israel, only that Luke was using this as a religio-political argument to defend Christianity. However, it is uncertain whether Judaism was viewed as a *religio lecita* at the time. Tertullian (*Apol.* 21:1) argued this was the case, but the evidence for such in Luke's period is dubious (see Talbert, *Luke*, 104; Witherington, *Acts*, 541–44). Further, since this work is written in proximity to the time of the Jewish War, the Jewish-Roman relationship would have been at a low point. Identity with the Jews would run counter to an apology before Romans.

139. Pesch, *Apostelgeschichte*, I, 290.

140. So Haenchen, *Acts*, 315; Pesch, *Apostelgeschichte*, I, 292; Schneider, *Apostelgeschichte*, I, 503.

141. Pesch, *Apostelgeschichte*, I, 291.

man at the appropriate time.[142] Thus, every feature in this encounter points to a divine appointment.[143]

That God initiates Paul's Damascus experience is evident to the reader through the theophanic encounter (9:3), and divine control over the event is seen in how the Lord Jesus' commands to Saul (9:6, 8) and to Ananias (9:11–12, 17) prescribe actions for each to take. Paul is dependent on the Lord's command and the details in the instructions to Ananias show that the Lord knows the actions that will follow.[144] In 9:24 a mysteriously revealed Jewish conspiracy leads to Paul going up to Jerusalem. Further, Lydda's nearness to Joppa when Peter is needed there (9:38) would seem providential.

Throughout the Cornelius episode (as in the encounter with the eunuch), the reader identifies God advancing the plot:[145] an angel commands action from Cornelius (10:3-5); Peter experiences a vision (10:10–16) and receives a command from the Spirit (10:19–20); and the Spirit is poured out even though Peter has not mentioned such an event (10:44). This divine action becomes the basis for Peter's argument against the objections found in Acts 11 and 15 (see chapter 5). Finally, the pre-Pauline mission portion ends with God's counter to Herod's action both in delivering Peter (12:7–12) and in punishing Herod (12:23). Several features draw the reader toward the conclusion that Peter's deliverance is divinely worked—community prayer is involved (12:5); an angel constantly directs Peter's action; the door opens by itself (a *topos* in deliverance stories);[146] multiple guards are involved; Peter states the divine involvement; and the community does not believe, so they had no hand in the rescue.[147]

As discussed earlier, the reader finds that the Spirit's role in sending out Paul and Barnabas is emphasized (13:2, 4). In Lystra it is God's healing act that prompts the conflict (14:9–10). After the apostolic decree, Paul and Silas arrive in Philippi because God has denied them access to two different areas (Asia and Bithynia, 16:6–7), before finally making plain their call to Macedonia (16:10). In a narrative where divine guidance is

---

142. Haenchen (*Acts*, 310) and Schille (*Apostelgeschichte*, 209–10) find this translation doubtful, but it is preferred by Barrett (*Acts*, 423) since divine activity is prevalent in the scene.

143. In suggesting that Philip "initiates" the Samaritan and gentile missions, Tannehill (*Narrative*, 110) fails to comprehend the way the divine interventions make God the initiator. O'Toole ("Philip," 28–30) points out that conversion scenes are filled with divine interventions, showing them as divinely caused events.

144. Haenchen, *Acts*, 322–23.

145. Pesch (*Apostelgeschichte*, I, 287; also Haenchen, *Acts*, 315) considers the two narratives "kinsmen" in style and content. Many scholars (Barrett, *Acts*, 529; Gaventa, *Acts*, 173; Haenchen *Acts*, 347, 358; Jervell, *Apostelgeschichte*, 304–16; Johnson, *Acts*, 186; Kieffer, "Linguistic," 83; Matera, "Acts 10:34–43," 63; Pesch, *Apostelgeschichte*, I, 334, 346) note some or all the features mentioned here. Bibb ("Characterization," 217) mistakenly identifies this as God changing the course of events. Since this is presented as the unfolding divine will, the course is *set*, not *altered*.

146. See Haenchen, *Acts*, 384, fn. 5; Schille, *Apostelgeschichte*, 271.

147. Pesch, *Apostelgeschichte*, I, 366. Such intervention is similar to that portrayed in 2 Maccabees. There, God defends the temple and the people through angelic figures (2 Macc 3:24–29; 5:1–4; 10:24–31; 11:7–12). This portrayal differs from Josephus, who prefers not to mention angelic figures and direct divine intervention (Haenchen [*Acts*, 388] fails to note this factor). The Acts narrative, therefore, seems to fit better (at least in how it presents divine intervention) with 2 Maccabees than with Josephus.

commonplace,[148] the rapid pace in this short section should suggest to Luke's reader that not only is God determining where Paul and Silas should go,[149] but also when—now is the time to go to Macedonia. In Philippi, God converts Lydia (16:14), and Luke emphasizes that Paul does not actively seek the following conflict (16:18). In Corinth, another divine vision commands an extended stay by Paul (18:9–11). Just as God-in-conflict scenes enclose Paul's second journey, so the reader finds this journey framed by divine visions (16:6–10/18:9–11).[150] The double-framing places special emphasis on divine control over this journey. This may be designed to alleviate any doubt the reader might have had about Paul after the dispute with Barnabas. Finally, the dramatic scene when Paul arrives in Ephesus provides divine witness to Paul that this is the proper time to operate here (see chapter 3). Acts 8:4—19:20, then, ends with God's "extraordinary miracles" (19:11) that set the conflict with the exorcists.

In addition to the reversal-of-persecution and removal-from-authorities themes found in Acts 19:21—28:31, the necessary witness in Jerusalem and Rome drives the plot throughout this section. Along the way, there are providential rescues from conspiracies (20:3; 23:12–22; 25:3) that cause Paul to be moved progressively from Jerusalem to Rome. Barrett speculates that Paul's nephew was "inadvertently included in the group,"[151] but Luke consistently declines to provide information about how these conspiracies are discovered. Given that the divine hand protects and guides throughout the narrative, these discoveries appear to the reader as evidence for providential action.

Even a shipwreck has its necessity (27:26) since God uses it to demonstrate the divine protection under which Paul exists. In such cases, although human action or natural forces may appear as immediate causes, the reader is made aware that divine involvement ultimately directs the events.[152] Further, Paul ends up on Malta (the island mentioned in 27:26) only because God has saved him and his companions from shipwreck. All this leads to Paul's joyful arrival in Rome—uncondemned by the authorities and obedient to the divine will.

Likewise, the reader finds Rome and its soldiers used in providing divine protection (21:31; 23:17–24; 27:43).[153] However, since the reader consistently sees Paul removed from Roman authorities, these Roman "deliverances" would not point to Rome's favorable response to Paul and Christianity.[154] Roman authorities are generally characterized

---

148. In Luke's narrative world, divine guidance is not unusual behavior in human history (*contra* Marguerat, *First*, 86). Schille (*Apostelgeschichte*, 340) accurately characterized Acts as a divine "Führungsgeschichte."

149. The episode is not a "commissioning episode" (*contra* Hubbard, "Role," 190–91; Talbert, *Reading*, 148). In Acts 13:2–4, the Spirit required that Barnabas and Saul (Paul) be "set apart" for the work to which the Spirit has called them. No setting apart is found here. No laying on of hands (cf. 13:3) takes place, and Paul has been "committed" by the brethren (15:40; cf. 14:26, Pesch, *Apostelgeschichte*, II, 93) well prior to 16:10. Paul's call in 16:9–10 is not a new commission, but the continuing work to which he was called in 9:15.

150. Noted by Pesch, *Apostelgeschichte*, II, 151.

151. Barrett, *Acts*, 1075.

152. See Tannehill, *Narrative*, 293–94, 338–39.

153. Rome becomes Paul's "unwissentlicher Schutzmacht" (Roloff, *Apostelgeschichte*, 331).

154. *Contra* Haenchen, *Acts*, 650.

as flawed—Felix's willingness to accept a bribe is a factor in Paul remaining a prisoner.[155] Felix (24:27) and Festus (25:9) seek to use Paul as a political tool (putting the Jewish leadership in their debt by agreeing to their demands).[156] Lysias (23:27) and Festus present their cases differently from the narrator in a way that the reader would determine they were seeking to make their actions seem more appropriate.[157] Julius (27:9–11) refuses to listen to Paul's warnings, which is all the more striking since Luke introduced him as a character friendly to Paul. Thus, the reader does not see Roman leaders as Paul's (or Christianity's) enlightened defenders. Further, while Paul stands trial before Roman officials, the reader's attention is on how the Way is related to Judaism (not Rome). The reader has found Rome consistently refusing to (18:14–15; 24:22), prevented from (Paul's absences—17:1–9; 19:23–41), or unable to (25:20; 26:24) enter into this theological debate, thus Roman favor is not the important issue.[158] Instead, the reader learns how God also controls Rome. From beginning to end, then, the reader finds God forging the plot and through this is assured that the events, message, and messengers are divinely ordained

Summary Portrait

Through the relationship between Scripture (God's words—cf. 1:16; 2:17; 4:24–25) and necessity (God's pre-ordained plan), God is consistently characterized as having planned and fulfilled the events related to Jesus and the community (1:16–21; 4:27), even choosing their timing. The divine will is made known in Scripture and demonstrated in the fulfilled promise concerning the messianic king's death and resurrection. Since these promises have been fulfilled, the reader can anticipate that those promises which remain unfulfilled, yet are expressed as part of the divine plan (i.e., the witness to "ends of the earth" and the "universal restoration"), are certain to come to completion. Luke's emphasis on divine control continues throughout 8:4—19:20. However, the way necessity is presented has changed, moving from a focus on the divine will revealed in Scripture to its present expression in the community. It is not simply that Scripture has revealed that God intends "light" to come to the gentiles (13:47), but that God is actively choosing the messengers and divine actions are reinterpreting Scripture. Throughout 19:21—28:31 the reader finds

---

155. Barrett, *Acts*, 1093.

156. See Tannehill, *Narrative*, 306–7

157. See Barrett, *Acts*, 1083, 1136. Festus takes a high moral tone in presenting the issue to Agrippa, but the use of χαρίζεσθαί (25:16) should remind the reader about his willingness to use Paul as a political tool (so Tannehill, *Narrative*, 311).

158. See Alexander, "Acts," 34–36; Jervell, *Apostelgeschichte*, 531–33; Witherington, *Acts*, 660. Conzelmann (*Theology*, 141–42) argued that Paul's defenses are always presented according to Roman procedure and Paul's appeal to his Roman citizenship before Romans indicates that the issue is about Paul's rights as a citizen (cf. 22:25). However, Paul's Roman citizenship is subordinated to his Jewish identity throughout the trial scenes. For example, Paul defends himself before Jews (22:1–21) before mentioning his Roman citizenship (his Tarsian citizenship even precedes this notice, but even that is subordinated to his Jewishness—21:39). Haacker ("Bekenntnis," 439–40) notes that only one time is Paul's appeal to Israel's hope expressed before a Roman ruler (Felix—24:15). Even King Agrippa is considered a Scripture-believing Jew (26:27). Thus, the issues are not Roman but Jewish.

God directing Paul. Paul is under divine necessity to go to Jerusalem and Rome. His witness to gentiles, kings, and eventually Caesar is divinely commissioned.

At the same time, the reader sees that God controls these events. Divine involvement in advancing the narrative from Jesus' ascension to the persecution begun with Stephen underscores this theme. So also, the underlying *reversal-of-fortune* (2:23–24; 3:13–15; 4:10–12; 5:30–31; 7:9–10, 35, 52) motif builds the reader's expectation that the entire narrative will turn out to be directed by God. In 8:4—19:20 God consistently initiates and directs the mission activities. Thus, divine control over the kingdom's "times and seasons" is maintained. In the final section, God uses persecution to bring Paul into Roman hands and, therefore, to the seat of Rome's power. The "silence" in Ephesus and from other justifying elements (shipwreck, "Justice") suggests that the reader should not consider these forces able to judge Paul. Even Rome does not have this responsibility since it cannot determine the crime with which to charge him and is unwilling to even decide issues of Jewish Law. Ultimately then, God has made Paul a prisoner and only God can judge him. This all points to God *ordaining* the kingdom's and its inhabitants' *times and seasons*.

The *God-in-conflict* scenes demonstrate that no power or religious belief is allowed to stand in opposition to God. God continues to direct the kingdom's advance, going before it in power and victory. Divine freedom cannot be constrained by Simon, so the message is not hindered by association with another power. God's way cannot be perverted by Bar-Jesus, so the "teaching about the Lord" is superior to the false-prophet's deceptions. The true message about God and salvation cannot be confused with other powers or messages. Finally, divine power cannot be appropriated by magical formulas, authenticating the "word of the Lord" (and its messenger Paul) since this power keeps it growing.

Adding the scenes that portray God as the Creator, one must consider what validation the reader would see for the message and its call for repentance. Is this support found through common religiosity? Although Paul tries to find common ground with his hearers (a *captatio benevolentiae*) by observing that the Athenians are very religious (17:22), the reader would find this statement ironic—their idolatry has already provoked Paul (17:16).[159] Further, every previous encounter with other religious beliefs illustrated attempts to misappropriate the divine message and power. Thus, religiosity is an obstacle not a help. Is it found through a common search for God? This conclusion may have some support in Paul's statement that all men are to search for God, but the blind groping for a God so near suggests this cannot support the message.[160] Is it found through appeal to philosophical concepts? Some note that Greek philosophers would agree with much in Paul's speech.[161] However, even though the statement about having life, movement, and existence is found in Stoic thought, Paul does not adopt the pantheistic (or panentheistic) viewpoint found in Stoicism—God is distinguished from creation. Luke's Paul takes contact points with Greek thought and reinterprets them by their place in a thoroughly

---

159. So Fitzmyer, *Acts*, 606; Schille, *Apostelgeschichte*, 355–56; Witherington, *Acts*, 520, 532; *contra* Davis, "Acts 17:16–34," 65; Gaventa, *Acts*, 250.

160. Ψηλαφω in classical and biblical texts suggests "the groping of the blind person" (Witherington, *Acts*, 528–29). Thus, the God who is near is not being found because, without divine revelation, people are blind.

161. So Pesch, *Apostelgeschichte*, II, 136–37; Schneider, *Apostelgeschichte*, II, 242.

monotheistic, Jewish/Christian framework.[162] Thus, the reader does not see Greek philosophy as a real dialogue partner.

In all these cases, the message is validated by divine power. God cannot be controlled by other powers and God controls all things, all people and all time, which means that only God can set the terms and the time for repentance.[163] Therefore, the call to repentance and belief in Jesus' name is supported by the demonstration that no other power or belief has a similarly authoritative claim to power and control.

Witherington comments that Luke uses the divine providence and plan to do "apologetics" for the early Christians.[164] If true, the presentation that Jesus' death and resurrection are necessary is intended to provide assurances to the reader that it is indeed God who has acted, and this action has restored the kingdom to Israel through the restored king. Since the divine plan continues to be worked out in the community and divine direction of narrative events remains constant, divine authority is offered to support this claim. The community is portrayed as the favored recipient of providential actions, obedient to divine commands, and provided with divine inspiration at appropriate points. Thus, it is ultimately divine action, favor, and direction that provide authority to the proclamation about the restored messianic king. God's sovereign will directs and controls the narrative, providing certainty for the reader.

By emphasizing God initiating events and the consequent control over the plot, Luke provides support to the salvation message. Divine visions were common features in the stories told about how ancient clubs and associations formed.[165] Similar occurrences are found in narratives about how cities were founded.[166] In both cases, these incidents provided divine authorization to the group/city. Thus, in looking for authorization for the message's expansion to Samaritans, gentiles, and the "ends of the earth," Luke's reader would expect divine guidance and initiation to have prominent roles; Luke does not disappoint.

The divine necessity surrounding Paul's trip to Jerusalem and Rome supports Paul's status as the innocent prisoner of God. God has made Paul a prisoner, so any doubts that the reader may have had about him because of this status are to be set aside.[167] Because Paul is a prisoner of God first, it is the divine will that authorizes Paul's appeal to Caesar. Paul must witness in Rome, therefore, God manipulates the conspiracies against Paul, leading to this demand. Paul has done nothing wrong, for it is the divine will that Paul "stand before the emperor" (27:24). So, Paul is a prisoner in Rome because God has ordained this circumstance. Still, Paul is not defended because he is the "driving force of the

---

162. Witherington (*Acts*, 524–30) suggests Luke offers a critique of Stoicism and Epicureanism. Various commentators point out that the Lukan Paul rejects the identification between creature and creator found in Stoicism—Fitzmyer, *Acts*, 602, 611; Schille, *Apostelgeschichte*, 358; Lake and Cadbury, *Beginnings*, 209.

163. Tannehill (*Narrative*, 219) thinks that Paul is encouraging a continued quest for God in 17:27–28. However, in announcing judgment by the "one," the time for ignorance is over and the search for God must end with that one.

164. Witherington, *Acts*, 201; also Rapske, "Opposition," 235–56.

165. See Ascough, "Formation" (1995); Witherington, *Acts*, 341.

166. See W. T. Wilson, "Urban," 81–87.

167. Haenchen (*Acts*, 693) suggests that Paul's imprisonment would have been a concern for the reader.

Christian mission."[168] Throughout Acts, God has *driven* the plot—reversing persecution and using Jews, Romans, and Paul for divine purposes. Paul's defense comes because the reader needs to have "certainty" concerning Paul (21:34), just as Luke has suggested his works are intended to convey (Luke 1:4).[169] Such assurance can only come from knowing that God has made Paul a prisoner, not for any crime, but because it was God's intention that he witness to Caesar in Rome. It is, then, divine control over the restored kingdom that assures the reader concerning the narrative events.

168. As Haenchen, *Acts*, 693.

169. Schille (*Apostelgeschichte*, 416) maintains that the use of ἀσφαλές at 21:34 suggests that this is the most important aspect in the Pauline trial scenes.

7

Conclusion

THE PRECEDING ANALYSIS HAS DEMONSTRATED THAT LUKE'S READER COMES TO SEE GOD as the Great King who restores the kingdom as the *ordainer of times and seasons*. God controls the rise and fall of kings and kingdoms, as well as all human affairs. This control is manifest in Jesus' resurrection and exaltation, the divine means for restoring the kingdom to Israel. The restoration, however, has taken place in a reinterpreted way—through the restored Davidic king, but national Israel is not the issue at present (chapter 4). Israel is initially redefined as those Jews who respond correctly to the message about divine salvation, leaving behind the "perverse generation" and entering into God's kingdom (chapter 5). This kingdom is also reinterpreted onto an ethical/pneumatic plane—kingdom people respond to divine rule under the messianic king, sharing divine standards for justice and social order, and piously revering and obeying their Great King (chapter 5). Further, God's kingdom now includes all those (Samaritan, gentile, Jew) who repent and believe in Jesus (chapter 5). Finally, divine control is evident in God ordaining, initiating, being involved in, and manipulating the events (human affairs) related to that kingdom's expansion and protection (chapter 6).

In this portrayal:

1. By raising Jesus from the dead and to the heavenly throne, God has (although something awaits a final restoration) restored the kingdom (chapter 4).

2. God retains rule over this kingdom despite Jesus sitting on the exalted throne as Lord and Christ (chapter 4).

3. This kingdom belongs to Israel as stressed by the proclamation to Israel and the fulfillment of covenant promises (chapter 5).

4. Yet, the kingdom includes Jew, Samaritan, and gentile, demonstrated not simply by God fulfilling scriptural promises, but by direct divine action (chapter 5).

5. God, nevertheless, has not allowed the Jews to become second-class citizens because Jewish piety and the Jew-first mission continue to receive emphasis (chapter 5).

6. Since God's newly expanded people share the divine concern for social order, welfare, and justice, citizens in the kingdom show that they live according to kingdom rule (chapter 5).

7. All God's people demonstrate piety and obedience, illustrating the appropriateness of their inclusion in the kingdom (chapter 5).

8. While such piety (i.e., law observance, Jewish customs) is an important characteristic for these people it is not an entrance condition. Repentance and faith, apart from, but not in contradiction to the Law or circumcision, qualifies the individual (chapter 5). Thus, divine, sovereign choice of the kingdom's citizens (cf. 9:15; 13:48; 15:7) remains paramount.

9. Also, despite the compelling force of the divine will, obedience is often difficult—illustrated by Paul's choice between heeding God and losing freedom (chapter 5).

10. Those who fail to obey God, refusing to repent and rejecting the forgiveness of sins offered in Jesus' name, mark themselves as divine enemies (chapter 5). In this way, God reserves the right to define enemies of the kingdom.

11. This presentation has a reverse side—God is the merciful Savior who offers deliverance in the face of rejection (chapter 5).

12. This overruling offer of salvation indicates hope even for those people (Jews in particular) who continue in their opposition (chapter 5).

13. The divine will and actions are intrinsic to plot development showing divine control over human affairs (chapter 6).

14. In particular, God encompasses the advancement of the kingdom in divine power so that there are no obstacles that God cannot overcome (chapter 6).

15. God decides the status (imprisoned or free, guilty or innocent) of the kingdom's citizens (chapter 6).

Thus, the events are seen to be those that God has planned and that God controls—God is the *ordainer of times and seasons* for the kingdom.

Johnson claims that Luke's narrative is an "*apologia* for God's work in history" where "God's mastery of history is available not to empirical test but to the eyes of faith."[1] However, in Acts God's work in history is assumed, not defended. Divine action is not argued *for*, but argued *from*. Divine exploits provide the *apologia* for the restored kingdom, the offer of salvation by entrance into it through faith, the inclusion of Samaritans and gentiles, and even Paul's status as a Roman prisoner. It is God, the *ordainer of times and seasons*, that determines all events and, therefore, provides authority to the witness concerning the restored (but reinterpreted) kingdom being present on earth.

---

1. Johnson, *Acts*, 458.

Bibliography

Abel, F. M. *Les Livres des Maccabées*. 2nd ed. Paris: J. Gabalda, 1949.

Albertz, Rainer. *A History of Israelite Religion in the Old Testament Period*. Vol. 2, *From the Exile to the Maccabees*. Translated by John Bowden. London: SCM, 1994. Originally published as *Religionsgeschichte Israels in alttestamentlicher Zeit*. Vol. 2, *Vom Exil bis zu den Makkabäern*. Grundrisse zum Alten Testament 8/2. Göttingen: Vandenhoeck & Ruprecht, 1992.

Alexander, Loveday. "The Acts of the Apostles as an Apologetic Text." In *Apologetics in the Roman Empire: Pagans, Jews, and Christians*, edited by Mark Edwards, Martin Goodman, and Simon Price, with Christopher Rowland, 15–44. Oxford: Oxford University Press, 1999.

————. "Fact, Fiction and the Genre of Acts." *New Testament Studies* 44 (1998) 380–99.

————. *The Preface to Luke's Gospel: Literary Convention and Social Context in Luke 1.1–4 and Acts 1.1*. Society of New Testament Studies Monograph Series 78. Cambridge: Cambridge University Press, 1993.

————. "Reading Luke-Acts from Back to Front." In *The Unity of Luke-Acts*, edited by J. Verheyden, 419–46. Bibliotheca ephemeridum theologicarum lovaniensium 142. Leuven: Leuven University Press, 1999.

Allen, O. Wesley, Jr. *The Death of Herod: The Narrative and Theological Function of Retribution in Luke-Acts*. Society of Biblical Literature Dissertation Series 158. Atlanta: Scholars, 1997.

Allison, Dale C., Jr. *The End of the Age Has Come: An Early Interpretation of the Passion and Resurrection of Jesus*. Philadelphia: Fortress, 1985.

Alter, Robert. *The Art of Biblical Narrative*. New York: Basic Books, 1981.

Amaru, Betsy Halpern. "Land Theology in Josephus' *Jewish Antiquities*." *Jewish Quarterly Review* 71 (1980) 201–29.

Anderson, Janice Capel. "Reading Tabitha: A Feminist Reception History." In *The New Literary Criticism and the New Testament*, edited by Edgar V. McKnight and Elizabeth S. Malbon, 108–44. Minneapolis: Trinity, 1994.

Arnold, Clinton E. "Magic and Astrology." In *Dictionary of the Later New Testament and Its Developments*, edited by Ralph P. Martin and Peter H. Davids, 701–5. Downers Grove, IL: InterVarsity, 1997.

————. *Power and Magic: The Concept of Power in Ephesians*. 2nd ed. Grand Rapids: Baker, 1997.

Ascough, Richard S. "The Formation and Propagation of Greco-Roman Associations." Paper presented at annual meeting for the Society of Biblical Literature, Philadelphia, PA, November 1995.

Attridge, Harold W. *The Interpretation of Biblical History in the Antiquitates Judaicae of Flavius Josephus*. Harvard Theological Review 7. Missoula, MT: Scholars, 1976.

————. "Jewish Historiography." In *Early Judaism and its Modern Interpreters*, edited by Robert A. Kraft and George W. E. Nickelsburg, 311–43. Philadelphia: Fortress, 1986.

Aune, David E. "Magic in Early Christianity." In *Aufstieg und Niedergang der römischen Welt: Geschichte und Kultur Roms im Spiegel der neueren Forschung*. Part 2 *Principat*, 23.2, edited by H. Temporini and W. Haase, 1507–57. Berlin: de Gruyter, 1980.

————. *The New Testament in Its Literary Environment*. Library of Early Christianity 8. Philadelphia: Westminster, 1987.

Bachmann, Michael. *Jerusalem und der Tempel: Die geographisch-theologischen Elemente in der lukanischen Sicht des judischen Kultzentrums*. Beiträge zur Wissenschaft vom Alten und Neuen Testament 109. Stuttgart: Kohlhammer, 1980.

Baer, Hans von. *Der Heilige Geist in den Lukasschriften*. Beiträge zur Wissenschaft vom Alten und Neuen Testament 3. Stuttgart: Kohlhammer. 1926.

Balch, David L. "Comments on the Genre and a Political Theme of Luke-Acts: A Preliminary Comparison of Two Hellenistic Historians." In the *SBL Seminar Papers, 1989*, 343–61. Society of Biblical Literature Seminar Papers 28. Atlanta: Scholars, 1989.

Baly, Denis. *God and History in the Old Testament: The Encounter with the Absolutely Other in Ancient Israel.* New York: Harper & Row, 1976.

Barrett, Charles. K. *The Acts of the Apostles.* 2 vols. International Critical Commentary. Edinburgh: T. & T. Clark, 1994.

―――. "Luke-Acts." In *Early Christian Thought in its Jewish Context*, edited by John Barclay and John Sweet, 84–95. Cambridge: Cambridge University Press, 1996.

Bartlett, John R. *The First and Second Books of the Maccabees.* Cambridge Bible Commentary. London: Cambridge University Press, 1973.

Bauckham, Richard. "The Acts of Paul as a Sequel to Acts." In *The Book of Acts in its Ancient Literary Setting*, edited by Bruce W. Winter and Andrew D. Clark. Vol. 1, *The Book of Acts in its First Century Setting*, edited by Bruce W. Winter, 105–152. Grand Rapids: Eerdmans, 1993.

―――. *God Crucified: Monotheism and Christology in the New Testament.* Carlisle, UK: Paternoster, 1998.

―――. "James and the Gentiles (Acts 15:13–21)." In *History, Literature, and Society in the Book of Acts*, edited by Ben Witherington III, 154–84. Cambridge: Cambridge University Press, 1996.

―――. "The Throne of God and the Worship of Jesus." In *The Jewish Roots of Christological Monotheism: Papers from the St. Andrews Conference on the Historical Origins of the Worship of Jesus*, edited by Carey C. Newman, James R. Davila, and Gladys S. Lewis, 43–69. Leiden: Brill, 1999.

Bauer, Walter, William F. Arndt, F. William Gingrich, and Frederick W. Danker. *Greek-English Lexicon of the New Testament and Other Early Christian Literature.* 2nd ed. Chicago: University of Chicago Press, 1979.

Bechard, Dean Philip. *Paul Outside the Walls: A Study of Luke's Socio-Geographical Universalism in Acts 14:8–20.* Analecta biblica 143. Rome: Biblical Institute Press, 2000.

Beck, David R. "The Narrative Function of Anonymity in Fourth Gospel Characterization." *Semeia* 63 (1993) 143–58.

Benoit, Pierre. "L'Ascension." In *Exégèse et Théologie*, 1:363–411. Cogitatio Fidei 30. Paris: Cerf, 1961.

Betz, Otto. "Miracles in the Writings of Flavius Josephus." In *Josephus, Judaism, and Christianity*, edited by Louis H. Feldman and Gohei Hata, 212–35. Leiden: Brill, 1987.

Bibb, Charles Wade. "The Characterization of God in Luke-Acts." PhD diss., The Southern Baptist Theological Seminary, 1996.

Bickerman, Elias. *The God of the Maccabees: Studies on the Meaning and Origin of the Maccabean Revolt.* Translated by Horst R. Moehring. Leiden: Brill, 1979. Originally published as *Der Gott der Makkabäer: Untersuchungen über Sinn und Ursprung der makkabäischen Erhebung.* Berlin: Schodken /Jüdischer, 1937.

Bilde, Per. *Flavius Josephus between Jerusalem and Rome: His Life, His Works, and Their Importance.* Journal for the Study of the Pseudepigrapha: Supplement Series 2. Sheffield: JSOT Press, 1988.

―――. "Josephus and Jewish Apocalypticism." In *Understanding Josephus: Seven Perspectives*, edited by Steve Mason, 35–61. Journal for the Study of the Pseudepigrapha: Supplement Series 32. Sheffield: Sheffield Academic, 1998.

Blass, Friedrich, and Albert Debrunner. *A Greek Grammar of the New Testament and Other Early Christian Literature*, translated and revised by Robert W. Funk. Chicago: Chicago University Press, 1961. Originally published as *Grammatik des neutestamentlichen Griechisch.* 9-10th ed. Göttingen: Vandenhoeck & Ruprecht.

Blomberg, Craig. "The Christian and the Law of Moses." In *Witness to the Gospel: The Theology of Acts*, edited by I. Howard Marshall and David Peterson, 397–416. Grand Rapids: Eerdmans, 1998.

Blue, Brad. "The Influence of Jewish Worship on Luke's Presentation of the Early Church." In *Witness to the Gospel: The Theology of Acts*, edited by I. Howard Marshall and David Peterson, 473–497. Grand Rapids: Eerdmans, 1998.

Bock, Darrell L. *Proclamation from Prophecy and Pattern: Lucan Old Testament Christology.* Journal for the Study of the New Testament Supplement Series 12. Sheffield: Sheffield Academic, 1987.

Bond, L. Susan. "Acts 10:34–43." *Interpretation* 56 (2002) 80–83.

Booth, Wayne C. *The Rhetoric of Fiction.* 2nd ed. Harmondsworth, NJ: Penguin, 1987.

Bovon, François. "The God of Luke." In *New Testament Traditions and Apocryphal Narratives*, translated by Jane Haapiseva-Hunter, 67–80. Allison Park, PA: Pickwick, 1995. Originally published as "Le Dieu de Luc." In *La parole de grace: Etudes lucaniennes à la memoire d' Augustin George*, edited by J. Delorme and J. Duplacy, 279–300. Paris: Recherches de science religieuse, 1981.

———. "Le Saint-Ésprit, l'Église et les relations humaines selon Actes 20,36—21,16." In *Les Actes des Apôtres: Traditions, rédaction, théologie*, edited by J. Kremer, 339–58. Bibliotheca ephemeridum theologicarum lovaniensium 48. Leuven: Leuven University Press, 1979.

———. *Luke the Theologian: Thirty-Three Years of Research (1950–1983)*. Translated by Ken McKinney. Allison Park, PA: Pickwick, 1987.

Brawley, Robert L. "Abrahamic Covenant Traditions and the Characterization of God in Luke-Acts." In *The Unity of Luke-Acts*, edited by J. Verheyden, 109–32. Bibliotheca ephemeridum theologicarum lovaniensium 142. Leuven: Leuven University Press, 1999.

———. *Centering on God: Method and Message in Luke-Acts*. Louisville: Westminster John Knox, 1990.

———. "The God of Promises and the Jews in Luke-Acts." In *Literary Studies in Luke-Acts: Essays in Honor of Joseph B. Tyson*, edited by Richard P. Thompson and Thomas E. Phillips, 279–96. Macon, GA: Mercer University Press, 1998.

Briend, Jacques. *Dieu dans l'Écriture*. Lectio divina 150. Paris: Cerf, 1992.

Brown, Raymond E. "Does the New Testament Call Jesus God?" *Theological Studies* 26 (1965) 545–73.

Bruce, F. F. *The Acts of the Apostles*. Grand Rapids: Eerdmans, 1970.

———. *The Book of Acts*. Rev. ed. New International Commentary on the New Testament. Grand Rapids: Eerdmans, 1988.

Brueggemann, Walter. *Theology of the Old Testament: Testimony, Dispute, Advocacy*. Minneapolis: Fortress, 1997.

Bryan, Christopher. "A Further Look at Acts 16:1–3." *Journal of Biblical Literature* 107 (1988) 292–94.

Buckwalter, H. Douglas. *The Character and Purpose of Luke's Christology*. Society for New Testament Studies Monograph Series 89. Cambridge: Cambridge University Press, 1996.

Burchard, Christian. "Joseph and Aseneth." In *Outside the Old Testament*, edited by Marinus de Jonge, 92–110. Cambridge Commentaries on Writings of the Jewish & Christian World 200BC to AD200 4. Cambridge: Cambridge University Press, 1985.

Burnett, Fred W. "Characterization and Reader Construction of Characters in the Gospels." *Semeia* 63 (1993) 3–28.

Cadbury, Henry J. *The Making of Luke-Acts*. London: SPCK, 1968.

Camponovo, Odo. *Königtum, Königsherrschaft und Reich Gottes in den Frühjüdischen Schriften*. Orbus biblicus et orientalis 58. Göttingen: Vandenhoeck & Ruprecht, 1984.

Capper, Brian J. "The Interpretation of Acts 5:4." *Journal for the Study of the New Testament* 19 (1983) 117–31.

———. "The Palestinian Cultural Context of Earliest Christian Community of Goods." In *The Book of Acts in its Palestinian Setting*, edited by Richard Bauckham. Vol. 4 of *The Book of Acts in its First Century Setting*, edited by Bruce W. Winter, 323–56. Grand Rapids: Eerdmans, 1995.

———. "Reciprocity and the Ethic of Acts." In *Witness to the Gospel: The Theology of Acts*, edited by I. Howard Marshall and David Peterson, 499–518. Grand Rapids: Eerdmans, 1998.

Carras, George P. "Observant Jews in the Story of Luke and Acts: Paul, Jesus and Other Jews." In *The Unity of Luke-Acts*, edited by J. Verheyden, 693–708. Bibliotheca ephemeridum theologicarum lovaniensium 142. Leuven: Leuven University Press, 1999.

Carroll, John T. *Response to the End of History: Eschatology and Situation in Luke-Acts*. Society of Biblical Literature Dissertation Series 92. Atlanta: Scholars, 1988.

Cassidy, Richard J. *Society and Politics in the Acts of the Apostles*. Maryknoll, NY: Orbis, 1987.

Chance, J. Bradley. *Jerusalem, the Temple, and the New Age in Luke-Acts*. Macon, GA: Mercer University Press, 1988.

Charlesworth, James H., editor. *The Old Testament Pseudepigrapha*. 2 vols. New York: Doubleday, 1983–85.

Chatman, Seymour. *Story and Discourse: Narrative Structure in Fiction and Film*. Ithaca, NY: Cornell University Press, 1978.

Chevallier, Max-Alain. *Souffle de Dieu: le Saint-Esprit dans le Nouveau Testament*, Vol. 1: Ancien Testament, hellénisme et judaïsme, la tradition synoptique, l'oeuvre de Luc. Le Point Théologique 26. Paris: Beauchesne, 1978.

Clark, Andrew C. *Parallel Lives: The Relation of Paul to the Apostles in the Lucan Perspective.* Paternoster Biblical and Theological Monographs. Carlisle, UK: Paternoster, 2001.

Cohen, Shaye J. D. *From the Maccabees to the Mishnah.* Philadelphia: Westminster, 1987.

———. "Was Timothy Jewish (Acts 16:1–3)? Patristic Exegesis, Rabbinic Law, and Matrilineal Descent." *Journal of Biblical Literature* 105 (1986) 251–68.

Collins, John J. *Between Athens and Jerusalem: Jewish Identity in the Hellenistic Diaspora.* 2nd ed. Grand Rapids: Eerdmans, 2000.

———. *Daniel, First Maccabees, Second Maccabees with an Excursus on the Apocalyptic Genre.* Old Testament Message 16. Wilmington, DE: Michael Glazier, 1981.

———. "The Kingdom of God in the Apocrypha and Pseudepigrapha." In *The Kingdom of God in 20th-Century Interpretation,* edited by Wendell Willis, 81–95. Peabody, MA: Hendrickson, 1987.

———. "The Testament (Assumption) of Moses." In *Outside the Old Testament,* edited by Marinus de Jonge, 145–58. Cambridge Commentaries on Writings of the Jewish & Christian World 200BC to AD 200 4. Cambridge: Cambridge University Press, 1985.

———. "Testaments." In *Jewish Writings of the Second Temple Period: Apocrypha, Pseudepigrapha, Qumran Sectarian Writings, Philo, Josephus,* edited by Michael E. Stone, 325–55. Philadelphia: Fortress, 1984.

Conzelmann, Hans. *Acts of the Apostles.* Translated by James Limburg, A. Thomas Kraabel, and Donald H. Juel. Hermeneia. Philadelphia: Fortress, 1987.

———. *The Theology of St. Luke.* Translated by Geoffrey Buswell. New York: Harper & Row, 1961. Originally published as *Die Mitte der Zeit: Studien zur Theologie des Lukas.* Beiträge zur historischen Theologie 17. Tübingen: Mohr, 1954.

Cook, Michael J. "The Mission to the Jews in Acts: Unraveling Luke's 'Myth of the 'Myriads.''" In *Luke-Acts and the Jewish People: Eight Critical Perspectives,* edited by Joseph B. Tyson, 102–23. Minneapolis, MN: Augsburg, 1988.

Cosgrove, Charles H. "The Divine δεῖ in Luke-Acts: Investigations into the Lukan Understanding of God's Providence." *Novum Testamentum* 26 (1984) 168–90.

Craig, Kenneth M., Jr. "The Character(ization) of God in 2 Samuel 7:1–17." *Semeia* 63 (1993) 159–76.

Cullmann, Oscar. *Christ and Time: The Primitive Christian Conception of Time and History,* translated by Floyd V. Filson. Rev. ed. London: SCM, 1962. Originally published as *Christus und die Zeit: Die urchristliche Zeit- und Geschichtauffassung.* Zollikon-Zürich: Evangelischer, 1946.

Dahl, Nils A. "'A People for His Name' (Acts XV.14)." *New Testament Studies* 4 (1957/58) 319–27.

———. "The Neglected Factor in New Testament Theology." In *Jesus the Christ: The Historical Origin of Christological Doctrine,* edited by Donald H. Juel, 153–63. Minneapolis, MN: Fortress, 1991.

Darr, John A. "Narrator as Character: Mapping a Reader-Oriented Approach to Narration in Luke-Acts." *Semeia* 63 (1993) 43–60.

———. *On Character Building: The Reader and the Rhetoric of Characterization in Luke-Acts.* Louisville: Westminster John Knox, 1992.

Davies, Philip R. *Daniel.* Sheffield: Sheffield Academic, 1985.

Davila, James R. "Of Methodology, Monotheism and Metatron: Introductory Reflections on Divine Mediators and the Origins of the Worship of Jesus." In *The Jewish Roots of Christological Monotheism: Papers from the St. Andrews Conference on the Historical Origins of the Worship of Jesus,* edited by Carey C. Newman, James R. Davila, and Gladys S. Lewis, 3–18. Leiden: Brill, 1999.

Davis, D. Mark. "Acts 17:16–34." *Interpretation* 57 (2003) 64–66.

Davis, P. G. "Divine Agents, Mediators, and New Testament Christology." *Journal of Theological Studies* 45/2 (1994) 479–503.

Denaux, Adelbert. "The Monotheistic Background of New Testament Christology: Critical Reflections on Pluralist Theologies of Religions." In *The Myriad Christ: Plurality and the Quest for Unity in Contemporary Christology,* edited by Terrence Merrigan and Jacques Haers, 133–58. Leuven: Leuven University Press, 2000.

Denis, Albert-Marie. *Introduction aux Pseudépigraphes Grecs D'Ancien Testament.* Studia in Veteris Testamenti pseudepigraphica 1. Leiden: Brill, 1970.

Dennis, Trevor. *Looking God in the Eye.* London: SPCK, 1998.

Derrett, J. Duncan M. "The Son of Man Standing (Acts 7, 55–56)." *Biblia e oriente* 30 (1988) 71–84.

deSilva, David A. *Introducing the Apocrypha: Message, Context, and Significance.* Grand Rapids: Baker Academic, 2002.

Dibelius, Martin. *Studies in the Acts of the Apostles.* Edited by Heinrich Greeven. Translated by Mary Ling. London: SCM Press, 1973. Originally published as *Aufsätze zur Apostelgeschichte.* Forschungen zur Religion und Literatur des Alten und NeuenTestaments 60. Göttingen: Vandenhoeck & Ruprecht, 1953.

Donelson, Lewis R. "Cult Histories and the Sources of Acts." *Biblica* 68 (1987) 1–21.

Doran, Robert. *Temple Propaganda: The Purpose and Character of 2 Maccabees.* Catholic Biblical Quarterly Monograph Series 12. Washington, DC: Catholic Biblical Association of America, 1981.

Duling, D. "Promises to David." *New Testament Studies* 20 (1973) 55–77.

Dunn, James D. G. *The Acts of the Apostles.* Peterborough: Epworth, 1996.

———. *Baptism in the Holy Spirit.* London: SCM, 1975.

———. "Pentecost." In *The Christ and the Spirit: Collected Essays of James D. G. Dunn.* Vol. 2: Pneumatology, 210–15. Edinburgh: T. & T. Clark, 1998. Originally published as "Pentecost, Feast of." In *New International Dictionary of New Testament Theology,* edited by Colin Brown, 783–88. Vol. 2. Exeter: Paternoster, 1975–1978.

———. *The Theology of Paul the Apostle.* Grand Rapids: Eerdmans, 1998.

———. "'They Believed Philip Preaching' (Acts 8:12)." In *The Christ and the Spirit: Collected Essays of James D. G. Dunn.* Vol. 2: Pneumatology, 216–21. Edinburgh: T. & T. Clark, 1998. Originally published as "'They Believed Philip Preaching' (Acts 8:12) A Reply." *Irish Biblical Studies* 1 (1979) 177–83.

Dupont, Jacques. "'Le Seigneur de tous' (Ac 10:36; Rm 10:12) Arrière-fond scripturaire d'une formule christologique." In *Tradition and Interpretation in the New Testament: Essays in Honor of E. Earle Ellis for His 60th Birthday,* edited by Gerald F. Hawthorne and Otto Betz, 229–36. Grand Rapids: Eerdmans, 1987.

———. *The Salvation of the Gentiles: Studies in the Acts of the Apostles,* translated by J. R. Keating. New York: Paulist, 1979.

Eades, Keith L. "Testament." In vol. 4 of *The International Standard Bible Encyclopedia,* edited by Geoffrey W. Bromiley, 796–97. Grand Rapids: Eerdmans, 1988.

Easterling, P. E. "Constructing Character in Greek Tragedy." In *Characterization and Individuality in Greek Literature,* edited by Christopher Pelling, 83–99. Oxford: Oxford University Press, 1990.

Eichrodt, Walther. *Theology of the Old Testament.* Vol. 1. Translated by John Baker. London: SCM, 1961. Originally published as *Theologie des Alten Testaments.* Vol. 1. 6th ed. Stuttgart: Ehrenfried Klotz, 1959.

Ellingworth, Paul. "'Men and Brethren . . .' (Acts 1.16)." *The Bible Translator* 55 (2004) 153–55.

Ellis, E. Earle. *Christ and the Future in New Testament History.* Novum Testamentum Supplements 97. Leiden: Brill, 2000.

———. *Eschatology in Luke.* Facet Books 30. Philadelphia: Fortress, 1972.

Eltester, Walther. "Israel im lukanischen Werk und die Nazarethperikope." In *Jesus in Nazareth,* edited by Erich Grässer and Walther Eltester, 76–147. Beihefte zur Zeitschrift für die neutestamentliche Wissenschaft 40. Berlin: de Gruyter, 1972.

Enermalm-Ogawa, Agneta. *Un langage de prière juif en grec: Le témoignage des deux premiers livres des Maccabées.* Coniectanea neotestamentica or Coniectanea biblica: New Testament Series 17. Stockholm: Almqvist & Wiksell, 1987.

Ernst, Josef. *Herr der Geschichte: Perspektiven der lukanischen Eschatologie.* Stuttgarter Bibelstudien 88. Stuttgart: Katholisches Bibelwerk, 1978.

Erwin, Ed. "Acts 10:34–43." *Interpretation* 49 (1995) 179–182.

Esler, Philip F. *Community and Gospel in Luke-Acts: The Social and Political Motivations of Lucan Theology.* Society of New Testament Studies Monograph Series 57. Cambridge: Cambridge University Press, 1987.

Farrell, H. "The Eschatological Perspective of Luke-Acts." PhD diss., Boston University, 1972.

Feldman, Louis H. "Josephus' Portrayal of the Hasmoneans Compared with 1 Maccabees." In *Studies in Hellenistic Judaism,* 136–63. Arbeiten zur Geschichte des antiken Judentums und des Urchristentums 30. Leiden: Brill, 1996.

————. *Studies in Josephus' Rewritten Bible.* Journal for the Study of Judaism in the Persian, Hellenistic, and Roman Periods Supplement 58. Leiden: Brill, 1998.

Fenske, Wolfgang. "Aspekte biblischer Theologie dargestellt an der Verwendung von Ps 16 in Apostelgeschichte 2 und 13." *Biblica* 83 (2002) 54–70.

Fernández Marcos, Natalio. *The Septuagint in Context: Introduction to the Greek Version of the Bible,* translated by Wilfred G. E. Watson. Leiden: Brill, 2001.

Fischer, Ulrich. *Eschatologie und Jenseitserwartung im hellenistischen Diasporajudentum.* Beihefte zur Zeitschrift für die neutestamentliche Wissenschaft 44. Berlin: de Gruyter, 1978.

Fitzmyer, Joseph A. *The Acts of the Apostles: A New Translation with Introduction and Commentary.* Anchor Bible 31. New York: Doubleday, 1998.

————. *The Gospel According to Luke.* Vol. 1. Anchor Bible 28A. New York: Doubleday, 1981.

————. "The Role of the Spirit in Luke-Acts." In *The Unity of Luke-Acts,* edited by J. Verheyden, 165–83. Bibliotheca ephemeridum theologicarum lovaniensium 142. Leuven: Leuven University Press, 1999.

Fokkelman, Jan P. *Reading Biblical Narrative: An Introductory Guide,* translated by Ineke Smit. Louisville, Ky.: Westminster John Knox, 1999. Originally published as *Vertelkunst in de bijbel: Een handleiding bij literair lezen.* Zoetermeer: Uitgeverij Boekencentrum, 1995.

Forster, E. M. *Aspects of the Novel.* Harmondsworth, NJ: Penguin, 1963.

Fowler, Robert M. "Characterizing Character in Biblical Narrative." *Semeia* 63 (1993) 97–104.

France, R. T. "The Worship of Jesus: A Neglected Factor in Christological Debate?" In *Christ the Lord: Studies in Christology presented to Donald Guthrie,* edited by Harold H. Rowdon, 17–36. Leicester: InterVarsity, 1982.

Francis, Fred. O. "Eschatology and History in Luke-Acts." *Journal of the American Academy of Religion* 37 (1969) 49–63.

Franklin, Eric. *Christ the Lord: A Study in the Purpose and Theology of Luke-Acts.* London: SPCK, 1975.

Fretheim, Terrence E. *Deuteronomic History.* Interpreting Biblical Texts. Nashville: Abingdon, 1983.

————. *The Suffering of God: An Old Testament Perspective.* Overtures to Biblical Theology 14. Philadelphia: Fortress, 1984.

Fusco, Vittorio. "Luke-Acts and the Future of Israel." *Novum Testamentum* 38 (1996) 1–17.

————. "'Point of View' and 'Implicit Reader' in Two Eschatological Texts: Lk 19,11–28; Acts 1,6–8." In *The Four Gospels 1992: Festschrift Frans Neirynck,* edited by F. Van Segbroeck, C. M. Tuckett, G. Van Belle and J. Verheyden, 1677–96. Vol II. Bibliotheca ephemeridum theologicarum lovaniensium 100. Leuven: Leuven University Press, 1992.

Gadamer, Hans-Georg. *Truth and Method.* Translated by Garret Broden and John Cumming. 2nd ed. New York: Crossroad, 1982.

Garrett, Susan R. *The Demise of the Devil: Magic and the Demonic in Luke's Writings.* Minneapolis, MN: Fortress, 1989.

————. "Light on a Dark Subject and Vice Versa: Magic and Magicians in the New Testament." In *Religion, Science, and Magic: In Concert and In Conflict,* edited by Jacob Neusner, Ernest S. Frerichs, and Paul Virgil McCracken Flesher, 142–65. Oxford: Oxford University Press, 1989.

Gaventa, Beverly Roberts. *The Acts of the Apostles.* Abingdon New Testament Commentaries. Nashville: Abingdon, 2003.

————. "The Eschatology of Luke-Acts Revisited." *Encounter* 43 (1982) 27–42.

————. "Initiatives Divine and Human in the Lukan Story World." In *The Holy Spirit and Christian Origins: Essays in Honor of James D. G. Dunn,* edited by Graham N. Stanton, Bruce W. Longenecker, and Stephen C. Barton, 79–89. Grand Rapids: Eerdmans, 2004.

Giblin, Charles H. *The Destruction of Jerusalem According to Luke's Gospel: A Historical-Typological Moral.* Analecta biblica 107. Rome: Biblical Institute, 1985.

Gilbert, Gary. "The List of Nations in Acts 2: Roman Propaganda and the Lukan Response." *Journal of Biblical Literature* 121 (2002) 497–529.

Gill, David W. J. "Acts and Roman Religion: A. Religion in a Local Setting." In *The Book of Acts in its Graeco-Roman Setting,* edited by David W. J. Gill and Conrad Gempf. Vol. 2 of *The Book of Acts in Its First Century Setting,* edited by Bruce W. Winter, 80–92. Grand Rapids: Eerdmans, 1994.

Gnuse, Robert Karl. *Dreams and Dream Reports in the Writings of Josephus: A Traditio-Historical Analysis.* Arbeiten zur Geschichte des antiken Judentums und des Urchristentums 36. Leiden: Brill, 1996.

Goldsmith, Dale. "Acts 13:33–37: A Pesher on 2 Samuel 7." *Journal of Biblical Literature* 87 (1968) 321–24.

Goldstein, Jonathan A. *II Maccabees: A New Translation with Introduction and Commentary.* Anchor Bible 41A. Garden City, NY: Doubleday, 1983.

Gowler, David B. *Host, Guest, Enemy, Friend: Portraits of the Pharisees in Luke and Acts.* Emory Studies in Christianity 2. New York: Peter Lang, 1991.

Grässer, Erich. *Das Problem der Parusieverzögerung in den synoptischen Evangelien und in der Apostelgeschichte.* Beihefte zur Zeitschrift für die neutestamentliche Wissenschaft 22. Berlin: A. Töpelmann, 1957.

———. "Die Parusieerwartung in der Apostelgeschichte." In *Les Actes des Apôtres: Traditions, rédaction, théologie,* edited by J. Kremer, 99–127. Bibliotheca ephemeridum theologicarum lovaniensium 48. Leuven: Leuven University Press, 1979.

———. *Forschungen zur Apostelgeschichte.* Wissenschaftliche Untersuchungen zum Neuen Testament 137. Tübingen: Mohr Siebeck, 2001.

———. "Ta peri tès basileias (Apg 1,3; 19,8)." In *A cause de l'Evangile: etudes sur les Synoptiques et les Actes: Offertes au P. Jacque Dupont, O.S.B. à l'occasion de son 70e anniversaire,* 709–25. Lectio divina 123. Paris: Publications de Saint-Andres, 1985.

Green, Joel B. "Salvation to the End of the Earth: God as the Saviour in the Acts of the Apostles." In *Witness to the Gospel: The Theology of Acts,* edited by I. Howard Marshall and David Peterson, 83–106. Grand Rapids: Eerdmans, 1998.

Grelot, Pierre. *L'Espérance Juive à L'Heure de Jésus.* Jésus et Jésus-Christ 6. Paris: Desclée, 1978.

Gross, Heinrich. "'Motivtransposition' als Überlieferungsgeschichtliches Prinzip im Alten Testament." In *Sacra Pagina: miscellanea biblica Congressus Internationalis Catholici de Re Biblica,* edited by J. Coppens, A. Descamps, and E. Massaux, 325–34. Bibliotheca ephemeridum theologicarum lovaniensium 12-13. Paris: J. Ducolot, 1959.

Gunn, David M., and Danna Nolan Fewell. *Narrative in the Hebrew Bible.* Oxford Bible Series. Oxford: Oxford University Press, 1993.

Guttenberger, Gudrun. *Die Gottesvorstellung im Markusevangelium.* Beihefte zur Zeitschrift für die neutestamentliche Wissenschaft 123. Berlin: de Gruyter, 2004.

Haacker, Klaus. "Das Bekenntnis des Paulus zur Hoffnung Israels nach der Apostelgeschichte des Lukas." *New Testament Studies* 31 (1985) 437–51.

Haenchen, Ernst. *The Acts of the Apostles,* translated by Bernard Noble and Gerald Shinn. Oxford: Blackwell, 1970. Originally published as *Die Apostelgeschichte.* 14th ed. Göttingen: Vandenhoeck & Ruprecht, 1965.

———. "Judentum und Christentum in der Apostelgeschichte." *Zeitschrift für die neutestamentliche Wissenschaft und die Kunde der älteren Kirche* 54 (1963) 155–87.

Hahn, Ferdinand. *Theologie des Neuen Testaments.* 2 vols. Tübingen: Mohr Siebeck, 2002.

Hamm, Dennis. "The Tamid Service in Luke-Acts: The Cultic Background behind Luke's Theology of Worship (Luke 1:5–25; 18:9–14; 24:50–53; Acts 3:1; 10:3, 20)." *Catholic Biblical Quarterly* 65 (2003) 215–31.

Handy, David A. "Acts 8:14–25." *Interpretation* 47 (1993) 289–94.

Hansen, G. Walter. "The Preaching and Defence of Paul." In *Witness to the Gospel: The Theology of Acts,* edited by I. Howard Marshall and David Peterson, 295–324. Grand Rapids: Eerdmans, 1998.

Harrelson, Walter. "The Significance of 'Last Words' for Intertestamental Ethics." In *Essays in Old Testament Ethics: (J. Philip Hyatt, In Memoriam)* edited by James L. Crenshaw and John T. Willis, 203–13. New York: Ktav, 1974.

Harrill, J. Albert. "The Dramatic Function of the Running Slave Rhoda (Acts 12.13–16) A Piece of Greco-Roman Comedy." *New Testament Studies* 46 (2000) 150–57.

Harrington, Daniel J. *The Maccabean Revolt: Anatomy of a Biblical Revolution.* Old Testament Studies 1. Wilmington, DE: Michael Glazier, 1988.

Hauser, H. J. *Strukturen der Abschlußerzählung der Apostelgeschichte (Apg 28,16–31).* Analecta biblica 86. Rome: Biblical Institute, 1979.

Havelaar, Henriette. "Hellenistic Parallels to Acts 5.1–11 and the Problem of Conflicting Interpretations." *Journal for the Study of the New Testament* 67 (1997) 63–82.

Haya-Prats, G. J. *L'Esprit Force de l'Église: Sa nature et son activité d'apres les Acts des Apôstres.* Lectio divina 81. Paris: Cerf, 1975.

Hayes, John H. "Resurrection as Enthronement." *Interpretation* 22 (1968) 333–45.

Hengel, Martin. *Acts and the History of Earliest Christianity.* Philadelphia: Fortress, 1979.

———. "Proseuche und Synagoge: Jüdische Gemeinde, Gotteshause und Gottesdienst in der Diaspora und in Palästina." In *Tradition und Glaube: Das frühe Christentum in seiner Umwelt: Festgabe für Karl Georg Kuhn,* edited by G. Jeremias, H-W. Kuhn, and H. Stegemann, 157–83. Göttingen: Vandenhoeck & Ruprecht, 1971.

———. "'Sit at My Right Hand!' The Enthronement of Christ at the Right Hand of God and Psalm 110:1." In *Studies in Early Christology,* 119–225. Edinburgh: T. & T. Clark, 1995.

Hengel, Martin, and Anna Maria Schwemer. *Paul Between Damascus and Antioch: The Unknown Years.* Translated by John Bowden. Louisville: Westminster John Knox, 1997.

Henten, Jan Willem van. *The Maccabean Martyrs as Saviours of the Jewish People: A Study of 2 and 4 Maccabees.* Journal for the Study of Judaism in the Persian, Hellenistic, and Roman Periods Supplement 57. Leiden: Brill, 1997.

Hiers, R. H. "The Problem of the Delay of the Parousia in Luke-Acts." *New Testament Studies* 20 (1974) 145–55.

Hill, Craig C. "Acts 6:1—8:4: Division or Diversity?" In *History, Literature, and Society in the Book of Acts,* edited by Ben Witherington, III, 129–53. Cambridge: Cambridge University Press, 1996.

———. *Hellenists and Hebrews: Reappraising Division Within the Earliest Church.* Minneapolis: Fortress, 1992.

Hochman, Baruch. *Character in Literature.* Ithaca, NY: Cornell University Press, 1985.

Hoet, Hendrik. "Ἐξ ἐθνῶν λαόν (Ac 15,14)." In *Luke and His Readers: Festschrift A. Denaux,* edited by R. Bieringer, G. Van Belle, and J. Verheyden, 397–413. Bibliotheca ephemeridum theologicarum lovaniensium 182. Leuven: Leuven University Press, 2005.

Holladay, Carl R. "Acts and the Fragments of Hellenistic Jewish Historians." In *Jesus and the Heritage of Israel: Luke's Narrative Claim upon Israel's Legacy,* edited by David P. Moessner, 171–98. Harrisburg, PA: Trinity, 1999.

Horst, Pieter W. van der. "Hellenistic Parallels to Acts (Chapters 3 and 4)." *Journal for the Study of the New Testament* 35 (1989) 37–46.

———. "Hellenistic Parallels to the Acts of the Apostles 2:1–47." *Journal for the Study of the New Testament* 25 (1985) 49–60.

Hubbard, Benjamin J. "The Role of Commissioning Accounts in Acts." In *Perspectives on Luke-Acts.* Edited by Charles H. Talbert, 187–98. Perspectives in Religious Studies 5. Danville, VA: Association of Baptist Professors of Religion, 1978.

Hui, Archie W. D. "Spirit-Fullness in Luke-Acts: Technical and Prophetic?" *Journal of Pentecostal Theology* 17 (2000) 24–38.

Hull, J. H. E. *The Holy Spirit in the Acts of the Apostles.* London: Lutterworth, 1967.

Humphreys, W. Lee. *The Character of God in the Book of Genesis: A Narrative Appraisal.* Louisville: Westminster John Knox, 2001.

Hur, Ju. *A Dynamic Reading of the Holy Spirit in Luke-Acts.* Journal for the Study of the New Testament: Supplement Series 211. Sheffield: Sheffield Academic, 2001.

Hurtado, Larry W. "First-Century Jewish Monotheism." *Journal for the Study of the New Testament* 71 (1998) 3–26.

———. *One God, One Lord: Early Christian Devotion and Ancient Jewish Monotheism.* 2nd ed. Edinburgh: T. & T. Clark, 1998.

Iser, Wolfgang. *The Act of Reading: A Theory of Aesthetic Response.* London: Routledge & Kegan Paul, 1978.

Jackson, F. J. Foakes. *Josephus and the Jews: The Religion and History of the Jews as Explained by Flavius Josephus.* London: SPCK, 1930.

Jervell, Jacob. "Das gespaltene Israel und die Heidenvölker: Zur Motivierung der Heidenmission in der Apostelgeschichte." *Studia theologica* 19 (1965) 68–96.

———. *Die Apostelgeschichte.* 17th ed. Kritisch-exegetischer Kommentar über das Neue Testament (Meyer-Kommentar) 5. Göttingen: Vandenhoeck & Ruprecht, 1998.

————. "The Future of the Past: Luke's Vision of Salvation History and Its Bearing on His Writing of History." In *History, Literature, and Society in the Book of Acts*, edited by Ben Witherington, III, 104–26. Cambridge: Cambridge University Press, 1996.

————. "Gottes Treue zum untreuen Volk." In *Der Treue Gottes trauen: Beiträge zum Werk des Lukas: für Gerhard Schneider*, edited by Claus Bussmann and Walter Radl, 15–27. Freiburg: Herder, 1991.

————. *Luke and the People of God.* Minneapolis: Augsburg, 1972.

————. *The Theology of the Acts of the Apostles.* Cambridge: Cambridge University Press, 1996.

————. *The Unknown Paul: Essays on Luke-Acts and Early Christian History.* Minneapolis: Augsburg, 1984.

Johnson, Luke Timothy. *The Acts of the Apostles.* Sacra Pagina 5. Collegeville, MN: Liturgical, 1992.

Jones, Donald L. "The Title *Huios Theou* in Acts." In *SBL Seminar Papers, 1985,* 453–63. Society of Biblical Literature Seminar Papers 24. Atlanta: Scholars, 1985.

Jonge, Marinus de. *Christology in Context: The Earliest Christian Response to Jesus.* Philadelphia: Westminster, 1988.

————. *The Testaments of the Twelve Patriarchs: A Study of their Text, Composition and Origin.* 2nd ed. Amsterdam: Van Gorcum, 1975.

Kampen, John. *The Hasideans and the Origin of Pharisaism: A Study in 1 and 2 Maccabees.* Society of Biblical Literature Septuagint and Cognate Studies 24. Atlanta: Scholars, 1988.

Keener, Craig S. *The Spirit in the Gospels and Acts: Divine Purity and Power.* Peabody, MA: Hendrickson, 1997.

Kieffer, René. "From Linguistic Methodology to the Discovery of a World of Metaphors." *Semeia* 81 (1998) 77–93.

Kilgallen, John J. "'The Apostles Whom He Chose Because of the Holy Spirit' A Suggestion Regarding Acts 1.2." *Biblica* 81 (2000) 414–17.

————. "Clean, Acceptable, Saved: Acts 10." *Expository Times* 109 (1998) 301–2.

————. "The Function of Stephen's Speech (Acts 7:2–53)." *Biblica* 70 (1989) 173–93.

————. *The Stephen Speech: A Literary and Redactional Study of Acts 7.2–53.* Analecta biblica 67. Rome: Biblical Institute, 1976.

Knibb, Michael A. "The Ethiopic Book of Enoch." In *Outside the Old Testament*, edited by Marinus de Jonge, 26–55. Cambridge Commentaries on Writings of the Jewish & Christian World 200BC to AD200 4. Cambridge: Cambridge University Press, 1985.

Koch, Dietrich-Alex. "Geistbesitz, Geistverleihung und Wundermacht: Erwägungen zur Tradition und zur lukanischen Redaktion in Apg 8:5–25." *Zeitschrift für die neutestamentliche Wissenschaft und die Kunde der älteren Kirche* 77 (1986) 64–82.

Koester, Craig R. *The Dwelling of God: The Tabernacle in Old Testament, Intertestamental Jewish Literature, and the New Testament.* Catholic Biblical Quarterly Monograph Series 22. Washington, DC: Catholic Biblical Association of America, 1989.

Koet, B. "Simeons Worte (Lk 2,29–32,34c–35) und Israels Geschick." In *The Four Gospels 1992: Festschrift Frans Neirynck*, edited by F. Van Segbroeck, C. M. Tuckett, G. Van Belle and J. Verheyden, 1149–69. Vol. II. Bibliotheca ephemeridum theologicarum lovaniensium 100. Leuven: Leuven University Press, 1992.

Kolenkow, Anitra Bingham. "The Genre Testament and the Testament of Abraham." In *Studies on the Testament of Abraham*, edited by George W. E. Nickelsburg, Jr, 139–52. Society of Biblical Literature Septuagint and Cognate Studies 6. Missoula, MT: Scholars, 1976.

Korn, Manfred. *Die Geschichte Jesu in veränderter Zeit: Studien zur bleibenden Bedeutung Jesus im lukanischen Doppelwerk.* Wissenschaftliche Untersuchungen zum Neuen Testament 2, 51. Tübingen: Mohr Siebeck, 1993.

Kort, Wesley A. *Story, Text, and Scripture: Literary Interests in Biblical Narrative.* University Park: The Pennsylvania State University Press, 1988.

Krieger, Klaus-Stefan. *Geschichtsschreibung als Apologetick bei Flavius Josephus.* Texte und Arbeiten zum neutestamentlichen Zeitalter 9. Tübingen: Francke, 1994.

Kümmel, Werner G. *Heilsgeschehen und Geschichte: Gesammelte Aufsätze 1933–1964,* edited by Erich Grässer, Otto Merck, and Adolf Fritz. Marburger theologische Studien 3. Marburg: N. G. Elwert, 1965.

————. *Promise and Fulfilment: The Eschatological Message of Jesus*, translated by Dorothea M. Barton. Studies in Biblical Theology 23. London: SCM, 1957.

Kurz, William S. "Effects of Variant Narrators in Acts 10–11." *New Testament Studies* 43 (1997) 570–86.

————. "Promise and Fulfillment in Hellenistic Jewish Narratives and in Luke and Acts." In *Jesus and the Heritage of Israel: Luke's Narrative Claim upon Israel's Legacy*, edited by David P. Moessner, 147–70. Harrisburg, PA: Trinity, 1999.

Ladd, George E. *A Theology of the New Testament*. Grand Rapids: Eerdmans, 1974.

Ladouceur, David J. "Hellenistic Preconceptions of Shipwreck and Pollution as Context for Acts 27–28." *Harvard Theological Review* 73 (1980) 435–49.

Lake, Kirsopp and Henry J. Cadbury. *The Beginnings of Christianity: Part 1 The Acts of the Apostles*. Edited by F. J. Foakes Jackson and Kirsopp Lake. Vol. IV. London: Macmillan, 1933.

Lambrecht, J. "Paul's Farewell-Address at Miletus (Acts 20, 17–38)." In *Les Actes des Apôtres: Traditions, rédaction, théologie*, edited by J. Kremer, 307–37. Bibliotheca ephemeridum theologicarum lovaniensium 48. Leuven, Leuven University Press, 1979.

Lampe, G. W. H. *God As Spirit: The Bampton Lectures 1976*. Oxford: Clarendon, 1977.

————. "The Holy Spirit in the Writings of St. Luke." In *Studies in the Gospels: Essays in Memory of R. H. Lightfoot*, edited by D. E. Nineham, 159–72. Oxford: Blackwell, 1957.

Landau, Tamar. "Out-Heroding Herod: Josephus, Rhetoric and the Herod Narratives." PhD diss., University of Oxford, 2003.

Lang, Bernhard. *The Hebrew God: Portrait of an Ancient Deity*. New Haven, CT: Yale University Press, 2002.

Larsson, Edvin. "Temple-Criticism and the Jewish Heritage: Some Reflexions on Acts 6–7." *New Testament Studies* 39 (1993) 379–95.

Lee, David. *Luke's Stories of Jesus: Theological Reading of the Gospel Narrative and the Legacy of Hans Frei*. Journal for the Study of the New Testament: Supplement Series 185. Sheffield: Sheffield Academic, 1999.

Levinson, John R. "The Debut of the Divine Spirit in Josephus's *Antiquities*." *Harvard Theological Review* 87 (1994) 123–38.

————. "The Prophetic Spirit as an Angel According to Philo." *Harvard Theological Review* 88 (1995) 189–207.

Lindemann, Andreas. "Herrschaft Gottes/Reich Gottes IV: Neues Testament und spätanikes Judentum." In *Theologische Realenzyklopädie*, edited by G. Krause and G.Müller, 196–218. Vol. 15. Berlin: de Gruyter, 1986.

Lindsay, Dennis R. *Josephus and Faith: Πίστις and Πιστεύειν as Faith Terminology in the Writings of Flavius Josephus and in the New Testament*. Arbeiten zur Geschichte des antiken Judentums und des Urchristentums 19. Leiden: Brill, 1993.

Lohfink, Gerhard. *Die Himmelfahrt Jesus: Untersuchungen zu den Himmelfahrts- und Erhöhungstexten bei Lukas*. Studien zum Alten und Neuen Testaments 26. Munich: Kösel, 1971.

————. *Die Sammlung Israels: Eine Untersuchungen zur lukanischen Ekklesiologie*. Studien zum Alten und Neuen Testaments 26. Munich: Kösel, 1975.

Loisy, Alfred. *Les Actes des Apôtres*. Paris: E. Nourry, 1920.

Longenecker, Bruce W. "Moral Character and Divine Generosity: Acts 13:13–52 and the Narrative Dynamics of Luke-Acts." In *New Testament Greek and Exegesis: Essays in Honor of Gerald F. Hawthorne*, edited by Amy M. Donaldson and Timothy B. Sailors, 141–64. Grand Rapids: Eerdmans, 2003.

Lucchesi, Enzo. "Précédents non bibliques à l'expression néo-testamenttair: 'Les temps et les moments.'" *Journal of Theological Studies* 28 (1977) 537–40.

Luz, Ulrich. "βασιλεία." In vol. 1 of *Exegetical Dictionary of the New Testament*, edited by H. Balz and G. Schneider, 201–5. Grand Rapids: Eerdmans, 1990.

Lygre, J. G. "Exaltation: Considered with Reference to the Resurrection and Ascension in Luke-Acts." PhD diss., Princeton Theological Seminary, 1975.

Lyons, William J. "The Words of Gamaliel (Acts 5:38–39) and the Irony of Indeterminacy." *Journal for the Study of the New Testament* 68 (1997) 23–49.

Mach, Michael. "Concepts of Jewish Monotheism During the Hellenistic Period." In *The Jewish Roots of Christological Monotheism: Papers from the St. Andrews Conference on the Historical Origins of the*

Worship of Jesus, edited by Carey C. Newman, James R. Davila, and Gladys S. Lewis, 21–42. Leiden: Brill, 1999.

Maddox, Robert. *The Purpose of Luke-Acts*. Edinburgh: T. & T. Clark, 1982.

Maile, J. F. "The Ascension in Luke-Acts." *Tyndale Bulletin* 37 (1986) 29–59.

Malina, Bruce J. *The New Testament World: Insights from Cultural Anthropology*. Atlanta: John Knox, 1981.

Maloney, Linda. *"All that God had Done with Them": The Narration of the Works of God in the Early Christian Community as Described in the Acts of the Apostles*. New York: Peter Lang, 1991.

Marguerat, Daniel. "The Enigma of the Silent Closing of Acts (28:16–31)." In *Jesus and the Heritage of Israel: Luke's Narrative Claim upon Israel's Legacy*, edited by David P. Moessner, 284–304. Harrisburg, PA: Trinity, 1999.

———. *The First Christian Historian: Writing the "Acts of the Apostles."* Society for New Testament Studies Monograph Series 121. Cambridge: Cambridge University Press. 2002.

———. "The God of the Book of Acts." In *Narrativity in Biblical and Related Texts*, edited by G. J. Brooke and J.-D. Kaestli, 159–81. Bibliotheca ephemeridum theologicarum lovaniensium 159. Leuven: Leuven University Press, 2000.

Marshall, I. Howard. *The Acts of the Apostles*. Grand Rapids: Eerdmans, 1980.

———. *The Gospel of Luke: A Commentary on the Greek Text*. New International Greek Testament Commentary. Exeter: Paternoster, 1978.

———. *Luke: Historian and Theologian*. Exeter: Paternoster, 1970.

Martin, L. H. "Gods or Ambassadors of God? Barnabas and Paul in Lystra." *New Testament Studies* 41 (1995) 152–56.

Mason, Rex. *Old Testament Pictures of God*. Regent's Study Guides 2. Oxford: Regent's Park College, 1993.

Mason, Steve. *Josephus and the New Testament*. 2nd ed. Peabody, Mass.: Hendrickson, 2003.

———. "'Should any Wish to Enquire Further' (*Ant.* 1.25) The Aim and Audience of Josephus's Judean Antiquities/Life." In *Understanding Josephus: Seven Perspectives*, 64–103. Journal for the Study of the Pseudepigrapha Supplement Series 32. Sheffield: Sheffield Academic, 1998.

Matera, Frank J. "Acts 10:34–43." *Interpretation* 41 (1987) 62–66.

Mattill, Andrew J. *Luke and the Last Things: A Perspective for the Understanding of Lukan Thought*. Dillsboro, NC: Western North Carolina Press, 1979.

———. "Naherwartung, Fernerwartung, and the Purpose of Luke-Acts: Weymouth Reconsidered." *Catholic Biblical Quarterly* 34 (1972) 276–93.

———. "The Way of Tribulation." *Journal of Biblical Literature* 98 (1979) 531–46.

Mayer, Bernhard. "ἐλπίς κτλ." In vol. 1 of *Exegetical Dictionary of the New Testament*, edited by H. Balz and G. Schneider, 437–41. Grand Rapids: Eerdmans, 1990.

McKenzie, John L. *A Theology of the Old Testament*. London: Geoffrey Chapman, 1974.

Mealand, David L. "Community of Goods and Utopian Allusions in Acts 2–4." *Journal of Theological Studies* 28 (1977) 96–99.

Meeks, Wayne A. *The Prophet-King: Moses Traditions and the Johannine Christology*. Novum Testament Supplements 14. Leiden: Brill, 1967.

Menzies, Robert P. *Empowered for Witness: The Spirit in Luke-Acts*. Journal of Pentecostal Theology Supplement Series 6. Sheffield: Sheffield Academic, 1994.

Merenlahti, Petri, and Raimo Hakola. "Reconceiving Narrative Criticism." In *Characterization in the Gospel: Reconceiving Narrative Criticism*, edited by David Rhoads and Kari Syreeni, 13–48. Journal for the Study of the New Testament Supplement Series 184. Sheffield: Sheffield Academic, 1999.

Merk, Otto. "Das Reich Gottes in den lukanischen Schriften." In *Jesus und Paulus: Festschrift für Werner Georg Kümmel zum 70. Geburtstag*, edited by E. Earle Ellis and Erich Grässer, 201–20. Göttingen: Vandenhoeck & Ruprecht, 1975.

Merkel, H. "Die Gottesherrschaft in der Verkündigung Jesus." In *Königherrschaft Gottes und himmlishcer Kult in Judentum, Urchristenum und in der hellenistischen Welt*, edited by Martin Hengel and Anna Maria Schwemer, 119–61. Wissenschaftliche Untersuchungen zum Neuen Testament 55. Tübingen: Mohr Siebeck, 1991.

———. "Israel im lukanischen Werk." *New Testament Studies* 40 (1994) 371–98.

Mettinger, Tryggve N. D. *In Search of God: The Meaning and Message of the Everlasting Names*. Translated by Frederick H. Cryer. Philadelphia: Fortress, 1988.

Metzger, Bruce M. *A Textual Commentary on the Greek New Testament*. Corrected ed. Stuttgart: Biblia-Druck, 1975.

Michel, H-J. *Die Abschiedsrede des Paulus an die Kirche Apg 20, 17–38: Motivgeschichte und theologische Bedeutung*. Studien zum Alten und Neuen Testaments 35. Munich: Kösel, 1973.

Miesner, Donald A. "The Missionary Journeys Narrative: Patterns and Implications." In *Perspectives on Luke-Acts*, edited by Charles H. Talbert, 199–214. Perspectives in Religious Studies 5. Danville, VA: Association of Baptist Professors of Religion, 1978.

Miles, Jack. *God: A Biography*. London: Touchstone, 1998.

Miles, Gary B. and Garry W. Trompf. "Luke and Antiphon: The Theology of Acts 27–28 In the Light of Pagan Beliefs about Divine Retribution, Pollutions, and Shipwreck." *Harvard Theological Review* 69 (1976) 259–67.

Mills, Mary E. *Images of God in the Old Testament*. London: Cassell, 1998.

Mitchell, Alan C. "The Social Function of Friendship in Acts 2:44–47 and 4:32–37." *Journal of Biblical Literature* 111 (1992) 255–72.

Moessner, David P. "'Completed End(s)ings' of Historiographical Narrative. Diodorus Siculus and the End(ing) of Acts." In *Die Apostelgeschichte und die hellenistische Geschichtsschreibung: Festschrift für Eckhard Plümacher zu seinem 65. Geburtstag*, edited by Cilliers Breytenbach and Jens Schröter with David S. Du Toit, 193–221. Leiden: Brill, 2004.

———. "The Ironic Fulfillment of Israel's Glory." In *Luke-Acts and the Jewish People: Eight Critical Perspectives*, edited by Joseph B. Tyson, 35–50. Minneapolis, MN: Augsburg, 1988.

———. *Lord of the Banquet: The Literary and Theological Significance of the Lukan Travel Narrative*. Minneapolis, MN: Fortress, 1989.

———. "'Managing' the Audience: Diodorus Siculus and Luke the Evangelist on Designing Authorial Intent." In *Luke and His Readers. Festschrift A. Denaux*, edited by R. Bieringer, G. Van Belle, and J. Verheyden, 61–80. Bibliotheca ephemeridum theologicarum lovaniensium 182. Leuven: Leuven University Press, 2005.

———. "Paul in Acts: Preacher of Eschatological Repentance to Israel." *New Testament Studies* 34 (1988) 96–104.

Moffatt, James. "The Second Book of Maccabees: Introduction." In vol. 1 of *The Apocrypha and Pseudepigrapha of the Old Testament*, edited by R. H. Charles, 125–31. Oxford: Clarendon, 1913.

Morton, Russell. "Acts 12:1–19." *Interpretation* 55 (2001) 67–69.

Motyer, J. A. *The Day of the Lion: The Message of Amos*. Leicester: InterVarsity, 1976.

Moule, C. F. D. "The Christology of Acts." In *Studies in Luke-Acts*, edited by Leander E. Keck and J. Louis Martyn, 159–85. Philadelphia: Fortress, 1980.

Mowery, Robert L. "Direct Statements Concerning God's Activity in Acts." In *SBL Seminar Papers, 1990*, 196–211. Society of Biblical Literature Seminar Papers 29. Atlanta: Scholars Press, 1990.

———. "The Disappearance of the Father: The References to God the Father in Luke-Acts." *Encounter* 55/4 (1994) 353–58.

———. "The Divine Hand and the Divine Plan in the Lukan Passion." In *SBL Seminar Papers, 1991*, 558–75. Society of Biblical Literature Seminar Papers 30. Atlanta: Scholars Press, 1991.

———. "Lord, God, and Father: Theological Language in Luke-Acts." In *SBL Seminar Papers, 1995*, 82–101. Society of Biblical Literature Seminar Papers 34. Atlanta: Scholars Press, 1995.

Munck, Johannes. *The Acts of the Apostles: Introduction, Translation and Notes*, revised by William F. Albright and C. S. Mann. Anchor Bible. Garden City, NY: Doubleday, 1967.

———. "Discours d'adieu dans le Nouveau Testament et dans la literature biblique." In *Aux Sources de la Tradition Chrétienne: Mélanges Maurice Goguel*, edited by O. Cullmann and P. Menoud, 155–70. Neuchatel: Delachaux et Niestle, 1950.

Munoa, Phillip B. "Jesus, the *Merkavah*, and Martyrdom in Early Christian Tradition." *Journal of Biblical Literature* 121 (2002) 303–25.

Mussner, Franz. "Die Idee der Apokatastasis in der Apostelgeschichte." In *Lex Tua Veritas: Festschrift für Hubert Junker*, edited by Heinrich Gross and Franz Mussner, 293–306. Trier: Paulinus, 1961.

Neudorfer, Heinz-Werner. "The Speech of Stephen." In *Witness to the Gospel: The Theology of Acts*, edited by I. Howard Marshall and David Peterson, 275–94. Grand Rapids: Eerdmans, 1998.

Neyrey, Jerome H. *Render to God: New Testament Understandings of the Divine*. Minneapolis: Fortress, 2004.

Nickelsburg, George W. E. *Jewish Literature Between the Bible and the Mishnah: A Historical and Literary Introduction*. Philadelphia: Fortress, 1981.

————. *Resurrection, Immortality, and Eternal Life in Intertestamental Judaism*. Harvard Theological Studies 26. Cambridge, MA: Harvard University Press, 1972.

Nickelsburg, George W. E., and Michael E. Stone. *Faith and Piety in Early Judaism: Texts and Documents*. Philadelphia: Fortress, 1983.

Noack, Bent. *Das Gottesreich bei Lukas: Eine Studie zur Luk. 17,20–24*. Symbolae biblicae upsalienses 10. Uppsala: Gleerup, 1948.

Nolland, John. "A Fresh Look at Acts 15:10." *New Testament Studies* 27 (1980) 105–15.

————. "Luke's Readers: A Study of Luke 4:22–8; Acts 13:46; 18:6; 28:28 and Luke 21:5–36." PhD diss., University of Cambridge, 1977.

————. "Salvation-History and Eschatology." In *Witness to the Gospel: The Theology of Acts*, edited by I. Howard Marshall and David Peterson, 63–81. Grand Rapids: Eerdmans, 1998.

Noth, Martin. *Deuteronomistic History*. 2nd ed. Journal for the Study of the Old Testament: Supplement Series 15. Sheffield: JSOT Press, 1981. Originally published in *Überlieferungsgeschichtliche Studien*, 1–110. Tübingen: Max Niemeyer, 1957.

O'Neill, J. C. *The Theology of Acts in Its Historical Setting*. 2nd ed. rev. London: SPCK, 1970.

O'Toole, Robert F. "Acts 2:30 and the Davidic Covenant of Pentecost." *Journal of Biblical Literature* 102 (1983) 245–58.

————. "Philip and the Ethiopian Eunuch (Acts 8:25–40)." *Journal for the Study of the New Testament* 17 (1983) 25–34.

————. "The Kingdom of God in Luke-Acts." In *The Kingdom of God in 20th-Century Interpretation*, edited by Wendell Willis, 147–62. Peabody, MA: Hendrickson, 1987.

————. *The Unity of Luke's Theology: An Analysis of Luke-Acts*. Wilmington, DE: Michael Glazier, 1984.

Oepke, A. "ἀποκαθίστημι, ἀποκατάστασις." In vol. 1 of *Theological Dictionary of the New Testament*, edited by G. Kittel and G. Friedrich, translated by G. W. Bromiley, 387–93. Grand Rapids: Eerdmans, 1964.

Palmer, Darryl W. "Acts and the Ancient Historical Monograph." In *The Book of Acts in Its Ancient Literary Setting*, edited by Bruce W. Winter and Andrew D. Clarke. Vol. 1 of *The Book of Acts in Its First Century Setting*, edited by Bruce W. Winter, 1–29. Grand Rapids: Eerdmans, 1993.

Parker, James III. *The Concept of Apokatastasis in Acts: A Study in Primitive Christian Theology*. Austin, TX: Schola Press, 1978.

Parsons, Mikeal C. *The Departure of Jesus in Luke-Acts: The Ascension Narratives in Context*. Journal for the Study of the New Testament: Supplement Series 21. Sheffield: JSOT Press, 1987.

————. "The Place of Jerusalem on the Lukan Landscape: An Exercise in Symbolic Cartography." In *Literary Studies in Luke-Acts: Essays in Honor of Joseph B. Tyson*, edited by Richard P. Thompson and Thomas E. Phillips, 155–71. Macon, GA: Mercer University Press, 1998.

Patrick, Dale. "The Kingdom of God in the Old Testament." In *The Kingdom of God in 20th-Century Interpretation*, edited by Wendell Willis, 67–79. Peabody, MA: Hendrickson, 1987.

————. *The Rendering of God in the Old Testament*. Overtures to Biblical Theology 10. Philadelphia: Fortress, 1981.

Payne, J. Barton. *The Theology of the Older Testament*. Grand Rapids: Zondervan, 1962.

Pelling, Christopher, editor. *Characterization and Individuality in Greek Literature*. Oxford: Oxford University Press, 1990

Pervo, Richard I. *Profit with Delight: The Literary Genre of the Acts of the Apostles*. Philadelphia: Fortress, 1987.

Pesch, Rudolf. *Die Apostelgeschichte*. 2 vols. Evangelisch-katholischer Kommentar zum Neuen Testament 5. Neukirchen-Vluyn: Neukirchener Verlag, 1986.

Plümacher, Eckhard. "Cicero und Lukas: Bemerkungen zu Stil und Zweck der historischen Monographie." In *The Unity of Luke-Acts*, edited by J. Verheyden, 759–75. Bibliotheca ephemeridum theologicarum lovaniensium 142. Leuven: Leuven University Press, 1999.

————. "Die Apostelgeschichte als historische Monographie." In *Les Actes des Apôtres: Traditions, rédaction, théologie*, edited by J. Kremer, 457–66. Bibliotheca ephemeridum theologicarum lovaniensium 48; Leuven: Gembloux, 1979.

————. *Lukas als hellenistischer Schriftsteller: Studien zur Apostelgeschichte*. Studien zur Umwelt des Neuen Testaments 9. Göttingen: Vandenhoeck & Ruprecht, 1972.

Plunkett, Mark A. "Ethnocentricity and Salvation History in the Cornelius Episode (Acts 10:1—11:18)." In *SBL Seminar Papers, 1985*, 465–79. Society of Biblical Literature Seminar Papers 24. Atlanta: Scholars, 1985.

Porter, Stanley E. "The 'We' Passages." In *The Book of Acts in Its Graeco-Roman Setting*. Edited by David W. J. Gill and Conrad Gempf. Vol. 2 of *The Book of Acts in Its First Century Setting*, edited by Bruce W. Winter, 545–74. Grand Rapids: Eerdmans, 1994.

Praeder, Susan Marie. "Luke-Acts and the Ancient Novel." In *SBL Seminar Papers, 1981*, 269–92. Society of Biblical Literature Seminar Papers 20. Chico, CA: Scholars, 1981.

Prieur, Alexander. *Die Verkündigung der Gottesherrschaft: Exegetische Studien zum lukanischen Verständnis von βασιλεία τοῦ θεοῦ*. Wissenschaftliche Untersuchungen zum Neuen Testament 2, 89. Tübingen: Mohr Siebeck, 1996.

Rad, Gerhard von. *Old Testament Theology*. Translated by D. M. G. Stalker. 2nd ed. 1 The Theology of Israel's Historical Traditions 1. Edinburgh: Oliver & Boyd, 1962. Originally published as *Theologie des Alten Testaments. Die Theologie der geschichtilichen Überlieferungen Israels 1*. Munich: Kaiser, 1957.

Räisänen, Heikki. "The Redemption of Israel." In *Luke-Acts: Scandinavian Perspectives*, edited by Petri Luomanen, 94–114. Helsinki: Helsinki University Press, 1991.

Rapske, Brian M. "Acts, Travel and Shipwreck." In *The Book of Acts in Its Graeco-Roman Setting*, edited by David W. J. Gill and Conrad Gempf. Vol. 2 of *The Book of Acts in Its First Century Setting*, edited by Bruce W. Winter, 2–47. Grand Rapids: Eerdmans, 1994.

————. "Opposition to the Plan of God and Persecution." In *Witness to the Gospel: The Theology of Acts*, edited by I. Howard Marshall and David Peterson, 235–56. Grand Rapids: Eerdmans, 1998.

Rashkow, Ilona N. "In Our Image We Create Him, Male and Female We Create Them: The E/Affect of Biblical Characterization." *Semeia* 63 (1993) 105–13.

Ravens, David. *Luke and the Restoration of Israel*. Journal for the Study of the New Testament: Supplement Series 119. Sheffield: Sheffield Academic, 1995.

Rehm, Martin. *Das Bild Gottes im Alten Testament*. Würzburg: Echter, 1951.

Reimer, Ivoni R. *Women in the Acts of the Apostles: A Feminist Liberation Perspective*. Minneapolis, MN: Fortress, 1995.

Reinhartz, Adele. "Anonymity and Character in the Books of Samuel." *Semeia* 63 (1993) 117–41.

Rese, Martin. *Altestamentliche Motive in der Christologie des Lukas*. Bonn: Rheinische Friedrich Universität Bonn, 1965.

Richard, Earl. *Acts 6:1—8:4: The Author's Method of Composition*. Society of Biblical Literature Dissertation Series 41. Missoula, MT: Scholars, 1978.

————. "The Divine Purpose: The Jews and the Gentile Mission (Acts 15)." In *SBL Seminar Papers, 1980*, 188–209. Society of Biblical Literature Seminar Papers 19. Chico, CA: Scholars, 1980.

Rimmon-Kenan, Shlomith. *Narrative Fiction: Contemporary Poetics*. 2nd ed. London: Routledge, 2002.

Robbins, Vernon K. "By Land and By Sea: The We-Passages and Ancient Sea Voyages." In *Perspectives on Luke-Acts*, edited by Charles H. Talbert, 215–42. Perspectives in Religious Studies 5. Danville, VA: Association of Baptist Professors of Religion, 1978.

Robinson, J. A. T. *Jesus and His Coming: The Emergence of a Doctrine*. London: SCM, 1957.

Roloff, J. *Die Apostelgeschichte*. Göttingen: Vandenhoeck & Ruprecht, 1981.

Romm, James S. *The Edges of the Earth in Ancient Thought: Geography, Exploration, and Fiction*. Princeton, NJ: Princeton University Press, 1992.

Rosner, Brian S. "The Progress of the Word." In *Witness to the Gospel: The Theology of Acts*, edited by I. Howard Marshall and David Peterson, 215–33. Grand Rapids: Eerdmans, 1998.

Rowland, Christopher. *The Open Heaven: A Study of Apocalyptic in Judaism and Early Christianity*. London: SPCK, 1982.

Russell, D. S. *Divine Disclosure: An Introduction to Jewish Apocalyptic*. Minneapolis, MN: Fortress, 1992.

Ryken, Leland, James C. Wilhoit, and Tremper Longman III, editors. "Fear of God." In *Dictionary of Biblical Imagery*, 277–78. Downers Grove, IL: InterVarsity, 1998.

Salmon, Marilyn. "Insider or Outsider? Luke's Relationship with Judaism." In *Luke-Acts and the Jewish People: Eight Critical Perspectives*. Edited by Joseph B. Tyson, 76–82. Minneapolis: Augsburg, 1988.

Salo, Kalervo. *Luke's Treatment of the Law: A Redaction-Critical Investigation*. Annales Academiae Scientiarum Fennicae 57. Helsinki: Suomalainen Tiedeakatemia, 1991.

Sanders, E. P. *Jesus and Judaism*. Philadelphia: Fortress, 1985.

Sanders, Jack T. "The Jewish People in Luke-Acts." In *Luke-Acts and the Jewish People: Eight Critical Perspectives*, edited by Joseph B. Tyson, 51–75. Minneapolis, MN: Augsburg, 1988.

———. *The Jews in Luke-Acts*. London: SCM, 1987.

———. "The Salvation of the Jews in Luke-Acts." In *Luke-Acts: New Perspectives from the Society of Biblical Literature Seminar*, edited by Charles H. Talbert, 104–28. New York: Crossroad, 1984.

———. "Who is a Jew and Who is a Gentile in the Book of Acts." *New Testament Studies* 37 (1991) 434–55.

Schille, Gottfried. *Die Apostelgeschichte des Lukas*. Theologischer Handkommentar zum Neuen Testament 5. Berlin: Evangelische, 1983.

Schlatter, Adolph von. *Die Theologie des Judentums nach dem Bericht des Josefus*. Beiträge zur Förderung christlicher Theologie 26. Gütersloh: C. Bertelsmann, 1932.

Schlier, Heinrich. "Jesus Himmelfahrt nach den lukanischen Schriften." In *Besinnung auf das Neue Testament: Exegetische Aufsätze und Vorträge 2*, 227–41. Vienna: Herder, 1964.

Schmidt, Daryl D. "Rhetorical Influences and Genre: Luke's Preface and the Rhetoric of Hellenistic Historiography." In *Jesus and the Heritage of Israel: Luke's Narrative Claim upon Israel's Legacy*, edited by David P. Moessner, 27–60. Harrisburg, PA: Trinity, 1999.

Schneider, Gerhard. *Die Apostelgeschichte*. 2 vols. Herders theologischer Kommentar zum Neuen Testament 5. Freiburg: Herder, 1980–82.

———. "Urchristliche Gottesverkündigung in hellenisticher Umwelt." In *Lukas, Theologe der Heilsgeschichte: Aufsätze zum lukanischen Doppelwerk*, 280–96. Bonner biblische Beiträge 59. Bonn: Peter Hanstein, 1985.

Schreiber, Stefan. "Aktualisierung göttlichen Handelns am Pfingsttag: Das frühjüdische Fest in Apg 2,1." *Zeitschrift für die neutestamentliche Wissenschaft und die Kunde der älteren Kirche* 93 (2002) 58–77.

Schürer, Emil. *The History of the Jewish People in the Age of Jesus Christ (175B.C.–A.D. 135)*. Vol. 3. Edited by Geza Vermes, Fergus Millar, and Martin Goodman. Rev. ed. Edinburgh: T. & T. Clark, 1986–87.

Schwarz, Daniel R. "The End of the ΓH (Acts 1:8) Beginning or End of the Christian Vision?" *Journal of Biblical Literature* 105 (1986) 669–76.

Schweizer, Eduard. "πνεῦμα κτλ." In vol. 6 of *Theological Dictionary of the New Testament*, edited by G. Kittel and G. Friedrich, translated by G. W. Bromiley, 396–453. Grand Rapids: Eerdmans, 1968.

Schwemer, Anna M. "Gott als König und seine Königsherrschaft in den Sabbatliedern aus Qumran." In *Königsherrschaft Gottes und himmlischer Kult: im Judentum, Urchristentum und in der hellenisticher Welt*, edited by Martin Hengel and Anna M. Schwemer, 45–118. Wissenschaftliche Untersuchungen zum Neuen Testament 55. Tübingen: Mohr Siebeck, 1991.

Scott, James M. "Acts 2:9-22 As an Anticipation of the Mission to the Nations." In *The Mission of the Early Church to Jews and Gentiles*, edited by Jostein Ådna and Hans Kvalbein, 87–123. Wissenschaftliche Untersuchungen zum Neuen Testament 127. Tübingen: Mohr Siebeck, 2000.

———. "Luke's Geographical Horizon." In *The Book of Acts in Its Graeco-Roman Setting*. Edited by David W. J. Gill and Conrad Gempf. Vol. 2 of *The Book of Acts in Its First Century Setting*, edited by Bruce W. Winter, 483–544. Grand Rapids: Eerdmans, 1994.

Seccombe, David. "The New People of God." In *Witness to the Gospels: The Theology of Acts*, edited by I. Howard Marshall and David Peterson, 349–72. Grand Rapids: Eerdmans, 1998.

Segal, A. F. "Heavenly Ascent in Hellenistic Judaism, Early Christianity and their Environment." *Aufstieg undNiedergang der römischen Welt: Geschichte und Kultur Roms im Spiegel der neueren Forschung*. Part 2 Principat, 23.2, edited by H. Temporini and W. Haase, 1334–94. New York: de Gruyter, 1980.

Sharp, D. S. "The Meaning of μεν ουν in Acts xiv,3." *Expository Times* 44 (1932–33) 528.

Sheeley, Steven M. *Narrative Asides in Luke-Acts*. Journal for the Study of the New Testament: Supplement Series 72. Sheffield: Sheffield Academic, 1992.

Shelton, James B. *Mighty in Word and Deed: The Role of the Holy Spirit in Luke-Acts*. Peabody, MA: Hendrickson, 1991.

Shepherd, William H., Jr. *The Narrative Function of the Holy Spirit as a Character in Luke-Acts*. Atlanta: Scholars, 1994.

Snowden, F. M. *Before Color Prejudice: The Ancient View of Blacks*. Cambridge, MA: Harvard University Press, 1983.

————. *Blacks in Antiquity: Ethiopians in the Graeco-Roman Experience*. Cambridge, MA: Harvard University Press, 1970.

Soards, Marion L. *The Speeches in Acts: Their Content, Context, and Concerns*. Louisville, KY: Westminster John Knox, 1994.

Spencer, F. Scott. *The Portrait of Philip in Acts: A Study of Roles and Relations*. Journal for the Study of the New Testament Supplement Series 67. Sheffield: Sheffield Academic, 1992.

Spilsbury, Paul. "God and Israel in Josephus: A Patron-Client Relationship." In *Understanding Josephus: Seven Perspectives*, edited by Steve Mason, 172–91. Journal for the Study of the Pseudepigrapha Supplement Series 32. Sheffield: Sheffield Academic, 1998.

Squires, John T. *The Plan of God in Luke-Acts*. Society for New Testament Studies Monograph Series 76. Cambridge: Cambridge University Press, 1993.

Stählin, G. "Τὸ πνεῦμα Ἰησοῦ (Apostelgeschichte 16:7)." In *Christ and Spirit in the New Testament: Essays in honour of C. F. D. Moule*, edited by Barnabas Lindars and Stephen S. Smalley, 229–52. Cambridge: Cambridge University Press, 1973.

Stanton, Graham N. *Jesus of Nazareth in New Testament Preaching*. Society for New Testament Studies Monograph Series 27. Cambridge: Cambridge University Press, 1974.

Stemberger, Günter. *Der Leib der Auferstehung: Studien zur Anthropologie und Eschatolgie des palästinischen Judentums im neutestamentlichen Zeitalter (ca. 170 v. Cr.–100 n. Chr.)*. Analecta biblica 56. Rome: Biblical Institute Press, 1972.

Stempvoort, P. A. van. "The Interpretation of the Ascension in Luke and Acts." *New Testament Studies* 5 (1958/59) 30–42.

Sterling, Gregory E. "'Athletes of Virtue': An Analysis of the Summaries in Acts (2:41–47; 4:32–35; 5:12–16)." *Journal of Biblical Literature* 113 (1994) 679–96.

————. *Historiography and Self-Definition: Josephos, Luke-Acts and Apologetic Historiography*. Novum Testamentum Supplements 64. Leiden: Brill, 1992.

————. "The Invisible Presence: Josephus's Retelling of Ruth." In *Understanding Josephus: Seven Perspectives*, edited by Steve Mason, 104–71. Journal for the Study of the Pseudepigrapha: Supplement Series 32. Sheffield: Sheffield Academic, 1998.

————. "'Opening the Scriptures': The Legitimation of the Jewish Diaspora and the Early Christian Mission." In *Jesus and the Heritage of Israel: Luke's Narrative Claim upon Israel's Legacy*, edited by David P. Moessner, 199–217. Harrisburg, PA: Trinity, 1999.

Sternberg, Meir. *The Poetics of Biblical Narrative: Ideological Literature and the Drama of Reading*. Bloomington, IN: Indiana University Press, 1985.

Strauss, Mark L. *The Davidic Messiah in Luke-Acts: The Promise and its Fulfillment in Lukan Christology*. Journal for the Study of the New Testament: Supplement Series 110. Sheffield: Sheffield Academic, 1995.

Strom, Mark R. "An Old Testament Background to Acts 12:20–23." *New Testament Studies* 32 (1986) 289–92.

Stronstad, Roger. *The Charismatic Theology of St. Luke*. Peabody, Mass.: Hendrickson, 1985.

Stroup, George W. *The Promise of Narrative Theology*. London: SCM, 1984.

Sylva, Dennis D. "The Meaning and Function of Acts 7:46–50." *Journal of Biblical Literature* 106 (1987) 261–75.

Talbert, Charles H. "Again: Paul's Visits to Jerusalem." *Novum Testamentum* 9 (1967) 26–40.

————. *Literary Patterns, Theological Themes, and the Genre of Luke-Acts*. Society of Biblical Literature Monograph Series 20. Missoula, MT: Scholars Press, 1974.

————. *Luke and the Gnostics: An Examination of the Lucan Purpose*. Nashville: Abingdon, 1966.

————. *Reading Acts: A Literary and Theological Commentary on the Acts of the Apostles*. New York: Crossroad, 1997.

—————. *What is a Gospel?: The Genre of the Canonical Gospels.* Philadelphia: Fortress, 1977.

Tannehill, Robert C. "Israel in Luke-Acts: A Tragic Story." *Journal of Biblical Literature* 104 (1985) 69–85.

—————. *The Narrative Unity of Luke-Acts: A Literary Interpretation.* Vol. 2: The Acts of the Apostles. Minneapolis: Fortress, 1990.

—————. "The Narrator's Strategy in the Scenes of Paul's Defense: Acts 21.27—26.32." *Foundations and Facets Forum* 8 (1992) 245–69.

—————. "Rejection by Jews and Turning to Gentiles: The Pattern of Paul's Mission in Acts." In *Luke-Acts and the Jewish People: Eight Critical Perspectives*, edited by Joseph B. Tyson, 83–101. Minneapolis: Augsburg, 1988.

Thackeray, H. St. John. *Josephus: The Man and the Historian.* New York: Ktav, 1967.

Thompson, Marianne Meye. *The God of the Gospel of John.* Grand Rapids: Eerdmans, 2001.

—————. "'God's Voice You Have Never Heard, God's Form You Have Never Seen': The Characterization of God in the Gospel of John." *Semeia* 63 (1993) 177–204.

Thompson, Richard P. "Believers and Religious Leaders in Jerusalem: Contrasting Portraits of Jews in Acts 1–7." In *Literary Studies in Luke-Acts: Essays in Honor of Joseph B. Tyson*, edited by Richard P. Thompson and Thomas E. Phillips, 327–44. Macon, GA: Mercer University Press, 1998.

Thornton, Timothy C. G. "To the End of the Earth: Acts 1.8." *Expository Times* 89 (1977–78) 374–75.

Tiede, David L. "Acts 11:1–18." *Interpretation* 42 (1988) 175–80.

—————. "'Glory to Thy People Israel': Luke-Acts and the Jews." In *Luke-Acts and the Jewish People: Eight Critical Perspectives*, edited by Joseph B. Tyson, 21–34. Minneapolis: Augsburg, 1988.

—————. *Prophecy and History in Luke-Acts.* Philadelphia: Fortress, 1980.

Tompkins, Jane P. "The Reader in History: The Changing Shape of Literary Response." In *Reader-Response Criticism: From Formalism to Post-Structuralism*, edited by Jane P. Tomkins, 201–32. Baltimore: Johns Hopkins University Press, 1980.

Trebilco, Paul R. "Paul and Silas—'Servants of the Most High God' (Acts 16:16–18)." *Journal for the Study of the New Testament* 36 (1989) 51–73.

Trémel, B. "A propos d'Actes 20, 7–12: Puissance du thaumaturge ou du témoin?" *Revue de théologie et de philosophie* 112 (1980) 359–69.

Turner, Max. *Power from on High: The Spirit in Israel's Restoration and Witness in Luke-Acts.* Journal of Pentecostal Theology Supplements 9. Sheffield: Sheffield Academic, 1996.

—————. "The Spirit and Salvation in Luke-Acts." In *The Holy Spirit and Christian Origins: Essays in Honor of James D. G. Dunn*, edited by Graham N. Stanton, Bruce W. Longenecker, and Stephen C. Barton, 103–16. Grand Rapids: Eerdmans, 2004.

—————. "The 'Spirit of Prophecy' as the Power of Israel's Restoration and Witness." In *Witness to the Gospel: The Theology of Acts*, edited by I. Howard Marshall and David Peterson, 327–48. Grand Rapids: Eerdmans, 1998.

Tyson, Joseph B. "Jews and Judaism in Luke-Acts: Reading as a Godfearer." *New Testament Studies* 41 (1995) 19–38.

—————. "The Problem of Jewish Rejection in Acts." In *Luke-Acts and the Jewish People: Eight Critical Perspectives*, edited by Joseph B. Tyson, 124–37. Minneapolis, MN: Augsburg, 1988.

Unnik, Willem C. van. "Der Ausdruck ἕως ἐσχάτου τῆς γῆς (Apostelgeschichte I 8) und sein alttestamentlicher Hintergrund." In *Sparsa Collecta, Part 1: Evangelia, Paulina, Acta*, 386–401. Novum Testamentum Supplements 29. Leiden: Brill, 1973.

Vanhoozer, Kevin J. "The Reader in New Testament Interpretation." In *Hearing the New Testament: Strategies for Interpretation*, edited by Joel B. Green, 301–28. Grand Rapids: Eerdmans, 1995.

Vielhauer, Phillipp. "Gottesreich und Menschensohn in der Verkündigung Jesus." In *Aufsätze zum Neuen Testament*, 55–91. Theologische Bücherei: Neudrucke und Berichte aus dem 20. Jahrhundert 31. Munich: Kaiser, 1965.

Viviano, B. T. "The Kingdom of God in the Qumran Literature." In *The Kingdom of God in 20th-Century Interpretation*, edited by Wendell Willis, 97–107. Peabody, MA: Hendrickson, 1987.

Völkel, M. "Zur Deutung des 'Reiches Gottes' bei Lukas." *Zeitschrift für die neutestamentliche Wissenschaft und die Kunde der älteren Kirche* 65 (1974) 57–70.

Volz, Paul. *Die Eschatologie der jüdischen Gemeinde im neutestamentlichen Zeitalter: Nach den Quellen der rabbinshen, apokalyptischen und apocryphen Literatur.* Hildesheim: Olms, 1966.

Wainwright, A. W. "Luke and the Restoration of the Kingdom to Israel." *Expository Times* 89 (1977–78) 76–79.

Walter, Nikolaus. "Apostelgeschichte 6:1 und die Anfänge der Urgemeinde in Jerusalem." *New Testament Studies* 29 (1983) 370–93.

Walworth, Allen James. "The Narrator of Acts." PhD diss., The Southern Baptist Theological Seminary, 1985.

Weder, Hans. "Hoffnung II: Neues Testament." In vol. 15 of *Theologische Realenzyklopädie*, edited by G. Krause and G. Müller, 484–91. Berlin: de Gruyter, 1986.

Weinert, F. D. "The Meaning of the Temple in Luke-Acts." *Biblical Theology Bulletin* 11 (1981) 85–89.

Weiser, A. "'Reich Gottes' in der Apostelgeschichte." In *Der Treue Gottes trauen, Beiträge zum Werk des Lukas: für Gerhard Schneider*, edited by Claus Bussmann and Walter Radl, 127–35, Freiburg: Herder, 1991.

Wendt, H. H. *Kritisch Exegetisches Handbuch über die Apostelgeschichte*. Göttingen: Vandenhoeck & Ruprecht, 1880.

Wenk, Matthias. *Community-Forming Power: The Socio-Ethical Role of the Spirit in Luke-Acts*. Journal of Pentecostal Theology Supplement Series 19. Sheffield: Sheffield Academic, 2000.

Westerman, Claus. *Elements of Old Testament Theology*. Translated by Douglas W. Stott. Atlanta: John Knox, 1982. Originally published as *Theologie des Alten Testaments in Grundzugen*. Göttingen: Vandenhoeck & Ruprecht, 1978.

Wicks, Henry J. *The Doctrine of God in the Jewish Apocryphal and Apocalyptic Literature*. London: Hunter & Longhurst, 1915.

Williams, Charles S. C. *A Commentary on the Acts of the Apostles*. Black's New Testament Commentaries. London: Black, 1957.

Wilson, Stephen G. *The Gentiles and the Gentile Mission in Luke-Acts*. Society for New Testament Studies Monograph Series 23. Cambridge: Cambridge University Press, 1973.

————. *Luke and the Law*. Society for New Testament Studies Monograph Series 50. Cambridge: Cambridge University Press, 1983.

Wilson, Walter T. "Urban Legends: Acts 10:1—11:18 and the Strategies of Greco-Roman Foundation Narratives." *Journal of Biblical Literature* 120 (2001) 77–99.

Winter, Bruce W. "Official Proceedings and the Forensic Speeches in Acts 24–26." In *The Book of Acts in Its Ancient Literary Setting*, edited by Bruce W. Winter and Andrew D. Clarke, 305–36. Vol. 1 of *The Book of Acts in Its First Century Setting*, edited by Bruce W. Winter. Grand Rapids: Eerdmans, 1993.

Witherington, Ben, III. *The Acts of the Apostles: A Socio-Rhetorical Commentary*. Grand Rapids: Eerdmans, 1998.

————. *The Many Faces of the Christ: The Christologies of the New Testament and Beyond*. Crossroad Companions to the New Testament Series. New York: Crossroad, 1998.

————. *Women in the Earliest Churches*. Society for New Testament Studies Monograph Series 59. Cambridge: Cambridge University Press, 1988.

Wolter, Michael. "Israel's Future and the Delay of the Parousia, according to Luke." In *Jesus and the Heritage of Israel: Luke's Narrative Claim upon Israel's Legacy*. Edited by David P. Moessner, 307–24. Harrisburg, PA: Trinity, 1999.

————. "'Reich Gottes' bei Lukas." *New Testament Studies* 41 (1995) 541–63.

Woods, Edward J. *The 'Finger of God' and Pneumatology in Luke-Acts*. Journal for the Study of the New Testament: Supplement Series 205. Sheffield: Sheffield Academic, 2001.

Zeitlin, Solomon and Sidney Tedesche. *The Second Book of Maccabees*. New York: Harper & Brothers, 1955.

Zeller, Dieter. "New Testament Christology in its Hellenistic Reception." *New Testament Studies* 47 (2001) 312–33.

Zimmerli, Walther. *Old Testament Theology in Outline*, translated by David E. Green. Scranton, PA: John Knox, 1978. Originally published as *Grundriss der alttestamentlichen Theologie*. Stuttgart: Kohlhammer, 1972.

Zumstein, Jean. "L'apôtre comme martyr dans les Actes de Luc." *Revue de théologie et de philosophie* 112 (1980) 371–90.

Zwiep, Arie W. *The Ascension of the Messiah in Lukan Christology*. Novum Testamentum Supplements 87. Leiden: Brill, 1997.

Made in the USA
San Bernardino, CA
23 February 2016